AF600438

About Face

Kritik: German Literary Theory and Cultural Studies

Liliane Weissberg, EDITOR

A complete listing of the books in this series can be found online at wsupress.wayne.edu

About Face

German Physiognomic Thought from Lavater to Auschwitz

Richard T. Gray

WAYNE STATE UNIVERSITY PRESS DETROIT

Manufactured in the United States of America.
ISBN-13: 978-0-8143-3179-8 ISBN-10: 0-8143-3179-3

Library of Congress Cataloging-in-Publication Data

Gray, Richard T.
About face : German physiognomic thought from Lavater to Auschwitz / Richard T. Gray.
p. cm. — (Kritik)
Includes bibliographical references (p.) and index.
ISBN 0-8143-3179-3
1. Physiognomy—German—History. I. Title. II. Series: Kritik (Detroit, Mich.)
BF851.G73 2004
138'.0943—dc22
2003017664

∞ The paper used in this publication meets the minimum requirements of the American National Standard for Information Sciences—Permanence of Paper for Printed Library Materials, ANSI Z39.48–1984.

Grateful acknowledgment is made to the University of Washington Graduate School Fund for their generous support of the publication of this volume.

Dedicated to the Memory of My Father

Richard Arthur Gray (1920–1997)

Contents

Illustrations

Preface

About Face

Physiognomics, broadly understood as the hermeneutic (re-) constitution of the internal character, desires, and dispositions of human beings based on the interpretation of the body as a system of meaningful signs, names a branch of knowledge that has displayed a certain currency throughout Western intellectual history. From the ancient physiognomic studies attributed to Aristotle, to Paracelsus's doctrine of signatures, to the physiognomic boom characteristic of the final decades of the eighteenth century, to the physiognomic characterologies prominent in the early twentieth century, through finally to the popularized lexica of "body-language" to be found in bookstores yet today, physiognomics has remained a pursuit that has attracted considerable attention in both scholarly and popular domains. In a recent *New York Times Magazine* article on the physiology of anxiety, Stephen S. Hall writes: "[D]octors are approaching the day—not soon, but foreseeable—when imaging machines may ultimately reveal a broken psyche with as much routine precision as an X-ray shows a broken bone" (44). Hall gives expression here to one of the most persistent fantasies held by the human intellect—the notion of developing a kind of penetrating interior vision that would infallibly reveal the psychological constitution of any human being at which it is directed. One of the earliest versions of this utopian dream is the lament attributed to Momus, the ancient Greek god of ridicule and fault-finding, that human beings unfortunately are not born with windows in their chests that reveal the secret workings of their hearts.

The very persistence with which this interest in physiognomics resurfaces throughout human history leads quite naturally to the conjecture that the urge to decipher and assess the "essential" nature of one's fellow human beings represents a universal human compulsion. In fact, the Swiss pastor Johann Caspar Lavater, whose monumental *Physiognomische Fragmente, zur Beförderung der Menschenkenntniß und Menschenliebe* (Physiognomic fragments for the promotion of human understanding and human love; 1775–1778) unleashed a Europe-wide rage for physiognomics in the final quarter of the eighteenth century, appeals precisely to the universality of this spontaneous physiognomic propensity as proof for the verity and validity of physiognomics. In a fragment entitled "Von der Wahrheit der Physiognomik" (On the truth of physiognomics) from the first volume of this work, Lavater programmatically maintains "that knowledge of physiognomy guides all human beings, whether they know it or not, on a daily basis—that . . . every human being, whether he knows it or not, understands something about physiognomics." Lavater extends this claim for the innate character of a physiognomic sensibility to all living organisms, adding "there is not *one single* living creature that, in its own way, does not draw conclusions about the internal on the basis of the external, that does not pass judgment, on the basis of empirical data, about things that cannot be empirically perceived" (1: 50–51). Lavater thus asserts the existence of a primordial sensitivity to the natural "language" of physiognomics as a kind of sixth sense that unconsciously guides all living creatures in their day-to-day interactions with the life world. Lavater's physiognomic project, in this sense true to the epistemological and disciplinary ambitions of the European Enlightenment, seeks to elevate this unconscious physiognomics to the level of a consciously understood and practiced methodology.

The title of the present work, *About Face,* does not merely point to the obsession with facial interpretation that is part and parcel of physiognomics; it also alludes to the idea of dialectical reversal, of a fundamental turnaround or change in direction, that is inherent in the history of modern German physiognomic thought. This "about face" occurs on two distinct levels, one methodological, the other anthropological. If prior to the end of the eighteenth century physiognomics was traditionally identified with such esoteric and "irrational" pursuits as chiromancy and oneiromancy, and hence associated with occultist prophetic practices, the physiognomic doctrines of Lavater—something one might not otherwise expect of this devout Pietist minister—mark a notable turn toward codifying physiognomics as a strictly positivistic and empirical science in the Enlightenment sense. Lavater unleashed an entirely new brand of physiognomics, pursued with disciplinary and methodological zeal throughout Enlightenment and post-Enlightenment Europe, but in particular in the German-speaking regions. This is particularly curious, since one might reasonably expect concerns with issues of physiognomic interpretation to be banished, with the dawn of bourgeois Enlightenment, from the sphere of accepted scholarly pursuits and recede even further into the shadowy realm of occultism. The contemporary German critical philosopher Peter Sloterdijk seems to be relying heavily on this intuition—rather than on historical fact—when he writes: "Enlightenment, which strives for the reification and objectification of knowledge, imposes absolute silence on the physiognomic world" (*Kritik der zynischen Vernunft* 1: 268). In fact, the opposite is the case: it is precisely in the post-Enlightenment period of bourgeois modernism that physiognomics emerges not only as a rigorously scientific discipline whose laws and methodologies can be codified and systematically practiced, but, moreover, as a veritable intellectual obsession that commandeers the fantasies of some of the most prominent thinkers of the period. Finally, it is in the rationalist, yet metaphysically fertile soil of German intellectual discourse that physiognomics experiences its most pronounced and most persistent boom, one that lasts from the end of the eighteenth through the first half of the twentieth century.

One of the primary motivations for the studies contained in the present volume is the pursuit of the question as to why physiognomic theory enjoyed such uncommon vitality in the sociocultural and intellectual atmosphere of modern Germany in particular. My investigations attempt to elucidate the reasons why the discipline of physiognomics was especially cultivated in the German intellectual tradition, and in particular why it engaged some of the most critical and creative minds of German thought—people like Lavater, Lichtenberg, Herder, Goethe, Gall, Hegel, Carus, Schopenhauer, Klages, Spengler, Kassner, and Kretschmer. Over the course of these investigations I came to realize that physiognomics was able to flourish in this intellectual climate in part because, the perfect parasite, it was able to feed off a significant number of robust and influential hosts endemic to the German intellectual-historical tradition. Spawned by German Protestant Pietist thought, it gathered energy in the nineteenth and early-twentieth centuries: 1) from German *Naturphilosophie*, the philosophy of nature propounded especially by the Romantic philosopher Friedrich von Schelling (1775–1854), but practiced most effectively and influentially by Goethe in his role as anti-Newtonian natural scientist; 2) from German *Lebensphilosophie*, the philosophy of life and dynamic vitalism advanced by Wilhelm Dilthey (1833–1911) and advocated by an entire generation of German intellectuals, not least among whom the young Friedrich Nietzsche (1844–1900) must be numbered; 3) from the cultural pessimism concretized in Arthur Schopenhauer's (1788–1860) philosophical program, which had a profound impact on intellectuals of the Weimar Republic such as Oswald Spengler (1880–1936); 4) from Edmund Husserl's (1859–1938) phenomenological method, which championed a form of intuitive observation that revealed the essence of the phenomenal world; 5) from Sigmund Freud's (1856–1939) psychoanalytic theory, which insisted on an unconscious, primordial layer of "truth" underlying conscious acts and intentions; 6) and finally, and most perniciously, from the racial-genetic turn German biology and anthropology underwent in the early decades of the twentieth century, leading up to the catastrophe of the Nazi racial state. The convergence of these diverse intellectual forces occurred during the years of the Weimar Republic, leading to an explosion of physiognomically-oriented theories in diverse academic and intellectual disciplines in the years from 1918 to 1935 and beyond (see Schmölders/Gilman).

The trajectory marked off by this catalogue of central intellectual-historical impeti already hints at the curious "about face" that operates in the anthropological self-understanding of modern German physiognomics: this is the trenchant irony that, born with the theories of the Protestant preacher Lavater as a manner for promoting human love and understanding, as the subtitle to Lavater's magnum opus itself suggests, German physiognomic science quickly reverted to a principally misanthropic and homophobic ideology that sought to establish narrow characterological and behavioral norms, while stigmatizing all the traits or behavioral patterns that fell outside this closely circumscribed taxonomy of the acceptable. The present study attempts to investigate the perverse dynamic of this dialectical reversion. There is, as I seek to demonstrate, a profound affinity—although certainly no *necessity*—that connects Lavater and his theories with the atrocities of Auschwitz. This is related, above all, to Lavater's insistence on the inherently natural and biological—as opposed to accidental and historico-cultural—basis of physiognomic significance. For Lavater, the fundamental Being of every individual, his or her capacities and potentials, is given and unalterable from birth: according to his theory, each of us is biologically—later thinkers will say "genetically"—predetermined, and this predetermined nature expresses itself, for those who can read it, in our physiognomy, in the form and structure of our face and body. The affinity of this idea with the racial ideology that asserted its prominence in Germany during the Weimar Republic and the years of Nazi rule is obvious, and this fact was not lost on nationalist and *völkisch* thinkers of the time. Shortly after the beginning of the Second World War, for example, a certain Richard Trebeck published an article in the respected and widely circulated *Zeitschrift für Psychologie* entitled "Die Anthropologie des Johann Caspar Lavater," which portrays Lavater as a significant precursor to the genetic-deterministic racial anthropology practiced in Germany at the time. Indeed, the ferocious attacks on the theories of "milieu" and environmental influence voiced by twentieth-century racial ideologues echo in many respects arguments already made by Lavater a century and a half earlier. But the relationship between the German physiognomic tradition and Nazi racial policy runs much deeper than this.

Histories of German racial thought have long cited the nationalist sentiment and irrationalist leanings of Romanticism as two of the seminal historical harbingers of National Socialism; these same studies tend, however, to treat the German physiognomic tradition as a mere footnote to this larger intellectual-historical complex (see, for example, Mosse, *Crisis of German Ideology* 13–107). In my view, what these cultural historians have thus far tended to overlook is that the existence in Germany of a sustained and thriving physiognomic tradition—a tradition, moreover, that was viewed as intellectually mainstream, and even as scientifically legitimate—lent a significant new dimension to German nationalism and racism: the dimension, namely, of an applied hermeneutics, a concrete interpretive *practice.* This is one of the other primary contentions of this book: that the deadly effectiveness of German racism was predicated at least in part on its ability to translate racial theory into a set of specific practices that allowed for the segregation of racially desirable and undesirable individuals on the basis of somatic, physiognomically derived evidence. For if the proclivity of the Germans for a nationalistically defined "inwardness" indubitably had its roots in political Romanticism, it has generally passed unnoticed that this focus on inwardness was dialectically tied to an obsession with disciplined observation and a trained spectatorial gaze, a fundamentally *physiognomic* gaze, capable of establishing inward qualities based on the study of outward traits. From the eighteenth century onward, physiognomics was instrumental in the process of creating a public sphere of like-minded—or like-emotioned, like-gened, like-countried—subjects whose sense of community was largely grounded in the exclusion of those Others who were determined not to fit the moral, intellectual, racial, or other paradigm to which these judging subjects themselves subscribed. At the same time as these excluded groups were subjected to absolute transparency by the disciplined physiognomic gaze, the observing, spectatorial subjects who formed the community of the like were born qua mastering, coercive subjects. The existence of a vital and respected physiognomic heritage in German science, philosophy, psychology, and humanistic study helped ultimately to support the emergence of a racially motivated physiognomic practice, and it is no coincidence that the two most prominent racial physiognomists of the Weimar and Nazi periods, Hans F. K. Günther (1891–1968) and Ludwig Ferdinand Clauss (1892–1974), tended to focus their attention on the pragmatic dimension of physiognomic identification and segregation rather than on underlying theoretical issues. In short, it was, among other things, their ability to encourage participation in physiognomic spectatorship, the application of disciplined physiognomic observation, that helped the Nazi leadership congeal the German populace into a community of self-policing, spectatorial subjects able to stylize itself as the "master race."

In his *Die geistige Situation der Zeit* (The intellectual situation of the contemporary age; 1931), the existential philosopher Karl Jaspers (1883–1969) recognizes physiognomically based anthropology as one of the three primary intellectual movements—the other two being sociology and psychology—with which his nascent existentialist philosophy had to vie in the intellectual landscape of 1930s Germany. Jaspers gives one of the most astute analyses of this racially oriented physiognomics, a critique that culminates in the assertion that it mingles scientific fact and intuitive understanding in a wholly questionable and irresponsible manner. According to Jaspers, in the works that represent this line of thought, "compelling objective knowledge and the possible intuitive understanding of [somatic] expression are so closely intertwined that the validity of the one suggests for the readers the type of validity expected of the other. Measurements are taken, but what is actually studied eludes all acts of measurement and any quantitative definition" (140). Jaspers puts his finger on one of the central characteristics of all German physiognomic theories from Lavater onward: the peculiar manner in which they marry intuitive perception to the empirical, quantifying techniques of positivistic science. Again, this is a tendency first introduced to physiognomic study by Lavater.

In her 1990 film *Europa, Europa,* Agnieszka Holland thematizes, among other things, the interpretation of the human body as the physiognomic site at which nature and culture inscribe the signs of their determining influence. Based on the autobiography of Salomon Perel, a Jewish youth caught up in the political tensions of Europe after the German attack on Poland, the film recounts how its protagonist manages, by deftly switching loyalties from Judaism to Communism to Nazism, to survive the horrors of the Holocaust. The tensions generated by the film derive from the omnipresent danger that Perel's true identity—his Jewishness—will be revealed to the Nazi perpetrators who have mistakenly adopted him as one of their own. In a central scene from the movie, where Perel attends a mandatory class on racial ethnology in the educational institution for Hitler Youth in which he is receiving his training, Holland mercilessly satirizes the racial-physiognomic theories practiced throughout Germany at this time. The teacher in charge of this racial-anthropological demonstration begins his lesson by asserting the absolute infallibility of the quantifying methods this "science" has developed. Behind him stands a physiognomic chart, complete with "typical" photographs, portraying the various "races" represented on the European continent—a chart of the sort found in classrooms throughout Germany at this time. Relying on such anthropometric tools as a skull caliper, the teacher sets out to demonstrate the reliability of these methods. Of course, he chooses Perel, whose Jewish heritage is unknown, as his guinea pig. A close-up of the protagonist's face reveals the unspoken anxiety he experiences as he is subjected to cranial measurements and the comparison of his eye and hair color with the range of colors listed in the appropriate racial-physiognomic charts: he clearly anticipates that his Jewishness is about to be divulged. His fears subside when the teacher confidently pronounces Perel's Aryan heritage, situating him physiognomically as a representative of the "East Baltic" race. To be sure, this race does not stand as high as the so-called "Nordic" one in the Nazi racial hierarchy, but its inherent value is at least recognized—it is not subject to Nazi persecution or extermination. By means of trenchant dramatic irony, this scene lays bare the absurdities and ideological illusions of the racial-physiognomic practices applied throughout the Third Reich.

The broader importance of this scene becomes evident in the context of a counter-theme that dominates the structural and thematic makeup of *Europa, Europa:* the motif of circumcision, played out most emphatically in the episodes in which Perel furiously attempts to hide his circumcised penis, the only "physiognomic" sign that could truly expose his Jewish identity. The importance of circumcision for the events of the film, as well as its definition as a *religious-cultural* ritual, is emphasized by the fact that the movie opens with a scene depicting the ceremonial circumcision with which the life of its protagonist begins. Throughout the film, Perel identifies this "small piece of foreskin" as the only feature that sets him apart from his "fellow" Germans from whom he fears persecution. Holland's screenplay makes a forceful counterargument against the position of racial physiognomics—indeed, against the entire tradition of modern, post-Lavaterian physiognomics, with its insistence that a person's biological constitution shapes his or her characterological destiny—by asserting the priority of those signs inscribed on the body by *culture*—Perel's circumcision—over those deposited there by nature and genetic makeup: the protagonist's racial "physiognomy." The film thereby invokes, and enters into, one of the primary intellectual debates around which modern German physiognomic theory crystallized throughout its history: whether the somatic signs interpreted by physiognomists are indicative of biological constants or cultural variables. This is the central terrain on which the critical struggle over physiognomics is waged, beginning with the so-called *Physiognomikstreit,* the controversy over physiognomics that emerged in the wake of Lavater's theories in the final decades of the eighteenth century, and continuing through the nineteenth and twentieth centuries. This study attempts to identify the participants in this battle, in addition to outlining the deeper philosophical issues at stake in this debate.

Although the focus of the present book is largely historical, relating a history of German physiognomic theory and practice from Lavater to racism, it does not set about this task by relying on a traditional historiography grounded in linear narration. Instead, my approach employs a procedure schooled on Nietzschean perspectivism, and as such its movement is more that of a historiographic spiral. Beginning each chapter at a new thematic starting point and with a distinct set of questions, it seeks to interrogate and re-interrogate the central representatives of the German physiognomic tradition by coming at them and the positions they represent from diverse perspectives. This nonlinear, more thematically oriented approach gives rise to some overlaps in the discussion of particular authors and materials in some of the chapters. I have, of course, attempted to keep repetitions to a minimum by referring backward or forward to relevant discussions in other sections. My hope, however, is that the continual re-scrutinizing of the German physiognomic tradition, in particular of certain key theoreticians, on the basis of different issues and problems will help reveal facets of this intellectual-historical complex that linear analysis would be forced to pass over in silence. Above all, my methodological aim has been constantly to reconfigure and recontextualize the constellation of German physiognomic thought so as not only to highlight certain common themes but also bring out aspects of the tradition—for example, the central role the reception of Goethe played in revitalizing physiognomics in the late nineteenth and early twentieth centuries—that scholars have hitherto ignored. Moreover, this nonlinear methodological procedure is intended to discourage any implication that eighteenth-century physiognomic thought and twentieth-century racism are linked by a relationship of teleological necessity. Martin Blankenburg has correctly insisted ("Rassistische Physiognomik" 136) that physiognomics itself is not inherently racist: it requires certain historical determinants in order to take a virulent racist turn. My study seeks to interrogate in particular the intellectual-historical conditions that support such a turn.

The introduction, the only attempt at a rough linear historiography, recounts in broad outline the intellectual-historical development of physiognomics from Lavater to Husserlian phenomenology and Freudian psychoanalysis, stressing its ties to the ideological program of Enlightenment and post-Enlightenment German civil society. Chapter 1 discusses the emergence of physiognomics as a scientific discipline in Lavater's theory, highlighting the semiological impulses he derived from German Enlightenment philosophy as the crucial disciplinary backdrop. Chapter 2 takes a socio-pragmatic approach, examining the debate that raged around Lavater's physiognomic program in the context of Enlightenment theories of individuality. Chapter 3 investigates how the theories of early physiognomists like Lavater and Carus already prefigure, in certain key respects, the racial turn German physiognomics would take in the early twentieth century. Chapter 4 treats the reception of Goethe's writings on physiognomics and morphology as an invigorating force in the emergence of modern German physiognomics and the primary intellectual cause for its renaissance among humanistic thinkers in the early twentieth century. Chapter 5 traces the development of a broadly defined physiognomic worldview in Weimar Germany, a movement that embraced and articulated many of the antirationalist, antimodern themes typical of the cultural pessimism characteristic of this period. Chapter 6 studies the materialist brand of racial physiognomics made popular by Hans F. K. Günther, one of the primary ideologues of race, who collaborated in the development of Nazi racial thought and policy. Chapter 7 examines the metaphysical counterpart to Günther's racial ethnology, the physiognomic theories of Ludwig Ferdinand Clauss, which emerged as a conscious application of Husserl's phenomenological method to the contemporary problematic of race. The conclusion outlines the exploitation of technological advances, especially in the realm of illustrative print media, throughout the history of physiognomics and the role these technologies played in lending legitimation, conviction, and credibility to physiognomic theories.

This book has emerged over the course of several years, and I am indebted to many individuals and institutions for their support. I began my research into physiognomics almost ten years ago in the context of an altogether different project related to the role of semiotic theory in the institutionalization of scientific disciplines in Germany at the end of the eighteenth century. This larger project, which was generously supported by a research grant from the Alexander von Humboldt Foundation, was never completed; instead, what was initially conceived as a chapter on physiognomics and semiotic theory was spun off as an independent project and expanded into the present book. I also received research support for a year of release-time from teaching due to the generosity of the German-American Fulbright Commission, to which I would like to express my sincere gratitude. Much of the research for this project was conducted in libraries and archives in Germany. Among the institutions that provided the most useful and the most interesting material, I would like to make special mention of the Bundesarchiv (German Federal Archive) in Coblenz, the Hessische Landesbibliothek (Hessian State Library) in Darmstadt, and the library of the Medizin-Historisches Institut (Department of Medical History) at the University of Mainz. I also profited greatly from the collection in the Suzzallo/Allen Library at the University of Washington, as well as from the Rare Books and Special Collections division of the Health Sciences Library at the University of Washington. I want to express my special gratitude to the Graduate School Fund of the University of Washington, which generously supported the publication of this book with a grant to help defray the costs of the illustrations.

Parts of some chapters of this book appeared previously in gestational form: segments of the introduction in the *Lessing Yearbook* 23 (1991); an early version of chapter 2 in the *Deutsche Vierteljahrsschrift für Literaturwissenschaft und Geistesgeschichte* 66 (1992); a German rendition of chapter 1 in *Poetica* 23 (1991) and of chapter 3 in *Archiv für Kulturgeschichte* 81 (1999); and a German version of chapter 4 in *Körper, Diskurse, Praktiken* (Synchron Verlag, 2003). I wish to thank the editors of these journals and books for permission to reprint those ideas here in revised form.

I want to thank my wife Sabine Wilke and my daughter Cora for putting up with me and all my inane jokes about physiognomy and physiognomics over the past several years. Without their inspiration and support, this book would never have been finished. I also want to express my profound thanks to Liliane Weissberg, the editor of the Kritik series, and to Jane Hoehner, the Director of the Wayne State University Press, for their gracious support in expediting the review of the manuscript and for their extraordinary patience in seeing the project through to its completion. Finally, I have dedicated this book to the memory of my father, Richard Arthur Gray.

RTG
Seattle, January 2003

Introduction

Physiognomic "Surface Hermeneutics" and the Ideological Context of German Modernism

> False consciousness is simultaneously correct; internal and external existence are torn asunder.
>
> Theodor W. Adorno ("Zum Verhältnis von Soziologie und Psychologie" 45)

> *Physiognomics,* the knowledge of and acquaintance with the relationship of the external with the internal, of the visible surface with the invisible content, of what is *visible* and perceptibly *animated* with what is *invisible* and imperceptibly *animates,* of the visible effect to the invisible force.
>
> Johann Caspar Lavater (*Physiognomische Fragmente* 1: 13)

Physiognomics and German Civil Society

The years 1770 to 1780 can with certain justification be designated the physiognomic decade of German intellectual and cultural history. To be sure, the study of the human physiognomy as symptomatic of character, fate, and talents of the individual subject was no eighteenth-century invention. Indeed, as an intellectual discipline, physiognomics has venerable roots that are commonly traced back as far as the Greek philosopher Aristotle (384–322 B.C.), to whom an early Greek physiognomic treatise, entitled *Physiognomica,* is often attributed. But traditional physiognomics received revolutionary new impulses and was substantially revitalized by the physiognomic theories of the Swiss pastor Johann Caspar Lavater (1741–1801) in what I designate as the physiognomic decade of German intellectual-cultural history. (Fig. 1) Lavater sought to dissociate physiognomics from such prophetic avocations as chiromancy, the guise it took in the ancient tradition carried on by Antonius Polemo (88–145) and Adamantius (184–253), elevating it to the status of a positivistic empirical science. As such, physiognomics was considered capable of supplying valid and accurate information about the supersensual character of the human "soul" based on interpretive conclusions drawn from its sensual manifestations.

While from today's perspective it is perhaps tempting merely to decry Lavater as a quack and shake our heads over the apparent naiveté and simplicity of his physiognomic notions, such responses fail to come to grips with the tremendous appeal the man and his theories held for his contemporaries. Beyond being generally accepted as a legitimate academic-scientific discipline, physiognomics also assumed the character of one of the first widely dispersed movements of modern popular culture. During this period the interpretive "reading" of the facial features of one's social contacts acquired the status of a parlor game that was de rigueur in the social circles of emergent German civil society,[1] and the exchange of character-revealing silhouettes as a sign of intimacy and friendship became a veritable fad. These (pseudo-)intellectual physiognomic crazes proliferated among the representatives of civil society not only in German-speaking lands, but throughout Europe. By 1810, less than forty years after the publication of Lavater's magnum opus, the *Physiognomische Fragmente, zur Beförderung der Menschenkenntniß und Menschenliebe* (Physiognomic fragments for the promotion of human understanding and human love; 1775–1778), no fewer than sixteen German, fifteen French, and twenty English editions had appeared, and even two Russian, one Dutch, and one Italian translation had been published (Herrmann 27). In his *Physiognomische Reisen* (Physiognomic travels), first published in 1778–1779, Johann Karl August Musäus (1735–1787) both documents and scathingly satirizes the prominence that physiognomic practices had assumed in the social intercourse of European civil society in the wake of Lavater's reception.[2]

Lavater unleashed and fueled this physiognomic vogue with the publication of a series of treatises between the years 1772 and 1778. The first of these, an essay entitled "Von der Physiognomik" (On physiognomics), represents the script of a lecture Lavater read before the Scientific Society of Zurich. It is

Fig. 1. Portrait of Johann Caspar Lavater, from Rudolf Kassner, *Physiognomik,* 1932.

one of the ironies of the history of physiognomics that Lavater himself apparently did not at first sense that the time was especially auspicious for the propagation of his theories. Indeed, he cannot be credited with initiating the publication of these first reflections on physiognomics. This honor falls to his friend and mentor, the physician and cultural dilettante Johann Georg Zimmermann (1728–1795), who published Lavater's essay anonymously and without the consent of its author in the *Hannoverisches Magazin* of February 1772. When Lavater reissued—in book form and under his own name—this disquisition that sought to establish the positivistic foundations of physiognomy, he appended to it an outline of the various subfields into which he imagined this new "scientific" discipline could be divided.[3] But it was ultimately the four costly, profusely illustrated folio volumes of the *Physiognomische Fragmente,* which appeared from 1775 to 1778, with which Lavater placed his stamp on the intellectual physiognomy of this decade. (Fig. 2)

The popular reception of the *Physiognomische Fragmente* stands in a relationship of ironic paradox with Lavater's own stated intentions for these volumes. Already in the preface to the first volume he openly asserts: "It [this volume] is not written for the large mass of common people. It is costly in its very

Physiognomische Fragmente,
zur Beförderung
der Menschenkenntniß und Menschenliebe,
von
Johann Caspar Lavater.
Vierter Versuch.
Mit vielen Kupfern.

Leipzig und Winterthur, 1778.
Bey Weidmanns Erben und Reich, und Heinrich Steiner und Compagnie.

Fig. 2. Title page, volume 4 of Johann Caspar Lavater, *Physiognomische Fragmente,* 1778.

nature . . . ; and anyway, different people can pitch in, buy it together, and own it as a group" (1: "Vorrede" [unpaginated]). Although it was not expressly written for the masses, the *Fragmente*'s receptive history is marked above all by its mass circulation. To be sure, Lavater perhaps piqued the interest of the general readership by asserting the very distinction of these volumes and their readers: who would not want to number themselves among those distinguished few for whose eyes these richly illustrated volumes were composed?

The innovative distribution method of this work also contributed to its dissemination. It was among the first in Germany to be published based on the principle of subscription; indeed, the first volume contains a list of two hundred sixty-nine subscribers, for a total of more than three hundred volumes, that includes the names of many prominent aristocrats and the principal representatives of German civil society. The tactic of subscription allowed Lavater and his publisher to leverage the exorbitant cost of the volumes up-front, thereby guaranteeing from the outset the financial success of this publishing venture. Moreover, Lavater proved to be an enormously effective salesman: he persuaded many individuals to subscribe by requesting that they send him a portrait or silhouette, in return for which he promised to analyze the contributor's physiognomy in a future volume (Swoboda 93). By playing on the vanity-driven desires of individuals who might attain a certain public stardom by being featured in the *Fragmente,* Lavater found a shrewd way of insuring the success of this grandly conceived project. This ploy of requesting portraits or silhouettes from his contemporaries was so well orchestrated that Lavater ultimately assembled a collection of more than twenty-two thousand images.[4] It is symptomatic of Lavater's shrewd sense of commodity value and of his belief in his own self-worth that he added value to these images by adorning them with hand-written titles and interpretive comments. By means of this practice Lavater transformed these simple images into Baroque-like *emblemata* (Rauchensteiner and Swoboda 112). And by presenting them to friends and supporters as gifts, he consciously developed a clever marketing strategy for his physiognomic theories and interpretations (see Siegrist, "Nachwort" 379). These physiognomic *emblemata* ultimately acquired the status of highly regarded cultural artifacts that circulated among the German cultural elite, who collected and displayed them with pride. Lavater thereby instituted a subtle and highly successful marketing campaign that both fueled and played off of the emerging discourse of fashion and the nascent consumerism it promoted.[5] In this sense Lavater brilliantly exploited the mechanism and the media of the public sphere in order to underwrite the dissemination of his physiognomic theories and practices.

One further element related to the marketing and reception of the *Fragmente* is relevant here: the community-building function of these volumes, hinted at by Lavater's comment that people might pool their money to purchase these works as a group. As Isabel Hull notes, reading societies were among the major institutions of late eighteenth-century German civil society, and Lavater's remark would seem to be directed at these societies. In fact, the *Physiognomische Fragmente* were often purchased by reading groups, which then met not only for communal reading but also to practice their interpretive physiognomic skills.[6] As Ingrid Goritschnig has shown ("Faszination des Porträts" 138), the *Physiognomische Fragmente* called forth a true cult of personality; people began to meet, in the fashion of the modern social game, for communal "Lavaterizing," seeking to characterize individuals on the basis of their images or silhouettes. In a very concrete sense, then, Lavater's rich and expensive volumes came to be regarded as cult objects that formed the focal point of small, self-sustaining communities. These societies modeled in microcosm the larger community-building function, the definition of social-physiognomic insiders and outsiders, that physiognomic theory and practice sought to institute on a wider scale.

The inherent vitality of any upstart intellectual movement is perhaps best measured by the significance and vehemence of the critical opposition it evokes, rather than by its ability to attain broad appeal. Measured by this standard as well, Lavaterian physiognomics truly represented a thriving intellectual phenomenon. Indeed, it acquired the status of a scholarly event that the erudite of the day simply could not ignore. The claim that Lavater's theories divided the bourgeois intelligentsia into two camps, physiognomists and supporters of Lavater on the one side, antiphysiognomists and more circumspect critics of his theories on the other (Siegrist, "Nachwort" 387–88), is no exaggeration. A great deal was at stake in the controversy over physiognomy that raged in these years, as is best demonstrated by the vociferousness of Lavater's most zealous critic, the Göttingen physicist Georg Christoph Lichtenberg (1742–1800). In the caustically satirical treatise "Über Physiognomik; wider die Physiognomen. Zu Beförderung der Menschenliebe und Menschenkenntnis" (On physiognomics; against the physiognomists. For the promotion of human love and human understanding; 1778),[7] Lichtenberg initiated a crusade against the popularization of Lavater's physiognomic hermeneutics. He later ridiculed Lavater's interpretive practices in the parodistic piece "Fragment von Schwänzen: Ein Beitrag zu den Physiognomischen Fragmenten" (Fragment on tails: A contribution to the Physiognomic Fragments; 1783),[8] in which the purported character traits of pigs are derived from

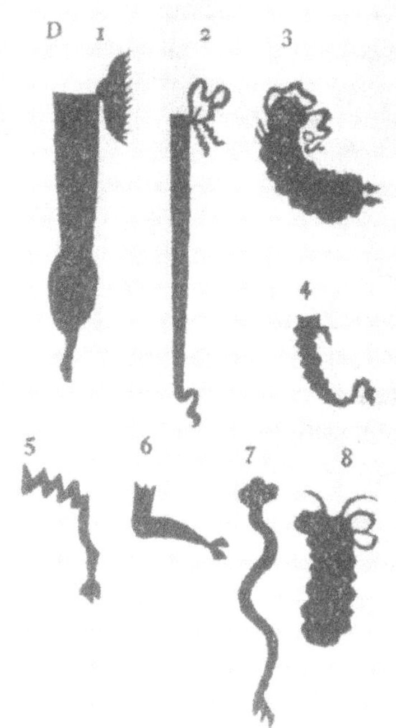

Fig. 3. "Eight Silhouettes of Pig Tails for Practice," from Georg Christoph Lichtenberg, "Fragment von Schwänzen," 1783.

interpretations of the kinks in their tails. (Fig. 3) Yet despite the wittiness of these attacks, in the final analysis physiognomics was no laughing matter, even for Lichtenberg, and Lavater and his disciples went to great lengths to refute his objections.[9]

In literary and cultural histories the phenomenon of physiognomics is commonly reduced to this high-pitched dispute between Lichtenberg and Lavater. Their exchange is somewhat simplistically interpreted as a confrontation between the rationality of the physicist Lichtenberg and the irrational eruptions of the Storm-and-Stress "genius" Lavater—a conflict, moreover, in which the Enlightenment dragon-killer successfully if viciously subdues the beast of prejudice and unreason.[10] This reductive understanding ignores the fact that Lavater himself conceived physiognomics all too rationally as a positivistic, empirical science in the Enlightenment tradition (see Pestalozzi, "Physiognomische Methodik" 137–53). Moreover, it fails to register both the breadth and complexity of Lavater's physiognomic project, as well as the degree to which it is interwoven with the ideological fabric of German civil society. Indeed, what constitutes physiognomics as a significant historico-cultural "event" is precisely the fact that it managed to gather into a single unitary economy the diverse intellectual currencies in circulation at the time.

It is well known that physiognomics found substantial support among the chief "enthusiasts" of the so-called "genius" generation: Johann Wolfgang von Goethe (1749–1832), Johann Gottfried Herder (1744–1803), and Johann Michael Reinhold Lenz (1751–1792) all defended Lavaterian physiognomics and even contributed actively to the composition of the *Physiognomische Fragmente.*[11] But even such leading critical spirits of the German Enlightenment as Moses Mendelssohn (1729–1786) and Friedrich Nicolai (1733–1811) could not resist the seductive power that emanated from Lavater's theories. To be sure, Nicolai assailed Lavater's zealotry, but only because to his mind it threatened to undercut the scientific basis of physiognomics, in which, by his own admission, he firmly believed.[12] Nicolai even contributed to the institutionalization of physiognomics as a serious intellectual discipline by assigning it a separate disciplinary heading in his *Allgemeine Deutsche Bibliothek,* the central scholarly publishing organ of Enlightenment culture in Germany, thereby implicitly setting it equal to such traditional disciplinary classifications as the fine arts and mathematics. Even Lichtenberg could not stop short of admitting his own proclivity to interpret character out of people's faces (see "Über Physiognomik" 260); while he denied the validity of Lavater's physiognomic readings, he refused to question the essential readability of physical creation ("Über Physiognomik" 265).

The emergence and popular reception of physiognomics in the 1770s and beyond was intimately connected with the ideological substance of German civil society. If, as Hull has argued, the private/public split generated "a powerful symbol system used to bring order to emerging posttraditional relations" (5), then the power of physiognomic discourse in this period stemmed in large part from the fact that it was ideally suited to inhabiting a theoretical space at the interstice of the public and the private. Indeed, the revelatory thrust of physiognomic practice can be conceived as a disclosure of the private, its "publication," or making-public through the physiognomist's interpretive practices. The very ardor with which individuals sought to turn themselves and their graven images over to public viewing and interpretation in the volumes of Lavater's *Physiognomische Fragmente* indicates the perverse pleasure associated with this revelatory hermeneutic. We must imagine the practitioners of civil society as moral "flashers," individuals who experience titillation at the exposure of their private selves to the unobstructed view of the public. To be sure, the discourse of revelation and authenticity associated with the belief that physiognomic interpretation uncovers the genuine core of the individual actually disguises the fundamentally constructivist principle at work in physiognomic theory and practice: rather than *uncovering* the self hidden behind the public façade, physiognomic interpretation in fact participates in the *construction* of this private self.

One of the commonplaces among scholars studying the history of modern physiognomics is the recognition that it thrives in particular during times of social and political disorientation.[13] The transition from the absolutist state to civil society marked a period of particular disorientation with regard to the self-understanding and self-definition of the individual. As Helmut König has pointed out (59), absolutist society had no conception of the individual as individual; instead, each person was the representative of a trans-individual system of reference that detected personal essence not in terms of psychological or physiological traits, but rather on the basis of external identifiers such as clothes, hairstyle, manner of speech, gestures, and general habitus.

This situation changed radically with the emergence of civil society in the last half of the eighteenth century in Germany. Now the individual steps out of the social fabric woven by the order of estates. Instead of identifying itself by means of an affiliation with a social group, it seeks these identifying traits in its own self. Because outward appearance no longer gives a clear indication of whom one is dealing with, the order of visibility that had previously permitted sure orientation in everyday interactions disappears. One consequence of this is that the equality of civil society is not automatically accompanied by new, freer social contacts; it can also culminate in uncertainty and lack of orientation. Where previously a system of visible coordinates ensured the existence of transparency and order, confusion and uncertainty are now the rule. One can no longer clearly distinguish people from one another (König 60).

Given this collapse of the previously valid system of visibility, physiognomics emerges as an attempt to ordain a new system of visibility in line with the ideological mechanisms underpinning the new order of civil society. As Daniel Purdy has shown for the case of German civil society, the demise of sumptuary laws dictating the attire appropriate to a given estate goes hand in hand with the consumerism that powers the mercantile economy and the discourse of fashion that identifies clothes not with class representation, but as indicators of the vital internal self (79). As a manner of redefining the relationship between the human body and personal identify, fashion contributes to the production of the civil subject. This civil subject is the reflex not of the larger social group, but of an individually defined *style.* Indeed, under the hegemony of fashion it is not so much the case that clothes make the (wo)man, as that he or she is a function of a personally choreographed *style.*[14] This distinction is important, because style is attached not simply to external adornments; it penetrates to the internal essence of the self. In this sense, the discourse of physiognomics plays a role that is complementary to that of fashion: both operate toward the production of different aspects of the civil subject, fashion constructing its external, physiognomics its internal substance.

The relationship between physiognomics and fashion is particularly complex, for this element of complementarity only captures one aspect of their interaction. Viewed from another perspective, physiognomics can also be interpreted as a countermeasure against the stylistic flourishes of fashion. Here again physiognomics relies on its greater authority as the arbiter of personal authenticity, predicated above all on the dialectic of surface and depth that defines its ideological crux. Several considerations come into play here. One is that fashion is largely, although by no means exclusively, addressed to and carried by women, whereas physiognomics is a distinctly male discipline—practiced by males, and for the most part applied to males. If Hull is correct in her judgment that the most significant sociological observation about this period is that Enlightenment discourse was produced exclusively by and for men (207), then this also helps explain the obsessiveness with which physiognomic theory—not merely in the eighteenth century, but throughout its modern history—concentrates on men, glosses over questions of gender, and marginalizes examinations of and observations about women.[15] To be sure, Lavater dedicated one small section of *Physiognomische Fragmente* to the study of women (3: 239–330), but instead of generating criteria for the differentiation of individuality, his observations there reduce women to the prejudices and stereotypes typical of the time and hence simply reinforce the prevalent societal consensus about women (Lachs, "Frauenbild" 152–54). In its general exclusion and marginalization of women, then, the discipline of physiognomics repeats that more concrete act of exclusion typical of the institutions of civil society, its lodges, associations, and reading societies (see Hull 211–12). By the same token, this did not prevent women from subscribing to the tenets of physiognomics and engaging in its practices; indeed, Lavater and his works enjoyed particular popularity among women (Lachs, "Frauenbild" 160). But the general suppression of gender matters in the discourse of modern physiognomics explains why such questions go unaddressed in the present historical examination.

The relationship between physiognomics and the ideology of consumption is just as paradoxical as that between this hermeneutics of the body and fashion. Hull has convincingly made the case that civil society replaced an ethic of abstention that previously governed the self-understanding of the non-aristocratic classes with an ethic of production and consumption (4). This is the place, of course, at which economic issues impinge directly on the evolution and ideology of civil society. But once again the relationship between physiognomics and the drive for production and consumption seems problematic. As a primer for the recognition and cultivation of an "essential self" untouched by the artifacts of emergent consumerism, physiognomics appears as a potential antidote to the ideology of consumption. It would not be surprising if the reversal in the evaluation of luxury, once considered a sin but in the context of civil society now viewed as the useful motor behind a developing economy, called forth a bad conscience in those who began to embrace this new, more positive evaluation. Physiognomics could be interpreted as the expression of this bad conscience to the extent that it can be read as a neutralization of the relationship between consumption, acquisition, and personal style: it preaches, in a word, the virtues of abstention in the service of an ideology of authenticity. On the other hand, as we have seen, Lavater cleverly manipulated the mechanisms and the mentality of consumer culture to promote his physiognomic project and disseminate his theories. He might be regarded as an incipient televangelist, someone who exploited the consumer market as a vehicle for propagating a Christian anti-consumerist, essentialist ideology that identified moral substance as its structural cornerstone.

If the major practitioners of civil society were an intelligentsia who produced and mediated meaning (Hull 216), then the discipline of physiognomics was central to the ideological self-constitution of civil society insofar as it invoked and reinforced the two pillars on which this new sociopolitical formation rested: morality and rationality. Lavater's reliance on the methods and discourse of enlightened science will be the subject of the next chapter and need not be developed here. More important than this scientific dimension is the role of physiognomic discourse in generating and buttressing not only a set of clearly defined moral values—honesty, empathy, intelligence, ingenuousness, constancy, sensitivity, grace, and so on—but also a *language* capable of transmitting and manifesting this new moral substance. A further reason for the tremendous popularity of Lavater's writings on physiognomics was their engagement of the new language of sentimentalism, emotion, and intimacy. As Purdy has astutely observed, the empathy that formed the core of this ideology of sentimentalism presumed the existence of a universal moral psychology (41–42). To physiognomics fell the significant task of producing the tenets of this universal moral psychology and disseminating them among the populace in the form not simply of a body of knowledge, but as a set of practices that could be employed to identify those individuals with whom one shared this palette of characterological virtues. The body became the vehicle for projections of and about that individual private core that constituted communal identity beyond all individual difference.

Although ostensibly glorifying the human body by conceiving it as the sensual concretization of divine significance, Lavaterian physiognomics in fact pursues a strategic program for the negation of the body, the repression of its sensual being in the very process by which it is lent "significance." As such, physiognomics as discipline manifests one of the significant ideological drives of civil society, what Michel Foucault has termed the "docility" of the body (*Discipline and Punish* 135–69). Similarly, Herbert Marcuse has argued that the hypostatization of the "soul" as the supersensual essence that escapes the structures of a reifying socioeconomic practice represents the fundamental reflex in what he terms the "affirmative" culture of modernism (78). While the obsession with the ethereality of this innerworldly spiritual domain must be considered, as Foucault so clearly demonstrates, to be a critical response to the waxing oppression of the subject in emerging civil society, it simultaneously "affirms" these concrete structures of alienation insofar as it, at the very least, passes over them in silence. Instead of intervening in the conditions responsible for its physical coercion, the civil subject reacts by denying the significance of the physical, empirical sphere, substituting for it the fantasy of the all-important life of the soul. This internal domain is hypostatized as the sphere of the "private" self that must be set apart and shielded from the public domain. The irony of physiognomic theory and practice is that in order to *identify* this isolated kernel that is the passport to acceptance in civil society, it must explode the barrier between private and public life and expose the private core to the public eye. The keen *empirical* observation on which this hypostatization of the metaphysical soul and its revelation is based ultimately turns into a form of omnipresent surveillance, a universalized panopticism in which the social subject is coerced into compliance with a certain set of norms. In the words of Michel Foucault:

> Our society is one not of spectacle, but of surveillance; under the surface of images, one invests bodies in depth; . . . the play of signs defines the anchorages of power; it is not that the beautiful totality of the individual is amputated, repressed, altered by our social order, it is rather that the individual is carefully fabricated in it, according to a whole technique of forces and bodies. . . . We are neither in the amphitheatre,

> nor on the stage, but in the panoptic machine, invested by its effects of power, which we bring to ourselves since we are part of its mechanism. (*Discipline and Punish* 217)

Physiognomics became one of the primary tools deployed by civil society for this fabrication of the individual according to preordained ethical, characterological, national, or racial definitions. Its prominence throughout the modern epoch is tied to the fact that, as instrument both for the promulgation of ideological values and the coercive policing of their implementation, it represents an impressively efficient disciplinary mechanism. As Richard Sennett persuasively argues, "[w]hen everyone has each other under surveillance, sociability decreases, silence being the only form of protection" (15). Paradoxically, then, physiognomics, which styles itself as a strategy for increased intimacy, actually increases the isolation of the individual by subjecting it to a totalizing regime of visibility. But whereas Sennett views the open-floor office plan as the culmination of this paradox of visibility and isolation, modern physiognomics, as systematized scrutiny of the social Other, is certainly the most effective and insidious—because least obvious—manifestation of this paradox.

The ideological program for the tactical segregation of the "soul" from all empirical, sociopolitical facticity is paradigmatically manifest in Gottfried Wilhelm Leibniz's (1646–1716) conceptualization of the human subject as a "windowless monad": "Monads do not have any windows through which things can enter or exit. . . . Thus neither external substance nor external accident can ever have any influence on a monad," he unequivocally asserts in the *Monadologie* (440). This absolute self-containment of the monad constitutes its autonomy, its total isolation from all impulses that derive from the physical world of the senses. Lavater's physiognomic theories operate from this Leibnizian presumption of the civil subject as a windowless monad upon whose entelechy external forces, be they of historical, sociological, or merely of accidental nature, can by definition have no impact. Lavater sets himself the somewhat paradoxical task of extending this monadic quality to the human body itself, thereby liberating it from all worldly conjunctures. This belief will resurface, of course, in the racial theories of the late-nineteenth and early-twentieth centuries as an argument against environmental influences on the human individual and the thesis of the absolute genetic predetermination of every human being. But what makes Lavater's physiognomic project especially noteworthy is that it goes about this autonomization of the body as reflection of the monadic "soul" by drawing specifically on *semiotic* arguments. This suggests that Lavater's physiognomics is particularly well suited for an analysis of the role of emergent semiotic theory in the ideological program of self-mastery endemic of civil society.

Physiognomics operates by semioticizing the body, by transforming it into a discursive system composed explicitly of *natural* signs, which, according to the semiotic understanding current in Lavater's day, are utterly transparent and hence vanish behind their (spiritual) signifieds. This insistence on the requisite transparency of signs, which dominated semiotic thought in Germany in this period (Wellbery 7–8), is appropriated in Lavaterian physiognomics as a tactic for the de-substantialization of the body, the sublation of its sensual being by means of its "en-signment," its reduction to the transitory token of the supersensual "essence." It is important not to confuse this semiotic transparency with a doctrine of immanence, which would hold that things—in this case the body—have meaning in and of themselves. This error is committed, for example, by Hans-Georg von Arburg, who views physiognomic traces as hieroglyphs rather than as signs (49), as well as by Claudia Schmölders (*Der exzentrische Blick* 16), who claims that physiognomics treats the body as simple embodiment *(Inbegriff)* of transsensual Being. Modern physiognomics always assumes—if with reluctance and a wistful nostalgia for the immediacy of immanence—a fundamental split between transsensual essence and bodily appearance. This forces it to divide the body into distinct "texts" that operate according to their own codes and read these texts as representational signs, with all their attendant advantages and disadvantages. The necessary corollary of this semiotics of somatic representation—body parts as *signifiers* that point to transsensual signifieds—is the demand that these somatic signifiers be decoded according to a systematic hermeneutic, the organized and disciplinarily codified interpretive methodology that informs physiognomic practice.

With this broader historico-cultural context in mind I have coined the phrase "surface hermeneutics," in conscious allusion to the concept of depth hermeneutics associated with Freudian psychoanalysis, to describe the interpretive practice Lavater, as the founder of modern physiognomics, pursued in his analyses. A comparison of the Lavaterian and Freudian interpretive projects, which mark the historical inception and culmination of cultural modernism, as well as a look at the relation between physiognomics and Edmund Husserl's (1859–1938) phenomenology, will allow us to throw into relief certain continuities and discontinuities in this intellectual-historical formation. We must keep in mind, of course, that Lavaterian physiognomics is no isolated phenomenon in the history of modern German culture. But perhaps the persistence with which the star of physiognomics reappears on the cultural horizon of German-speaking Europe during the modern age testifies more convincingly than anything else to the manner in which it is fundamentally interwoven into the fabric of German civil society.

Lavater's Physiognomic Project

The aim of Lavaterian physiognomics was to develop a unifying theory of the human subject, one able to establish an ineluctable interconnection between body and soul, between the entelechy of the spirit and the external existence of the empirical being subject to natural, sociopolitical, economic, and other laws. What distinguishes Lavater's undertaking as a peculiarly modern enterprise was his desire to conceive the human physiognomy specifically in terms of a *language* whose seemingly inscrutable signs can ultimately be deciphered.[16] In the early essay "Von der Physiognomik" he explicitly invokes the linguistic nature of this physiognomic idiom when he ends his defense of the aesthetic harmony of the human body with the assertion: "From this one can incontrovertibly conclude, in my opinion, that everything about the human body, small and large, is significant, that nature possesses a tenthousandfold language in which it speaks to us simultaneously, that it principally speaks in a very comprehensible, very unequivocal manner, and that it is not nature's fault, but our own, if we fail to understand it or if we understand it incorrectly" (160). Especially significant is Lavater's insistence on the absolute unequivocality of this natural language of the body, which leads him to the corollary that all physiognomic misunderstandings are simply misreadings attributable to the hermeneutic deficiencies of human beings. As a corrective to this interpretive inadequacy, physiognomics takes on the specific character of a hermeneutics of the body—a "surface hermeneutics," as I have chosen to call it—which Lavater defines as *"the facility for being able to recognize the inner nature of a human being on the basis of his or her external qualities,* the ability to perceive what does not immediately appear to the senses by means of some natural form of expression" (*Physiognomische Fragmente* 1: 13).

Lavater recognizes that the elaboration of such an infallible hermeneutic practice invariably depends on the identification of a semiotic theory that governs the constitution of the natural signs that make the sensual body "significant," that is, that cause it to signify. In order to provide physiognomics with an adequate theory of bodily signs Lavater appeals to semiotic conceptions widely disseminated in the German Enlightenment. In particular he invokes the discipline of medical semiotics, which concerns itself with the localization of specific physical symptoms as the index of particular illnesses, expanding its "symptomatic" theory of the interconnection between external sign and internal signified to encompass the moral, characterological, and intellectual spheres as well (see Pestalozzi, "Physiognomische Methodik" 140–42). "Are we not able to demonstrate on the basis of reason alone that consumption, due to its very nature, modifies our face in such and such a way; that excreted gall must color the eyes in such and such a manner; that a more violent seething of the blood calls forth this specific color? Are these purely arbitrary signs, or signs that are founded in nature, in the immediate connection of the external and the internal?" ("Von der Physiognomik" 151–52).

As this passage makes amply clear, Lavater's contention that the language of the human physiognomy is wholly unequivocal leads him necessarily to the claim that its signs are not *arbitrary;* they are explicitly *natural* or *motivated*—that is, the connection between signifier and its signified is grounded in a relation of cause and effect. He thus adopts in toto the semiotic principles propagated by Enlightenment philosophy in an attempt to legitimate "scientifically" the reading strategies of his physiognomic surface hermeneutics. In his physiognomic theories Lavater "en-signs" the human body by grafting this semiotic doctrine onto his understanding of its "significant" sensual features. He thereby establishes the secondariness and transparency of the body, in its status as signifying medium, to an underlying, meaning-producing human "spirit": "One should never forget," he asserts in the *Physiognomische Fragmente*, "that external expression *exists precisely for the purpose* of making the internal recognizable by means of it!" (1: 165; emphasis added). The only purpose of the body, it would seem, is to serve as a sensual manifestation of the soul; the body becomes a text whose decoding is the business of physiognomic hermeneutics. In chapter 1 I will examine in detail the relevant tenets of Enlightenment semiotics and the aporias into which the adoption of these principles leads Lavater's physiognomic theory and practice.

The ideological dialectic of Lavater's physiognomics crystallizes around an all-out war against the principles of (semiotic) arbitrariness that constitute the condition of possibility of the enlightened episteme.[17] This arbitrary relation is Lavater's nemesis, and he envisions its eradication as the ultimate aim of all culture ("Von der Physiognomik" 150; *Physiognomische Fragmente* 1: 47). The *Natursprache*, or language of nature "spoken" by the human physiognomy, represents for Lavater the paradigm of a non-arbitrary code in which sensually discernible features function as natural signs for supersensual characteristics. But clearly Lavater cannot designate *all* external bodily features as symptoms of genuine internal traits; indeed, he admits that dissimulation and mimicry, "the capacity to imitate everything by applying reason, arbitrariness, and choice" (*Physiognomische Fragmente* 2: 30), are fundamental to human nature. This recognition leads him to voice a critique of the fascination with superficialities he senses among his contemporaries, an assault on the alienated state of enlightened culture that rings similar to the typical denunciations articulated by the generation of Storm-and-Stress poets. "The great mass of human beings constantly feast on and satiate themselves with words without meaning, externalities without energy, bodies without spirit, structure and form without animating essence— . . . and yet this is the most universally valid assertion . . . : *it is the spirit that breathes life into these things, the flesh is good for nothing*" (*Physiognomische Fragmente* 1: 144–45). The sociocultural context that Lavater invokes is marked by a widening breach between semblance and essence, surface and depth, external sign and internal significance. Symptomatic of this cultural phenomenon is the vigorous proliferation of arbitrary, dissimulative signs; there is a near-pathological obsession with such empty externalities.

It is against this backdrop that Lavater formulates his physiognomic theories, conceiving them as an antidote to the cultural malaise of emergent civil society. A preoccupation with the sensuality of the body is indicative for him of this degenerate cultural state, and his critique culminates with ideological necessity in a typically Christian condemnation of the flesh.[18] The attempt to establish the human physiognomy as, strictly speaking, *significant* leads Lavater to theorize the body as a malleable shell that is shaped and animated—in effect *created*—by the spirit that occupies it. Thus he defines physiognomics as "the acquaintance with the relationship of the external with the internal, of the visible surface with the invisible content, of what is *visible* and perceptibly *animated* with what is *invisible* and imperceptibly *animates*" (*Physiognomische Fragmente* 1: 13). Taking this organic unity of body and soul as his point of departure, Lavater's aim is the generation of a hermeneutic science that cannot be misled by the dissimulations of arbitrary signs; physiognomics represents for him a hermeneutics to end all hermeneutics in the sense that it performs the interpretive acid test capable of infallibly segregating genuineness and authenticity from falsehood and dissemblance. Physiognomics, as a surface hermeneutics that decodes the natural traces the supersensual essence engraves upon the sensual body, circumscribes a discipline in which one can pursue metaphysics as an *empirical* science. This tension between transrational metaphysical faith and scientistic rationality lends Lavaterian physiognomics its fundamentally paradoxical character. This curious blend of scientific self-understanding with a metaphysical, sometimes even mystical line of thought is one of the defining features of modern, post-Lavaterian physiognomics.

It is no coincidence that the attack Georg Wilhelm Friedrich Hegel (1770–1831) launched against Lavater in the section entitled "Physiognomik und Schädellehre" (Physiognomics and phrenology) in his *Phänomenologie des Geistes* (Phenomenology of mind) takes aim specifically at the semiotic underpinnings of physiognomics. Indeed, Hegel undercuts Lavater's theory precisely by asserting the absolute arbitrariness of the semiotic relationship on whose non-contingency Lavater insisted (*Phänomenologie des Geistes* 236). Hegel's critique is aimed primarily at Lavater's contention that physiognomic significance expresses itself involuntarily, employing the body as a purely passive medium. Lavater's dogmatic insistence that only those expressions not subject to the arbitrariness of human intentionality constitute determinate signs of supersensual "spirit" opened up physiognomics to the charge that it amounted to nothing but a theory of human determinism. For Hegel, by contrast, the a priori givens of *stable* character in no way reflect the essence of the individual; rather, this essence is *self*-created in the very process by which the human being externalizes and transmutes its physical givenness in intentional acts such as speech and labor (*Phänomenologie des Geistes* 235). In stark contrast to the essentialist and conservationist position of Lavater, which locates individuality in a transsensual and a priori Being called the "soul," Hegel argues that individuality arises only when this Being, in its givenness, is sacrificed to a process of becoming that manifests itself externally in words and deeds. According to Hegel, these externalizations are the only noncontingent, nonarbitrary signs of authentic character because they are inherently bound up with it in a dialectical process of reciprocal self-determination. Moreover, Hegel stresses that the physiognomic conception of a given and stable physical being that is tailored by a soul so as to serve as its sensual sign is not only far more arbitrary than Lavater is willing to concede; it further robs the physical body of its *actuality,* transforming it merely into the passive index of this supersensual other. Thus Hegel recognizes that to conceive the body as *sign* is to deny it any Being-in-itself, demoting it to the incidental status of a being-(sign)-for-something-other. In other words, Lavater's en-signment of the body is tantamount to a monumental act of repression in which the sensuality, freedom, and creativity of the human being as individual are fundamentally negated.

Lavater, Freud, Husserl

It may at first glance strike one as an exaggeration or oversimplification to situate Lavater's physiognomic surface hermeneutics in a single intellectual-historical continuum with Freud's psychoanalytical depth hermeneutics and Husserl's phenomenology. By the same token, the possibility that physiognomics and psychoanalysis exhibit a certain historical interwovenness is suggested by the fact that the same Carl Gustav Carus (1789–1869) who attempted to rehabilitate physiognomics in the nineteenth century also composed a significant psychological treatise, which in many respects anticipates Freud's central theories, including his conceptions of the unconscious and the preconscious.[19] The natural affinities between physiognomics and empirical psychology can also be witnessed in their close imbrication in the characterology of Ludwig Klages (1872–1956). Now, although it is obvious, to be sure, that Lavater's wholly nondynamic conception of human character knows none of the complexity and conflict characteristic of the modern Freudian view of the psyche, there is at least one important respect in which Lavaterian physiognomics resembles Freud's psychoanalytic project: the common force behind these theories is the irrepressible urge to uncover a genuine, authentic level of expression and internal Being that exists *beyond* the active will and conscious intentions of the human subject. Lavater's crusade against all that is arbitrary *(willkürlich)* is inadequately comprehended if this concept is limited to the connotation of semiotic arbitrariness; indeed, Lavater understood this word to signify quite literally that which is *will-kürlich,* that is, to describe whatever is subject to the discretion *(küren)* of the human will *(Wille)*. This fundamental distrust of human intentionality, a distrust that we perhaps take for granted in the post-Freudian era, strikes one as particularly paradoxical in a figure such as Lavater, who is otherwise steeped in the joyous optimism of a Christian anthropology. Yet his interest in physiognomy as an authentic, super-intentional expression of the genuine, "true" sentiments of the human subject represents but one variation on a theme that forms a persistent leitmotif in the thought of his contemporaries and is omnipresent throughout German modernism in general. The fascination with gesture, mime, and other forms of nonverbal communication at the end of the eighteenth century is only one of the symptoms of this obsession with authentic expression,[20] as is the valorization of the "naive" over whatever is deliberate and reflective.[21] Freud is the modern heir to this strain of thought that seeks ideologically to reconcile the external and internal dimensions of human subjectivity, to rejoin those two halves of the integral being that modern life praxis tears asunder. Only in a life world in which interpersonal obligation and interhuman trust have ceased to be dependable intersubjective bonds, a world whose mechanisms are concealed behind the playful if illusory simulacra of arbitrary signs, can such a fixation on modes of verity, untouched by intention, will, reflection, or consciousness, take hold. According to Sennett, this belief in the involuntary disclosure of the emotions and the self was one of the principal developments of the nineteenth century, leading to a blurring of the lines between the public and the private spheres (24–25). Ironically, this blurring made the creation of such hermeneutic tools as physiognomics all the more necessary, which in turn sought to expose the private life to ever greater public scrutiny, thereby further erasing the line that separated these two domains.

Physiognomy as theorized by Lavater can be understood as a kind of *Fehlleistung,* an unintentional "slip" in the Freudian sense: it circumscribes the domain of human self-expression in which the individual is not master in his or her own house. Lavaterian physiognomy and Freudian psycho-theory have this involuntaristic, deterministic element in common—with the noteworthy difference, of course, that the authoritative voice that Lavater's "transcendental ventriloquism" (Lichtenberg, "Über Physiognomik" 257) projects into a *meta*physical beyond, Freud's "psychological ventriloquism," if we may call it that, locates in an *intra*physical, an intra*psychical* agency, namely in the unconscious. Physiognomics as the science of this super-intentional language is a surface hermeneutics that resembles in kind the dream analyses on which Freud's depth hermeneutics is predicated: both seek to reconstitute the noncontingent, uncensored "text" of authentic human character. Lichtenberg, the enlightened crusader against the prophetic quality of physiognomy, unwittingly becomes a prophet in his own right when he observes in one of his notebooks: "If people would honestly relate their dreams, we could surmise their character better from this than from the interpretation of their face" (*Sudelbücher* 447).

Lichtenberg obviously could not know that this sarcastic remark, which belittles physiognomics by comparing it disfavorably with oneiromancy, anticipates what Freud would argue little over a century later in his groundbreaking study *Die Traumdeutung* (The interpretation of dreams). And in fact what Lavater attempted in the four volumes of his *Physiognomische Fragmente* has—relatively speaking, of course—further rather astonishing parallels to Freud's psychoanalytic program. Like Freud, Lavater was concerned with the systematization of a symbolic language, with the ascertainment of its semantics or semiotics, and with the determination of its syntax. To be sure, whereas Lavater modestly promises only to provide a few letters of the physiognomic alphabet (*Physiognomische Fragmente* 1: "Vorrede" [unpaginated]), Freud seeks to reconstruct the language of the unconscious in its entirety by pinpointing the laws that govern its deep structure. Moreover, both sought to rehabilitate interpretive disciplines traditionally disparaged as groundless prophetics, and each pursued this aim by appropriating the methodological procedures and empirical credibility of positivistic sciences. Both Lavaterian physiognomics and Freudian psychoanalysis thereby succumb to that scientistic self-misunderstanding that, according to Jürgen Habermas, is endemic to the human sciences in the modern epoch (see *Erkenntnis und Interesse* 88–233).

Despite these similarities we cannot fail to note that Lavater and Freud could scarcely be farther apart where their conceptions of sensuality and the body are concerned. For Freud, of course, it is precisely the repressed sensual needs and desires of the body that authorize the super-intentional language of the unconscious, which thereby functions as the custodian of repressed sensuality. For Lavater, on the other hand, the en-signment of the body signals precisely the repressive moment inherent in "Protestant ethics," in which sensuality is strategically reduced to a negligible epiphenomenon of the "soul."[22] Whereas for Lavater the body is nothing but the sensual sign of a supersensual signified, Freud reverses the roles of sign and signified in this semiotic equation: the super- or intrasensual psychic "text" constitutes the sign that marks the place once held by negated, absent sensuality. Insofar as Freud's hermeneutics attempts to liberate the sensual from this chain of repressive denial, of which physiognomics is but one prominent link, its thrust is directed decidedly against one of the mainstays of modern ideology. On the other hand, it simultaneously replicates the structure of false consciousness in that it seeks to purchase the liberation of sensuality at the price of disregarding the sociopolitical and economic structures that triggered this repressive self-mastery in the first place. In Freudian depth hermeneutics this moment of ideological self-deception is marked by the masking of sociopolitical coercion behind the interpersonal demands of the patriarchal family.[23]

Lavaterian surface hermeneutics and Freudian depth hermeneutics share the overriding paradox that while they are initially conceived as neutralizers of the ideological cleavage between internal and external existence in modern life praxis, each ultimately reveals itself to be the agent of a repression that serves to buttress this rift. Lavaterian physiognomics as surface hermeneutics writes the body large, paradoxically, only so as to be able better to erase it by means of its reduction to transparent signs: it trans-scribes the body, so to speak, in invisible ink. By contrast, Freudian depth hermeneutics attempts to rescue the script of that sensuality that Lavater would expunge. We can perhaps best throw this mechanism into relief by borrowing from Freud the image of the "magic writing pad" that he employed in the late essay "Notiz über den 'Wunderblock'" (Note on the magic writing pad) in order to illustrate the operation of the psyche. The *Wunderblock* is a simple apparatus consisting of a dark wax pad covered by a transparent cellophane sheet. Under the pressure of a stylus the wax sublayer leaves traces on the surface sheet that can be erased simply by separating it from this backing (363–64). Taking this magic pad as a metaphor for the body-soul dichotomy of the human subject, Lavaterian physiognomics can be imagined writing the text of the body on this transparent cellophane surface only in order better to wipe away its traces in a flurry of hermeneutic activity. Lavater overlooks, however, that this writing leaves a permanent inscription on the underlying wax pad. Psychoanalytic hermeneutics concerns itself with this inscription as the return of the repressed, the indelible remainder and reminder of an act of self-coercion that suppresses human sensuality. In this sense we can view Lavater's physiognomic surface hermeneutics as one of the ideological-historical conditions of possibility constitutive of psychoanalytic depth hermeneutics. On the other hand, however, Freud's attempted intervention in the ideology of the civil subject, much like Lavater's, amounts to a mystification that ultimately contributes to the perpetuation of that ideological self-deceit it aims to dismantle. This self-abrogating dialectic is the most profound trait shared by physiognomic surface hermeneutics and psychoanalytic depth hermeneutics. This deep-structural commonality points to the resilience and continuity- constitutive power of ideology in the intellectual-historical conglomerate we designate as cultural modernism.

Husserlian phenomenology, which, along with Freudian psychoanalysis, represents one of the major intellectual-historical contributions of twentieth-century German thought, has close affinities with both physiognomics and psychology. However, while Husserl openly acknowledges what he calls "the intimate connection between phenomenology and psychology" (*Ideen I* 177), the proximity of phenomenology to the physiognomic tradition remains largely unarticulated. The major point of overlap is, of course, the conception of the human being as an entity in which body and soul, external and internal being, form an inherent unity. Thus in the second book of his *Ideen zu einer reinen Phänomenologie und phänomenologischen Philosophie* (Ideas for a pure phenomenology and phenomenological philosophy), which focuses on the constitution of materiality, Husserl stresses that the ego "encompasses the 'entire' human being, body and soul" (94). Moreover, like physiognomics, phenomenology understands the soul as an active, animating power, and the body as the more or less passive medium of its expressions. Indeed, the material body, for Husserl, is the condition of possibility for the objective manifestation of the psychic domain as such: "In order to be experienced objectively," he asserts in *Ideen*

II, "spirit must be animation of a material body" (96). The human body, then, as a living entity, is always a body animated by the psyche, the soul, or the internal, non-perceptible essence. Husserl employs the German word *Leib* to designate this animate body, which he distinguishes from *Körper* as purely material, inanimate body. Hence *Leib,* as the animate, animated body, always manifests the expressions of the internal spirit. "The animate body is not just a thing, but rather the expression of spirit," Husserl insists, and he goes on to maintain in absolute terms that "*everything* about the animate body can assume psychic significance" (*Ideen II* 96). The body thus becomes the sole indicator of the psychic life, and as such it is the vehicle by means of which we gain access to this internal domain. Indeed, for Husserl intersubjective experience would be impossible without a hermeneutics of the body that uncovers or projects psychic meanings on the basis of bodily expressions (see *Ideen II* 95).

Phenomenology's understanding of the expressive connection between soul and body, psyche and the realm of physicality, reads like the foundations for a theoretical physiognomics. Moreover, Husserl, like Lavater, even draws a comparison between the psychic expressions of the body and language, claiming that there is a certain "analogy between this sign system for the 'expression' of psychic events . . . and the sign system of language for the expression of thoughts" (*Ideen II* 166). Yet whereas he suggests that one ought to be able to "systematically study the 'expression' of the psychic life" and "establish the grammar of this expression" (*Ideen II* 166), Husserl himself never embarks upon such a project; if he had, he would have produced a practical physiognomics. As we will see, this move from phenomenological theory to physiognomic practice was reserved for one of Husserl's students, Ludwig Ferdinand Clauss (1892–1974), who consciously sought to develop a pragmatic physiognomics based on the theory and methodology of Husserlian phenomenology. More important, perhaps, is that, in contrast to Lavater, who stressed the significance of the firm and unchanging features of the body, for Husserl it is the body in motion, the animate, animated body, that manifests psychic significance. Like Lavater's two critics Lichtenberg and Hegel, Husserl will take sides with pathognomics, which ascribes significance solely to the motive, dynamic body.

Husserl's lack of practical application and systematization for his theory of the animate body as expressive medium of the psyche and the stress he places on pathognomic expression over the meaning of stable bodily form comprise two features that distinguish phenomenology from Lavaterian physiognomics. A third difference can be found in the self-understanding of phenomenological theory vis-à-vis the positivism of the natural sciences. Whereas Lavater sought to appropriate the methods and the discourse of the empirical sciences in order to lend scientific validity to his physiognomic interpretations, Husserl explicitly distances himself from the natural sciences. If science is concerned with empirical "facts," phenomenology, according to Husserl, concentrates on the discernment of "essences" (*Ideen I* 6). Taking up Wilhelm Dilthey's (1833–1911) distinction between the human sciences (*Geisteswissenschaften;* literally: "sciences of spirit or mind") from the natural sciences *(Naturwissenschaften),* Husserl explicitly locates phenomenology in the realm of the human sciences (*Ideen II* 191). As such, phenomenology does not rely on empirical data, as do the natural sciences, but depends instead on intuition, or *Anschauung.* This German term is key to phenomenological theory. Derived from the German verb *schauen,* meaning to see or to view, *Anschauung* has both the concrete meaning of "visual perception" and the more figurative significance of "intuition." The fusion of these two meanings in the word *Anschauung* is essential to phenomenological practice. Indeed, one could argue that the marriage of concrete and abstract meanings in this central term parallels the fusion of concrete body and supersensual psyche in the phenomenological understanding of the human body. Just as the psyche only makes itself manifest through the medium of the body, intuition of transsensual essence—what Husserl calls *Wesensanschauung* or *Wesenserschauung*—can only transpire as a corollary to visual perception. Sight, seeing, vision, and their metaphors become the key terms of phenomenological discourse. Husserl acknowledges the prominence of this transsensual seeing when he writes: "*Immediate 'seeing,'* not merely sensual, experiential seeing, but *seeing as such as an originary dative consciousness of any sort whatever,* is the ultimate source of grounding for all reasonable assertions" (*Ideen I* 43). For phenomenology as for physiognomics, "vision" implies both concrete visual perception and intuitive discernment. Indeed, for both the physiognomist and the phenomenologist every act of empirical seeing simultaneously entails a moment of supersensual intuition. Thus phenomenology rejects the positivistic, natural-scientific impulse of modern physiognomics only in order to highlight more emphatically the intuitive dimension that is always inherent in physiognomic practice.

When we recognize the intermediary position physiognomics assumes between Freudian psychoanalysis and Husserlian phenomenology we can begin to appreciate its significance as an intellectual-historical phenomenon in the fabric of German modernist thought. Physiognomics is wedded so closely with the emergence and development of modern culture in Germany that the issues around which it turns help to spawn some of the most notable positions of modern German intellectuals. Clearly, there is more at stake in the phenomenon of physiognomics, especially given its persistence in modern German thought, than just the interpretation of character out of the face. Physiognomics is about more than just the face. The chapters that follow will attempt to explore some of the many dimensions of physiognomics and physiognomic theory in German thought from Lavater through to the racist physiognomics of the Weimar Republic and National Socialism.

1

Science and Semiotics in the Physiognomic Theories of Johann Caspar Lavater

> In the Enlightenment, the metaphor of legibility is the thread that marks a history of the constant infiltration of reason, which conceived itself as incorruptible, by the secret wish that the world might have more meaning for the human being and disclose more to him or her than might reasonably be expected.
>
> Hans Blumenberg (*Die Lesbarkeit der Welt* 199)

Physiognomics and the Spirit of Enlightenment

The publication of Johann Caspar Lavater's *Physiognomische Fragmente zur Beförderung der Menschenkenntniß und Menschenliebe* was one of the major intellectual events of the final decades of the eighteenth century. Despite his criticism of Lavater's lack of scientific rigor, Johann Wolfgang von Goethe laudingly acknowledged the timeliness of Lavater's thought when he asserted in his autobiography, *Aus meinem Leben: Dichtung und Wahrheit* (From my life: Poetry and truth): "No one drew as much from this time and wrote for this time in the way he [Lavater] did: his writings are genuine chronicles that can only truly be comprehended in the historical context of the time itself" (157). With this statement Goethe ascribes a key historical, dialectical position to his former friend: Lavater's creations not only drew heavily on the intellectual tendencies of the historical period in which he lived, they actively contributed to the intellectual constitution of this epoch itself. According to this assessment—and keeping within the terminological fashion of the day—Lavater can be considered both as "imitator" and "original genius." Fusing intellectual appropriation and creativity, this position corresponds perfectly with Lavater's own definition of intellectual originality. "The most magnificent original thinkers," he remarks in the third volume of the *Physiognomische Fragmente,* "are nevertheless mere copiers. . . . They merely perceived nature in an individual manner, through the medium of the works produced by its masters and through exemplary models—that is what made them original thinkers and geniuses" (3: 41). Like all his portraits of the vital intellectual contained in these volumes, this ideal image is based on Lavater's own self-understanding. Nevertheless, questions remain: which "masters" and "exemplary models" guided the evolution of Lavater's physiognomic thought, and did Lavater actually succeed in transcending these models in his physiognomic theory.

Intellectual history, especially literary history, has given an unequivocal answer to this question: Lavater's physiognomic project is viewed in a configuration with the primary spokesmen of the so-called "genius generation"—Johann Gottfried Herder (1744–1803), Johann Georg Hamann (1730–1788), Goethe, Jakob Michael Reinhold Lenz (1751–1792), to name just the most significant representatives. And indeed, one does not need to look far to find the traces of their influence in the *Physiognomische Fragmente,* an influence Lavater proudly acknowledged. In fact, Lavater opens the first volume of the *Fragmente* with an introduction in which Herder's *Älteste Urkunde des Menschengeschlechts* (Oldest document of the human race) is extensively quoted (1: 3–6). This text celebrates the human being from an overindulgently homocentric perspective, which we find it difficult to identify with today, as the crowning achievement of divine creation. It is clear, of course, that this Christian anthropomorphism, which expressly views the human body as the mirror of the divine soul, constitutes both the point of departure and the aim of Lavater's physiognomic studies. And yet, especially with regard to its theoretical foundations, Lavater's physiognomics by no means exhibits the monolithic character commonly ascribed to it. On the contrary, what distinguishes Lavater's project, especially from the traditional physiognomic works of antiquity and the Renaissance, is its astonishing combination of fanaticism and hyperemotional rhetoric—so typical of the writings of the Storm-and-Stress "geniuses"—with a claim to positivistic objectivity and scientific exactitude in the spirit of Enlightenment thinking. This latter tendency accounts not only for the peculiar attraction Lavater's theories held for his contemporaries, but also for the ferocity with which Lavater was attacked by some of his critics.

Lavater's most outspoken antagonist, the Göttingen physicist Georg Christoph Lichtenberg, brings the inherent contradictions of Lavater's physiognomics into precise focus when, in the introduction to the second edition of his polemical treatise "Über Physiognomik; wider die Physiognomen: Zu Beförderung der Menschenliebe und Menschenkenntnis" (On physiognomics; against the physiognomists: For the promotion of human love and human understanding), he summarizes the point of his campaign against Lavater in the following words: "Now that crude superstition has been banished from the more refined world, I wanted to make sure that a more subtle form of prejudice did not sneak its way back in, one that would prove even more dangerous than crude superstition because of the mask of rationality it wore" (257). With typical enlightened optimism Lichtenberg presupposes the existence of a rational "world"—the reference is presumably to the "republic of scholars" made up of the intelligentsia or the enlightened public sphere of civil society—in which reason reigns supreme and from which all superstition, the nemesis of the Enlightenment, has been successfully banished. But Lichtenberg fears that this "more refined world" is threatened by the possibility of contagion through its contact with the cunning irrationalism of Lavater's physiognomics, an irrationalism that is all the more dangerous because it wears the mask of reason. Thus for Lichtenberg it is precisely the presumption to scientific validity that makes Lavater's physiognomic theories especially insidious: the semblance of scientific objectivity in which they are packaged might allow them to penetrate the island of enlightened reason and infect it with the fatal disease of irrationalism.

This insight marks a significant functional shift in the cultural politics of the German Enlightenment, one that will have a determining influence on its historical development. For the aim of Enlightenment is no longer simply the colonization of the intellectual world by means of the ever wider dissemination of healthy reason; rather, it is a matter of fortifying and defending that territory already under the reign of reason—that is, of protecting Enlightenment ideology itself from the debilitating invasion of unreason. On the example of Lavater's physiognomics, in other words, Lichtenberg gains a prescient insight into what Theodor Adorno and Max Horkheimer will diagnose, almost two centuries later, as a "reversion of Enlightenment to mythology" or a "dialectical reversal of Enlightenment into positivism, into the myth of that which is the case" (*Dialektik der Aufklärung* 3, ix). Horkheimer and Adorno, like Lichtenberg, understand their critique of a form of reason that succumbs to unreason as an attempt to rescue all that is healthy and emancipatory in Enlightenment thought from this aberration.

It is obvious that the subjectivity and the rejection of normativity typical of the Storm-and-Stress rhetoric, both of which are amply represented in Lavater's physiognomic writings, represent the expression of an incipient protest against the all-inclusive positivistic codification of the intellectual and material life world. But the very obviousness of this assertion has led to a failure to recognize the extent to which Lavater himself fell victim to the coercive power of positivism and Enlightenment scientism. For example, when he holds out the possibility that some day physiognomics will become the "science of all sciences" (*Physiognomische Fragmente* 1: 55), or when he maintains that the discipline of physiognomy should be viewed as a training program in which human beings learn to elevate their naturally-given, but obscure, physiognomic "feeling" to the level of conceptual clarity (1: 166), these are signs that the drive to codify rigorously scientific knowledge in the Enlightenment sense must take its place alongside the emotional rhetoric of the genius generation as something that, as Goethe suggests, Lavater drew from the intellectual atmosphere of the contemporary age.

Indeed, Lavater adopts point for point the telos of the Enlightenment epistemology, as it was disseminated in the wake of thinkers such as Gottfried Wilhelm Leibniz (1646–1716) and Christian Wolff (1697–1754), the explicit aim of which was to raise the "confused" and "obscure" judgments of the "lower" or sensual faculty of knowledge to the level of "clarity" and "precision" they attributed to the "higher" or conceptual, rational faculty. Lavater's attempt to transform a "naturally-given" physiognomic feeling into scientifically valid knowledge corresponds to the scientific codification of sensual knowledge pursued in eighteenth-century aesthetics, as formulated above all by Alexander Gottlieb Baumgarten (1714–1762) and his successor Johann Georg Sulzer (1720–1779). This helps explain why Lavater repeatedly appeals to Baumgarten and Sulzer as spokespersons whose authority can be summoned in support of his own physiognomic theories (see, for example, *Physiognomische Fragmente* 1: 27, 50, 52, 135; 2: 53, 78; 4: 486). It is also symptomatic that Lavater attempts to deflect attacks against the scientific presumptions of physiognomics by defining it as an "artistic" discipline that can be subsumed under the arts, which were termed the "sciences of beauty" *(schöne Wissenschaften)* in the academic discourse of Lavater's day (*Physiognomische Fragmente* 1: 52). Clearly, for Lavater the emphasis on the role that subjective insights play in his physiognomic judgments did not contradict his conviction that physiognomics would "certainly become a science definable in mathematical terms" (4: 481). With this claim Lavater pays deference to the fact that scientific disciplines structured according to mathematical calculation formed the exemplary model of knowledge as such at the inception of the modern age (see Foucault, *Order of Things* 50–58), and that for this reason mathematics became the standard against which any intellectual discipline that wanted to be taken seriously needed to measure and compare itself. Only in the intellectual-historical context of this burgeoning drive toward positivistic codification, which aimed at reducing both the sensual existence of human beings and the supersensual life of the soul and the intellect to rationally calculable laws, can we explain how Lavater could silently embrace this apparent contradiction in his own project. This inconsistency seems all the more surprising in the case of Lavater, as one of the primary representatives of the Storm-and-Stress generation, a group that, in the annals of literary history, has consistently been defined in terms of its resistance to and protest against the normativity of Enlightenment thought. The example of Lavater's physiognomic writings makes evident that this literary-historical portrayal has been much too one-sided.

Lavater's dependence on Enlightenment conceptions is largely disguised by the rhetorical and emotional excesses of his language, as well as by the religious zealotry expressed in the

Physiognomische Fragmente. But the dispute between Lavater, the Zurich preacher, and Lichtenberg, the Göttingen physicist with solid scientific credentials, has tended to cause critics to overlook the degree to which Lavater also appealed to enlightened, scientific principles. The immediate contemporary reception of the *Fragmente* demonstrates that their language earned Lavater both the greatest praise and the most vehement condemnation. In a review of the first volume of the *Fragmente,* which appeared in 1775 in the important and popular journal *Der Teutsche Merkur,* Christoph Martin Wieland (1733–1813), the journal's editor and one of the leaders of the German intelligentsia of the time, called Lavater's physiognomics "one of the most significant products of our century" and "one of the classical works written in the German language" (Wieland 184, 185). Moreover, it is striking that Wieland not only acknowledges the mixture between emotional enthusiasm and analytical, empirical observation in Lavater's text, he even cites this as one of its greatest merits: "I, at least, have never encountered such profound insight—into the very inner being of nature—such a calm power of observation, such a refined, exact capacity for discrimination, combined with such a fiery imagination, with such warmth of heart, with such a high degree of poetic genius, as I find in the whole of this work" (185).

Even the Swiss poet-scientist Albrecht von Haller (1708–1777), who otherwise was very critical of Lavater's physiognomics, wrote in an anonymous review of the third volume, published in the *Göttingische gelehrte Anzeigen:* "One of the merits of this work resides in the manner in which it is written and the large number of powerful expressions that Herr Lavater has invented. These new expressions are nonetheless comprehensible and define totally new concepts. He is without doubt an enricher of the German language" (54). The popularity and influence of Lavater's physiognomics can thus be partially attributed to the fact that, at a time when the German language was just beginning to develop as a literary-cultural medium, Lavater's writing was seen as an exemplary manifestation of the status of German as a powerful, culturally expressive language.

In contrast to this praise of Lavater's linguistic innovations, an anonymous review published in the *Neue Bibliothek der schönen Wissenschaften und der freyen Künste* criticizes above all the expressive abuses of Lavater's language, noting primarily his frequent use of highly individual, even peculiar metaphors. According to this unknown reviewer, Lavater's metaphors appear at first glance to elucidate the situations they are intended to describe; but this first impression is actually erroneous, and his use of seemingly apt but ultimately infelicitous metaphors renders Lavater's treatise especially deceptive. Following up on this criticism, the reviewer goes on to formulate his objection in more general terms: "That is why a cautious use of [metaphors] must be recommended, especially in works where precision and the use of correct concepts is particularly significant, in works in which one makes pretenses to philosophizing. Herr Lavater's comparisons often introduce a great degree of confusion and stiffness into his text."[1] According to this assessment, Lavater commits the cardinal sin of transgressing the law that forbids metaphors in scientific and philosophical discourse—a law that would culminate a century and a half later in the antimetaphorical language of analytical philosophy. Once again, then, it is the peculiar mixture of rational, philosophical claims with emotional, even poetic language of which Lavater's critics take special note.

Friedrich Nicolai (1733–1811), a Berlin publicist and one of the leading representatives of Enlightenment culture in Germany, was another figure who recognized—and, surprisingly, regretted—that Lavater's proclivity for emotional outbursts and rhetorical overstatement undermined the "scientific" quality of his physiognomic treatise. In a review of the *Fragmente* published in the prominent scholarly journal *Allgemeine deutsche Bibliothek,* which Nicolai himself edited, he openly admits that he holds "physiognomics to be a significant art that is capable of being grounded in the truth of nature" (Review 393); but he goes on to deny that Lavater's approach to this "art" of physiognomics will elevate it to the level of a pragmatic science. For Nicolai, it is once again primarily Lavater's "peculiar" manner of thinking and writing that inhibits this aim, and he summarizes the faults of Lavater's style in the following way: "The desultory, declamatory nature of his style, his love of the unusual and the marvelous, the leaps of imagination . . . , the logical reasoning that is often mingled in the most peculiar way with profound mysticism, the insightful philosophy that often crosses over into zealous piety, soulful enrapturement, and prophecy. . . . All of this serves to make this work extremely original, but it cannot be denied that it also makes it less useful" (Review 382–83). For Nicolai, the enlightened intellectual, it was obviously a matter of the "usefulness" of physiognomics as a practical and mathematical science. Lavater had gambled away the opportunity for establishing this pragmatic discipline, and thereby undermined the entire project of a scientifically based physiognomics, by placing too much emphasis on "whimsies, foundationless hypotheses, and exaggerated promises" (Review 406).

The severity of Nicolai's criticism has its source in the singular ambivalence of his position, which seeks to affirm the possibility that physiognomics could become a rigorous science but which also recognizes Lavater's efforts in this direction as ineffective and faulty, indeed, as inimical to the development of a physiognomic theory with pretensions to scientific validity. This ambivalence expresses itself most forcefully in a letter Nicolai wrote to his friend Lichtenberg, dated 15 April 1778, in which Nicolai reacts to his reading of Lichtenberg's polemic "Über Physiognomik; wider die Physiognomen," a copy of which Lichtenberg had sent to Nicolai.

> I'm not sure if you are aware that the belief in physiognomics is one of my weaknesses. I myself have practiced it for many years, and I believe that it permits one to recognize certain things apodictically, many other things with a high degree of probability. Lavater's method is worlds removed from my own. Nevertheless, I have to admit to having learned some things from him. I'm sure you can understand that I have no patience for his whimsies, of which the text is full. Still, I must frankly admit that it appears to me as if we at times have done him an injustice. He is certainly not completely inexperienced in this area. If he only were not bent on advancing theological hypotheses (for it can be proven that his physiognomics develops out of his *Aussichten [in die Ewigkeit]*,[2] in the third volume of which one finds the unfortunate traces), if instead of writing four folio volumes in three years he had only filled twenty sheets in ten years, then he could really have reawakened this nearly lost science and made a name for himself in this endeavor. (Letter to Lichtenberg 815–16)

The fact that one of the most significant representatives of Enlightenment culture in Germany designates physiognomics as a personal "weakness" suggests that the concern with the potential enshrinement of physiognomics as a scientific discipline reveals one of the faults of the German Enlightenment in general: namely, its fascination with the unreasonable, with the explanation of the inexplicable, which is part and parcel of Enlightenment thinking from the outset. For contrary to Nicolai's expectations, Lavater did indeed "make a name for himself" in the discipline of physiognomics, and he accomplished this, moreover, in the period of German modernism that is defined by the objectives of Enlightenment science. Ultimately Lavater initiates the drive to found physiognomics on a scientific basis, a drive that recurs with leitmotivic persistence throughout German intellectual history through to the racial physiognomics of German fascism.

It is precisely Lavater's role as a precursor to Nazi racial physiognomics that motivates Richard Loewenberg, in the crisis years of 1932–1933, to recall to scholars the dispute about physiognomics that raged between Lavater and Lichtenberg. "It is all the more important to remind ourselves [of this debate]," Loewenberg writes, "since today untested, unproven prejudices and assertions are immediately translated into political and concrete effects in daily life" ("Der Streit um die Physiognomik" 15). Loewenberg follows in the critical footsteps of Lichtenberg, who already in 1778 raised doubts about whether physiognomics was likely to promote human love, as Lavater claimed. That is why Lichtenberg defends the vociferousness of his attack on Lavater by asserting "I wanted to prevent people from practicing physiognomics for the promotion of human love just as in earlier times people had ravaged and burned to promote the love of God" ("Über Physiognomik" 257). Loewenberg reiterates this point when he maintains that in the science of physiognomics, as practiced in 1933, people do not formulate their interpretations of other human beings "out of responsibility and love," but rather for the purpose of "attaining mastery" over them ("Streit" 31–32). What these two critics expose in the purportedly "humane" science of physiognomics is a disguised will to overpowerment and self-empowerment. However, this will to mastery does not derive from the theological "whimsies" in Lavater's texts, as Nicolai believes; rather, it is inscribed in the scientific understanding of the Enlightenment itself, in which, in the words of Horkheimer and Adorno, "power and knowledge are synonymous" (8). The inconsistencies in Lavater's physiognomic discourse are produced by the attempt to practice a kind of pragmatic mimesis of the ruling forms of thought and argument characteristic of the German Enlightenment. Lavater seeks to justify his mystico-theological belief that the Christian divinity makes itself manifest in the human being by lending it the guise of positivistically and empirically grounded facticity.

Karl Pestalozzi was the first to demonstrate that Lavater's reliance on the discourse and apparatus of enlightened science makes itself most evident in the early, preliminary treatise "Von der Physiognomik" (On physiognomics), which was initially given as a lecture before the Scientific Society of Zurich ("Physiognomische Methodik" 137). Its original presentation in this forum, of course, helps explain its reliance on scientific terminology and argumentation. But Lavater does not abandon this claim to scientific exactitude in the *Physiognomische Fragmente;* on the contrary, this empiricist, positivist methodology remains present as his fundamental legitimation strategy, although over the course of the publication of the *Fragmente* this basic core is buried in increasingly heavy layers of declamatory rhetoric. Pestalozzi points correctly to the fact that the invocation of medical semiotics and its extension into the moral and intellectual spheres constitute Lavater's original contribution to physiognomic theory ("Physiognomishe Methodik" 140–42). According to Pestalozzi, Lavater is following ideas laid out by the Enlightenment philosopher Christian Wolff, who in his *Philosophica practica universalis* (Universal practical philosophy) first sketched the idea of a moral semiotics. Lavater's contemporaries already made this connection between his physiognomic conceptions and Wolff's moral semiotics. Gotthold Ephraim Lessing (1729–1781) makes a statement to this effect, for example, in a letter to Friedrich Nicolai dated 9 July 1776, in which he attempts to explain why Lavater has succeeded in lending physiognomics the appearance of a rationally founded discipline. After perusing all the books on physiognomics available in the extensive library in Wolffenbüttel, where he served as librarian, Lessing writes to Nicolai:

> Lavater conceives physiognomics in such a broad way that it no longer deserves this name. No other author has ever dealt with it in this way; and recently several people distinguished this model from genuine physiognomics by giving it the designation moral semiotics. And that accounts for how Lavater has successfully dressed up and disguised physiognomics, which is destined to remain uncertain and unreliable unto eternity, by cloaking it in so many less debatable and wholly certain assertions, so that its detractors are the ones who take on the appearance of being unreasonable. (*Gesammelte Werke* 9: 680)

Lessing stresses that in the domain of moral semiotics, Lavater has not made an original contribution; rather, he is simply following unnamed predecessors. Lavater's sole achievement, in Lessing's mind, is the rather questionable one of having confused the thoroughly legitimate sphere of knowledge circumscribed by moral semiotics with the unreliable art of physiognomics. According to Lessing, this alone accounts for the fact that Lavater has been able to lend his hypotheses the credibility of scientific theories.

Lessing's claim that moral semiotics is a recognized philosophical discipline independent of its appropriation by physiognomics is confirmed by Johann Walch's *Philosophisches Lexikon* of 1775, one of the standard encyclopedic works of the German Enlightenment. Under the entry "semiotics" Walch notes that this concept originated in the field of medicine, where it designates a subdiscipline dealing with the physical symptoms of particular illnesses. He continues his description by explaining exactly how this concept came to be transferred to philosophical discourse: "Due to the fact that some people modeled their moral theories on the method used by physicians . . . , this word entered the language of philosophy. Here moral semiotics designates the part of moral philosophy that defines the attributes according to which one can investigate the moral state of the soul" (2: 894). It is noteworthy that Walch's entry ends here, without even mentioning the adoption of the term "semiotics" by epistemology and linguistics, which represents an important accomplishment of Enlightenment thought already well established at the time Walch's lexicon was published. As early as 1764—that is, more that ten years before the appearance of the fourth edition of Walch's lexicon, which I have cited here—the philosopher Johann Heinrich Lambert (1728–1777) defined semiotics as one of the four fundamental branches of philosophy and devoted a major section of his *Neues Organon* to its description (2: 3–214). Be that as it may, Lavater, at least, was well aware of the profound interconnection of his own physiognomic project with this broader definition of semiotics, a conception that enjoyed wide recognition in intellectual circles of the day.[3] To be sure, the word "semiotics" itself scarcely occurs in Lavater's writings, and when it does, it is used almost exclusively in connection with the older conception of medical semiotics, one of the historical roots of physiognomic thought itself. In these contexts Lavater summons medical semiotics as a witness for the defense, brought forward to testify to the validity of his own readings of the signs of human physiognomy (see *Physiognomische Fragmente* 4: 365–68; "Von der Physiognomik" 150–52). Aside from this context, the word "semiotics" occurs only one other time in Lavater's physiognomic texts, in a footnote to the fragment entitled "Die Physiognomik, eine Wissenschaft" (Physiognomics, a science) in the first volume of the *Physiognomische Fragmente* (1: 52). Here Lavater points to Baumgarten's integration of semiotics into aesthetics in order to make the case that physiognomics also merits being ranked, like aesthetics, as a branch of science. He thereby draws an implicit comparison between semiotics and physiognomics, identifying the latter, as was the case for Baumgarten's aesthetic theory, as a subcategory of the former.

The semiotic theory on which Lavater's physiognomics is based is derived directly from Leibniz, Wolff, and Lambert, the triumvirate of philosophers principally responsible for the development of German Enlightenment philosophy. In what follows I will demonstrate in detail the extent to which Lavater simply appropriates, without great reflection on the consequences, the Enlightenment theory of semiotics for his physiognomic hermeneutics. Many of the contradictions inherent in Lavater's theories are already evident in the semiotic conceptions of the German Enlightenment. In this sense, Lavater's physiognomics brings the semiotic principles of the Enlightenment to their logical culmination—and drives them, as it were, *ad absurdum*—by applying them in a manner and a context that expose their inherent deficiencies.

The Aporias of Enlightenment Semiotics

For Enlightenment semiotic theory, whatever functions as a sign is by definition relegated to the status of a secondary, nonessential phenomenon. The sign serves principally as a dispensable mark whose only purpose consists in pointing to the existence of some other thing or concept: it is in effect but a *waysign,* the insubstantial indicator of some more substantial Being. The philosopher Christian Wolff stresses this subordination of the sign to the essential substance that it "signifies" when he writes: "A sign is a thing on whose basis I can discern either the presence or the arrival of another thing" (*Vernünfftige Gedancken von Gott, der Welt und der Seele des Menschen* 160). The sign, in other words, is a means to an end, not an end in itself—a conception that dominates Western semiotics at least until the theories of Charles Sanders Peirce (1839–1914) and the advent of High Modernist aesthetics. Modernism's glorification of the opacity and autonomy of signs obtains theoretical codification in the linguistic and philosophical doctrines of structuralist and poststructuralist thought. For the Enlightenment, by contrast, the sign operates basically as though it were a telescopic lens through which one can gaze in order to recognize with more clarity the objects or sensations it signifies. As Christian Wolff maintains: "Since our sensations are by and large unclear and obscure, words and signs serve the purpose of greater clarity by helping us to distinguish the different aspects of the things themselves, as well as the differences among those things" (*Vernünfftige Gedancken von Gott* 177). The more transparent the sign—the more it itself ceases to be an object to be perceived and instead takes on the character of an instrument *through which* one perceives—the more effective and efficient it is. It is wholly in keeping with this semiotic understanding that Lavater attributes to his physiognomic surface hermeneutics the capacity to transform obscure feelings into clear judgments (*Physiognomische Fragmente* 1: 166), a process that forms the core of the Enlightenment theory of progressive knowledge. Moreover, it is no coincidence that Lavater compares his physiognomic practices to "eyeglasses" that assist one's perceptions of human character ("Von der Physiognomik" 165): his cultivated physiognomic sensitivity permits him to "peer through," and thus to transcode, the physiognomic signs of the body in order better to recognize the spiritual traits they signify.

This demand for a semiotic transparency holds sway especially in the aesthetic theories of the Enlightenment. In his *Metaphysica*, for example, Alexander Gottlieb Baumgarten, the founding father of modern aesthetic theory, defines the sign as "a means for the knowledge of some other thing, and the purpose of the sign is its signified. Thus the sign is the ground *[principium]* for the knowledge of the signified" (97). The sign is not autonomous, it does not entail its own purpose; rather, it is strictly heteronomous, serving as the ground for something else. To adopt a metaphor employed by Ludwig Wittgenstein (1889–1951) in the closing paragraphs of his *Tractatus* (paragraph 6.54), the sign is a ladder that can be thrown away once one has climbed over it to knowledge of its signified. Lessing transposes this problematic of transparency into a temporal schema when, in notes for the treatise *Laokoön,* he criticizes what he terms a "symbolic picture"—that is, a representation in which the mimetic signs do not perfectly duplicate their original—because its opaque signs stand in the way of an immediate cognition of their signified: "in such an instance I am more conscious of the signs than the signified thing," Lessing objects, "and this accomplishment of my soul . . . always prevents my intuition of the signified thing from being able to occur simultaneously with the intuition of the sign itself" (423). The irrepressible awareness of the signs themselves threatens to blot out apperception of what they signify, and thus for Lessing perfect semiosis can be said to occur only when no lag-time separates sign-intuition from signified-intuition—that is, when the sign is co-temporaneous to and thereby merges indistinguishably with its signified.

In the third volume of his *Aussichten in die Ewigkeit* (Outlooks on eternity), published in 1773 in the midst of his preoccupation with the issues of human physiognomy, Lavater supplies his readers with what amounts to a crash course in Enlightenment epistemology and semiology, outlining the distinction between intuitive and symbolic cognition and the differences between the types of signs with which they operate: "If an object has an immediate effect on our senses, then the impression of which we are conscious is called *sensual, intuitive [anschauende]* cognition, *perception,* experience. If an object does not have an immediate effect on our senses, but instead is presented to us by means of *arbitrary* signs, then our cognition is *non-sensual, logical, symbolic.* Hence we either have knowledge of the *thing* or of a *representation* of the thing" (3: 2–3). Lavater's portrayal of symbolic knowledge as specifically reliant on *arbitrary* signs reiterates the standard position of Enlightenment semiotics. However, his definition of intuitive cognition as immediate recognition of the thing itself appears at first blush somewhat anomalous insofar as it suggests that this mode of thought is *trans*-semiotic, wholly independent of the intermediacy of signs.

Enlightenment epistemology had, of course, long since recognized and accepted—admittedly, not without considerable reluctance—the fact that there is no such thing as trans-semiotic knowledge, except perhaps in the absolute cognition of God. Thus in the epistemological theories of Leibniz, Wolff, and Lambert, the differentiation between natural and arbitrary signs serves to distinguish between intuitive and symbolic cognition. To be sure, in the Enlightenment understanding, natural signs, because they are motivated and hence exhibit a high degree of transparency to their signifieds, most closely approximate the ideal of trans-semiotic knowledge. The philosophic-historical telos of Enlightenment culture turns on a process of "progressive semiosis," as David Wellbery felicitously calls it (41), by which human cognition, as it becomes successively more reliant on natural signification, will gradually approach this trans-semiotic ideal.[4] What is noteworthy about Lavater's definition of intuitive cognition is that it essentially elides the Enlightenment recognition that this mode of thought functions by means of natural *signs* by overemphasizing the teleological projection of a trans-semiotic utopia as the ultimate goal of all culture. Whereas Enlightenment thinkers tend to be rather circumspect in their evaluations of both the arbitrary and the natural sign, cognizant that each possesses certain advantages and disadvantages,

Lavater will have none of this ambivalence. Thus while Wolff, for example, can laud the arbitrary signs of symbolic cognition as instruments that magnify the distinctness and clarity of our knowledge (*Vernünfftige Gedancken von Gott* 176–77), Lavater asserts unequivocally "that symbolic cognition is incomparably less consummate than intuitive, or immediate cognition" (*Aussichten* 3: 17).

As Lavater's terminology indicates, his valorization of the natural signs of intuitive cognition is grounded in the belief that they are "immediate" in the literal sense of non-mediated and hence utterly transparent to their signifieds: they disappear without remainder once they have fulfilled their signifying function, thus constituting a form of knowledge that for all intents and purposes is sign-less. He thereby radicalizes the Enlightenment theory of natural signification, and in doing so telescopes or even collapses the historical telos of Enlightenment culture. To be sure, Lavater, like the Enlightenment philosophers, recognizes that the state of human knowledge attained by enlightened Western culture operates to a large part through symbolic cognition and thus is reliant on the intermediacy of arbitrary signs. Furthermore, he shares their belief that the philosophic-historical aim of all culture is the return to a state in which human cognition is nonreflective, intuitive, and immediate, and in which semiosis hence is perfectly transparent, motivated, and natural. But he differs from them in two respects: on the one hand, he believes that if not humanity at large, then at least certain "geniuses"—among whom, of course, Lavater numbers himself—are already close to the attainment of such perfect cognition; on the other hand, he construes physiognomics as the sole science with the potential for cultivating in humanity an understanding of the non-mediated language of nature.

Enlightenment philosophers identified aesthetics as the realm that had managed to preserve the ideal of natural signification, and this in turn led them to hold up the arts as the "medium" through which, paradoxically, humankind could be reintroduced to this non-mediate mode of cognition. Friedrich Schiller's (1759–1805) *Ästhetische Erziehung des Menschen* (Aesthetic education of humankind) represents perhaps the most significant manifestation of this Enlightenment program. For Lavater, by contrast, physiognomics, as the science that rediscovers and explicates the primordial, natural, and divine significance of the human body, functions as the motor driving this philosophic-historical teleology. As a hermeneutic praxis that "reads" on the surface of the sensual being so as to decipher its supersensual significance, physiognomics takes on the character of a fundamental pedagogical tool by which humanity will be trained in the skill of immediate, intuitive cognition. Physiognomics for Lavater thus practices a kind of phenomenological *Wesenserschauung,* a perceptual intuition of essences, not unlike that propagated by Edmund Husserl a century and a half later—with the important difference, of course, that Lavater's physiognomic-phenomenological reduction is totally homocentric, directing its intuitive gaze solely at the human being, which it conceives, moreover, in strictly ontotheological terms.[5] Already in the *Aussichten in die Ewigkeit* Lavater asserts, much in this vein: "thus every human being—an image of God and Christ—is entirely expression, simultaneous, truthful, comprehensive, inexhaustible, inimitable expression that cannot be arrived at by means of words; he is wholly natural language [*Natursprache*]" (*Aussichten* 3: 109). Once the human physiognomy is comprehended as the paradigm for a pure and transparent *Natursprache,* or, indeed, as *the* primordial language of nature, physiognomics becomes the interpretive primer by means of which humanity will be instructed in the comprehension of this discourse of immediate, non-mediated knowledge.

Enlightenment semiotic theory is characterized by two apparently contradictory conceptions of the sign, oriented around the traditional distinction between "natural" and "arbitrary" signs. On the one hand we have the dream of a return to a completely natural "language"—understood in the widest sense—in which the signifier and what it signifies stand in a wholly transparent relationship to one another. On the other hand there is the attempt to invent an entirely artificial language, based on the model of mathematical calculus, that would make the entire world, in all its complexity, accessible to human knowledge. What both theories share is the desire to make a virtue of the necessity that all human thought is mediated by signs.

The resonance of these contrary semiotic conceptions is nearly omnipresent in the philosophy of language and the epistemology of seventeenth- and eighteenth-century Germany. As an example, let us take the theory of language and the sign developed by Gottfried Wilhelm Leibniz, as formulated in his *Unvorgreifliche Gedanken, betreffend die Ausübung und Verbesserung der teutschen Sprache* (Impartial thoughts about the use and improvement of the German language; 1717). Here Leibniz emphasizes that words, as signs both of concepts and of the things to which they refer, are simply arbitrary, that is, conventionally established devices that greatly augment human understanding by helping to promote memory and cogitation. In order to elucidate the arbitrary nature of linguistic signs, Leibniz chooses a particularly revealing comparison. He equates verbal signs with the paper notes that in economic commerce are often used as a substitute for specie: "For just as in large commercial cities, as well as in games and in other instances, one does not always pay with money, but instead makes use of paper or tokens until the final bill is due, reason operates in the same way with the images of things, especially when it must perform a great deal of cogitation; namely, it uses signs for these images so that it is not necessary to conceive of the thing anew each time it occurs" (*Unvorgreifliche Gedanken* 520). In this conception verbal signs function as mere placeholders for ideas and things themselves, and one employs these placeholders, like the symbols in a mathematical formula, "as ciphers, or as counters, in place of the images and things, until one moves step by step to the final result, and once reasoning comes to its conclusion it arrives at the thing itself" (521). For Leibniz, the role of the counters or signs remains completely unproblematic throughout this "calculative" process: at the beginning one replaces the things by specific signs, completes certain logical operations, and at the end one replaces the signs that appear in the final result by the things to which they refer. The signs themselves are mere mediative aids that make it easier to arrive at the logical conclusion. Moreover, according to Leibniz, by virtue of this employment of arbitrary signs "one can discover things today that the ancients were unable to arrive at, and yet the entire artistry consists of nothing but the use of appropriate signs" (536). It is interesting to note that Leibniz compares this creative application of signs, which ultimately promotes the expansion of knowledge, with a "cabala" that possesses the capacity to resolve arcane riddles through the simple application of linguistic signs. This metaphor—one might rather expect to find it in Lavater's than in Leibniz's writings—points precisely to the mysterious, even mystical moment in this calculative thought process that is conceived as strictly rational. This mysticism is grounded in the inexplicable relationship between the sign and the thing, in the presumed adequacy of the sign as a placeholder for the thing, which forms the basis for their remainderless exchangeability.

Leibniz appears to have been aware that the calculative semiotic relationship he theorized suffered from a lack of motivation, for later in the same treatise he reduces the relationship between verbal sign and signified thing to an a priori natural-mimetic correspondence that has been obscured by the historical development of language. On the example of the word *Welt* (world), Leibniz tries to show that the articulated sounds of these letters have an originary mimetic connection to what the word itself means. He advances the hypothesis that the Old German word *Werelt* alludes to the rotation of the earth and that the root of this word can be found in the letter "W." He goes on to surmise that the pronunciation of this letter produces a motion that mimetically imitates the motion of the earth. After supporting this theory with the addition of further examples, Leibniz concludes "that words are not as arbitrary or unmotivated as some people suppose, just as there is nothing unmotivated in the world except where there is lack of knowledge, and this only because the causes remain hidden to us" (*Unvorgreifliche Gedanken* 536). Whereas the theory of linguistic-semiotic calculation stresses the arbitrariness of signs in their function as "paper notes" or "tokens," here Leibniz ultimately seeks to derive this arbitrary connection from some prior, but historically obscured, natural, mimetic relationship. He thereby sketches the primary concerns that characterize the interest of eighteenth-century philosophers in issues of language and semiotics: on the one hand, the discovery of an artificial language of signs that could serve the purpose of analysis—an *ars characteristica* or *ars combinatoria*—and on the other hand, the investigation of the origin of language and the localization of this origin in a natural and a priori relationship between human beings and their life world. As we will see, these two aims become the pillars of Lavater's physiognomic theories. But before we turn to an examination of this fundamental semiotic problematic in Lavater's physiognomic texts, we must deal with the question if—and if so, then how—Enlightenment thought was able to bring these two opposing semiotic conceptions into harmony with one another.

In his "archaeology of the human sciences" *The Order of Things*, Michel Foucault examines these contrary conceptions in the semiotic understanding of the Enlightenment (in his terminology the "Classical *episteme*"). He claims that this obvious discrepancy did not appear to be a contradiction for Enlightenment thought itself.

> In its perfect state, the system of signs is that simple, absolutely transparent language which is capable of naming what is elementary; it is also that complex of operations which defines all possible conjunctions. To our eyes, this search for origins and this calculus of combinations appear incompatible, and we are only too ready to interpret them as an ambiguity in seventeenth- and eighteenth-century thought. The same is true of the interaction between the system and nature. In fact, there is no contradiction at all for thought at that time. More precisely, there exists a single, necessary arrangement running through the whole of the Classical *episteme:* the association of a universal calculus and a search for the elementary within a system that is artificial and is, for that very reason, able to make nature visible from its primary elements right to the simultaneity of all their possible combinations. (62)

According to Foucault, Enlightenment thought harmonizes these two divergent semiotic functions by declaring one of them to be the aim or telos of thought and establishing the other as the means to this end. In other words, the nostalgic project of transcending all of culture and its signs and returning to a primitive state in which nature is revealed to the human being in all its immediacy and elementary significance can only be reached by making a detour through the medium of arbitrary signs, whereby the expectation is that this *ars combinatoria* will ultimately lead back to an elementary and immediate, non-mediated relation to the world. Immediacy, in short, will be achieved by an insistence on the mediate; artificiality and arbitrariness become a self-sublating maneuver that returns to the origin of a natural and elementary understanding. By passing through the detour of arbitrary signs humanity will ultimately return to the immediacy of natural signification. In this dialectical structure it is not difficult to identify a manifestation, transposed into the realm of semiosis, of the philosophic-historical project of a dialectical return to a state of natural understanding that was especially pronounced in the German Enlightenment. In his essay "Über das Marionettentheater" (On the puppet theater) Heinrich von Kleist (1777–1811) played out the paradox inherent in this idea, expressed in the conclusion drawn by his first-person narrator—itself formulated tentatively, in the form of a question: "so human beings must eat once more from the tree of knowledge in order to return to a state of innocence?" (807). Kleist thereby extends this utopian philosophic-historical project into the domain of myth.

As we have seen in the example of Leibniz, despite the valorization of an analytical, calculative system that operated with arbitrary signs, motivated or "natural" signs remained the ideal semiotic aim of eighteenth-century thought. Contrary to Foucault, I am inclined to read this disparity as the symptom of a fundamental ambivalence in the attitude of Enlightenment intellectuals vis-à-vis their own semiotic theories. The insistence on a causally motivated, or on a mimetic-iconic relation between signs and their signifieds—a relationship intended to guarantee their original meaning—is both utopian and nostalgic in the sense that it attempts to revivify the doctrine of signatures that, according to Foucault, was typical of the sixteenth-century epistemic formation. This would mean that "Classical" thought—at least in the German-speaking realm—is not nearly as monolithic as Foucault believes it to be. On the contrary, the system of a semiotic calculus is from the very outset countered by the dream of arriving at an authentic and immediate form of knowledge. No doubt, the Enlightenment strives to resolve this semiotic duality into a unitary theory. Ultimately, the teleological moment in Enlightenment semiotic theory is rooted in the—irrational—desire to identify the aim of all human history as the dialectical sublation of the arbitrary signs instituted by human cultural production into divine natural signs. Enlightenment thinkers conceived the mechanism driving this philosophic-historical process in different ways; however, it is possible to distill from them two fundamental models, which I will call the mimetic and the structural paradigms.

We are familiar with the mimetic connection of arbitrary verbal signs with an original, natural significance from the predominant theories on the origin of language promulgated in the seventeenth and eighteenth centuries, in which onomatopoeia is identified as the motivation behind the creation of the first articulated sounds. A modification of this hypothesis appears in Leibniz's "affective theory" of the relation of words to things, which presumes a metaphorical relationship between the form of articulation and the expressed content or meaning.[6] In its teleological, philosophic-historical manifestation this hypothesis appears above all in the domain of Enlightenment aesthetics, in which a privileged status is ascribed to the mimetic signs with which art operates. The best, and best-known example of this is Lessing's vindication of the verbal arts in *Laokoön.* Expanding on the semiotic conception presented in this text, he writes in a famous letter to his friend Friedrich Nicolai dated 26 May 1769: "Literature must ultimately attempt to elevate its arbitrary signs to the status of natural signs. . . . The means it applies to accomplish this are sound, words, the placement of words, meter, figures and tropes, metaphors, etc." This argument culminates for Lessing in a valorization of dramatic art as the "highest genre of literature," since it succeeds in transforming "its arbitrary signs completely into natural signs" (*Gesammelte Werke* 9: 319–20). When the arbitrary signs of verbal art, which qua arbitrary signs have certain advantages over natural signs, appropriate a mimetic or metaphorical function, they become, as it were, consummate signs. This semiotic consummateness of dramatic literature authorizes the privileged status of the theater in the educational conceptions of the time.

The structural model that proposes a natural correspondence between sign configurations and the structure of the subject matter they signify is the fundamental idea behind the Enlightenment theory of an *ars combinatoria,* and it consequently finds expression most frequently in the realms of logic and epistemology. For Christian Wolff, by way of example, the truth of figural or symbolic knowledge, which operates solely with arbitrary signs, is based on the manner in which the signs are combined. Although for Wolff symbolic cognition has certain advantages over intuitive *(anschauende)* cognition, he readily admits that the more accidental semiotic relation characteristic of symbolic knowledge brings with it the disadvantage that we can "take empty words, which are not connected to any concept, to be knowledge, and thereby pass words off as things" (*Vernünfftige Gedancken von Gott* 177). In short, symbolic cognition is constantly threatened by the possibility that meaningless signs, which have the mere appearance of genuine significance, can be mistaken for true knowledge. Without the guarantee of a natural connection that allows one to test the truth content of signs in a concrete and immediate manner, the danger of empty, meaningless expressions is constantly present wherever arbitrary signs are employed. According to Wolff, because of this tendency to foster illusion and dissemblance, the concepts of symbolic cognition lack clarity and precision. In order to circumvent this potential for deception and provide distinctness and exactitude for symbolic knowledge, Wolff introduces the notion of a structural correspondence—an idea, we should note, that remains central for a certain strain of modern epistemology through to the conceptions of the logical positivists.

In paragraph 324 of his *Vernünfftige Gedancken von Gott, der Welt und der Seele des Menschen* (Rational thoughts about God, the world, and the human soul), Wolff maintains: "It is possible that even figural cognition provides clarity and precision by placing immediately before our eyes the represented content of the state of affairs so that one can distinguish it from others. It accomplishes this by structuring its combined signs, which have a wholly arbitrary relation to the signified things, in such a way that one can recognize from this structure the relationship that the things have to one another" (179). We recognize in Wolff's metaphor of placing things "immediately before our eyes" that the immediacy of intuitive knowledge provides the only standard by which truth can be measured, and that this standard must be applied to symbolic cognition as well. The unreliability of the arbitrary semiotic relation thus must be compensated by ordering the signs in such a way that they provide a model whose structure is congruous with the structure of the represented state of affairs. The absence of a mimetic or iconic guarantee at the level of the individual signs themselves is compensated by a form of structural mimesis at the level of sign combination: the relation among the signs mirrors the interrelation among the signified things. To be sure, Wolff is well aware of the practical weakness of this otherwise elegant solution; this *ars combinatoria,* despite its promise of a consummate semiotic system, has not yet been realized, and hence symbolic cognition still contains for him a discomforting inadequacy.

As Wellbery has persuasively argued, Wolff's principal ambivalence with regard to symbolic cognition is representative of the profound suspicion Enlightenment intellectuals had of the calculative, scientific system of arbitrary signs that constituted the condition of possibility for the "progressiveness" of their own thought (5). For them the arbitrary sign is not only, as Foucault maintains, "the sign at the peak of its activity" and as such immensely productive (*Order of Things* 62); it is also the source of deception and error. This bitter recognition was already expressed by John Locke (1632–1704) in his *Essay Concerning Human Understanding;* here he lauds human language as a system of arbitrary signs, "the great instrument and common tie of society" (229), yet he also criticizes it as a distorting glass that stands between our faculty of knowledge and the things themselves. Verbal signs, according to Locke, "interpose themselves so much between our understandings, and the truth which it would contemplate and apprehend, that, like the medium through which visible objects pass, the obscurity and disorder do not seldom cast a mist before our eyes, and impose upon our understandings" (274).

Johann Heinrich Lambert is the philosopher of the German Enlightenment who most consistently follows in Locke's footsteps by defining semiotics as a fundamental science of truth and setting about an examination of its principles. In the preface to his *Neues Organon* he defends his expansion of epistemology, which traditionally was divided into dianoiology, or the doctrine governing the laws of thought, and alethiology, or the doctrine of truth, by two further disciplines: semiotics, which is concerned with the understanding of signs and words; and phenomenology, which addresses the issue of semblance. "These two disciplines [dianoiology and alethiology]," Lambert writes, "would be sufficient if human understanding were not necessarily tied to *words* and *signs,* and if truth did not often present itself in a wholly different *semblance,* from which one must distinguish it as one distinguishes truth from error" (1: unpaginated preface). Still, the doctrine of semblance is closely tied to the discipline of semiotics, as Lambert later explains, to the extent that one can discriminate between "semiotic" or "hermeneutic" semblance, which are related, respectively, either to the use or to the interpretation of signs (2: 236). As did Wolff before him, Lambert resolves the issue of unreliability in the employment of arbitrary signs by appealing to a structural notion of congruence. Indeed, he goes beyond Wolff's conception to the extent that he expressly locates the usefulness of signs for *scientific* purposes in this structural relation. Lambert thus writes in paragraph 23 of his section of the *Organon* devoted to semiotics: "Moreover, the signs for concepts and things are *scientific* in the narrow sense when they not only represent these concepts or things, but also indicate the relationships in such a way *that the structure of the thing and the structure of its signs can be interchanged*" (2: 16). According to this proposition, scientific knowledge becomes possible when the arbitrariness of signs is annulled to the extent that they become (structurally) interchangeable with their signifieds—that is, to the extent that they accurately render in structural microcosm the formal relationship of the state of affairs they signify.

Ultimately it was this deep-seated semiotic insecurity, which produced a widely sensed uneasiness about the nature of signs, that motivated Enlightenment thinkers to formulate their utopian conceptions of a "return" to the certainty of natural signs, a belief that was at home in the epistemic formation of the sixteenth century. In this earlier thought formation, according to Foucault, there is "no difference between the visible marks that God has stamped upon the surface of the earth, so that we may know its inner secrets, and the legible words that the Scriptures, or the sages of Antiquity, have set down in the books preserved for us by tradition. The relation to these texts is of the same nature as the relation to things: in both cases there are signs that must be discovered" (*Order of Things* 33). For Renaissance thinking, divine and humanly created signs, natural signs, and cultural signs are one and the same, and their reliability is metaphysically guaranteed by the godhead as the transcendental producer of all signs. It is in part the search for such a guarantee that leads to Leibniz's famous postulate that the given world is the best of all possible worlds. The persistence of this belief in the universal legibility of the (divinely created) world marks the bad conscience of Enlightened thought about its own purposive and rational paradigms for acquiring knowledge, especially as they are manifest in the theories of scientific positivism. The stubbornness with which the age of reason held onto this mystical faith in the legibility of the divine script of creation is best exemplified, perhaps, in Lichtenberg's refusal, in his polemic against Lavater's physiognomic interpretations, to abandon the metaphor of the legible world (see Blumenberg 199–213). "No one has any doubts about this absolute legibility of everything in everything," Lichtenberg unequivocally asserts ("Über Physiognomik" 265). But with the skepticism typical of Enlightenment thinkers in general, especially with regard to questions of semiotics, he nevertheless admits that the attempt to decipher these natural signs leads to errors. The fact that the world consists of nothing but signs that beg to be interpreted obviously does not guarantee for Lichtenberg that human beings will be able to interpret these signs correctly. Lichtenberg by no means doubts, *theoretically,* that divine creation is, in its entirety, meaningful and consistent; rather, he merely doubts that the (contemporary) state of human knowledge is capable, *in practice,* of heremeneutically comprehending this meaning.

This insecurity with regard to the semiotic-hermeneutic conditions of possibility of its own thought structures motivates the myth of a return to natural signification in Enlightenment semiotic theory. The nucleus of Enlightenment epistemology is shaped by this tension between the need to accept the fact of semiotic mediation, with its resulting limitations on human knowledge, and the desire to wish away or ignore this fact: these poles produce the energy that drives the teleological thought of the era. Moreover, this myth of a teleological return to absolute knowledge, as we have seen in the case of Lambert, is intimately tied to the Enlightenment conception of science. It is the irrational moment inherent in this Enlightenment myth that Lichtenberg—in this regard, at least, probably the most consistent of the German Enlightenment thinkers—attacks as it manifests itself in Lavater's "science" of physiognomics. What this means, ultimately, is that the dispute over physiognomics between Lichtenberg and Lavater should no longer be understood as a campaign of enlightened reason against the irrationality and enthusiasm of the Storm-and-Stress generation, but rather as an attempt to exorcise the ghost of irrationality that has taken up residence in the body of Enlightenment thought itself.

Lavater's physiognomics represents a suitable medium for this Enlightenment self-critique for two reasons: first, because the contradictions of a "science" supported by the subjective judgments of a fanatic are especially obvious in Lavater's physiognomics; second, and more importantly, because the identification of Lavater with the sentimental irrationalists of the Storm-and-Stress "geniuses" presented a strategic opportunity to launch this self-critique under the guise of attacking a prominent opponent from the irrationalist camp. Clearly, Lichtenberg's aim was not to voice an annihilating critique but to enunciate a form of *salvaging* criticism that would rescue at least the foundation, although not the entire edifice, of Lavater's physiognomic surface hermeneutics.

Enlightenment Semiotics as Theoretical Foundation of Lavater's Physiognomics

As a scientific hermeneutics that determines the relationship between body and soul on the basis of the interpretation of physical signs, Lavaterian physiognomics is firmly rooted in one of the principal conceptions of the early Enlightenment: namely, in the hypostatization of the human soul as the harmonious middle term between divine reason and its objectified worldly creation. Leibniz had paradigmatically expressed in his *Monadologie* this belief that the human soul mirrors in microcosm the entire worldly universe (475). This implicit physiognomics is explicitly developed by Christian Wolff in the fourth chapter of his ethics, *Vernünfftige Gedancken von der Menschen Thun und Lassen* (Rational thoughts on human actions and omissions). Under the heading "universal rules on how to recognize human dispositions" Wolff investigates "physiognomy," which he characterizes as "the art of recognizing the disposition of human beings based on the form of their limbs and of the entire body" (137). Lavater was well aware of the physiognomic convictions of his enlightened predecessors; indeed, he quotes an excerpt from Wolff's deliberations on physiognomics in the first volume of the *Physiognomische Fragmente* in order to bring testimony for the scientific claims of this discipline. Hence it is not surprising to discover that some of the central principles of Lavater's physiognomics are already present in rudimentary form in Wolff's text. What is especially striking is Wolff's insistence on the *naturalness* of physiognomic expression, for this thought will form one of the primary contentions of Lavater's theories. Beginning with the assumption that body and soul stand in an a priori and unalterably harmonious relationship to one another, Wolff arrives at the following conclusion:

> Hence the construction of the body, and therefore its form and the form of its parts, must correspond with the nature of the soul. And on this basis the differences among human dispositions must reveal themselves in the differences in their bodies. In short, the body must contain something, both in its form and in the form of its parts, through which one can determine, in nature, the character of a person's disposition. I have deliberately stipulated in *nature*; for I am specifically not referring to things that are acquired through upbringing, interaction with others, good education, etc. (*Thun und Lassen* 137)

The distinction on which Wolff deliberately insists is nothing other than that between nature and culture, necessity and accident, divine givenness and human adaptation. The human body is conceived as a text onto which the a priori subjective nature of the individual, prior to all cultivation, is inscribed and made hermeneutically legible.

As Friedrich Nicolai correctly diagnosed, it is already clear from Lavater's *Aussichten in die Ewigkeit* that his interest in physiognomics is motivated by the desire to discover the natural connection of the human being with the Christian divinity, a connection that transcends all the manifestations of culture. In the sixteenth section of this work, composed in epistolary form, Lavater takes it upon himself to describe the heavenly language in which he believes all inter-spiritual communications will occur after death. Here he repeats in condensed form the paradigmatic features of the Enlightenment's telos of semiotic progress. He begins with the assertion that all arbitrary languages are nothing other than "garbled versions of an original language of nature" (*Aussichten* 3: 102–3), and goes on to describe this process of historical distortion in the following manner: "Gradually all that was natural was suppressed and obscured by imitation [Lavater is referring here to onomatopoeia], and this in turn by arbitrary designations. Verbal language suppressed the natural language of the whole human being—physiognomic language, the language of gestures—just as the phonetic alphabet most likely suppressed images" (103–4). Thus the goal of Lavater's engagement with human physiognomy is to reverse this progressive history of the alienation of natural meaningfulness. Physiognomics is supposed to become the central science permitting human beings to learn once more the original "language of nature" and thereby return them to a utopian state of pre-cultural paradise. This (re-)discovery of the primal physiognomic language thus bears all the characteristics of a semiotically grounded telos, much like that theorized by Enlightenment epistemology.

The critique of symbolic cognition and the arbitrary signs on which it is based, which was inherent in Enlightenment epistemology, recurs in Lavater's thought in exaggerated form. In contrast to Wolff and Leibniz, who, while acknowledging the deficiencies of symbolic knowledge, also pointed to its potential for discovering hitherto unrecognized truths, Lavater is convinced "that symbolic cognition is immeasurably more defective than intuitive, or immediate cognition; that symbolic cognition as such possesses no true inherent value, but rather only a relative value that is predicated on the current limitations of our perceptual faculties; that it is nothing but a crutch for those who are lame, and that, like such a crutch, it will be sct aside when we have learned to walk on our own, when we can perceive many things simultaneously and with precision" (*Aussichten* 3: 17). Symbolic cognition is not conceived here, as it by and large was for Enlightenment thinkers, as a medium that builds a bridge to immediate intuitive understanding; instead it is viewed purely as an artificial tool whose usefulness is obviated once intuitive cognition is, as it were, reinstituted by divine revelation. For Lavater, in short, symbolic cognition itself plays no instrumental role in helping to achieve this perfected form of knowledge. This can be recognized especially well on the basis of Lavater's metaphor; symbolic cognition is not equated with a ladder that can be thrown away once one has climbed up with its aid, but instead with a "crutch" that becomes superfluous once human beings are granted, by divine providence, the ability to walk again.

Lavater himself, apparently, is not entirely satisfied with this assertion, since he immediately qualifies it by maintaining at least the possibility that even once they attain this manner of ideal, divine cognition, human beings will not be completely weaned of arbitrary signs. However, he restricts the arbitrariness of these signs in a typical manner when he assumes that "these arbitrary signs would be much more proximate to the things they represent, would call forth much more similar impressions, and hence would be much less arbitrary than today" (*Aussichten* 3: 21). It becomes perfectly apparent just how much Lavater's semiotic conceptions are derived from those of Enlightenment philosophers when he concludes by comparing these arbitrary, but somehow less arbitrary signs of the future with algebra; with this he takes up the primary example used by Enlightenment thinkers to explain the paradoxical notion of arbitrary signs that have the power and effectiveness otherwise attributed to natural signs.

A direct line leads from these epistemological and semiotic deliberations contained in the *Aussichten in die Ewigkeit* to the vehement attack on arbitrariness in all its forms that constitutes one of the primary objectives of Lavater's physiognomics. Already in the early essay "Von der Physiognomik" he emphatically asserts: "One cannot reiterate it often enough: arbitrariness is the wisdom of fools, a plague for the healthy doctrine of nature, philosophy, and religion. The task of wisdom and truth is to banish it from all three spheres" (150). There can be little doubt that Lavater's obsession with physiognomics derives from the fact that he conceives it precisely as a "healthy doctrine of nature" that will ultimately expel all arbitrariness from the domains of wisdom and truth. Moreover, it seems obvious that this drive to identify a form of knowledge free of all accident and uncertainty closely corresponds with the Enlightenment's demand that reason be reduced to its purest, most "healthy" form.

One of the most gnarly problems of theoretical physiognomics proves to be nothing other than the segregation of the "natural" signs that are present in the primal "text" of the body from the arbitrary signs of affect, intention, and mood, which also leave their semiotic traces on the somatic form. Lavater is forced to comprehend the human body as a kind of palimpsest in which a natural and original physiognomic text is always already overwritten by secondary, arbitrary texts produced by human intentionality. In his physiognomic theory, this necessarily leads to the distinction between two fundamentally different layers of bodily significance: on the one hand, the body as such functions as a divinely ordained natural sign, and this constitutes for Lavater its strict physiognomic aspect; on the other hand, it serves merely as the accidental bearer of signs that carry a cultural content. Lavater demands that a rigorously "scientific" physiognomics be able to uncover the original physiognomic text of the body—that it possess, in other words, the capacity to strip the body of all the contingencies impressed upon it by incidental cultural and emotional conditions. In this regard, as well, Christian Wolff must be seen as Lavater's immediate precursor; for Wolff also insists on a definition of physiognomics that limits it to the a priori and natural predispositions and aptitudes of the individual. Thus Wolff asserts without qualification that "one can only discern from the constitution of the body and its parts the natural inclination of the human being, not what he or she will undertake by applying reason or inveterate habit to withstand these natural proclivities" (*Thun und Lassen* 138). Similarly, Lavater maintains that "the originary form of the human being will always be visible through all its contingencies" (*Physiognomische Fragmente* 4: 32), that is, that the original physiognomic form cannot be covered over by culture or climate, nor by the blows of fate or by willful acts. In contrast to Lavater, however, Wolff acknowledges the almost insurmountable difficulties attendant upon such a conception; indeed, he shrinks before the complex task of discriminating between the a priori natural signs of the body and the arbitrary signs that it subsequently expresses.

Thus he appends the following qualifying deliberation to the statement cited above:

> It is probably true that no changes can occur in the soul without corresponding changes taking place in the body as well. And yet just as one recognizes that natural proclivities constantly run counter to reason and habit . . . , so too must we conclude that the change occurring in the body cannot completely alter the structure of the body and its parts. This is an extremely complex issue, and I am quite afraid that physiognomy demands more insight than existed in the world at the time when people attempted to supply it with rules. (*Thun und Lassen* 138–39)

What Wolff touches on here is the profound contradiction between the presupposition, which he shares with Lavater, that soul and body stand in a relationship of pre-established harmony, and the fact that the body is subject to changes that can have no possible influence on the soul. That is why Wolff proposes the hypothesis—and Lavater most likely appropriated this idea from him—that there must be a primordially given and unalterable bodily form that is the pure expression of the individual's dispositions or "soul." Unlike Lavater, however, Wolff is at a loss when it comes to determining precisely what constitutes this primordial form of the body. This leads him to the evasive conclusion that the physiognomic rules established by previous theoreticians are inadequate. There can be little doubt that Lavater understood his attempt to turn physiognomics into a science as a way of correcting these inadequacies. In his search to resolve this problem he formulates his most significant, but also most controversial, contribution to physiognomic theory: the hypothesis that the authentic, primordial form of the human being manifests itself in the "firm features" of the body, particularly in the structure and shape of the bones. The fundamental distinction between the "firm" and the "soft" parts of the body—which, as we will see, operates with a conceptual apparatus modeled on the semiotic notions of Enlightenment philosophy—was the solution at which Lavater arrived in order to escape the aporia Wolff identified.

It is remarkable that a fundamentally different, even contrary solution to this dilemma is outlined in the "Addendum" to the fragment entitled "On Physiognomics" in the first volume of the *Physiognomische Fragmente.* This addendum is not a product of Lavater's pen; it was written by his friend Goethe, who was given free hand in making additions and alterations to Lavater's manuscript (von der Hellen, *Goethes Anteil* 33–39). It is worth examining Goethe's alternative solution to this problem in some detail, not merely because it is diametrically opposed to Lavater's own position, but also because it brings out in particularly poignant fashion the basic terms of this dilemma. Moreover, as will be elucidated in chapter 4, Goethe's ideas have a profound impact on the development of modern German physiognomics through their reception by such significant twentieth-century figures as Ludwig Klages, Oswald Spengler, and Rudolf Kassner.

Goethe and Lavater share the view that physiognomics is a science capable of drawing inferences about the human psyche on the basis of interpreting physical signs. Lavater reacts to Wolff's insight that the body represents, as it were, the battlefield on which nature and culture vie to impress their signs upon the body by restricting what is physiognomically meaningful to specific bodily features. Goethe, by contrast, reacts in the opposite manner, expanding the field of what is physiognomically significant to the point that it transcends the human body itself. Goethe responds to his own question "But what exactly constitutes the external side of the human being?" with the unequivocal answer: "Certainly not his or her naked form, unconscious gestures that designate his or her inner energies and their interaction!" (*Physiognomische Fragmente* 1: 15). With this Goethe sweeps away the doctrine of the physiognomic significance of the firm features and appears to do away with the semiotics of the body in its entirety, including its "pathognomic" elements. In contrast to Lavater (and Wolff) he explicitly admits that "class, habit, possessions, clothes" have the capacity to modify human appearance and conceal the individual's nature. Moreover, he confesses that this is precisely what causes difficulties for any theory of physiognomics that seeks to exclude what is arbitrary. He writes in conscious opposition to Lavater's doctrine: "It appears extremely difficult, even impossible, to penetrate all of these veils to a person's innermost being, or even to discover stable points in these alien modifications on the basis of which one could draw inferences about his or her nature." But he then goes on to give his own answer to this problem, adding:

> But take heart! The things that surround human beings do not only have an impact on them; they also have an influence on these things, and at the same time as people let themselves be modified by these things, they also make their own modifications in their immediate environment. As a result, we can draw sure conclusions about a man's character from his clothes and household effects. Nature forms human beings, but they in turn transform themselves, and these transformations are once again natural; those who find themselves placed in a wide, expansive world erect fences and walls to create their own small world within it, and they design and furnish this world according to their own image. (*Physiognomische Fragmente* 1: 15)

Goethe does not deny that the external appearance of the human being is always caught up in specific culturally defined codes that disguise the signs of authentic internal being and make physiognomic interpretation difficult or impossible. However, he stops short of completely rejecting physiognomics by interpreting the cultural inscriptions of the human being as things that, although they contribute to the determination of the individual, are in turn also shaped and determined *by* the individual. In other words, according to Goethe the human subject tailors its appropriation of external cultural codes to fit its own nature, which explains why even these seemingly arbitrary signs can be taken as symptoms of a person's true nature. Goethe's position, it is important to note, is entirely coherent with the discourse of fashion that was rapidly gaining prominence at this time in Germany. Daniel Purdy has convincingly demonstrated how for Goethe's Werther, the eponymous protagonist of his novel *Die Leiden des jungen Werthers* (The sorrows of young Werther), fashion assumed the function of "a semiotic system in which clothes and personal property operated as signs of emotions, moral character, political commitment, and capacity for productive work" (154). This position is paradigmatically represented already in Goethe's addendum to the fragment "On Physiognomics": If Lavater's physiognomic theories can be read as a protest against the semiotic of fashion that decries it as arbitrary and deceptive masks that hide the authentic individual, Goethe, by contrast, subscribes to the capacity of fashion to express the projections and emanations of personal identity.

Goethe's position undermines the entire theoretical foundation upon which Lavater sought to erect the edifice of his physiognomic science. It casts off the semiotically based distinction between the natural and the arbitrary that serves as the cornerstone of Lavater's physiognomic theory. According to Goethe, it is impossible to identify absolutely natural, non-arbitrary, culturally independent or autonomous signs on the surface of the human body; every natural sign inscribed on the body already bears the traces of its individual-cultural transformation based on the choices and actions of the individual. But for Goethe this insight does not deal a deathblow to physiognomics itself, for the simple reason that the complement to this assertion is also valid, namely that there are also no arbitrary, cultural signs that are imposed upon the individual beyond his or her own will. This theory assumes, of course, an autonomous, free-willed subject who extends its metaphysical presence and its authentic character to everything in its immediate environment, including "clothes" and "household effects." In this conception the human subject becomes the scene of a dialectical process in which the conflict between the semiotic codes of nature and those of culture is waged—a thesis, we should note, that anticipates the cultural theory of Sigmund Freud in seminal points. To be sure, Goethe views this process of conflict with a great deal more optimism than Freud, writing a century and a half later. In Goethe's view, human beings, as creative creatures, inherently possess a transformative power that allows them to appropriate cultural signs according to their own choice and design, to modify them so as to make them suitable and appropriate to their inner "nature."

No doubt, the ideology of individualism and human genius, which was especially promoted by the Storm-and-Stress writers, underwrites Goethe's conception of the physiognomic significance of fashion. To be sure, in this addendum he only expresses the self-certain, optimistic side of this ideology, free of all the Werther-like pathos of the suffering individual who must sacrifice himself to the heartless cultural codes of the established social order. Nonetheless, in the case of Goethe, Lavater's theological point of departure, which sees the human being as the reflection of the Christian divinity, experiences a significant secularization. Goethe begins with a conception of the Promethean human being who transforms everything in his or her immediate environment: much like a positive variant of the myth of King Midas, Goethe's human beings place their own individual stamps on all the objects of culture with which they come into contact. This "physiognomic" conception—if, in fact, it still even deserves this attribute—is immeasurably more progressive than is Lavater's insofar as it substitutes for the latter's image of a passive human being subject to divine determination a picture of an active, creative individual who has the power to be or to become the master of his or her own fate. This discrepancy marks a veritable quantum leap in the development of the bourgeois ideology of the individual: individuality is no longer conceived, as it is by Lavater, as a divine gift that is already preordained in the "monad" and hence develops independent of any subjective actions of the individual; instead it takes the form of an autonomous self-creation, as the free and independent transformation of everything that is "objectively" given. In this sense, Goethe's position—which is, paradoxically, literally inscribed into the very text of Lavater's *Physiognomische Fragmente*—already anticipates the critiques that Lichtenberg, and after him Hegel, will direct at Lavater's physiognomic theories. We will see in the next chapter how the controversies surrounding Lavater's physiognomic theories culminate in a conflict that turns on the semiotics of the self and the very definition of individuality.

If we now take a closer look at Lavater's segregation of the "firm" from the "soft" parts of the body, we will see that this distinction is based on the semiotic opposition between natural and arbitrary signs. This is already evident in the terminology Lavater employs when, in the essay "Von der Physiognomik," he first addresses this distinction. He does this while laying down rules for practitioners of what he here calls "empirical physiognomics": "We must first begin with whatever is certain and reliable. Hence we must make ourselves familiar above all with the extremes or the outermost points and signs and attempt to gain a good impression of them. We must segregate what is firm from what is soft, what is permanent from what is accidental" (167). The firm features are equated with what is certain and reliable, the soft tissues with what is accidental, arbitrary, or contingent. Muscles, expressions, gestures—everything that is malleable and alterable—Lavater sees as arbitrary, "willkürlich" in the true sense of the German word, which means, taken literally, subject to the determination and the free will of the individual. It is precisely this subjectively determined intentionality that makes these "accidental" signs doubtful and unreliable. Arbitrariness designates for Lavater the negative side of emergent human freedom, which injects an element of unpredictability into human deeds and actions and thereby threatens to destabilize intersubjective relations. Lavaterian physiognomics seeks to strip away this layer of intentional action so as to reveal, like Freudian psychoanalysis, the authentic core that underlies it.

This is precisely the point with which Lichtenberg will take issue in his scathing critique of Lavater's physiognomic theory. For him Lavater's version of physiognomics not only throws into question the free will and autonomy of the human being. It also places unacceptable restrictions on the transformative capacity of the individual, both in its positive aspect as perfectibility, and in its negative form as corruptibility. Obviously, such a static, deterministic conception threatens to undermine the entire progressivist, teleological project of the Enlightenment, for the infinite freedom of the human being to choose between good and evil is placed in the straightjacket of physiognomic predetermination (see Lichtenberg, "Über Physiognomik" 267–69, 287). Nevertheless—and this in itself is significant—Lichtenberg does not want to deny completely the existence of an unintentional body language. On the contrary, he maintains that there exists "a non-arbitrary language of gesture, one that is spoken throughout the world by the emotions in all their degrees." He calls this transhistorical and transcultural language of nature "pathognomics," defining it explicitly as the manifestation of "transitory action" as opposed to the "standing character" that forms the interpretive basis for Lavater's physiognomics (278). As opposed to physiognomics, pathognomics makes no claim to permanence; it does not point to something that is firm and unalterable in someone's character. Instead, it interprets spontaneous, ephemeral facial expressions, gestures, and the like as the symptoms of specific actions. With this Lichtenberg actually moves closer than Lavater to the Freudian view of the subject; in contrast to Lavater, Lichtenberg's non-arbitrary language of "nature" does not have a divine, transcendental quality, but instead is traced back to an internal, psychic agency that is inherent to the individual subject.

One of the most brilliant discursive skills evident in Lavater's physiognomic writings is the talent for engaging the objections of his antagonists and transforming them into fruitful tenets in support of his own argument. Surely it is in part this art of rhetorical-discursive appropriation that explains the persuasive power physiognomics had for many of Lavater's contemporaries. One sees this appropriative mechanism operating at its best in Lavater's response, contained in the fourth volume of the *Physiognomische Fragmente,* to Lichtenberg's devastating critique. Especially typical is the way in which Lavater embraces the distinction between physiognomics and pathognomics, which Lichtenberg employed as one of his primary critical tools, and transmogrifies it so that it supports his own position. He accepts without contradiction Lichtenberg's assertion that physiognomics studies "standing character," but he emphasizes that this expresses itself in nothing other than the firm features of the face and head. Similarly, he agrees that pathognomics deals with "character in motion," and he adds that this manifests itself in the soft tissues of the face (see *Physiognomische Fragmente* 4: 39). He thereby exploits Lichtenberg's critical objection in order to lend support to his own segregation of the significance attributable respectively to the firm and to the soft parts of the body. This then leads him to a conclusion that inverts Lichtenberg's hierarchy, which stresses the importance of pathognomics over that of physiognomics, into its very opposite: physiognomics becomes for Lavater "the root and the stem" of pathognomics, "the soil in which [pathognomics] is planted" (4: 39). Lavater uses strategically chosen metaphors to give physiognomics priority over pathognomics, making the former into the necessary basis or precondition for the latter. In so doing, he takes steps toward limiting the value of pathognomics. He continues with this line of thought by claiming that pathognomics is nothing but an artificial language, and one, moreover, that is spoken above all in the degenerate atmosphere of the aristocratic court. He maintains, in addition, that pathognomic signs are highly unreliable, since they can be imitated and dissimulated at will, as every theater performance makes clear. By contrast, according to Lavater, only physiognomics possesses the capacity to penetrate and unmask such arts of dissimulation and reveal the authentic sentiments of the human being.

This is exactly what Lavater hopes to accomplish by hypostatizing the firm parts of the body as non-arbitrary, absolutely reliable signs of human character. He admits that the capacity "to imitate everything by employing the powers of reason, will, and choice" is essential to human nature (*Physiognomische Fragmente* 2: 30); however, he views this "essential" capacity as nothing but a dissimulating fog that the sun of physiognomic science must dissipate so as to reveal the actual individual it hides. In the fragment entitled "On Dissimulation, Falsehood, and Honesty" in the second volume of the *Fragmente*, Lavater seeks to dispel the notion that "the human being's universal art of dissimulation, which has been exaggerated to the extreme" (2: 55), can be used as an objection against the effectiveness of physiognomic interpretation. He counters the undeniable truth that human beings "can dissimulate and deceive, they can dissolve and remove any doubt, any suspicion about their honesty" (2: 55) with the assertion that "there are innumerable things in the external appearance of the human being where no dissimulation is effective, and it is precisely these things that constitute reliable signs of the person's inner character" (2: 55). He immediately goes on to cite skeleton and bone structure as the quintessence of these features that escape dissimulation. In short, it is the resistance of the firm parts of the body to falsification, feint, and dissimulation that makes them the appropriate concern of a physiognomics that wants to disclose the authentic inner character of the human being.

Although Lavater recognizes the need to develop a "theoretical" physiognomics that would support his empirical physiognomic practice by defining the precise relationship between a particular external sign and the internal character trait it signifies (see "Von der Physiognomik" 146–47), he himself never delivers such a systematic code. Instead he relies completely on the theory of natural signification as it was hypothesized in Enlightenment epistemology. I now want to examine on the basis of some concrete examples the aporias in which Lavater's theory becomes ensnared through the uncritical appropriation of this semiotic system.

Enlightenment semiotic theory develops two principally different definitions of natural signs, distinguished by their mode of signification. In the first instance, the relationship constituting natural signification is conceived as causal—in current semiotic terminology one calls such signs "symptoms"; in the second case, the manner of signification is understood to be mimetic, that is, it is presupposed that the sign shares a relationship of similarity with the content it is intended to signify—today such signs are termed "iconic." It is not surprising to discover that these two definitions occur in diverse philosophical contexts; symptoms predominate in the field of epistemology, while icons are the preferred type of natural sign in discussions of aesthetics. Lavater makes use of both conceptions in his physiognomics, and in both instances this has far-reaching, ultimately aporetic consequences.

Christian Wolff succinctly summarizes the understanding of natural signs as symptoms in the following words: "Thus, if two things always occur together simultaneously, or one always follows from the other, then the one is forever the sign of the other. And such signs are called *natural signs*. For example, smoke is a natural sign of fire" (*Vernünfftige Gedancken von Gott* 161). It is either *spatial* proximity in the form of a metonymic contiguity or *temporal* connection in the form of causal consequence that determines a natural relation between a sign and its signified. Lavater's attempt to appropriate this firm but empirically testable semiotic relation for his physiognomic theory leads to especially complex problems. Above all, it seduces him into conceiving the significance of physiognomic signs exclusively in terms of a *semantics* rather than trying to understand it as the product of a more complex physiognomic *syntax*. He tends, in other words, to limit physiognomic meaning to the paradigmatic axis of referentiality, without paying enough attention to the syntagmatic axis of immediate context. This is already indicated in the metaphor of the "alphabet" that he uses to circumscribe the systematic results of his physiognomic investigations. To be sure, in the preface to the first volume of the *Physiognomische Fragmente* Lavater sets certain limits on his task when he admits that he cannot promise "to deliver the entire alphabet for decoding the non-arbitrary natural language of the face, which contains thousands of letters"; rather he merely hopes "to sketch out a few letters of this alphabet so legibly that every healthy eye will be able to find and recognize them wherever they occur" (1: "Vorrede" [unpaginated]). Lavater's apparent ideal would be the compilation of a physiognomic lexicon in which one could "look up" any somatic trait in order to discover the psychic significance attributed to it in nature (that is, by God). Such a conception abstracts the meaning of physiognomic signs from any context by viewing them as unconditionally subordinate to a determined referential meaning. This absolutely fixed identification of the somatic sign with a specific psychic quality forces Lavater to evaluate every alteration in the anatomical exterior as an index for parallel changes in the corresponding psychic content. He formulates this iron law already in his early essayistic outline of a scientific physiognomics: "Every modification of my body has a certain relation to my soul. . . . The fact that my hand is shaped in such and such a way, and in no other way, immediately points to the fact that I possess a soul that is determined in such and such a way" ("Von der Physiognomik" 159). Lichtenberg satirizes this position with biting sarcasm when, in his attack on Lavater, he poses the rhetorical question: "Does the soul fill up the body, much like an elastic fluid always takes the form of the vessel in which it is contained, so that, if a flat nose is indicative of maliciousness, anyone whose nose is pressed flat will become malicious?" ("Über Physiognomik" 267). Lichtenberg humorously points out the problems inherent in a physiognomic-semiotic conception that demands an absolute causal connection between a particular somatic sign and its purported psychic significance, above all the fact that such a relationship is fundamentally reversible: it is not (only) the content of the soul that produces particular anatomical signs, as Lavater would like to contend; rather, the presence of a specific somatic indicator, even if artificially created, would necessarily also have to be indicative of the psychic characteristic with which it is causally connected. This merely reiterates on the level of semiotics the dilemma that Christian Wolff identifies as the result of any physiognomic connection based on a presupposed harmony between body and soul. Lichtenberg's example reveals the absurdity of this idea once it is conceived in the semiotic terms that Lavater adopts from Enlightenment philosophy and unquestioningly applies to his physiognomic theories.

We can see even more clearly the dead-end into which this uncritical appropriation of Enlightenment semiotics inevitably leads Lavater's physiognomics by examining the principles of this symptomatic understanding of the natural sign in more detail. For this purpose it is useful to look at the more rigorous definition of natural signs provided by Johann Heinrich Lambert in the section of his *Neues Organon* dedicated to semiotics. In paragraph 47 of this treatise, after having sketched a crude typology of signs on the basis of selected examples, he writes:

> There are, moreover, a great many other signs of different sorts and with different purposes. *Natural* signs stand in a specific connection to the signified subject matter in terms of causes, effects, etc., as, for example, smoke is a sign of the presence of fire, a red evening sky is a sign of the pleasant weather that will follow it. To be sure, natural signs must be capable of being theorized in such a way that their connection to the signified subject matter is definite and provable. In the absence of such a theory, one would at the very least have to establish on the basis of precise empirical observations whether this relationship indeed always holds or not. Since these things are called signs because they are symptoms of a change in nature that is present, has already occurred, or whose future occurrence they foretell, the primary requirement should be that they are absolutely reliable. They should hence not be deceptive, as are most of the signs of developing weather, which in former times people passed off as certain. Instead, in natural science, as in the case of symptoms of illness in medicine, an increasing effort is made to discover more reliable signs. (2: 30)

This discussion summarizes those advantages of natural signs that Lavater wants to transpose to the semiotic significance of the human body, above all the causal relation between sign and signified and the absolute reliability and infallibility of such signs. Beyond this, Lambert appeals, as does Lavater as well, to medical semiotics as the paradigmatic example of a firmly codified system of natural signs. In addition, he distinguishes signs according to their temporal mode, that is, whether they refer to past, present, or future events or states of affairs. This type of categorization is typical for the time. For example, Walch's *Philosophisches Lexikon* distinguishes three types of signs: those that relate to something future *(signa prognostica)*; those that point to something in the present *(signa demonstrativa)*; and those that recall something that lies in the past *(signa rememorativa)* (2: 1684). Although Lavater never refers to this distinction, it plays an important role for his scientific renewal of physiognomics insofar as one of his main goals is to strictly segregate his physiognomic science from traditional forms of prophetic physiognomics such as chiromancy. As a subdivision of heraldry, prophetic physiognomics reduces somatic signs to their prognosticating function. Already in the essay "Von der Physiognomik" Lavater condemns this brand of physiognomics as "charlatanism," calling it "tasteless, with pretensions to being an art that foretells the particular and individual fates of human beings on the basis of their faces"; and he insists that this has no place in the "realm of true science" in which he seeks to situate his own physiognomics (155–56; cf. *Physiognomische Fragmente* 1: 17). In order strictly to uphold this distinction, Lavater would have to reject any prognosticative function whatsoever for physiognomic signs; yet he cannot bring himself to accept such a position. On the contrary, he ascribes to his physiognomic method an undeniably prophetic character when he justifies the physiognomic expressiveness of the bone structure with the claim that it represents the "only genuine *pure form of predestination*" (*Physiognomische Fragmente* 2: 146). And in the fourth volume of the *Fragmente,* Lavater uses the description of physiognomic intuition as an opportunity to elucidate the prognosticative function of his physiognomic judgments. Here he claims that the physiognomist (that is, of course, Lavater himself) possesses a sensibility "*not only for the present character of the human being, but also for his future character, which is still hidden in the present*" (4: 130). Assertions of this type ultimately persuade one to associate Lavater's physiognomics—against Lavater's own protestations—with heraldry and prophecy. This also has its semiotic aspect, for it is obvious that Lavater wants to understand the physiognomic signs of the firm body parts as nothing other than *signa prognostica,* as prognosticative signs.

Indeed, as is clear above all from his deliberations in *Aussichten in die Ewigkeit,* Lavater conceived the non-arbitrary language of physiognomics in general as a sign system that pointed forward to a paradisiacal, utopian future.[7]

Lavater appears to have sensed that this insistence on the prophetic function of physiognomic knowledge exposes his own theories to the danger of being confused with the older physiognomic "charlatanism" from which he seeks to distance them. Thus he attempts to find another type of criterion that will help him distinguish his scientifically grounded physiognomic hermeneutics from unfounded physiognomic prophecy. We are no longer surprised to discover that in this context Lavater once again turns to those semiotic arguments that perform such a crucial theoretical service for his physiognomics. The craft of physiognomic prophecy, he maintains, is nothing other than "charlatanism and empty fantasy . . . because it appears to depend entirely on arbitrary signs, and not on natural connections of cause and effect" ("Von der Physiognomik" 156). Whenever the ship of scientific physiognomics begins to take on water, Lavater turns to semiotic arguments to patch the hole.

In his critique of Lavater, Lichtenberg succeeds—once again—in finding an image that exposes both the prophetic as well as the materialistic, deterministic aspect of physiognomics: he compares Lavater's practice with forecasting the weather. Although meteorology, according to Lichtenberg, operates solely with natural signs—which, moreover, are codified in a relatively mechanical system—it has nevertheless not attained any degree of reliability. However, whereas the principles of weather forecasting can at least be determined in theory, despite the fact that it lacks the apparatus to become a science in practice, physiognomics lacks both the theoretical and the practical determinants to make it into an objective, calculable science. For Lichtenberg, the reason for this is that the subject matter of physiognomics, the human being itself, is not composed of a set of calculable natural occurrences. On the contrary, human beings are free, self-determining, and hence unpredictable and incalculable subjects ("Über Physiognomik" 266). Here Lichtenberg exposes the essential mechanism of reification that emerges out of Lavater's insistence on the establishment of physiognomics as a science based on Enlightenment principles. It is certainly no coincidence that Lambert, in the above-cited passage, also appealed to meteorology when he sought an example for signs that appear to be natural and motivated but in fact are deceptive; weather served—and still serves—enlightened reason as the paradigm of a theoretically determinate but for all practical purposes unpredictable natural phenomenon. At any rate, Lavater's physiognomic theory irredeemably suffers precisely from the lack of any theoretical conception for the relation between anatomical features and characterological dispositions that goes beyond the semiotic notions of Enlightenment philosophy. Lavater's strategy of appropriating the semiotic conceptions developed by Enlightenment epistemology, which had won relatively wide circulation in German intellectual circles of the day and hence wielded strong persuasive power, is intended to cover over his own lack of a suitable theory. This also explains Lavater's tendency to explain physiognomics by appealing to the example of medical semiotics (see "Von der Physiognomik" 152); for already Lambert, as we have seen, viewed the physical "symptoms" that the physician reads as signs of organic illness as paradigmatic examples of natural signs firmly anchored in a causal relationship to their signified. But Lavater ignores the fact that medical semiotics, which concerns itself solely with the organic body, does not entail a metaphorical move between two incommensurable domains, from body to "soul," as does physiognomics. At any rate, his very attempt to resolve the theoretical dilemmas of physiognomics by appealing to semiotic principles simply ensnares Lavater in contradictions that, far from leading his physiognomics toward its firm establishment as a positivistic science, instead merely points it down the road to absurdity.

Nowhere does the misguidedness of Lavater's semiotically based physiognomics become more clear than in the instances in which he explicitly appeals to the iconic (rather than the symptomatic) aspect of natural signs. He does this, for example, when he expresses the conviction that the physical size of the forehead is an indicator of a person's mental or cognitive capacity. In the context of his attempt to rescue a natural semiotic relation for physiognomics from Lichtenberg's critical attack, he supplies the following commentary on a portrait of the philologist Joseph Scaliger (1540–1609): "If there is a relationship between cause and effect, if we do not live in a fairy-tale world—then the high, arched, square forehead and the entire shape of the skull of Joseph Scaliger must stand in a natural, recognizable relationship to his intelligence, his incredible memory, and his immeasurable knowledge" (*Physiognomische Fragmente* 4: 14). What stands behind this plea for the infallibility of his physiognomic hermeneutics is an appeal to the authority of modern natural science, for which empirical phenomena can be traced back to a set of simple and predictable rules. Anyone who expresses doubt in the truth of physiognomics, Lavater would have us believe, ultimately places in question the entire worldview of modern natural science. For Lavater, the glue that holds together this worldview is a "natural" semiotic relation that is vouchsafed not only by causality, the goddess of enlightened reason, but also by the iconic relationship which suggests that the relative size of the forehead must be a sign of the relative mental capacity of the brain behind it. Lavater's invention of his *Stirnmaaß,* an instrument for measuring the shape and size of the skull, is based on this belief in an iconic relationship between the particular body part and the function of the organ in which it resides. (See Figs. 58 and 59 in the conclusion) Moreover, in his attempt to devise an instrument that makes this relationship empirically measurable, Lavater takes a decisive step in the direction of an anthropometrics that will lend physiognomics the credibility of positivistic science. It should be obvious that both in regard to his belief in the iconic relationship of the head to its mental "organs" and in his attempt to express these capacities in quantifiable terms, Lavater's physiognomics is a significant precursor to Franz Joseph Gall's phrenology. Indeed, Lavater is one of the first intellectuals of this period who subscribes to and actively promotes the specious association of skull size and shape with innate intelligence. Beginning at the very latest with the theories of Samuel Thomas Soemmerring (1755–1830), this linkage becomes one of the constituent ideas of racial anthropological theories.[8]

Examples in which the nature of the body is read as a sign for the disposition of the soul occur relatively infrequently in Lavater's physiognomic writings.[9] The theoretical underpinnings of physiognomics—the causal or symptomatic relation of signifier to its signified—simply predominates. But once Lavater turns to the more practical side of his physiognomic studies, this iconic-mimetic relationship takes on increased significance. This is especially true since Lavater specifically insists on the application of artistic representations of the human face, rather than the face in the flesh, as the ideal object for physiognomic study (see "Von der Physiognomik" 176). This is an argument, we should note, that, in Lavater's wake, becomes a widely held theorem of physiognomic investigators, one that motivates the frequent use of images, especially photographs, as the ideal object for analysis.[10]

The inconsistencies in Lavater's physiognomic praxis become evident once more when one investigates the problem of mimetic representation that necessarily arises out of Lavater's faith in the validity of artistic portrayals for his physiognomic investigations. Precisely because Lavater insists on the ultimate significance of even the most minute detail for the "language" of physiognomics, the question concerning the mimetic exactitude of the images he examines takes on central importance. He supports his assertion "that the smallest differences, scarcely noticeable to the untrained eye, often are indicators of most distinct character traits" with a line of examples intended to exemplify such minimal discrepancies that carry physiognomic significance: "A tiny curve or point, a lengthening or shortening, often only by the width of a thread, of a hair; the most minute displacement or distortion—how noticeably something like this can change a face, the expression of a character trait!" (*Physiognomische Fragmente* 1: 143). But it is almost impossible for any artist to achieve such perfection, and this fact, in an age that has not yet discovered photographic reproduction, calls into question the reliability of the very matter on which Lavater's physiognomic analyses are based.[11]

Even more problematic than this technical difficulty of producing mimetically exact representations is the accepted artistic ideology of portrait painting at the time, which maintained it was the artist's duty to correct the "errors" of nature by producing an idealized version of the portrayed subject.[12] Since physiognomics must demand naturalistic faithfulness from both the artists and their artistry, it is easy to understand why Lavater admonishes all the artists involved with the illustrations for his project to base themselves solely on nature and avoid all idealizing transformations (*Physiognomische Fragmente* 2: 270). This also explains Lavater's position with regard to the debate that emerged around Johann Joachim Winckelmann's (1717–1768) theory about the art of antiquity. We are not surprised to discover that Lavater steps up to defend Winckelmann; like him, Lavater explains the extraordinary beauty of antique Greek sculpture by assuming that it represents a true mimetic copy of a more beautiful kind of human nature than is present in the world of his day (see *Physiognomische Fragmente* 3: 40–47). Ultimately, of course, it was only by insisting on just such a theory of mimetic naturalness and objectivity that he could legitimate his own use of aesthetic representations for the investigation of human physiognomy.

The inconsistencies of Lavater's physiognomic praxis become even more apparent when one realizes that he was not even capable of adhering to this demand for exact mimetic representation. The four volumes of the *Fragmente* are full of physiognomic analyses of historical, sometimes mythic individuals for whom no living "original" can be ascertained with certainty. One only need think of his interpretations of the apostles or his obsession with representations of Christ. Lavater's interpretation of Hans Holbein's (1497–1543) Judas in the first volume of the *Fragmente* (see 1: 79–83) is perhaps the most instructive example for this problem. (Fig. 4) Here he criticizes Holbein for having produced an image of Judas completely out of his own fantasy, and he objects in particular to what he perceives as the one-sidedness of this portrayal, which emphasizes solely the negative features of the despicable betrayer, without showing any of the traits of the one-time apostle. Now it is obvious, of course, that Holbein's representation of Judas makes no pretense to mimetic portrayal—the flesh and blood Judas certainly did not sit for him—but Lavater treats the painting as though it were, or at least should be, an absolutely "true" rendering of Judas as historical, as *physiognomic* figure.[13] But Lavater fails completely to recognize the contradiction between the kind of analyses he presents here and his own requirement that the representations used for physiognomic investigation must be genuinely mimetic.

Fig. 4. "Judas, after Holbein," from volume 1 of Johann Caspar Lavater, *Physiognomische Fragmente,* 1775.

Lavater never recognizes that his attempt to establish a valid physiognomic "alphabet" on the basis of artistic representations is bound to throw into question the *scientific* basis of his experimental data. Indeed, far from seeing this as a problem, he argues that such investigation of drawings, silhouettes, copper etchings, and portraits constitutes the very condition of possibility for a *scientific* physiognomics. Here we become aware once more of his truly naive reliance on the Enlightenment theory of signs, for he appears to assume that just because signs employed by the visual arts are iconic and natural, this automatically implies that they are accurate. As we have seen, however, he himself does not uphold this principle in his critique of Holbein's Judas.

In his description of the methodology demanded by the study of the human physiognomy, Lavater relates the considerations that led him to adopt this practice of examining artistic representations rather than flesh-and-blood individuals.

> I want to discover in the mild-mannered person the traits of this mild manner, in the humble person the signs of humility. But my observations must be exact; they must be repeated and tested often. How can that be possible if I have to make these observations on the sly? Isn't it presumptuous to analyze faces? And if a humble person notices that

> she is being observed, won't she turn away and hide her face? Indeed, it is here that I encountered one of the greatest obstacles to my studies; anyone who notices that he or she is being observed either puts up resistance or dissimulates. How can I get around this problem? Perhaps in part in the following way.
>
> I retire into solitude; I place before me a medallion or a piece of antique sculpture, the sketches of a Raphael, the apostles as depicted by Van Dyck, the portraits of Houbraken. These I can observe at will, I can turn them and view them from all sides. ("Von der Physiognomik" 176)

The ideal of observation that Lavater has in mind is clearly that of the empirical scientist: like him, the physiognomist must strive to observe with precision; like the scientist, the physiognomist must be able to repeat his observational experiment under the same conditions; like the empirical researcher, the physiognomist must be able to investigate his object "from all sides"—that is, he must be able to manipulate it at will. In short, like the natural scientist, the physiognomist must be able to simulate the conditions for objective experimentation in order to guarantee the truth of his results. Not even the awareness by the subject under study that he or she is being observed can be allowed to interfere with or compromise this pose of objectivity. In other words, it is precisely the turn to artistic representations, which can be examined at will and withdrawn from the facticity of reality, that manifests most prominently Lavater's desire to establish a scientific laboratory for the physiognomist. From this perspective it becomes clear why a profuse amount of illustrations were critical for the four volumes of the *Physiognomische Fragmente:* they represent, as it were, the rudiments of this physiognomic laboratory, with the added advantage that they communicate this "empirical" data directly to Lavater's readers. Indeed, the so-called "physiognomic cabinet," the collection of portraits, silhouettes, sketches, and so on that Lavater collected over the course of many years, constitutes his attempt to realize as completely as possible this laboratory of experimental physiognomics.

Systematic physiognomic investigation is only possible under sterile conditions such as these, in which every potentially individual—and hence uncodifiable—element in the human object of analysis is eliminated so that what is "characteristic" can come more prominently to the fore. The scientific physiognomist can only analyze other human beings in effigy, so that all the contingencies of the moment, every passion, and every exertion of the will can be set aside and left out of consideration. Ultimately, then, the steely gaze of the empirical, scientific physiognomist, as conceived by Lavater, reifies the human being under the pretense of studying it in the interest of human love and understanding. The suppression of everything dynamic and vital in the human being, which is characteristic in general of Lavater's theory, makes itself manifest in his preference for paper representations of the human face.

Seen in this context, Lavater's peculiar insistence on silhouettes as especially appropriate objects for physiognomic analysis begins to make all too much sense (see *Physiognomische Fragmente* 2: 90–93). (Fig. 5) This form of representation has particular advantages for a scientific physiognomics of the kind Lavater seeks to establish. Since I will return to this issue in the concluding chapter of this book, where I will examine the function of illustrations and reproductions in modern physiognomic works in broader terms, a few general remarks will have to suffice here. First of all, the technique of the silhouette represents a first step in the direction of objective, mechanical reproduction, a direction that would culminate about a century later with the development of photographic methods. Thus, the silhouette conformed especially well to the conditions of mimetic objectivity Lavater demands for representations of the human physiognomy. Second, and perhaps more importantly, the silhouette excludes "pathognomic" features of the face, which Lavater discounted as "arbitrary" signs of character, while emphasizing precisely the firm features of the face and skull to which he ascribed central significance.

Lavater's preference for silhouettes demonstrates with particular clarity the tendency of his physiognomic method to reduce everything individual to a limited, quantifiable set of norms. The mode of representation practiced by the visual arts in general is well suited to this limited understanding of physiognomics to the extent that, according to the aesthetic understanding of Lavater's time, it was only able to portray the static, not the active human being. That fits, as we have seen, especially

Fig. 5. Silhouettes, from volume 2 of Johann Caspar Lavater, *Physiognomische Fragmente,* 1776.

well with Lavater's conception of the *natural* human being, who, to his mind, antedates the cultured person motivated by intentional drives. Lavater specifically wants to exclude human actions and willful acts from his physiognomic purview, because he sees them as secondary effects that can cover over the more "authentic" layer of natural physiognomic signification (see *Physiognomische Fragmente* 1: 137–38). This is the point that particularly raised the hackles of Lavater's critic Lichtenberg, and following him somewhat later, of Hegel.

This explicit devaluation of the expressions of human actions as unreliable signs of essential character exposes especially well the methodological *petitio principii* in which Lavater's physiognomics is invariably caught up. The inescapable circularity of his procedure expresses itself unmistakably in his statement, cited above, that the aim of his physiognomics is to "discover in the mild-mannered person the traits of this mild manner, in the humble person the signs of humility" ("Von der Physiognomik" 176). If actions, deeds, and accomplishments cannot be read as definite, unequivocal signs of authentic character, as Lavater presumes, then one wonders what criteria he will use to establish the humility and mild manner of individuals in the first place. He cannot accomplish this by applying his physiognomic hermeneutics, for this "science" is yet to be established and codified. There is only one way out of this vicious circle: an appeal to the immediate intuitive understanding of the physiognomic "genius." But even here Lavater needs to presuppose what he first must demonstrate: namely, that the physiognomist has access to a mode of intuitive cognition that rests, as the Enlightenment philosophers (and Lavater following them) believed, on a semiotic process grounded in natural signification.

The principles of philosophical hermeneutics had, of course, not yet been theorized at the time of Lavater's writing; the Romantic theologian and philosopher Friedrich Schleiermacher (1768–1834) would not take first steps in this direction for another two decades. But Lavater's physiognomic practice seems to anticipate in one key respect a central theorem of hermeneutics: namely, that interpretation can only begin with a first hypothetical judgment, which then must undergo subsequent modification once one has a better grasp of specific details.[14] The hermeneutic circle is not a vicious one—as Martin Heidegger was among the first to point out (153)—but rather a dialectical one in which the momentary understanding of the parts and the whole mutually condition and progressively redefine each other. The immediate intuitive insight of the physiognomist could be viewed as a hermeneutic hypothesis that "spontaneously," as it were, intuits the character of the human being under analysis. In a subsequent second, reflective step the physiognomist would then have to isolate the specific signs that constitute the unconscious basis for this intuitive hypothesis. If this is what Lavater had in mind, then he never made it explicit; and such a methodology still lacks the self-corrective dialectic that lends hermeneutic thought its sophistication. But above all, Lavater's persistent appeal to the unfathomable intuition of the physiognomic genius—which, no doubt, he saw exemplified in his own person—still bespeaks a lack of scientific objectivity. Whenever objective proof is absent, Lavater simply relied on subjective "intuitions" and sensibilities. This is the point at which physiognomics clearly ceases to be an exact and rigorous natural science, as Lavater sought to conceive it, and simply turns to a hermeneutics of empathy to underwrite its purportedly positivistic conclusions. Lavater failed to recognize this crucial aspect of his own theory, and this fundamental misprision is what allowed him to misconceive a physiognomic theory that basically operates according to the principles of *textual* (or hermeneutic) science as a science of nature.[15] This is, as we will see, one of the problems inherent in modern, post-Lavaterian physiognomics in general; and the creativity and credibility of any individual theory depends largely on how ingenious it proves in resolving this conflict between the reliance on intuitive insights and the appeal to scientific objectivity.

This brings us back to the central theme of this chapter, the similarities between Lavater's physiognomic project and the rationalizing enterprise of the Enlightenment. Lavater's campaign against every form of contingency in human existence, above all against all forms of (semiotic) arbitrariness, corresponds to the Enlightenment dream of codifying all of nature in a rigorous system, reducing the world to what is rationally "meaningful," and dispelling whatever is not calculable and predictable. It should be obvious, however, that Lavater's battle against whatever is arbitrary itself relies heavily on the arbitrariness of his own subjective judgments. This is the central contradiction of this—and any other—physiognomics that pretends to be able to formulate its conclusions with scientific exactitude.

What makes Lavater's procedure and methodology especially interesting and instructive is the way in which he attempts to plug the holes in the leaky semiotic logic borrowed from Enlightenment models with rhetorical filler modeled on the stance of the Storm-and-Stress geniuses. One need only think of his insistence on the "fragmentary" nature of his own procedure, or of his praise of "wit" as a guide to intuitive comprehension.[16] The subjectivist element, without which Lavater's physiognomics is practically inconceivable, plays the significant role of serving as a kind of discursive, rhetorical plaster with which he can try to seal the cracks that appear in the foundations of Enlightenment science when the edifice of physiognomics is erected upon it. This marriage of logic and rhetoric is one of the features that will characterize all modern German physiognomic theories that follow in Lavater's wake.

2

Sign and *Sein*

Physiognomics, Phrenology, and the Dispute over the Semiotic Constitution of Modern Individuality

> The word "*sein*" in German means two things: existence, and belonging to him.
>
> Franz Kafka ("Betrachtungen" 44)

> Facial expression and gesture, tone, even a pillar, a post driven into the ground on a desolate island, announce immediately that they mean something other than their simple and immediate *existence*. They declare themselves to be signs by possessing a determinacy that points to something else that does not inherently belong to them.
>
> Georg Wilhelm Friedrich Hegel (*Phänomenologie des Geistes* 251)

Franz Joseph Gall's Phrenology and Lavater's Physiognomics

Lavater's physiognomics was not the only hermeneutic of human character that would storm onto the intellectual scene of German-speaking Europe in the final quarter of the eighteenth century. Less than two decades after the fourth and final volume of Lavater's *Physiognomische Fragmente* appeared, rumors began circulating in 1796 about the lectures dealing with the functions of the brain that were being given in Vienna by a certain Dr. Franz Joseph Gall (1758–1828). By 1802 the stir caused by Gall and his lectures became so great it reached the ears of that Königsberg recluse, Immanuel Kant (1724–1804), who made note of the intense intellectual furor that was raging (Saltzwedel 42). But even as early as 1798, Gall published the first summary of his ideas in *Der neue Teutsche Merkur*, a prominent journal; here he refers to the heated debate these theories had evoked in Vienna and beyond ("Des Herrn Dr. Gall Schreiben" 311). Gall was later to become recognized, of course, as the founder of phrenology, the art of reading the inherent mental capacities and moral inclinations of people from the shape and contours of their skulls. The rudiments of Gall's theory were relatively simple: he argued that the brain was the seat of all human faculties, that each faculty could be localized at a certain place in the brain, and that by examining the skull one could make definitive claims about the strength and/or weakness of specific mental functions—and hence about an individual's innate character.

The proximity of Gall's phrenological studies to Lavater's physiognomics was generally acknowledged at the time. Indeed, as indicated by a published summary of Gall's lectures in Vienna, recorded by an anonymous listener, Gall himself was aware of the connection between his project and Lavater's. This summary begins with the statement: "Lavater's physiognomics and the furor it created, as well as the mischief made with his theories, are still so fresh in people's memories that any new attempt to establish and found a theory of physiognomics could not help but attract general attention" (Anon., *Darstellung* 3). This remark is noteworthy for several reasons. First, it documents Gall's awareness that he is, as it were, following in Lavater's footsteps and that he sees his phrenological studies as inherently related to physiognomics. Second, it registers the stir caused by physiognomics and acknowledges that Gall's own theories will inevitably be received in an intellectual atmosphere conditioned by this reception. Hence Gall was aware from the outset that his own ideas would provoke widespread public debate and that he was destined to become a famous, or perhaps infamous, individual. Given that Gall went to great lengths to popularize his theories—the forum of his lectures in Vienna, which were offered to the general public, is the first symptom of this—it seems likely that he was more than happy to exploit Lavater's notoriety in order to assure himself and his new science a large and engaged audience. Third, and perhaps most importantly, Gall's reported remark about the misuse of physiognomics suggests that he conceived his own theories not merely as an extension of Lavater's, but as an improvement that would correct the failings of his predecessor's physiognomic conceptions.

Since Gall's ideas, unlike Lavater's, have found broader dissemination and were shuttled widely into the popular imagination, they are not in need of a detailed general summation here.[1] Instead, I want to concentrate on the points of intersection between the theories and practices of Lavater and Gall so as to demonstrate the ways in which phrenology must be seen as a response to, and further development of, "scientific" physiognomics in its Lavaterian form.[2] Three issues will take center stage in this discussion: the heightened scientific self-understanding of Gall's phrenology; the connection between Lavater's insistence on the natural signs of physiognomics and Gall's understanding of the relationship of the skull to the brain; and Gall's role as a popularizer of both the theoretical and practical dimensions of phrenology, and, by extension, of physiognomics understood in the broadest sense.

Those who most vehemently opposed Gall's theories raised against them, not coincidentally, exactly the same objections that were initially brought against Lavater's physiognomics. Phrenology was accused, above all, of being deterministic, of setting limits to the freedom of the individual, and of crass materialism in the then fashionable French manner. Gall's antagonists believed his theory was inherently atheistic because it reduced the spiritual, metaphysical qualities of the human being to base physiological processes. As inimical to basic tenets of Christian religion, Gall's ideas were considered a threat to common morality. Even with several decades of Enlightenment behind them, average citizens in German-speaking Europe, not to mention a large portion of the intellectuals, were reluctant to embrace such an ostensibly desanctifying conception of the human being. Gall's phrenology was viewed as natural science with a vengeance, a form of science whose objective was the total demystification of the world, its reduction to physical laws and properties that did not require the mollifying, ennobling notion of the divine. Gall was painfully aware of this criticism, and in the early essay in which he summarized his ideas, he dedicated the first several pages to an attempt to assuage these general fears ("Des Herrn Dr. Gall Schreiben" 311–17). Ultimately, however, this reproach of fatalism and atheism led to the censure of Gall by the Austrian Emperor Franz II (1768–1835) in December of 1801. By imperial edict Gall was prohibited from holding any further public lectures and from publishing his ideas in Vienna or elsewhere in the Austro-Hungarian monarchy. As a result, Gall took his phrenological lecture series on the road, visiting all the major intellectual centers of continental Europe between 1805 and 1807, and finally settling in Paris, a city in which the intellectual atmosphere was generally receptive to his cranioscopic science.

Lavater, as we recall, expressed the hope and the expectation that physiognomics would ultimately become "a science definable in mathematical terms" (*Physiognomische Fragmente* 4: 481). Gall takes major steps in this direction, not only toward such quantification, as Barbara Stafford suggests (118), but—as its necessary prerequisite—also toward a closer circumscription of the material and data with which his cranioscopy would concern itself. One of Lavater's most serious problems was his broad, indistinguishably general conception of what might assume meaning for the physiognomic interpreter. The only distinction to which he adheres relatively religiously is that between the, strictly speaking, "physiognomic" signs of the firm features and the "pathognomic" signs of the fleshy tissues. But even this segregation opens up physiognomic analysis to the knees, the feet, the hands, the shoulders, and even the general physique. In fact, Lavater presented interpretive analyses of other somatic features aside from the head and face, in particular of the structures of the hand. (Fig. 6) It was, quite understandably, impossible for Lavater to provide any but the most crude systematic rules for the interpretation of these diverse somatic signs, and so he inevitably had to be satisfied with only "fragmentary" recognitions. The only rule Lavater applied with relative consistency was the association of straight lines with virtue and curved lines with vice (Goritschnig, "Faszination des Porträts" 145), whereby it is once again simple iconicity (straight line as equivalent to the moral straight and narrow; curved line as indicative of circumvention) that underwrites this association. Gall, by contrast, did not have such difficulty limiting the scope of his physiognomic purview; indeed, he solved this dilemma in an admittedly brilliant way: the only part of the body that concerns him is the brain, and the skull only insofar as he takes it to be the adequate reflection of the brain it houses. He thus maintains: "The object of my investigations is the brain; I only concern myself with the skull insofar as it presents an accurate imprint of the external surface of the brain, and hence it is only one part of my larger object of study" ("Des Herrn Dr. Gall Schreiben" 330). With this, Gall accomplishes much more than merely a significant reduction of his subject matter to a small and manageable set of data; he simultaneously transforms physiognomics with one stroke from a metaphysical preoccupation to a decidedly *physiological* endeavor. This was, of course, exactly what Lavater had sought to accomplish with his theory of physiognomics as reliant on the precepts of natural semiosis, but, as we have seen, his solution was woefully inadequate. What Lavater the preacher lacked, above all, was the necessary understanding of the human anatomy, something that Gall, a trained physician and physiologist, clearly mastered. Gall the scientist was, in short, immeasurably more qualified to lay out a design by which physiognomics could be pursued as a positivistic, empirical science.

Gall's second major initiative for giving his craniological physiognomics greater focus and specificity was his division of the human brain into a finite set of separate and wholly autonomous "organs," or particular localities, that were identified as the sources of specified mental functions.[3] (Fig. 7) Thus Gall unequivocally maintains: "Not only are our mental faculties essentially distinct and independent of our inclinations, but all the faculties are distinct and independent of each other, as are the inclinations as well. Hence their source must be found in different and independent sectors of the brain" ("Des Herrn Dr. Gall Schreiben" 313). Initially, Gall assumed that there were twenty-seven different autonomous faculties and inclinations that could be located in the human brain. This was eight more than he identified in the brains of the most sophisticated animals, and for Gall these eight purely human functions defined the superiority of the human being as species (Lesky 30). This significant physiological advance, the localization of certain functions at specified parts of the brain, marks the modern and progressive aspect of Gall's theory. Indeed, this is what, for some, defines his role as a significant precursor to the modern physiological and neurological sciences (Bruce and Young 224). When viewed from this perspective, Gall's phrenology is not the pseudo-science intellectual historians and popular thought often make it out to be; rather, it bears testimony to Gall's ability to formulate a theoretical advance that was far ahead of the technical possibilities

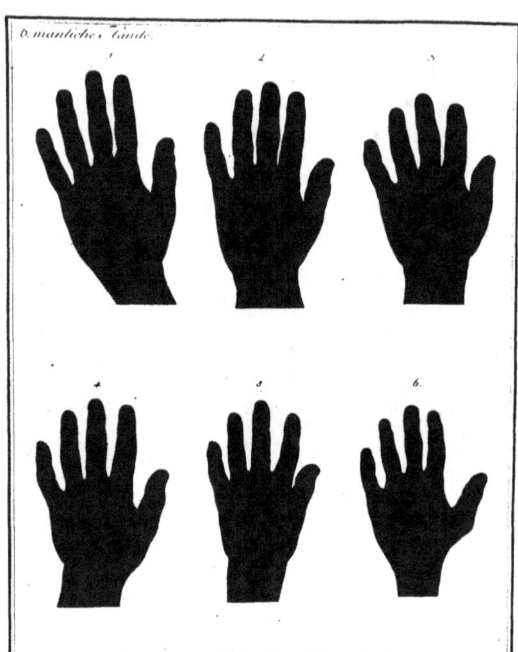

Fig. 6. "Six masculine hands," from volume 4 of Johann Caspar Lavater, *Physiognomische Fragmente.* 1778.

of contemporary science (Bruce and Young 225). Moreover, in this regard Gall also served as a theoretical model for the young Sigmund Freud, who, on the basis of his studies of phrenology, initially sought to locate the different psychic agencies, such as the ego and the id, in distinct parts of the brain (Sennett 173). Even in terms of intellectual impact and immediate influence on a changing worldview about the nature and constitution of the human being, it is no exaggeration to compare Gall's role at the inception of the nineteenth century with Freud's role at the beginning of the twentieth (see Borrmann 14).

Among the twenty-seven faculties and drives to which Gall assigned independent organs in the brain were the will to life, courage, cleverness, the power of observation, imagination, perseverance, and so on (see Anon., *Darstellung* 51–64). The number twenty-seven itself is not fortuitous, as we might expect, and curiously, it points to the Christian, almost mystic underpinnings of some aspects of Gall's thought. For twenty-seven is

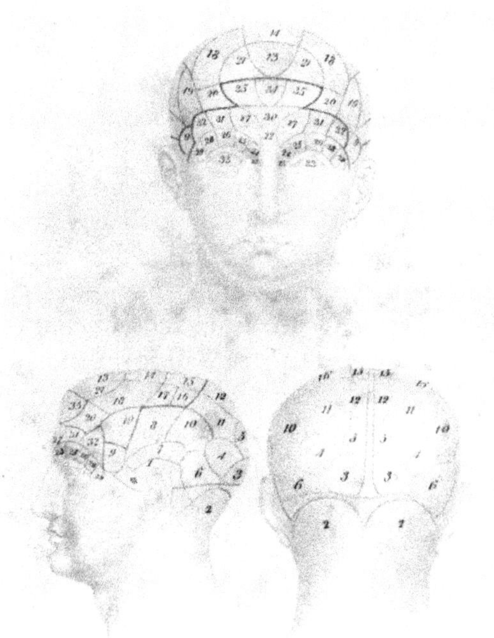

Fig. 7. Phrenological skull, from Johann Kaspar Spurzheim, *Phrenology, or the Doctrine of the Mental Phenomena,* 1846. (Courtesy of Special Collections, University of Washington Libraries)

the cube of the mystical number three, or three times three times three, and this systematic presupposition of a divinely ordained mathematical order indicates that Gall's theories did, in fact, as he constantly maintained, rest on certain Christian precepts (see Oehler-Klein, "Franz Joseph Gall" 98). On the other hand, Gall explicitly argued that size, and hence the strength or weakness, of these cranial organs was firmly established at birth, which fueled the accusation that his theory supported the notion of human predetermination. "*The faculties and proclivities are innate to their respective organs,*" Gall emphasized in his Vienna lectures, "*and they are not produced by education*" (Anon., *Darstellung* 12). This represents, of course, one of the closest bonds between Lavater's and Gall's theories: the presumption that the traits and characterological features identified by physiognomics or phrenology are innate, a priori givens that have a defining impact on the individual beyond any acts of will, consciousness, or rational choice. This appeared not only to go against accepted precepts of human choice and self-determination, but also to undercut the enlightened philosophy of progressive perfectibility.

In this regard, Gall's conception is not nearly as absolute and restrictive as is Lavater's. Indeed, Gall develops an argument to circumvent the unqualified determination of the individual by these preordained and innate faculties and inclinations—an argument that prefigures in significant ways the agonistic conception of the human psyche that Freud would theorize almost exactly a century later. There are, Gall asserts, certain qualities that set the human being apart from animals. The latter are, to be sure, wholly subject to their innate predispositions. Human beings, however, possess faculties that allow them to transcend their own characterological givenness.

> But aside from animalistic qualities, the human being has other traits, such as the capacity for language and the most extensive receptivity for education; these constitute two sources of inexhaustible knowledge and motivations. The human being has a sense for truth and error, for right and wrong, for the idea of an autonomous being; the past and the present can guide his actions; he is endowed with a moral sensibility and with intelligence. The human being employs these weapons in the struggle against his own inclinations. To be sure, these latter remain impulses that can lead him into temptations; but they are not impulses that cannot be mollified or repressed by opposing or stronger drives. ("Des Herrn Dr. Gall Schreiben" 315–16)

Gall lays out a rudimentary conceptualization of the human being as defined by a psychic space full of tensions and conflicts. The innate faculties and inclinations that his cranioscopy will identify and evaluate take on the permanence and relentlessness of the Freudian instincts, and they are countered, and partially controlled by, a set of other, more rational and circumspect capacities that have the potential for exercising a certain psychic governance. With this, freedom of choice, self-determination, and the possibility of progressive development and refinement of the individual enter into the equation. In this sense, Gall offers a much more differentiated picture of human beings and their potential for self-mastery than does Lavater; this conception is purchased at the price, however, of defining the human subject as a locus of repressive self-discipline and inherent conflict. For Gall, the advantages that can accrue from the knowledge of a person's innate faculties and drives, as discerned by phrenological analysis, perform an economic function in the process of individual cultivation. Once we recognize those drives that are strongest or weakest in the individual, Gall believes, we have access to a blueprint for the development of effective educational strategies. In order to cultivate our strengths and use them to counterbalance our frailties, we must first be able to identify them ("Des Herrn Dr. Gall Schreiben" 316–17). This, then, is the point at which the discoveries made by theoretical cranioscopy impinge on practical applications that can assist the individual in ordering his or her lifestyle, aims, and priorities.

The main practical problem that faces Gall's cranioscopy as physiological theory is the precise localization of the individual faculties at specified points or "organs" of the brain (see "Des Herrn Dr. Gall Schreiben" 324). As with Lavater, it is this transition from theory to practice that begins to muddy the waters of Gall's otherwise elegant conception. Like Lavater, however, Gall seeks to clarify this problem by outlining a methodology based on rigorous observation, experimentation, and the gathering of empirical evidence. Thus only after "tediously gathering experiences," Gall elucidates, does he move on to the next step of "building an edifice out of the laws of their interconnection" ("Des Herrn Dr. Gall Schreiben" 314). Gall describes his investigative procedure as an incremental progression from known to unknown facts (Anon., *Darstellung* 35–36). Similar in this regard to Lavater, who sought the physiognomic signs of humility in the person who was known to be humble, Gall also needs as his experimental basis individuals with known qualities, preferably powerful or exaggerated ones, whose heads he can examine in order to locate the cranial organ responsible for these traits. This is what motivates his seemingly macabre request that individuals with especially prominent characterological gifts bequeath their skulls to Gall for post mortem examination and study (Anon., *Darstellung* 38). Much as Lavater assembled a "physiognomic cabinet" that contained silhouettes, portraits, etchings, and so on, Gall meticulously collected the material for a phrenological "cabinet," in which he gathered the skulls of humans and animals, wax impressions, and plaster casts of the skulls of famous individuals (*Darstellung* 37; 40). He was, then, intent on establishing the most complete database of the empirical evidence that supported his theories. The kind of objectivity and laboratory conditions Lavater sought to establish by turning to the silhouette as mechanical reproduction, or to images that could be examined at will, Gall intended to provide for phrenology by relying on physiology—basing his studies on the investigation of real human skulls.[4]

Once Gall has established this physiological system that correlates particular faculties or proclivities with specifiable parts of the brain, the question becomes how he can gain access to these localizations without, as it were, dissecting the brain of a living person and thereby putting these functions out of commission. This is the point at which his central problem and the solution he proposes most resemble issues Lavater faced and resolved through his appeal to Enlightenment semiotics. Since Gall cannot examine the brain directly in order to gauge the size of certain organs, he turns instead to studying the skull as the cranial compartment that, according to his theory, conforms to the contours of the brain it houses. As Gall argues: "From the development of the skull bone onward, through to old age, the form of the inner surface of the skull is shaped by the outer form of the brain. Hence we are capable of drawing inferences about the existence of certain faculties and inclinations as long as the shape of the external skull is in conformity with that of the inner skull, or at least that it exhibits no exceptions to the otherwise known discrepancies" ("Des Herrn Dr. Gall Schreiben" 322–23). This is reminiscent of Lichtenberg's sarcastic remark about the Lavaterian soul as an elastic fluid that conforms to the contours of the static body, so that if we flatten someone's nose we also alter their personality ("Über Physiognomik" 267). It is almost as if Gall took his cue from Lichtenberg's joke, for this is precisely how he envisions the relationship between the brain and the skull. The major difference is that in this case the interconnection is by no means so absurd as in the instance of Lavater's "soul." For, as Gall is quick to point out—this argument, in fact, constitutes one of his major lines of defense—injuries to the head that alter the shape of the skull can, and do, in fact, have a harmful impact on the brain. Moreover, as Gall correctly argues, it is usually just one, or a small set, of mental capacities that are affected by such local injuries. Gall takes this fact as confirmation of his thesis that the organs for certain mental functions are localized in specific areas of the brain, and that when these areas are damaged the corresponding psychic faculty is impaired ("Des Herrn Dr. Gall Schreiben" 317–19).

It should be obvious that the relationship between skull and brain that Gall theorizes is identical to the one that Lavater attempted to establish for physiognomics by appropriating the Enlightenment theory of the natural sign. The connection of the bump on the skull, of the phrenological sign—if we may call it that—to its signified in the physiology of the brain is, like Lavater's physiognomic signs, both causally motivated and iconic. This is what allows one, after all, to determine, in Gall's words, "*the existence and the relative proportion of numerous faculties and inclinations based on the construction of the vessel that contains the brain*" ("Des Herrn Dr. Gall Schreiben" 321). Specifically, the existence or nonexistence of any particular capacity is signaled causally by the presence or absence of a protrusion on the skull at the specified place; the proportion, or *quantitative* degree, of this faculty is designated iconically, by a correspondence between the *size* of the protrusion on the skull and the *strength* or *power* of the mental function with which it is aligned (see Anon., *Darstellung* 26, 31).

If Lavater's theory of how the human body displays psychic meaning still depends on a semiotic theory, Gall accomplishes the same, indeed, a better effect by essentially desemioticizing the "signs" of phrenology. We are, in this instance, in fact, no longer dealing with signs in the strict sense, for the shape of the skull and that of the brain have been so closely correlated as to be identical. Where Lavater needed to rely, as it were, on a theory of "natural" *signification,* Gall can ground the correspondence of skull and brain in *nature* itself. This allows him to insist without equivocation "that in this life, spirit *[Geist]* is fettered *[gefesselt]* to somatic structure" ("Des Herrn Dr. Gall Schreiben" 319). The iron law of this causality between body and soul is expressed in Gall's metaphor of the fetter or shackle that irrevocably binds them to each other. With this, Gall succeeds in establishing precisely that absolute and determinate relationship between skull and brain function, between somatological indicator and psychic trait, that Lavater labored to concoct by turning to Enlightenment semiotics. Gall reduces the semiotic difference between signifier and signified to such a degree, however, that the skull is no longer a sign as such; it already *is* the psychic faculty it signifies. Sign and *Sein,* or Being, the interpreted somatological feature and the existential state of which it is indicative, have essentially been fused. As we will see, this is precisely the point that is up for debate in the controversy over physiognomics, a point against which Hegel will make the most persuasive arguments.

Before turning to this larger issue there is yet one further point of confluence between Lavater and Gall that requires brief discussion: their common role as popularizers of their distinct, yet related, physiognomic enterprises. Lavater's function as popularizer is closely tied to the media in which he presented his theories, especially in the lavishly illustrated and printed volumes of the *Physiognomische Fragmente.* Aside from the illustrations, which served to make his theories concrete and relatively accessible, Lavater's primary calling card was his effusive rhetoric. It was clear to all who read his physiognomic writings that Lavater, true to his calling as a preacher, was on a mission. His zeal was coupled with the right amount of rational argumentation and illustrative evidence to lend his theories persuasive force. Gall's case is somewhat different. Not that he sensed any less of a mission than did Lavater; indeed, he seems to have exuded confidence in his own convictions. But Gall's successes, and especially his ability to insure a wide dissemination of his theories, was predicated on the energy and initiative with which he traveled throughout Europe to deliver his lectures. Many of the greatest minds of the time made a point of attending these stimulating and controversial events—Goethe, Wilhelm von Humboldt (1767–1835), Hegel, and Samuel Thomas Soemmerring (1755–1830), the noted German anatomist, represent just a small cross section of his auditors. Gall brought in tow to these lectures his assistant Johann Kaspar Spurzheim (1776–1832) and a plethora of illustrative objects, from skulls to graphs and plaster casts, with which to demonstrate his principles. He was, in all likelihood, a gifted pedagogue, someone who could draw his audience along with him and punctuate his theoretical explanations with concrete examples at precisely the right moment. The power of Gall's presentation is perhaps best indicated by the fact that he actually charged—and that people gladly paid—for admission to his lectures (Lesky 30). Even under these conditions he regularly presented his ideas to overflowing lecture halls, and this was how he financed his travels and his research.

Presenting a kind of itinerant sideshow, complete with macabre but gripping props, Gall set an example that would become a norm for phrenologists worldwide. The prominence of such phrenological itinerants in rural America during the middle decades of the nineteenth century is just one of the most notable examples (see Davies 32–37). In Germany, this role was assumed around mid-century by the revivalist phrenologist Gustav Scheve (b. 1810). Like Gall, Scheve traveled throughout the country giving infamous public lectures on, and demonstrations of, the principles of phrenology. In addition, he published in 1851 a popularizing manual of phrenology, *Phrenologische Bilder: Zur Naturlehre des menschlichen Geistes und deren Anwendung auf Wissenschaft und Leben* (Phrenological pictures: On the natural doctrine of the human spirit and its application in science and life), a work that went into a second edition in 1855 and a third in 1863.[5] (Fig. 8) While Lavater initiated a physiognomic boom in the 1770s, and Gall fueled a fascination with phrenology in the first decade of the nineteenth century, Scheve led a phrenological revival that crested between 1840 and 1860 (Volrad Deneke 107). Figures like Lavater, Gall, and Scheve played no small part, then, in bringing an awareness of physiognomic and phrenological issues to a broad audience and insuring that a knowledge of the principles of their research transcended closely circumscribed disciplinary and academic boundaries.

Physiognomics and Individuality

Having sketched in broad outline the affinities between Lavater's and Gall's positions, I want to go back now to a more detailed

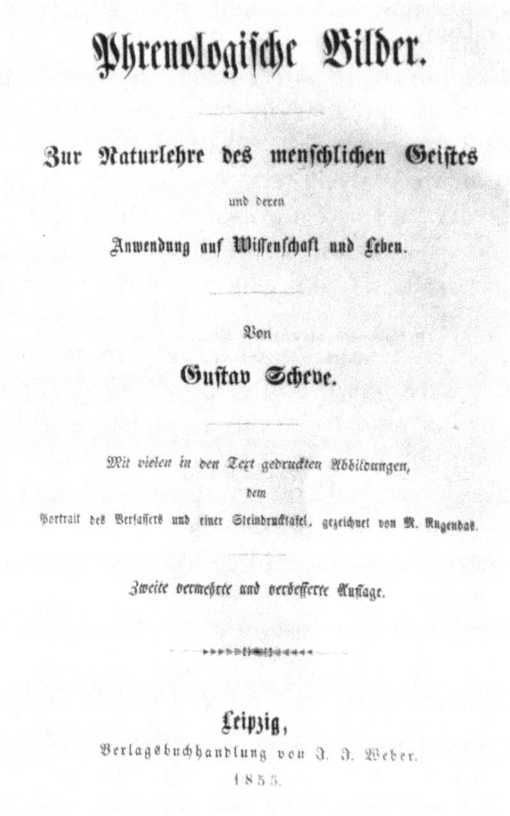

Phrenologische Bilder.

Zur Naturlehre des menschlichen Geistes

und deren

Anwendung auf Wissenschaft und Leben.

Von

Gustav Scheve.

Mit vielen in den Text gedruckten Abbildungen,

dem

Portrait des Verfassers und einer Steindrucktafel, gezeichnet von M. Rugendas.

Zweite vermehrte und verbesserte Auflage.

Leipzig,

Verlagsbuchhandlung von J. J. Weber.

1855.

Fig. 8. Title page, Gustav Scheve, *Phrenologische Bilder,* 1855.

study of the dispute over physiognomics that raged between Lavater and Lichtenberg in the late 1770s. There was, I hope to show, considerably more at stake in this debate than generally meets the eye. In fact, the terms of the debate recur throughout the nineteenth century in German intellectual culture whenever physiognomics or phrenology is at issue. Hegel launched perhaps the most destructive critical barrage against both Lavater and Gall in the section of the *Phänomenologie des Geistes* dealing with physiognomics and phrenology. But physiognomics finds a further defender in the person of Carl Gustav Carus (1789–1869), without doubt the most significant advocate of cranioscopy and general physiognomics in Germany in the nineteenth century.

And even the pessimistic philosopher Arthur Schopenhauer threw his substantial intellectual weight behind the cause of physiognomics. Why was this such a persistent and hotly-debated issue in the final decades of the eighteenth century and throughout the nineteenth in German intellectual history? The reason for this, I want to suggest, is that the debate over physiognomics thrashed out in disguise, as it were, certain fundamental issues about the very constitution of the civil subject as individual, issues that haunted the thought of the German intelligentsia of the time.

My thesis is that a fundamental intra-ideological debate over the constitution of the civil subject as individual crystallizes around this controversy over physiognomics. The parties in this dispute champion two distinct *semiotic* models for the theorization of human individuality. On the one hand, physiognomics and phrenology understand the individual as an eternally self-identical *re-presentational* construct in which a primordial, a priori Being—a transsensual "essence" or meta-physical "significance"—is mimetically *re*produced in the sensual signs of the body. On the other hand, those who oppose physiognomics or phrenology comprehend the individual subject as an autonomous, *self-productive* system in which the primordially given objectivity of self-identical Being is continually submitted to a process of (self-)transformation. According to this conception, word and deed, not mere corporeal Being, are the only reliable signs of genuine individual *Sein*, Being or personal existence.

Hans Blumenberg has sought to explain the fascination with physiognomics in the age of reason by arguing that the obsession with the "readability" of the natural world marks the secret, repressed desire of enlightened reason for a realm of significance that transcends the limited parameters established by the discourse of rationality itself (*Lesbarkeit* 199). This hypothesis, which is exceedingly illuminating from a psychological perspective, remains incomplete insofar as it fails to address the sociohistorical factors that helped make physiognomics one of the first widespread movements of modern popular culture.[6] We must keep in mind that the resurgence of physiognomics in the final three decades of the eighteenth century in Germany coincides not only with the rationalization of knowledge, its taxonomical segmentation into disciplinary divisions, but also with the solidification of the ideology of the autonomous civil subject into a powerful mechanism of sociocultural—if in Germany not yet political—mastery. It is this intermeshing of physiognomics with the ideological process of the civil subject's self-definition that largely accounts for those innovations that distinguish modern physiognomic theory from its historical antecedents.

Lavater passes on to his successors in the nineteenth and twentieth centuries his ambition to rationalize physiognomics, constituting it as a scientifically systematized discipline capable of laying claim to the discovery of accurate information regarding the inner, transsensual "essence" of the human subject. If Lavater was intent on rescuing his own brand of physiognomics from its denigrating association with popularistic forms of physiognomic prophecy (see "Von der Physiognomik" 147–60, 164–88; *Physiognomische Fragmente* 1: 52–56), his most immediate successors, Gall, on the one hand, and then the Romantic physiologist and psychologist Carl Gustav Carus, replicate this tactical move. On the very first page of his *Symbolik der menschlichen Gestalt,* Carus goes to some length to insist on the scientific nature of his human symbolics (1). Significantly, however, it is the supposed irrationality and nonscientific nature of Lavater's physiognomics that serves Carus as a foil with which he will contrast the unquestionable scientific basis of his own physiognomic theories. Carus himself is unaware of the irony that this very gesture betrays his own indebtedness to Lavater as the father of "scientific" physiognomics, since it replicates the manner in which Lavater himself sought to place distance between his own theories and the discredited ones of his predecessors. Moreover, Carus, similar to Lavater in this regard as well, concedes that his physiognomic "science" cannot in practice get by without the aid of a certain subjectivist "artistry": "In this regard one must note," he maintains in the introductory pages of his *Symbolik,* "that even such a *scientific* symbolics . . . can never, in its application, operate without a certain feeling that acts as a correct facilitator, without a refined tact that itself must be in-born. In short, like many sciences, when it is applied it must, as it were, be practiced as *an art*" (6). Carus fails to recognize the proximity of this assertion as well to Lavater's persistent invocations of "physiognomic genius" and the role "artistic feeling" plays in his physiognomic judgments ("Von der Physiognomik" 190–91; *Physiognomische Fragmente* 1: 52–53, 172–79). Carus thus unwittingly becomes in significant respects Lavater's most consequential successor, a fact that will be addressed at greater length below.

This scientistic-disciplinary orientation is one of the primary features that differentiates the physiognomic theories of post-Enlightenment German modernism, culminating in the psychology of expression in the early twentieth century, especially the works of Ludwig Klages (1872–1956), from their various antecedents in the history of physiognomics.[7] Closely tied to the scientistic-methodological penchant characteristic of physiognomics since the eighteenth century is its self-understanding as a *semiotic* discipline, its conception of the sensual body as a system of signs that signify transsensual essence. To be sure, Paracelsus's (1493–1521) doctrine of physiognomic signatures already turns on an implied semiotic (see Böhme 149–50); but beginning with Lavater, as we have seen, questions of semiosis come into the forefront of physiognomic investigations. Lavater addresses the semiotic design inherent in his physiognomics early in the first volume of the *Physiognomische Fragmente,* where he explicitly identifies it as the element capable of elevating physiognomics into the ranks of the natural sciences.

> As soon as a truth or an element of knowledge has signs, it becomes scientific; and it reaches this point as soon as it can be communicated using words, images, laws, determinations. Hence it is simply a matter of not merely obscurely perceiving the striking, undeniable distinctions among human facial features and forms, but rather of codifying them in characters, signs, expressions? Whether specific signs of strength and weakness, physical health and illness, stupidity and rationality, magnanimity and vileness, virtue and vice, etc. can be identified and communicated?—This is the only question under investigation for the current discussion. (*Physiognomische Fragmente* 1: 53)

Lavater's fragments draw their potency to a large degree from his ability to invoke the fundamental intellectual and scholarly values current in his day and line them up as unimpeachable witnesses in defense of physiognomics. One of the first demagogues of German modernism, Lavater knew exactly which buttons to push in order to marshal broad public and scholarly support for his theories. But before turning to a more detailed examination of the implications of this semiotic problematic for Lavater's theory of the constitution of individuality, we must examine one further feature that distinguishes modern physiognomics from antecedent physiognomic endeavors: this is what I will call its *sociopragmatic* dimension.

As a theory of authenticity that seeks to define self-identity in terms of a semiotic relationship presumed to obtain between the body as sensual sign and the transsensual essence of the individual as its signified, physiognomics plays a formative role in the ideological self-definition of the emergent civil subject. First of all, it establishes a criterion for a distinction between the self-identical, autonomous civil subject and the courtly aristocrat, who is viewed as a quintessentially non-self-identical being whose existence consists solely in the assumption and playing-out of inauthentic roles. If the critique of courtly society painted the picture of an artificial world held together by formalized social conventions rather than by genuine sentiment or intimate interpersonal attachment—a world in which mutual deceit, dissimulation, and dissemblance passed as social graces—then physiognomics provided the civil subject with a theoretical counter-model that defined individuality precisely in contradistinction to the counterfeit masquerade of courtly life. In this sense physiognomic theory functions as one of the mechanisms by which the practitioners of German civil society assert the precepts of their own authentic "culture" over the defamed "civilization" of the aristocracy.[8] Anthropological thought at the end of the eighteenth century is beset by the fear that the demands of the modern world threaten to open up an unbridgeable rift between the internal essence and the external appearance of the human subject. This anxiety expresses itself above all in an obsession with the notion of the counterfeit,[9] as well as in a fixation on the problems of deceit and dissimulation, issues that form the thematic core of much German literature of the period.[10] As a theory that appeals to the conception of natural semiosis in order to establish a firm connection between appearance and essential Being, physiognomics functions as a hermeneutic antidote to the threat of dissimulation; it thus is intended to shore up the sagging foundation of interpersonal relations in civil society (see Böhme 146). Physiognomics operates, in short, as a hermeneutics of disclosure: the physiognomically practiced gaze, functioning like a moral X-ray machine, reveals the "authentic" character of those individuals on whom it is trained by decoding their physiognomically significant features.

In response to this demand Lavater formulates his major contribution to physiognomic theory, the distinction between the "firm" and unalterable features of the human countenance and those characteristics such as bearing, demeanor, and facial expression that, being subject to human control, are capable of becoming the vehicles of dissimulation and deceit (*Physiognomische Fragmente* 2: 55–63; "Von der Physiognomik" 167). The first, as we have seen, Lavater associates with physiognomics in the strict sense, the second with pathognomics. The section in the fourth volume of the *Fragmente* that deals with this distinction alludes to the sociological dimension it implies. After asserting the priority of physiognomics over pathognomics by means of a series of illustrative metaphors, Lavater concludes with the assertion: "*Physiognomics* is the mirror of natural scientists and the wise. *Pathognomics* is the mirror of courtiers and the worldly-wise. The whole world reads according to *pathognomics*—very few read according to *physiognomics. Pathognomics* must struggle against the art of dissimulation; this is not the case for *physiognomics*" (4: 39). These remarks contain three especially revealing points. The first is Lavater's summary claim that the physiognomic traits of stable form are not subject to dissimulation and hence disclose authentic human essence. In effect, with this assertion Lavater establishes the object-character of the physiognomically analyzed face by decoupling it from all subjective, volitional acts, which he associates instead with pathognomics. Second, this fundamental proposition allows Lavater to valorize physiognomics, which he aligns with the "objective" world analyzed by the natural scientist, while simultaneously denigrating pathognomics, which he identifies with the subjective dissimulations that govern the world of the aristocratic court. Finally, Lavater further underwrites this hierarchy by contrasting the uniqueness of physiognomics to the mundanity and universality of pathognomics. Here in particular the sociopragmatic mechanism that drives Lavater's physiognomic theories makes itself evident; for Lavater is clearly concerned with delimiting the practitioners of, and believers in physiognomics on two fronts: both upward over against the degenerate nobility, and downward in contradistinction to the common masses. Physiognomics thereby stakes out a middle ground of social praxis in which the civil subject can attain self-definition and self-identification. The phenomenal popularity physiognomics enjoyed, especially among the practitioners of German civil society, in the years from approximately 1775 to 1790 evolves as a reflex of this drive toward self-distinction.[11] Physiognomics was uniquely suited to provide the civil subject with the claim to a moral monopoly on humanity as a way of legitimizing its struggle for sociopolitical self-empowerment.

Already the outline of an ideal physiognomic methodology that Lavater presents in the essay "Von der Physiognomik" manifests this complex mechanism that serves the double purpose of bourgeois self-approbation and social delimitation from the common rabble. Thus when it is a matter of establishing the physiognomic signs of unreason, that trait most despised by the enlightened subject, Lavater draws on the nameless faces of lunatics, proceeding synthetically in order to sketch a composite picture of the countenance of unreason ("Von der Physiognomik" 167–71). On the other hand, when his aim is the codification of the signs of intelligence, virtue, artistry, and so on—that is, when he concerns himself specifically with the physiognomic definition of those values hypostatized by civil society—Lavater examines portraits of famous individuals and proceeds analytically, identifying those physiognomic signs that correspond to the noteworthy accomplishments of these unique personalities ("Von der Physiognomik" 174–82).[12] The results at which Lavater will arrive are thus preprogrammed into the selection of the objects he studies: his physiognomic "method" confirms, on the one hand, that the anonymous lunatics are indeed part of a faceless mass and lack individual self-identity, and corroborates, on the other hand, that the deeds of certain world-historical individuals can be physiognomically demonstrated to be the reflex of a unique and self-identical character.

The sociopragmatic dimension of bourgeois physiognomics is in evidence in the popularization of physiognomic practice as a kind of parlor game. In this instance physiognomics serves the ends of a double-edged discrimination, permitting the practitioner of physiognomic hermeneutics to flatter its "objects" by passing lauding judgments, while simultaneously distinguishing himself or herself as a physiognomic "genius" in possession of unusual powers of discernment. This interactive, *dialogical* moment of physiognomic practice points to its function as a tool for social bonding in civil society. In this sense it is closely related to those other structures of social intimacy that are characteristic of the process by which the self-constitution of a group-specific social practice takes shape in civil society. The occupation with physiognomics also indicates the extent to which the evolution of sociocultural self-distinction occurs as the codification of a system of signs that serve a two-fold purpose: this semiotic is community-building in that it helps form a basis of mutual understanding for those who are initiated into its operation; and it functions as a means to segregate its initiates as a group from those "outsiders" who are not a part of this semiotic covenant. Physiognomics thus operates for the civil subject as a kind of *symbolon* in the original sense of this word: as a token or body of knowledge whose possession distinguishes and identifies the members of a secret fellowship. Much like the secret signs that both fuse and isolate such confraternities as the Freemasons—a movement, not coincidentally, that also attained prominence among the German bourgeoisie in this period (see Koselleck 53–68)—the "language" of physiognomics performs an essential community-constitutive function.

The paramount task of theoretical physiognomics from Lavater onward is the segregation of those corporeal features that can be deemed significant for an individual's metasensual essence from those traits that are merely "accidental" and hence not symptomatic of intrinsic character. In this sense physiognomics follows the lead of enlightened science, which sought to establish the essence of objects by differentiating between their "inherent characteristics" *(Eigenschaften),* and their coincidental "contingencies" *(Zufälligkeiten),* or nonessential features (see Lambert 1: 14). Lavater, as we have seen, goes about this discrimination by invoking the distinction between "physiognomic" traits in the narrow sense—that is, the relatively unchanging and stable structures of the "firm" body parts—and "pathognomic" characteristics, those mutable features connected with the malleability of the muscles and fleshy parts of the body.

Already in the essay "Von der Physiognomik" Lavater appeals to the discourse of authenticity in an attempt to ratify his physiognomic theory and practice. The physiognomist, he maintains, "segregates what is fixed in someone's character from what is habitual, the habitual from the accidental. He judges the human being *according to what he really is,* and not according to his exterior ornamentation" ("Von der Physiognomik" 163; emphasis added). In a subsequent paragraph he specifies this assertion by claiming that physiognomics reveals a dimension of the self that lies deeper, and hence is truer, than such products of the will as speech and action: "[Physiognomics] reveals more than all actions and words; it reveals the intellectual and moral predispositions" (164; cf. also *Physiognomische Fragmente* 1: 160). It is significant to note that here, too, Lavater is giving expression to a precept already laid down in the moral philosophy of the Enlightenment; Christian Wolff, for example, made a strikingly similar case for the priority of affects over actions as reliable indicators of human character.[13] Lavater merely supplements this Enlightenment theory by hypostatizing the dimension of physiognomic expression as the most primordial and genuine of all expressive functions. In Lavater's view, then, the human subject evinces a structure much like that of an onion: its authentic and individual core is submerged under various expressive layers, only one of which, namely the sub-intentional lineaments of the "firm" physiognomic features, is a valid sign of authentic Being. All other expressive dimensions, including affect, verbal expression, and action, represent nothing but external "ornaments," which at best are unreliable gauges of genuine character and at worst are purposive lies or dissimulations.

Lavater's conception of the individual basically conforms to a Pascalian worldview that stresses the virtues of absolute quietude: all sin, evil, and deception, his physiognomic theory suggests, derive from the fact that, to paraphrase a reflection from Pascal's *Pensées,* human beings do not simply remain alone in their rooms, but are called upon to act and interact (53). Lavater's penetrating physiognomic gaze seeks to bracket all volitional acts, thereby practicing a kind of phenomenological reduction that, like Husserlian *Wesenserschauung,* permits a reconstruction of the "stable" pre-actant essence that distinguishes the preconscious, authentic individual from the manifold guises of its willful, conscious counterfeit. Genuine individuality exists only in the state of absolute non-(e)motion, which is reflected in the physiognomically stable kernel that subtends all pathognomic and actantual mutation. As I have indicated, Lavater's practice of analyzing portraits and silhouettes rather than flesh and blood human countenances is consistent with this exclusion of all that is truly vital in the human subject from the sphere of what is physiognomically significant. The authentic Being that the language of Lavaterian physiognomics speaks is always already a mortified Being, stripped of all animate energy: in its drive to uncover authentic Being, physiognomics thus reifies subjective beings, transforming them into lifeless corpses.[14]

In a fragment bearing the title "On Human Freedom and Lack of Freedom," Lavater makes a vigorous effort to come to terms with the charge that his theories run counter to the ideals of human self-determination and liberty. He takes refuge in the paradoxical conception that humans are free to do what is necessary, an idea that he concretizes in an illustrative metaphor: "The human being is free, like a bird in a cage." Lavater explicates this image with these words: "[The human being] has a determinate and intransgressible sphere of influence and sensations. Just as every person's body has a specific contour, so too does that person have a circumscribed and unalterable space in which to maneuver" (*Physiognomische Fragmente* 4: 115). Each individual is defined by a given set of parameters that it can neither escape nor transcend. The measure of any particular individual's freedom resides in the degree to which it actualizes the limited potentials opened up within this confined space. Self-realization hence consists not in the establishment and subsequent accomplishment of autonomously defined aims, but rather in the effectuation of certain heteronomous, objectively given dispositions that function as the a priori determinants of one's character. The human being is "born," in other words, with a divinely pre-established temperament that, however, remains a mere potentiality; individual freedom extends only as far as the choice either to recognize and develop these preordained aptitudes, or to let them remain unrealized and unfulfilled by mistaking or ignoring them. Lavater's categorical imperative therefore reads: *"Be who you are, and become what you can"* (*Physiognomische Fragmente* 4: 117), whereby the physiognomist is commissioned with the crucial assignment of hermeneutically "divining" each person's predetermined inclinations. Becoming the acid test of authenticity, physiognomics assumes the role of an indispensable guide for those who wish to lead a life of "genuine" self-realization. In this physiognomic world, self-overcoming is by definition an exercise in futility. No degree of training, education, or labor can help one surpass one's "nature"; indeed, this "nature" is the individual's fate, an absolute, untranscendable horizon. The cult of physiognomics shares this fatalism with the cult of modern psychology, whose socially paralyzing effect Theodor Adorno has described in the following way: "The cult of psychology that is palmed off on humanity . . . is the complement to dehumanization, the illusion of the impotent that their fate is tied to their nature" ("Zum Verhältnis von Soziologie und Psychologie" 54). Charged with the delimitation of human "nature" as a realm of absolute necessity, physiognomics identifies the intransgressible boundary that divides nature from culture. By setting strict limits to the possible encroachment of the process of acculturation on this realm of necessity, it encourages passive acquiescence to the given and thereby helps shape the authority-oriented subject required by the social praxis of civil society.[15]

Lavater's conception of physiognomics as a hermeneutic practice that reads the sensual body as a sign of the primordial *Sein* or Being of the individual is reformulated some seventy years later by Carl Gustav Carus, who calls this re-presentational semiotics of Being a "symbolism" of the human form. In introductory remarks to his *Symbolik der menschlichen Gestalt* (Symbolism of the human form) that sketch the objectives of this corporeal symbolics, Carus names his two primary focuses. First, the central concern of this symbolics is not the actuality of the individual, what it in effect has become, but rather its predispositions, what it has the *potential* to become (12). Second, this symbolics must be able to distinguish between contingent, momentary impulses and essential, durable traits (13). Carus goes on to summarize the purpose of symbolics in these words: "The most important demand made of symbolics, at any rate, is that it represent the individual human being in all his or her *original particularity,* and that it aim for this regardless of what he or she attempts to accomplish and actually makes of this particularity" (13). The affinity of this program to that of Lavaterian physiognomics and Gallian phrenology is conspicuous: like Lavater and Gall before him, Carus is concerned with the identification, on the basis of a hermeneutic decoding of predetermined sensual signs, of the unalterable and untranscendable "essence" that lies at the core of each individual. Carus conceives this "original" essentiality as the underlying "idea" of the individual subject, and in accordance with Lavater's theories he views certain stable and unalterable "physiognomic" features as the sensual realization of this transsensual idea. In the psychological treatise *Psyche: Zur Entwicklungsgeschichte der Seele* (Psyche: On the developmental history of the soul), which appeared a few years prior to his *Symbolik* and which formulates in rudimentary fashion some of the principles elaborated there, Carus describes the soul as the "primordial ground" of the individual, the "idea of its existence" (10). He explicates this notion by providing an etymological interpretation of the word "person." Derived from the Latin verb *per-sonare,* which means "to sound or speak through," the "person," Carus maintains, must be understood as a vehicle through which the voice of some Other speaks. The sensual body of the "person" is like the actor's mask in the theater of the ancients: the "primordial ground" or metaphysical idea of the individual speaks through this physical mask (10–12). In Carus's understanding, in other words, the human subject is quite literally a *sub-iectum,* an entity that by definition is always already "thrown under"—that is, subjugated to—a divinely predetermined and immutable blueprint. For Lavater and Carus, then—and in a more limited sense for Gall—"individuality" is concretized in the human puppet who dances to a tune composed and chosen by someone else.

If Lavater's and Carus's visions of the individual as a Being controlled from within by transcendent impulses seem to approach the pessimistic metaphysics of Arthur Schopenhauer, this is no coincidence. In fact, Schopenhauer himself was one of the most adamant post-Lavaterian advocates of physiognomics, a fact that has received surprisingly little attention in scholarship on the subject.[16] In chapter 29 of his *Parerga und Paralipomena* (1851), under the ostensibly neutral heading "Zur Physiognomik" (On physiognomics), Schopenhauer proffers a spirited and engaged defense of the principles central to post-Enlightenment physiognomics. For example, he presumes, as do Lavater and Carus, that the human being is a semiotic construct in which an a priori, transsensual Being is represented in unalterable sensual signs. Furthermore, he asserts that this semiotic relationship is underwritten by the principle of causality, so that these signs are believed to stand in a necessary, nonarbitrary interconnection with their transsensual signifieds (744). The proximity of Schopenhauer's thoughts on physiognomics to those of Lavater is especially manifest in the following passage, in which he takes up one of the Swiss pastor's favorite themes: the denial of the "coincidentality" of the human countenance to the essential Being of the individual.

> Every human face is, rather, a hieroglyph; one, however, that we can decode, indeed, whose full alphabet we bear complete within us. In fact, a person's face usually says more, and more interesting things, than does his mouth: for the face is the compendium of everything that the mouth will ever say, since it is the monogram of this person's every thought and aspiration. Moreover, the mouth only communicates the thoughts of the human being, whereas the face communicates a thought of nature. (744–45)

Even in its figurative texture this passage echoes Lavater's writings on physiognomics. The metaphors of the hieroglyph, the alphabet, and the monogram or signature, for example, are all images familiar to readers of Lavater's *Physiognomische Fragmente.* In terms of thematic issues, Schopenhauer, like Lavater and Carus, pictures the human physiognomy as an object of "nature" through which a transcendental significance makes itself evident. Like them, he valorizes this physiognomic "thought of nature," ranking it above verbal expression, which he discredits as the mere "thought of a human being." Furthermore, he shares their deterministic tendency, envisioning the physiognomic dimension of the human subject as a symbolic map on which the intransgressible boundaries of its self-realization are ineradicably charted. Schopenhauer summarizes this semiotically grounded metaphysics of the physiognomically circumscribed individual when he writes: "a human being's face expresses precisely *what he is*. . . . By contrast, a human being's words merely express what he thinks, often simply what he has learned, or even what he only pretends to think" ("Zur Physiognomik" 748). This statement concisely formulates the notion of authenticity that underwrites modern physiognomics since Lavater: the objective *signs* of the human physiognomy transparently identify the primordial and ineluctable *Sein*, the Being of the individual. For Schopenhauer, as for Lavater, physiognomic interpretation is capable of divulging the authentic essence of the human subject precisely because it ignores all "arbitrary" expressive signs—those that emanate from the conscious, volitional subject—bringing into focus instead the "genuine," subconscious, sub-intentional signs that, attached to the very Being of the individual, infallibly signify "what he is."

It is consistent with this position that Schopenhauer argues, as did Lavater before him, that the physiognomist must observe the "object" he seeks to analyze only when it is in a state of absolute repose.

> For in order to grasp the physiognomy of a human being in all its purity and depth, one must observe him when he sits alone and is left to himself. Already any form of social contact, a discussion with someone else, throws an alien light upon him, usually to his advantage, because by means of this action and reaction he is set in motion and thereby elevated. However, alone and left to his own devices, swimming in the brew of his own thoughts and emotions—only then is he completely and absolutely *himself*. ("Zur Physiognomik" 749)

Only when sentenced to solitary confinement and reduced to the immobile state of total quietude is the transsensual essence of the individual perfectly and transparently represented in the *semes*, the signs, of its physiognomy. This authentic individual, devoid of all emotions and concerned solely with its own self-presence, is projected as quintessentially asocial. In its Schopenhauerian version the same physiognomic theory that was ostensibly formulated to further mutual human love and facilitate social bonding in civil society manifests a profoundly antisocial character. The philosophy behind physiognomics thus nourishes the drive toward privatization and self-encapsulation that is intrinsic to the social praxis of civil society. Schopenhauer unwittingly turns out this misanthropic underside that, from its very inception, is part and parcel of modern physiognomics.

Lichtenberg and Hegel, the most vociferous critics of post-Enlightenment physiognomics, both direct their critiques of Lavater's physiognomic hermeneutics at his belief that essential individuality is semiotically re-presented in the "firm" features of the sensual body. To reduce this controversy over physiognomics either to the opposition between the normativity of form and the articulation of action,[17] or to the conflict between "gaze" and "speech" as distinct modes for the disclosure of Being,[18] is to overlook the fact that this dispute centers on questions about the very constitution of subjectivity and its role within the life praxis of civil society. Whereas physiognomic theory postulates that the civil subject exists as a Being whose authentic core is always already established *prior* to its entrance into the domain of social practice and human interaction, Lichtenberg and Hegel defend a conception of human individuality that is *self*-constituted in a dialectical interface between the subject's intrinsic Being and the conditions of its material and social life world. Here individuality is identified not with predetermined durable Being, but rather with the *alterations* this Being undergoes as a result of this dialectical process. In other words, for these two critics of physiognomics, neither the *Sein* of the individual nor its expressive signs are indelibly stamped upon it from the moment of its conception: to this dictatorial, ahistorical Being they oppose a process of *historical* becoming in which the individual has autonomous input into its own determination.[19]

Lichtenberg marks off one of the most problematical areas of physiognomic theory when he points to the inherent difficulty of distinguishing between corporeal traits that reflect the a priori constitution of the "soul" and those that are historically produced in creative response to, and interaction with, external factors dictated by the socioempirical world.[20] "Our body thus stands in the middle between the soul and the rest of the world," he contends, "and mirrors the influences of both; it does not only tell of our inclinations and abilities, but also of the blows of fate, climate, illness, nourishment, and of a thousand hardships, to which we are not always subject due to our own bad decisions, but rather due to accident or even duty" ("Über Physiognomik" 266). The body, Lichtenberg recognizes, is not simply the external manifestation of internal essence; it is rather that dimension of the subject that is constituted at the intersection of two worlds, that of inner nature and that of empirical and sociocultural reality. The Being of any particular individual is neither identical with its givenness, nor with its sociocultural and empirical contexts, but is generated in the dialectical tension between these two spheres. Hence Lichtenberg can assert that one and the same human "nature," while retaining its predetermined physiognomy, would develop distinct character traits when confronted with extraordinarily different historico-empirical circumstances. "What can you possibly want to infer from the similarity of faces," he asks Lavater and his followers, "when the same fellow who has been hanged, with all his predispositions, under different circumstances could have earned laurels instead of the noose? Opportunity not only creates thieves, it also creates great men" (268). As opposed to the physiognomist, who believes he has captured the essence of an individual once he has deciphered its "natural" inclinations, Lichtenberg maintains that these factors remain secondary to the substantiality of *actual,* historically realized character: "I'm not interested in knowing what a person might have become. Might not anyone become anything? Instead, I want to know *what he is*" (271; emphasis added). Lichtenberg insists that Being arises only in the concrete actualization of options that are conditioned not by predetermined givens alone, but likewise by objective empirical circumstances as well as by volitional acts, that is, by *subjective* responses to various givens.

Lichtenberg attempts to decertify physiognomics by calling into question its most holy principle: the transparency and unequivocality of the signs it interprets. He sets about this task by highlighting the manner in which meaning is bound to context. Lichtenberg speaks with the experience and linguistic insight of the lifelong aphorist when he writes: "If in a short sentence I shift the meaning of every word just an inch, the meaning of the sentence can change by miles" ("Über Physiognomik" 276). The "language" of physiognomics, he perceives, stakes its fortunes on the wager that the referential meaning of "natural" signs is given and unalterable, and hence independent of their *use.* Lichtenberg holds up against this absolute referentiality, which orients language solely around the vertical or paradigmatic axis of semantics, the definitional strictures of the horizontal or syntagmatic axis. He recognizes, furthermore, that it is Lavater's absolute equation of sign and *Sein* that accounts for the prejudicial, blindly Eurocentric undercurrent evident in Lavaterian physiognomics. Against Lavater's proto-racist claim that "nature" could not possibly place the mind of a Leibniz or a Newton in the skull of a Lapp or a Moor ("Von der Physiognomik" 149; *Physiognomische Fragmente* 1: 46–47), Lichtenberg argues that it is the historico-cultural context in which these philosophers were embedded that, more than anything else, accounts for the distinctiveness of their thought. A Moor subject to the same upbringing, education, culture, sociopolitical environment, and so on, would in his opinion have the same basis for writing the *Theodicy* as did Leibniz ("Über Physiognomik" 272–74).

This insight into the dependence on context, and hence the transitoriness, mutability, and *historicity* of all referential significance, leads Lichtenberg to defend the pathognomic signs of affect as more meaningful and trustworthy than Lavater's physiognomic signs. This forms the crux of his polemic against physiognomics. Over against physiognomics as a semiotic of absolute and stable Being that examines the body for "signs of *standing* character," Lichtenberg asserts the priority of pathognomics as a semiotic of *ephemeral* emotions and "signs of *transitory* action" ("Über Physiognomik" 278; emphasis added). To be sure, when in the same context he refers to pathognomics as a "nonarbitrary language of gesture," Lichtenberg seems to transfer to pathognomics the claim of immediacy and authenticity that Lavater makes for physiognomics. But what Lichtenberg understands under affective language's lack of arbitrariness is not its unequivocality and trans-intentionality, as was the case for Lavater; rather, pathognomics for him is nonarbitrary or "natural" simply in the sense that it is transcultural, that is, universal to all humanity. Lichtenberg freely admits that because the signs of particular affects can be imitated at will, their expression is no guarantee for the presence of the affects they commonly signify (287).

According to Lichtenberg, there is a third, neither "physiognomic" nor "pathognomic" dimension of expressive signs transmitted by the human countenance; these he circumscribes as the traces of previous *actions,* and such signs, he asserts, can be interpreted with relative certitude. He argues, in fact, that it is only by unwittingly projecting data revealed by this expressive dimension onto more narrowly defined physiognomic traits that physiognomists are able to pass "correct" judgments at all.

> What often makes our judgments based on faces correct are the indubitable signs, which are neither physiognomic nor pathognomic, of previous actions, without which no person can ever appear on the street or in the company of others. Debauchery, greed, begging, etc. all have their own livery, in which they are just as recognizable as the soldier in his uniform or the chimney sweep in his. One false word betrays a bad education, and the form of a hat and the way we wear it can betray our entire deportment and the degree of our foppishness. Even the insane would often not be recognizable as such if they did not reveal themselves by means of actions. ("Über Physiognomik" 289)

Whereas according to physiognomics the genuine Being of the individual comes to light only in absolute solitude and in a state of total repose, Lichtenberg argues that authentic character manifests itself only when the individual acts and reacts within a sociocultural context. This means that individuality does not subsist in a transcendentally preordained, eternal, and durable Being; it is *generated* in encounters between the individual and the socioempirical life world. Furthermore, if character is subject to infinite unforeseeable mutations that derive from the subject's interaction with the external world, then its signs must likewise be conceived in terms of a series of displacements, not as stable referents. Both individual *Sein* and its signs, in other words, are established in a *differential* rather than in a *referential* system. Lichtenberg summarizes this differential semiotic, explicitly contrasting it to the representational semiotic of physiognomics, when he comments: "It is above all the *series of changes* in [the face], which no portrait and certainly no abstract silhouette can ever represent, that express character" ("Über Physiognomik" 287; emphasis added). Affect and action are more revealing signs of human character precisely because they betoken the transformations by which character is shaped. If for Lavater the "soul" antedates and resists all history, for Lichtenberg it evolves within history, as the traversal of different temporal and situational states of Being: individuality is Protean, defined not as Being eternally "what one is," but as the capacity for Becoming-other than one is in every new encounter with the socioempirical world.

Lichtenberg, of course, does not follow this historicization of individuality through to its most radical conclusion, namely to the postulate of the absolute non-identity—the fundamental "dividuality"—of the in-dividual. He locates self-identity, rather, in the consistency that obtains within a series of actions over time, and this *consequence*—understood both as effectuated "result," and as "con-sequence," that is, as the logical consistency of a certain set of actions—becomes for Lichtenberg the only reliable method for analyzing and predicting character. Following the summation of his arguments against Lavater's physiognomic hermeneutics, with which he concludes his anti-physiognomic treatise, Lichtenberg elucidates this alternative mode for deciphering human individual character.

> Another way of investigating the character of human beings would be more useful, and it could perhaps be studied in a scientific manner: namely, to discover from the known actions of a person, which he has no reason to try to conceal, other actions to which he would not readily confess. . . . Thus one can infer with greater certainty from orderliness in the living room the orderliness in a person's head, from a sure eye for proportion a powerful understanding, from the color and cut of the clothes people wear at a certain age their character, than one can infer anything from a hundred silhouettes made from a hundred different perspectives of one and the same head. . . . One judges the man by his mistress, or at least draws conclusions about many of his actions toward us. Those who are good to their servants are generally good people in principle. ("Über Physiognomik" 293)

Whereas physiognomics compares apples and oranges, so to speak, equating transsensual disposition with an arbitrary sensual "sign," thereby establishing character on the basis of semiotic fiat, Lichtenberg suggests that one can only draw valid conclusions about character by proceeding analogically through a comparison of like things: from the evidence of certain known actions we can infer, assuming the principle of con-sequence, other parallel and unknown actions. The examples Lichtenberg cites of such actions on which characterological inferences can reasonably be made, while all are specifically *inter*active, fall into two general categories: the relationships the individual sustains with its material environment, and those it entertains with its fellow human beings. Only in the latter case, where character is divulged by interactions in the intersubjective realm, for example between man and mistress or master and servant, does it hold that Lichtenberg understands individuality as a *social* phenomenon.[21] This intersubjective, social dimension must be supplemented by those exchanges between the individual and its objective environment—for example, the way it appropriates and organizes its living space. This interactive dimension divulges the manner in which the individual *acculturates* the natural world. For Lichtenberg it is the *subjective modification* of the natural environment—that is, *productive labor* that transforms the objects of nature into artifacts of culture—which best betokens individuality and character.

Lichtenberg nowhere expounds upon this productive, dialectical model of individuality which he sketches in his critique of Lavater; this task will be taken up instead by Hegel a quarter of a century later in the *Phänomenologie des Geistes* (1807), where once again it will be developed in counterpoint to the re-presentational semiotic of durable Being promulgated by modern physiognomics. But it is important to recall here that the view Goethe represented in his "Addendum" to the fragment "On Physiognomics" in the first volume of Lavater's *Fragmente* already contains the kernel of this dynamic, self-productive conception of the individual. Goethe, as we recall, extends the jurisdiction of physiognomics far beyond the limits set by Lavater, arguing that not only the individual's sensual body, but similarly all the objects it appropriates and acculturates can be read as signs of its inner character. These objects, according to Goethe, have been invested with the power of the individual, and it is this investment that renders them legible signs of its character. Individuality, Goethe suggests, is not something given in nature, but rather something that is generated at the dynamic intersection between nature and culture. Nature's stamp upon the human subject is not the sign of individuality; on the contrary, it is the human subject's stamp on nature, its cultivation or productive transformation of nature into cultural artifact, that becomes the token of individuality. It is precisely this Promethean image of the human subject as its own self-creator in a dynamic encounter with the empirical world that Immanuel Kant terms "having character." "It is . . . not a matter," Kant remarks in the *Anthropologie in pragmatischer Hinsicht* (Anthropology regarded pragmatically), "of what nature makes of the human being, but rather of what the human being *makes of himself;* for the former belongs only to temperament (whereby the subject is to a large degree passive), and only the latter reveals that he has character" (634). "Having character," or possessing individuality, is an attribute solely of the subject *in action.* Hegel develops this vision of individuality as self-creative encounter with the givenness of the objective life world in his theory of reflective *Geist* (spirit/mind).

Immediately before beginning the section in the *Phänomenologie des Geistes* that treats the relationship of self-consciousness to its immediate reality, in which is contained his critical discussion of physiognomics and phrenology, Hegel defines individuality as the dialectical union of a primordially given and a self-generated Being. "Individuality is what makes *its* world into *its own;* it is the circle of its own actions in which it presents itself as reality, and as such it is nothing other than the unity of *given* and *created* Being *[Sein]*" (232). Elaborating on this distinction, he identifies a priori Being as the "in itself" *(an sich)* of individuality, productive Being, or "free doing," as its "for itself" *(für sich):* "The individual exists in and for itself; it exists *for itself,* or it *is free action* [emphasis added]; but it also exists *in itself,* or it itself *has* [emphasis added] an original, determinate Being *[Sein]*" (233). The individual is a composite of two moments: of the active Doing that it *is* for itself, and the passive Being that it *has* or *possesses* in itself. Hegel gives priority to the first of these, to individuality as self-creation by means of deed, claiming that only through action does it constitute in actuality its *genuine* Being: "The *true Being [Sein]* of the human being is rather *his deed;* in this deed his individuality is *real*" (242). Deed as the Being-for-itself or "true Being" of the individual is not conceived as the simple *realization* of its Being-in-itself or passive Being as pure potential, as physiognomics would have it; rather, it is envisaged precisely as the dialectical negation of this primordial Being: "when it acts, individuality presents itself as the *negative* being *[Wesen]* that only *exists* insofar as it sublates

Being *[Sein]*" (243). Only in the active sublation of its passive *Sein* (its Being-in-itself) does individuality come into *act-ual* Being (Being-for-itself). The self-creation of the individual thus emerges as a process by which the human subject sacrifices the givenness of its Being-in-itself in order to become a Being-for-itself: individuality is produced only in that act in which the subject gives itself over to the moment of transformation and becomes "work," understood both as active labor and as the concrete product of such labor. "Individuality that entrusts itself to the element of objectivity by becoming work surrenders itself to the possibility of being altered and perverted" (243).

Before turning to the relevance of this conception of individuality to Hegel's critique of physiognomics, it is necessary first to examine the semiotic status he ascribes to these two moments of Being, which I will refer to as Doing or productive Being (Being-for-itself) and passive or primordial Being (Being-in-itself). Central to Hegel's valorization of Doing over passive Being is his hypothesis that primordial Being cannot have the a priori status of a sign; only to active Doing can one ascribe the dual status of being at once both genuine *Sein* and sign.

> An action is something simple and determinate, something general, something that can be contained in an abstraction; it is murder, theft or act of charity, courageous act, etc.; and we can *express* what *it is.* It *is* this, and its Being *[Sein]* is not just a sign, but rather the thing itself. The action *is* this, and the individual human being *is* what *this action is.* . . . Thus only action can be conceived as the person's *genuine Being [Sein]*—not his figure, which is supposed to express . . . what one thinks that he merely might do. (*Phänomenologie des Geistes* 243)

This remark is directed at Lavater's belief that the firm or "physiognomic" features of the human body—what Hegel elsewhere in this treatise derogatorily refers to as "dead Being" (*totes Sein,* 206)—are the signs of human predisposition. As the marks of pure potentiality, such "signs" are incommensurate with the individual comprehended as actualized substantiality. Earlier in the *Phänomenologie* Hegel expresses in the form of a general maxim the priority he gives to the actual and really existent over the merely potential and non-actualized: "what *is supposed* to be," he insists, "also *exists* in action, and what is merely *supposed* to be, without actually *existing,* has no truth" (192). Physiognomics consequently cannot lay claim to truth because it concerns itself solely with what *should* be, ignoring what in actuality *is*—that is, what has been realized in deed and action. Doing alone is genuine Being, and concrete deed or having-done is the sign of this true Being; by contrast, potential to do that which remains undone is merely "dead Being" and as such cannot function as a sign of individuality as Being-for-itself.

This differentiation between sign and *Sein* is fundamental to Hegel's critique of physiognomics. While it is possible, according to Hegel, for any natural object to be simultaneously both Being and sign, these two modes are distinct from one another insofar as the process by which any object becomes sign requires the input of human subjectivity: "Facial expression and gesture, tone, even a pillar, a post driven into the ground on a desolate island, announce immediately that they mean something other than their simple and immediate *existence.* They declare themselves to be signs by possessing a determinacy that points to something else that does not inherently belong to them" (251). A stake driven into the ground on a desolate island operates as a sign precisely because it has *been driven* into the ground *by* a human agent: its status as sign relates not to its Being as stake, but solely to the quality of being "driven into the ground," which signifies its having been acted upon by a human subject. Being functions as a sign, in short, only as a consequence of having become the object of productive *labor.* Taken to its logical conclusion, Hegel's remark implies that there are no such things as *natural* signs: no empirical entity serves in its mere natural and given Being as a sign; it acquires the attribute of "signness" only when subjected to a process of acculturation. All signs, in other words, are for Hegel "arbitrary" in the sense of "conventional": they are the products of subjective human attributions of meaning. This is consistent with the definition of the sign found elsewhere in Hegel's philosophy.[22]

This semiotic assumption forms the ground for Hegel's censure of physiognomics. Since Lavater founds the scientific "verity" of physiognomics on the assertion that the signs it interprets are natural, causally motivated, nonarbitrary, and hence trans-intentional, Hegel undermines the very foundation of physiognomics by denying the subsistence of such natural semiosis. He argues, in effect, that if a semiotic relationship were to obtain between passive Being and active individuality—a relationship which Hegel, as we have seen, explicitly refutes—then such a signifying relation could only be arbitrarily instituted.

> Now if the external form, insofar as it is neither an organ nor an activity, and as such just a *passive* totality, were truly capable of expressing internal individuality, then it would thereby function as an existing thing that would placidly receive this internal quality, as something foreign, in its passive being and thereby become its sign—an external, accidental expression whose *real* aspect would be meaningless for itself; a language whose sounds and sound combinations are not linked directly to the thing itself, but instead are connected by free choice *[freie Willkür]* and hence have an accidental relationship to the thing. (*Phänomenologie des Geistes* 236)

Hegel puts his finger on one of the major problems underlying physiognomic practice: namely, its tendency to interpret away the body, to declare its corporeal *reality* meaningless by means of its hypostatization as *sign*. Conceived as sign, the materiality of the body becomes secondary to and disappears behind the transsensual significance of which it is presumed to be the token. Hegel's use of the subjunctive mood in the quoted passage indicates that in his opinion such an en-signment of the primordial and passive body can make no claim to truthfulness. Thus wherever such en-signment is accomplished, as in physiognomics, the connection between sensual sign and its transsensual signified is by definition arbitrarily instituted. Hegel recognizes, in other words, that the supposedly "objective" interpretations proffered by physiognomic hermeneutics amount to nothing but subjective attributions of meaning.

We are now able to specify more precisely Hegel's conception of the relationship between sign and *Sein*. As the product of human activity, which Hegel identifies with Being-for-itself, signs can only refer to this active Being as Doing: to deed, action, self-production, and labor. That passive, primordial Being-in-itself that is not (yet) individuality, on the other hand, cannot have the value of a sign. Hegel elucidates this on the example of the human skull. "The skull bone as such is such an indifferent, disinterested thing," he observes, "that there is nothing one can immediately see in it or think about it than just itself; . . . it constitutes a reality that is purported to portray another side of individuality that is no longer Being *[Sein]* reflected in itself, but instead a purely *immediate Being [Sein]*" (251). Contrary to the presuppositions of physiognomics and phrenology, the Being of the skull cannot be taken as a sign for some transsensual significance: it has no other "meaning" than simply its pure "immediate Being." The skull is incapable of making any statement about the individuality it encompasses simply because this individuality, as *Being reflected in itself (sich in sich reflektiertes Sein),* is incommensurate with the immediate, primordial Being of the skull.

Hegel attacks physiognomics for attributing the value of a sign to the primordial Being of the body; the body, he objects, like the stake on the desolate island, only takes on the function of a sign when it becomes an object acted upon by human subjectivity. Only once it is *en-acted* by subjective spirit/mind *(Geist)* does the body become both sign and *Sein,* a semiotic indicator and a symptom of productive Being: "This *Being [Sein],* the *body* of the particular individual, is this individual's *primordialness,* his absence of having acted. But insofar as the individual only is what he has accomplished, the body is also the expression of the self that he *creates;* as such it is simultaneously a sign that has not remained immediate thing, but instead reveals what it is insofar as it has transformed an originary nature into its product" (*Phänomenologie des Geistes* 233). This passage brings us back to the problematic Goethe addressed in his "Addendum" to the fragment on the nature of physiognomics in the first volume of Lavater's *Physiognomische Fragmente.* The body, as Goethe and Hegel both recognize, does not simply reflect the immediate Being of the human subject; rather, it exists precisely at the intersection of this primordial Being and the actantual Doing initiated by *Geist.* This interaction alone constitutes its individuality. For Hegel this means that the body is a conglomerate of a priori Being and sign, these two marking distinct and incommensurate modes of its being. As passive Being the body does not function as a sign; as sign it is not a sign of this primordial Being, but rather a sign of that "genuine Being" produced when primordial Being is dialectically sacrificed and transformed by means of productive labor. Hegel's objection to physiognomics and phrenology thus is grounded in a fundamentally distinct conception of the

Being of individuality: over against Lavater's (and Gall's) heteronomously defined individuality anchored in predetermined "natural" Being, he defends an autonomously generated individual in which Being is self-created in a process of dialectical exchange between the empirical world as objective Being and the subjective world of spirit/mind *(Geist)*. The "essence" of individuality as *Geist* is constituted as the acculturation of the material world through the individual's productive labor: only as *work* and human *product* does the empirical world—the sensual body included—take on the status of a meaningful sign.

It is one of the central paradoxes of physiognomics since Lavater that, while it tends to glorify humanity as the image of the godhead, it is simultaneously steeped in an elemental cultural pessimism, displaying radical skepticism wherever human drives, desires, and intentions are at work. Human will, for modern physiognomists, is never identical with goodwill; thus they strive to uncover an expressive domain beyond—or below—all conscious and intentional acts of human subjectivity, a realm of immediate "nature" that underlies all culture. The "authentic" individual, for physiognomics as for psychoanalysis, always exists somewhere underneath everything the human subject *purposively* accomplishes in the process by which it acculturates the natural world. The opposite is the case for Hegel: here it is precisely the purposive acts of speech and deed that point irrevocably to the genuine Being of the individual.

> The speaking mouth, the laboring hand . . . are the realizing and accomplishing organs that portray action *as action* or the internal as such. . . . Language and labor are expressions in which the individual no longer keeps hold of and possesses himself, but in which he instead allows the internal to step completely outside itself and sacrifice itself to being other. . . . They do not merely *express* the internal, rather they are this internal in all its immediacy. . . . Because the internal transforms itself into something other in language and action, it thereby surrenders itself to the element of transformation, which perverts the completed deed and makes it into something other than what it is, in and for itself, as the action of this particular individual. (*Phänomenologie des Geistes* 235)

If for physiognomics the skull, the silhouette, the bone structure of the body are taken as the marks of essential Being, for Hegel it is the *speaking* mouth and the *laboring* hand that betoken genuine individuality. The individual comes into Being in that precarious moment when it ceases to *possess* itself, abandoning solitary, passive self-possession in favor of active ex-pression in speech and deed. This process of ex-pression has two discernible aspects: on the one hand, the inward self is opened up to transformation and change; on the other hand, its speech and deeds become externalities that take on an objectivity of their own, independent of the individual of which they were the subjective expression. This externalization of the internal, in other words, is simultaneously both the self-*realization* of the internal self and its self-*alienation*. In order to enter into the dimension of genuine individuality as self-reflective Being, the human subject must sacrifice self-possession as Being-in-itself to the mutations of externalization through speech and deed. Only by means of this detour over the empirical world as Other can the Self be constituted as *self*-consciousness: "But in fact self-consciousness is the reflection out of Being *[Sein]* of the sensual and perceived world, and as such essentially the return from *Being-Other [Anderssein]*. As self-consciousness it is motion" (*Phänomenologie des Geistes* 138). Physiognomics precludes such a process of coming to oneself, or self-realization, by means of becoming Other; it recognizes only a binary form of "self-reflection" in which the internal self is represented in the primordial Being of the sensual body. For Hegel, by contrast, only that complex dialectical process of self-reflection by which the individual hazards its Being to self-alienation, to Being-Other in speech and action, produces "genuine" individuality. Such an individual, to be sure, is not stable and eternal, but constantly caught up in this process of transmutation. The individual as historically mutable construct stands over against the ahistoricality of the preordained and durable individual advanced by physiognomics.

We can illuminate the difference in these two conceptions by enlisting the aid of an illustrative metaphor to which we turned previously. As I have indicated, physiognomics views the human body as a palimpsest in which an originary text, inscribed by a transcendent author, has been overwritten by later, less significant texts (see Blumenberg 230). As a hermeneutics of disclosure, physiognomics attempts to reconstitute this original writing, thereby identifying the essential core of the intrinsic individual. For Hegel and Lichtenberg, on the other hand, the originary text inscribed on the human palimpsest is strictly speaking in-significant; indeed, it is in the very process by which this transcendentally "authored" original text is constantly rewritten, overwritten, and blurred by new, self-authored texts over the course of history that individuality is constituted.

The foregoing archaeology of the relationships between sign and *Sein* as concretized in the dispute over physiognomics is, it seems to me, of more than simple intellectual-historical relevance. It manifests the emergence of a theoretical controversy over the constitution of subjectivity, especially with regard to its function vis-à-vis the determining factors of semiotic codes, that is still relevant today. This same problematic has informed the debate surrounding poststructuralist theories that tend to define the subject as a product of "discourse," or an effect of "structure"—that is, as something always already predetermined by an inviolable code. The critique of this position, which has drawn its arguments primarily from philosophical hermeneutics on the one hand[23] and Neo-Marxism on the other,[24] has stressed the creative potency of the subject, its ability to transgress and hence to alter discursive codes. It is not my intention to enter the fray of this controversy here; I wish merely to point out that the positions assumed in this current critical debate reiterate in striking ways those assumed by the adversaries in the controversy over physiognomics. As we will see in subsequent chapters, the historical power of physiognomic theory and discourse in the German-language tradition stems in part from the fact that over the course of its evolution physiognomics is ultimately able to incorporate the Hegelian critique into its own position. In particular, the racist physiognomics of the early twentieth century will bridge this divide, taking up positions on both sides of this eighteenth- and nineteenth-century dispute and making those arguments relevant for its respective theories of race and racial expression.

3

Physiognomics between Humanism and Racism

Johann Caspar Lavater and Carl Gustav Carus

Lavater as Forerunner of Racial Physiognomics

In the introduction to his "anti-physiognomics," the critical attack on Lavater's physiognomic practice, Georg Christoph Lichtenberg justifies the vehemence of his campaign against Lavater and his followers by alluding to the connection between their physiognomic judgments and the condemnations passed down by the Spanish Inquisition ("Über Physiognomik" 257). Lichtenberg expresses this idea even more emphatically in an entry from his "Sudelbücher," the diary-like notebooks he kept throughout his life: "If physiognomics ever becomes what Lavater hopes it will be, then we will begin to hang children before they commit the crimes that deserve the gallows; a new kind of confirmation ritual will be practiced every year. A physiognomic auto-da-fé" (*Sudelbücher* 1: 532). With this incisive critical remark Lichtenberg points to a curious dialectic inherent in Lavater's physiognomic practice: the reversion of a theory, derived from Christian theological roots, that ostensibly seeks to promote human love and understanding into a practical system for the denigration, condemnation, and even damnation of those defined as physically, morally, or characterologically "other." Lavater, we should not forget, entitled his physiognomic investigations "Physiognomic Fragments for the Promotion of Human Understanding and Human Love." Lichtenberg did not fail to notice that Lavater's title gave priority to human understanding over human love. He alludes to this questionable hierarchy when he inverts these terms in the subtitle to his own treatise on physiognomics, whose purpose he cites as the "promotion of human love and human understanding." It is significant that Lichtenberg, the representative of Enlightenment science, thereby throws a negative light on the project of human understanding. When put into *practice,* he suggests, this attempt to comprehend others on a physiognomic basis all too often devolves into strategies of disclosure that seek to unmask and lay bare the analyzed human "object."[1] Lichtenberg insists, moreover, that the extraordinary popularity of Lavater's physiognomics cannot be attributed to special powers of observation inherent in the German populace; on the contrary, "[t]his speedy dissemination can be explained much more easily and more naturally as a response to the tendency, which today has become so common, to exploit as little knowledge as possible to create the greatest possible appearance that one is knowledgeable" ("Über Physiognomik" 259). The debasement of other human beings, in other words, ultimately serves the ends of establishing and legitimating the superiority of the subject who passes physiognomic judgments. Lichtenberg seems to have had an inchoate insight into the disciplinary aspect of Lavater's physiognomic gaze, its manifestation of a panopticism that had the potential for disseminating the manipulative, controlling measures of Jeremy Bentham's (1748–1832) panoptic prison system throughout the fabric of society as a whole.

What Bentham's panoptic penitentiary and Lavater's physiognomic gaze have in common is their monologic structure of observation: while the observed human "object" is subjected to constant observation, made completely transparent by insistent and all-fathoming surveillance, the observing, judging subject assumes a privileged site of observation and remains hidden to its object (see Foucault, *Discipline and Punish* 195–228). This association of physiognomics with a form of criminal justice is already present in Lichtenberg's critical analogies, and this forensically oriented brand of physiognomics, as we know, was refined throughout the course of the nineteenth century, culminating in the criminalistic theories of Cesare Lombroso (1835–1909) and in the carefully orchestrated method of forensic identification and photography developed by Alphonse Bertillon (1853–1914).[2] (Fig. 9) But this censorious trajectory of the physiognomic tradition since Lavater reaches its culmination in the proto-fascist, racial anthropology of the "Nordic Movement" in Germany in the years immediately following the First World War. One need only think of the racial ethnology of Hans F. K. Günther (1891–1968), or of the racial psychology of Ludwig Ferdinand Clauss (1892–1974), both of whose theories will be discussed in subsequent chapters. However, Günther and Clauss are merely the best known, most influential representatives of a much broader, more complex, and far-reaching racial-physiognomic movement that emerged in the period of the Weimar Republic and flourished under Nazi rule—a movement whose scale and significance has not yet been adequately investigated.[3] Lichtenberg was the first to recognize the germ of this misanthropic trajectory in Lavater's physiognomic practice, despite its purported claim to promote a sense of Christian "brotherly love." The present chapter focuses on the role Lavater and his most prominent nineteenth-century German successor, the naturalist and psychologist Carl Gustav Carus (1789–1869), played as precursors to the physiognomically oriented racial ethnology so prominent in German letters at the beginning of the twentieth century. Lavater and Carus serve here as the principal physiognomic theorists in whose work one can recognize the curious "about face" of German physiognomic thought identified in the title of this book. They present instructive examples of physiognomic positions that begin with decidedly humanistic presuppositions and conceptions, but ultimately succumb, due largely to an underlying materialist tendency, to a prejudicial and racist hierarchy that establishes the inherent worth and unworth of different ethnic and cultural groups.

One of the peculiarities of the German physiognomic tradition is its close association with some of the leading representatives of German intellectual history. We have already noted the participation of people like Johann Gottfried Herder, Jakob Michael Reinhold Lenz, and Johann Wolfgang von Goethe in Lavater's physiognomic project, as well as the extension of the debate over physiognomics into the controversy between two of the greatest philosophical minds of nineteenth-century Germany, Georg Wilhelm Friedrich Hegel and Arthur Schopenhauer. But this list can be extended to include people like Franz Josef

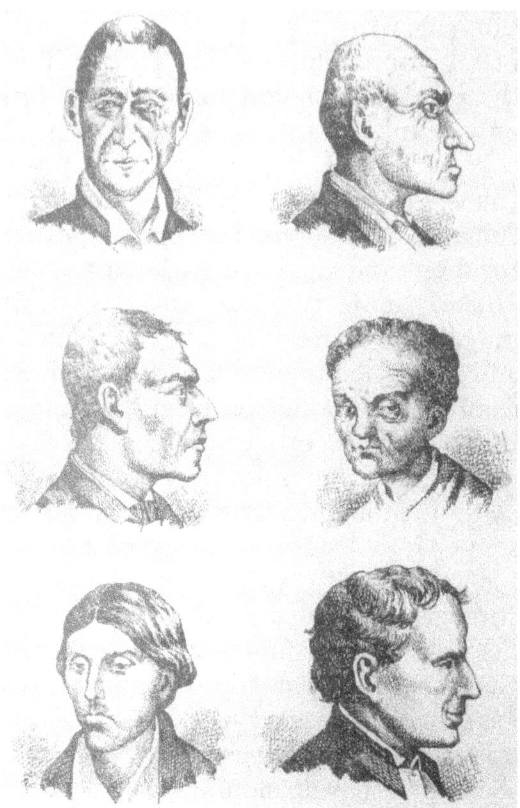

Fig. 9. "Criminal Types," from Cesare Lombroso, *Der Verbrecher,* 1890. (Courtesy of Special Collections, University of Washington Libraries)

Gall and Carus in the nineteenth century, Oswald Spengler and Rudolf Kassner in the twentieth century, and ultimately also Ernst Kretschmer and Ludwig Klages, who applied physiognomic principles to medicine and psychology respectively. Moreover, without exception all these thinkers believed their physiognomic projects were born of the spirit of a fundamentally humanistic tradition. My objective here is to examine the extent to which the dialectical reversion of physiognomics from a theory conceived to promote love and humanistic understanding into a philosophy that denigrates individuality and Otherness already has its seeds in the thought of Lavater and Carus. In this context I will concentrate on three principal issues that Lavater's and Carus's theories have in common: the attempt to establish physiognomics as a rigorously empirical scientific discipline; the priority of all that is natural, primordial, and unalterable over culturally acquired traits and environmental influences; and the fundamentally chauvinistic Eurocentrism that informs the physiognomic judgments of each.

Lavater, as we have noted, introduces a new epoch in the history of physiognomics insofar as he is the first theoretician who seeks to distance this art of characterological interpretation from occultist practices and tries instead to organize it as a strict natural-scientific discipline. In his first work dedicated to physiognomics, the essay "Von der Physiognomik," the substructure of positivistic, rationalistic science with which Lavater attempts to support his physiognomic edifice is most clearly in evidence. In this treatise Lavater's reflections are expressly guided by the leading figureheads of scientific empiricism: first by keen perception, which is charged with the registering of empirical facts, and second by reason, which is given the task of testing and organizing the natural facts established by the empirical attitude. Thus Lavater insists that one need only rely on "reason and empirical knowledge" in order to "confirm the truth of this science [of physiognomics]" (148). As a consequence, Lavater asserts, the physiognomist must be equipped with the very same abilities and talents requisite for the natural scientist: the physiognomist must be a "great and keenly observant analyst" (160), whereby the attribute "keenly observant" alludes to the physiognomist's special empirical abilities, while the designation "analyst" points to the requisite critical faculty.

When Lavater argues that the firm features of the human body, those not subject to will and intentionality, constitute the "primordial form" of the human being and hence are the somatic expression of the individual's "pure predestination" (*Physiognomische Fragmente* 2: 146), he reveals himself to be a pioneering champion of an understanding of the human being that stresses "natural," inherited, a priori qualities over those that are acquired or assumed through individual choices, environmental influences, or by means of cultural appropriations. Thus in the first volume of the *Physiognomische Fragmente* he explicitly states: "I can think of few errors that are more crass and more palpable . . . than this one: 'Everything about the human being is attributable to education, cultivation, models—and nothing is attributable to the organization and primordial structure of the human being, since these are the same for everyone'" (1: 71). Lavater denies not only the principle of the primordial equality of all human beings—decades before this position will be transformed into a racial ideology by Count Arthur Gobineau (1816–1882)—but also the possibility of any subsequent equalization or egalitarianism on the basis of education, training, self-fashioning, and so on. "The human being is free like the bird in a cage" (*Physiognomische Fragmente* 4: 115); this is Lavater's paradoxical conclusion, which subscribes to the materialist predetermination of the human being in all essential matters and establishes somatic nature as the ultimate indicator of every individual's fate.

There is an obvious connection between this materialistically grounded model of predetermination and the fanaticism with which the defenders of heredity and race in the early decades of the twentieth century struggled against the Lamarckian thesis that acquired traits can become part of an individual's genetic makeup.[4] The proponents of racial hygiene maintained that genes are the sole determinants of character, independent of any and all cultural or environmental influences, and hence they argued that all human beings were racially preconditioned from the moment of birth. "All is race; there is no other truth," the English statesman Benjamin Disraeli (1804–1881) baldly asserted (quoted in Poliakov 262), and this statement became the watchword of the modern racial movement. But already in the theories of Lavater this deterministic materialism is married to a Eurocentric, chauvinistic attitude that valorizes the "enlightened" intelligence of certain European peoples as the pinnacle of human evolution and juxtaposes it with select other races or nationalities that are taken to be "naturally" inferior. The traits of modern Europeans, in short, become the standard by which other peoples and alien cultures are measured and ultimately found to be woefully inadequate. This Eurocentric chauvinism already informs Lavater's essay "Von der Physiognomik," in which the Protestant preacher unequivocally asserts: "Human reason does indeed revolt against anyone who might claim that *Leibniz* or *Newton* could have become the metaphysician or mathematician they were in the body of an idiot, the body of a person from a lunatic asylum; or that the former could have conceived of the theodicy in the skull of a Laplander, or that the latter could have measured the planets and refracted light . . . in the head of a Moor" (149; cf. *Physiognomische Fragmente* 1: 46–47). *Dein Kopf—dein Charakter!* (Your head—your character!) is the title of a popularizing book on physiognomics, published by a certain Gerhard Venzmer (b. 1893) in 1934, one year after the Nazis seized power. (Fig. 10) A propaganda piece assembled by the Rassenpolitisches Amt der NSDAP (Nazi Office for Racial Policy) employs, significantly, both the same circular logic and rhetoric that is striking similar to Lavater's. Asking the rhetorical question "How can the same soul, the same mind, possibly exist in these different bodies?," this document juxtaposes portraits of two typical representatives of the so-called "Nordic" or "Aryan" race with images of two African tribespeople.[5] (Fig. 11)

One of the constant leitmotifs of physiognomics since Lavater is the belief that nature is fate, and that nature, moreover, has especially privileged those human beings who live on a certain part of the European continent. We should not forget, of course, that Lavater firmly believed in the Christian notion that human beings are created in the likeness of God, and that the human face, as Lavater maintains, represents a "mirror image of the divinity" (*Physiognomische Fragmente* 1: 46). It seems, however, that God was not wholly egalitarian when it came to distributing these divine traits among his human creations; for some human beings clearly enjoy physiognomies that manifest a greater likeness of the divine than do others. For Lavater this belief that humans are created in the image of God guarantees the causal correlation between internal and external, soul (or psychic constitution) and somatic blueprint. In the human being, as in all of God's creation, a pre-established harmony vouchsafes the causal relationship that defines the firm parts of the human body as indicators of specific predispositions, abilities, and character traits. Already for Lavater, then, the purported intellectual and moral superiority of Western Europeans is reflected in somatic features such as skin color, the shape of the nose, or the form of the skull.

Lavater's physiognomics goes well beyond mere allusions to a possible taxonomy of racial and national features. The fourth volume of the *Fragmente* brings, in fact, an entire section,

Dein Kopf – dein Charakter!

Was Schädelform und Antlitzbildung
über die Wesensart des Menschen verraten

Von Dr. med. et phil.
Gerhard Venzmer

Mit 14 ganzseitigen Bildtafeln
und 30 Abbildungen im Text

Sechste Auflage

Franckh'sche Verlagshandlung / Stuttgart

Fig. 10. Title Page, Gerhard Venzmer, *Dein Kopf—Dein Charakter!* 1934.

covering seventy-five pages, containing an explicit physiognomics of "nationalities and families" (*Physiognomische Fragmente* 4: 265–340).[6] One of the fragments in this section bears the title "Some Tables Containing Miscellaneous National Physiognomies," and depicts, side-by-side for the purpose of comparison, a group of portraits representing distinct nationalities (310–11). (Figs. 12 and 13) Although Lavater avoids establishing an explicit hierarchy, relative valuations are implicit in the adjectives he uses to describe these various faces. Not surprisingly, the Moor stands at the very bottom of his scale, with the "native American from Virginia," who represents a kind of noble savage in the Rousseauean sense, slightly higher up the ladder. The next position on the scale is shared by Russians, Poles, and Turks, and the top of the pyramid is occupied by the

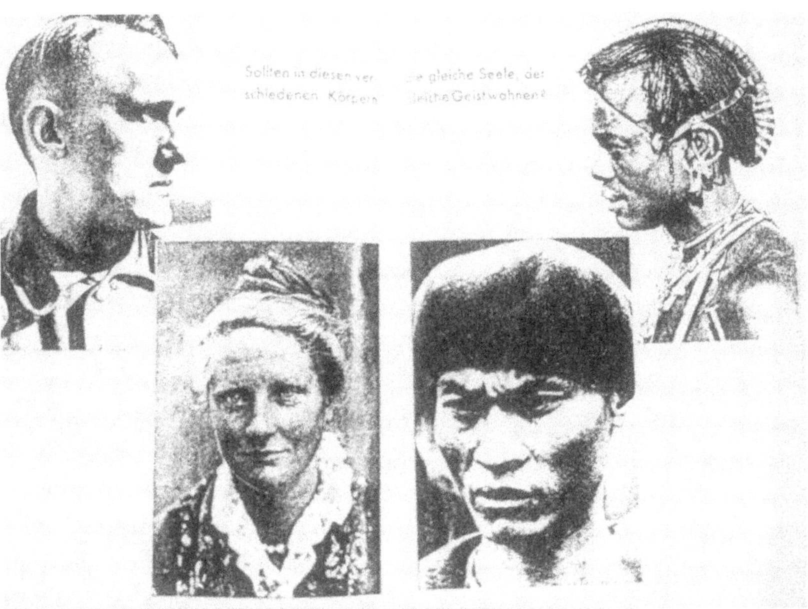

Fig. 11. "How Can These Bodies Be Inhabited by the Same Soul?" Propaganda piece produced by the Nazi Office for Racial Politics. (Courtesy of the Bundesarchiv, Coblenz)

German, who is characterized as "a strong, upright, daring, industrious man" (310). This fragment is representative of the arguments found in this section of Lavater's work, the purpose of which is to codify historically and culturally determined prejudices as natural, unassailable, and inalterable—that is, God-given facts.[7] Lavater's physiognomic interpretation of the head of a Moor, as presented in an etching by the famous artist Daniel Chodowiecki (1726–1801), is wholly in keeping with this design. Here we learn: "The stub nose and the protruding lips of the *Moor* testify, in conjunction with the fieriness of his eyes, to a peculiar mixture of dull animality in the intellectual sphere with powerful passions in the physical domain" (320). The attributes "animality" and "powerful passions" are, of course, ciphers for a pronounced sexual appetite, and in this sense Lavater's judgments often anticipate the prejudices associated with blacks still today.[8] Similarly, for Lavater people from Tierra del Fuego are

Fig. 12. "Miscellaneous National Physiognomies," from volume 4 of Johann Caspar Lavater, *Physiognomische Fragmente,* 1778.

characterized by their "*indifference*"—a code word for "laziness"—their "*stupidity,*" and their "*incapacity* to produce a culture" (318). Nor do the Jews escape the barbs of Lavater's damning commentaries: to his friend and collaborator Jakob Michael Reinhold Lenz he ascribes the statement, "that the *Jews* carry the sign of their fatherland, the Orient, around with them into all four corners of the globe. I am referring to their short, black, curly hair and their brownish skin color. The speed with which they talk, the quick but halting manner of their movements all seems to me to come from here as well. Indeed, I believe that Jews have greater amounts of gall than do other human beings." And Lavater immediately adds to this characterization: "I also number among the national characteristics of the Jewish face a pointed chin and thick lips with a well defined medial line" (272–74). All of these supposedly "typical" Jewish

Fig. 13. "Miscellaneous National Physiognomies," from Volume Four of Johann Caspar Lavater, *Physiognomische Fragmente,* 1778.

traits confirm long-held prejudices about the Jewish physiognomy, supplemented by an allusion to what the Germans call *Mauscheln,* the peculiar manner of speech associated with German-speaking Jews.[9]

There is an immediate connection between Lavater's physiognomic theories and the attempts by the Dutch anatomist Petrus Camper (1722–1789) to establish national and racial distinctions among human beings on the basis of measurements taken from human skulls.[10] To be sure, Camper limited his observations to anatomical facts and made no attempts to establish a racial hierarchy on the basis of empirical anatomy.[11] Camper's famous lecture about the facial angle established a gradation of humans and animal species based on the angle of facial prognathism, with the 100° angle of the idealized Greek face established as the high end and the 70° angle of the skull of the Negro as the dividing line between humans and apes. (Fig. 14) This lecture was first presented to the Amsterdam Drawing

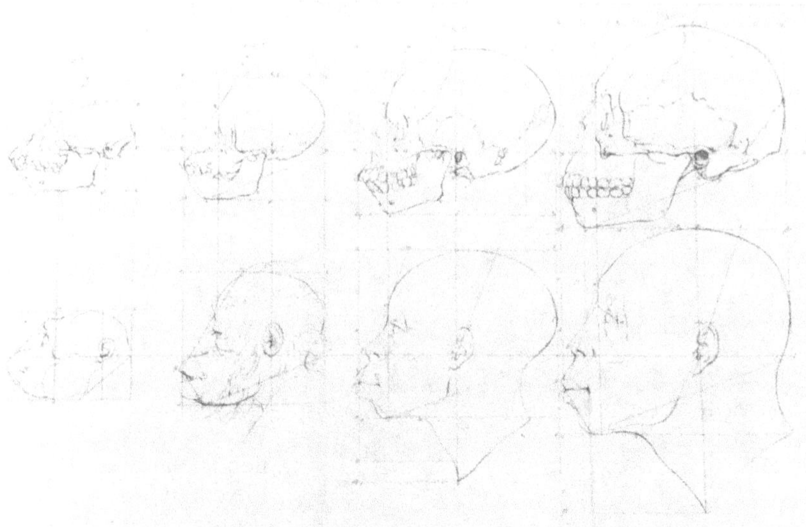

Fig. 14. Portrayal of the facial angle, ascending from apes to Negroes to Europeans, from Petrus Camper, *Dissertation physique, sur les différences réelles que présentent les traits du visage chez les hommes de différents pays et de différents âges,* 1791. (Courtesy of Special Collections, University of Washington Libraries)

Academy in 1770, and subsequently delivered in Paris in 1777 and London in 1785 (Meijer 5). It was only published posthumously by his son in 1791, but Lavater includes a letter by Camper in *Physiognomische Fragmente* (4: 281–83) that contains the rudiments of this theory. Thus Lavater's *Fragmente,* being one of the first places this theory appeared in print (Meijer 118), contributed in fundamental ways to its dissemination throughout Europe. Concern with cranial measurements that would help him develop a taxonomy of human and animal species was something that occupied Lavater even beyond the period in which he composed the *Physiognomische Fragmente,* as a passage from a letter to Goethe, dated 18 March 1780, clearly indicates. Here Lavater writes: "I am on the verge of making a new, highly significant physiognomic discovery—establishing in a *simple* manner the stages of animality as they progress to the most basic forms of humanity. At the same time, I have an inkling that this will allow me to demonstrate mathematically, on the basis of this medial line alone, the inherent and eternally untranscendable dividing line between human beings and animals" (*Goethe und Lavater* 106). Lavater had toyed with this idea several years earlier, at the time he was working on the fourth volume of the *Fragmente.* Here this concern expressed itself above all in the construction of a so-called *Stirnmaaß,* an instrument that would permit precise measurements of the human skull. Alluding to Camper's derivation of the *linea facialis,* Lavater writes that the employment of this instrument will make it possible to plot a series of vertical and horizontal lines on the human head from which, as Lavater believed, one would be able to determine any individual's mental capacities (see *Physiognomische Fragmente* 4: 23–24). Thus Lavater transfers the "objective" data arrived at by such quantifying principles to the schematic form of the silhouette to produce a graphic representation of an individual physiognomy and the qualities it signifies. (Fig. 15) Lavater expects that the implementation of such empirical practices will permit him to derive "objective" data about the psychic and mental attributes of human subjects, thereby helping him realize his dream of establishing physiognomics as "a science definable in mathematical terms" (481). The application of the *Stirnmaaß* introduces a rudimentary form of cranioscopy that makes possible the comparative examination of human skulls—a kind of comparative anthropology on the basis of cranial structures. Thus Lavater predicts that "the use of this [machine] will allow us to generate, over time, a universally comprehensible and practical proportional table for all the capacities of the human soul" (24). The realization of such a project was not as far away as Lavater perhaps presumed: it would be perfected just fifty years later in Carl Gustav Carus's treatises on cranioscopy, above all in his *Proportionslehre der menschlichen Gestalt* (Proportional theory of the human form), which appeared in 1854.[12] (Fig. 16)

If Lavater's physiognomic theories display a hybrid character that attempts, in an uncanny manner, to fuse a scientific methodology with metaphysical speculation, this, as I have tried to demonstrate, is no coincidence. Indeed, this hybrid quality is

Fig. 15. Silhouette used for facial measurements, from volume 2 of Johann Caspar Lavater, *Physiognomische Fragmente,* 1776.

one of the distinguishing traits of post-Enlightenment, post-Lavaterian physiognomics. On the example of Lavater one can discern with particular clarity my hypothesis that modern physiognomics attempts to pursue metaphysics by employing the strategies of empirical science. Subjective judgments are lent support through their association with objective facts; the free play of the imagination on the part of the physiognomic interpreter is justified by philosophical or pseudo-philosophical arguments; cultural prejudices are passed off as untranscendable states of affairs ordained in nature. These two dimensions—physiognomics as fantasy, art, and inherent "skill," on the one hand, and physiognomics as an empirically oriented discipline in the tradition of the positivistic sciences, on the other—form the obverse sides of a unitary if paradoxical phenomenon. Already the fundamental task that every physiognomics sets for itself, its aim of determining the metaphysical, internal features of an individual on the basis of his or her physical exterior, conjures up this paradox. The more physiognomics becomes a disciplinary and disciplining practice—and this is the central drive that fuels its historical evolution over the course of the nineteenth century and the first four decades of the twentieth—the more intense this contradiction becomes. It is complemented

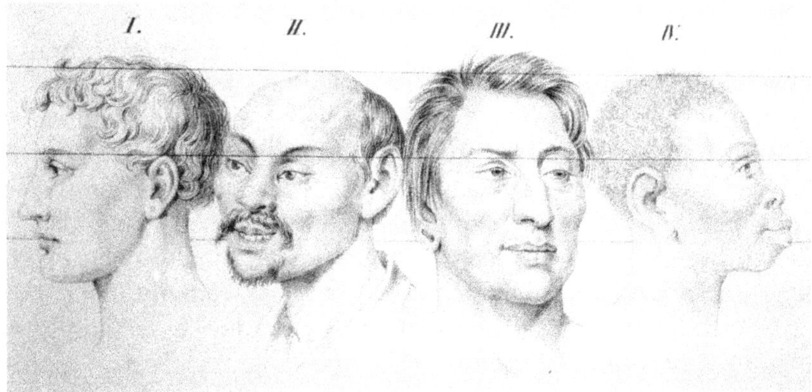

Fig. 16. Schematic heads representing the four primary races, from Carl Gustav Carus, *Die Proportionslehre der menschlichen Gestalt.* (Courtesy of the Hessische Landesbibliothek, Darmstadt)

and partially obscured by a further disparity: the clash between its explicitly stated pan-humanistic, even humanitarian motivations, which are often identified, as in Lavater's case, as its altruistic core, and the inhumane, demeaning, and destructive practices manifest in the concrete judgments it passes. This conflict between purported humanitarian design and the brutal extinguishing of "degenerate" human specimens was, we cannot forget, part and parcel of the racial hygienic theories defended and put into practice by the Nazis. The elimination of "inferior" people not only relieved—so the Nazis argued—these degenerate human specimens of their suffering and hence served a humanitarian purpose, but by purifying the gene pool they guaranteed the future health and happiness of the "race" as a whole.

Carl Gustav Carus: The Physiognomic Grounding of Racial Inequality

Carl Gustav Carus (1789–1869) is generally recognized as one of the greatest nineteenth-century humanist thinkers in German-speaking Europe. A man with broad talents, interests, and abilities, he made a name for himself as a natural scientist and physician, but he also gained renown as a physiologist and psychologist. Indeed, in the realm of psychology Carus is commonly viewed as a significant precursor of Freud, having developed a rudimentary theory of the unconscious. He was, moreover, a close friend of the prototypical Romantic painter Caspar David Friedrich (1774–1840), and was himself a landscape painter of considerable skill. As a great admirer of Goethe and a self-designated disseminator of Goethe's thought, Carus contributed to the vitality of the humanistic worldview of German Classicism during the latter part of the nineteenth century. His major physiognomic work, the *Symbolik der menschlichen Gestalt* (Symbolism of the human form), which bears the subtitle "Ein Handbuch zur Menschenkenntnis" (A handbook for understanding human beings), first appeared in 1853 and went into a second edition five years later, in 1858. There can be little doubt that this work was the most significant, and most influential, scientific physiognomics of the nineteenth century in German-speaking Europe.

Today the word "symbolism" in the title of an ostensibly scientific work may strike us as odd. For Carus and his contemporaries, however, this was by no means the case. On the contrary, this term signals Carus's indebtedness to the predominant tradition of German *Naturphilosophie,* the philosophy of nature, in particular the influence of Carus's great teacher, the philosopher Friedrich Wilhelm Joseph von Schelling (1775–1854). In *Idee zu einer Philosophie der Natur* (Idea for a philosophy of nature; 1797) and *Von der Weltseele* (On the world soul; 1798), Schelling developed a pantheistic conception of the natural world that envisioned it as the perfect and beautiful realization of an intangible "world reason," or the concretization of a universal "world idea." Schelling's philosophy of nature was decidedly holistic, conceiving the natural world as a harmonious totality in which each element stood in a definite, necessary, and harmonious relationship with the whole. Thus Carus's physiognomic "symbolism," while still viewing the human body—similar in this regard to Lavater's theory—as a reflection of the image of God (see *Symbolik* 2), also emphasizes its aesthetic character, the harmonious relation of each part to every other part and to the somatic structure as a whole. Summarizing this theory of the body as an organic totality, Carus comments in his subsequently published "Symbolische Rhapsodien: Fragmente zur Symbolik menschlicher Gestalt" (Symbolic rhapsodies: Fragments on the symbolism of the human form): "However, if one seeks to truly understand the form and structure of the human being, then it is not simply a matter of taking accurate measurements; rather it is simultaneously and primarily a question of correct interpretation and judgment of the relation of all the individual parts to the totality and vice versa—in other words, it is a matter of understanding the symbolism of the body" (103). The symbolism of the human body becomes indistinguishable, in other words, from its structure as a harmonious, holistic totality. Carus thus sees this symbolic mode of understanding as the condition for any proper understanding of the human somatic form: the natural-scientific procedure of measuring and deriving empirical, mathematical facts is joined by an act of human-scientific interpretation, by hermeneutics in the broader sense. The joining of these two perspectives distinguishes Carus's physiognomic methodology, but it is worth noting that this same marriage of empirical fact-finding with the free and liberal interpretation of these facts will later become the emblem of the racially oriented physiognomics that flourished in the early decades of the twentieth century.

Carus takes pains to distinguish his physiognomic endeavors from those of Lavater, whom he openly criticizes for his lack of scientific rigor and his tendency to regress into irrational prophecy. By contrast, he maintains that his own physiognomic practice can lay claim to scientific validity precisely because it makes use of the empirical method of measuring and comparing. At the same time, Carus admits that physiognomics, in this regard no different, in his mind, from sciences such as medicine, cannot forego a certain divinatory quality—indeed, an element of artistry—when it moves from pure theory to its practical application. "The organic structure of the human being," he remarks in *Symbolik der menschlichen Gestalt,* "is something so incommensurable, something so incomprehensible in all its profundity; it contains alongside the great power of rationality so much wholly indispensable irrationality, that acts of weighing, measuring, and counting are never by themselves sufficient for arriving at an understanding of it" (5). Carus's scientific exemplar,

Goethe, was more adamant about the inappropriateness of applying such quantifying techniques to living things: "The measurement of a thing is always a crude act," Goethe noted in the essay "Studie nach Spinoza" (Study on the model of Spinoza), "that can only be applied to living entities in the most imperfect way" (*Gedenkausgabe* 16: 841). Carus was clearly aware of this problem, but it never led him to forswear these empirical, quantifying techniques. Apparently Carus never perceived the fundamental reification of the human being, which necessarily accompanies its reduction to an object for the scientist's empirical gaze, as something that stood in contradiction to his valorization of the human body as a divine creation.[13] The reason for this is easily discerned: if his holistic philosophy guarantees that every living creature, but above all the highest living thing, the human being, must be an absolutely harmonious, aesthetically proportional construct, then the measurement of the human being ultimately serves the ends of establishing this proportionality in exact, mathematical terms. It is telling, then, that Carus's *Proportionslehre der menschlichen Gestalt* appeared just one year after the first edition of his *Symbolik*, demonstrating its role as a logical extension and culmination of this earlier work. By the same token, it is coherent with Carus's holistic theory, as well as with his belief in the autonomy of every organic creature, that he refuses to introduce a norm imported from outside as a standard for measuring the individual human being. Hence he seeks to establish a unit of measure that can be derived from the human body itself and universally applied as a standard, and he discovers this unit in what he calls the "module," defined as one-third of the length of the human backbone. He calls this module "a genuine and organic primordial measure *[Urmaß]*" (*Symbolik* 52), and he goes on to measure and compare the diverse parts of the human body in modules or in fractions of modules. (Fig. 17) The module becomes, in short, the unitary "idea," the overriding principle, from which the body in its harmonious totality can be derived.

Now, to be sure, Carus cannot be credited with introducing this holistic conception into the tradition of modern physiognomics; it is already present in rudimentary form, of course, in Lavater's physiognomic theories. But there are many further

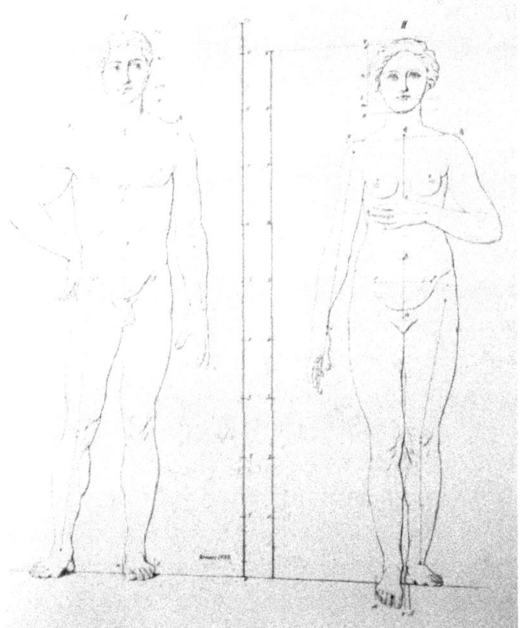

Fig. 17. Human anatomies with module units, from Carl Gustav Carus, *Die Proportionslehre der menschlichen Gestalt,* 1854. (Courtesy of the Hessische Landesbibliothek, Darmstadt)

themes—more, perhaps, than Carus would have cared to admit—that link Carus's physiognomic views with those of his Swiss forerunner. We have already seen how obsessed Lavater was with proving, in his own way, the scientific nature of his physiognomic enterprise. But whereas Lavater relies, for this purpose, on the semiotic theory of Enlightenment philosophy, Carus derives his principles for establishing physiognomics as a natural science from Schelling's philosophy of nature. Both Lavater and Carus, moreover, stress the necessity of a certain "artistic" sensibility or special physiognomic talent that is required before theory can be transformed into adequate interpretive practice. Lavater appeals to "the power of observation" and "imagination" ("Von der Physiognomik" 190), or describes his physiognomic ability as nothing but "a poetic feeling" (*Physiognomische Fragmente* 1: 269). Carus, for his part, maintains that "a particular natural feeling and a particular innate gaze" are prerequisites for the successful application of physiognomic precepts and for the development of the true skill in recognizing human character (*Symbolik* 350). What is certain, at any rate, is that the same mixture of subjective and objective assertions, of a theological point of departure with scientific legitimization, of metaphysical presuppositions with empirical methods, informs both Lavater's physiognomic theories and Carus's symbolism of the human form. To the extent that Carus develops and even exaggerates this quantifying tendency, whose germ was already evident in Lavater's thought, we are perhaps justified of speaking in his case not merely of a metaphysics pursued by empirical means, but even of a radically positivistic metaphysics. In this sense Carus builds a significant bridge between Lavater, as the founder of the modern physiognomic tradition, and the racial anthropology of the Weimar Republic and the Nazi era, which also conceived itself largely—but, as we will see, not solely—as a quantifying, positivistic science.[14] For despite Carus's attempts to place critical distance between Lavater's theories and his own, his physiognomic program in fact develops and, with a certain logical consistency, expands on thoughts and practices that are merely suggested or vaguely outlined in Lavater's works. This is true not only where methodological issues are concerned—in Carus's realization of Lavater's wish that physiognomics should become a quantifiable science—but also with regard to certain central ideas and precepts. Here I will focus only on Carus's genesis of a sophisticated racial typology based on physiognomic-symbolic hypotheses, a typology whose crass Eurocentrism and chauvinism anticipates in astonishing ways the perverse attitudes of the German racial anthropologists whose hierarchical theories of racial value will not emerge until over a half century later. What makes Carus's racial theory especially peculiar is the fact that it is expressly produced out of the spirit of a humanistic self-understanding purportedly based on the principles of Goethean Classicism.

In celebration of the centennial of Goethe's birth on 28 August 1849, Carus composed a little known "commemorative" essay that bears the title *Über ungleiche Befähigung der verschiedenen Menschheitsstämme für höhere geistige Entwickelung* (On the unequal capacities of the different human races for higher intellectual development). (Fig. 18) In the preface to this essay Carus explains the motivations behind publishing this piece in memory of Goethe:

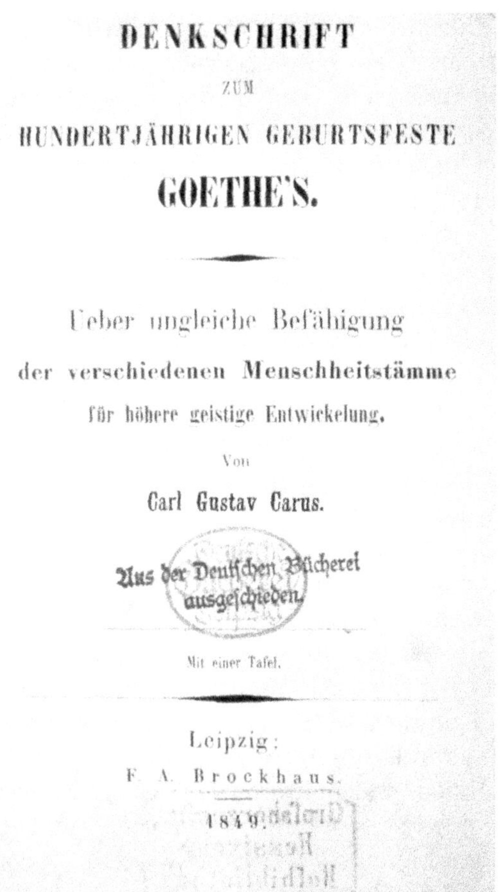

DENKSCHRIFT

ZUM

HUNDERTJÄHRIGEN GEBURTSFESTE

GOETHE'S.

Ueber ungleiche Befähigung

der verschiedenen Menschheitstämme

für höhere geistige Entwickelung.

Von

Carl Gustav Carus.

Mit einer Tafel.

Leipzig:

F. A. Brockhaus.

1849.

Fig. 18. Title page, Carl Gustav Carus, *Essay in Commemoration of Goethe: Über ungleiche Befähigung der verschiedenen Menschheitsstämme für höhere geistige Entwickelung,* 1849. (Courtesy of the Hessische Landesbibliothek, Darmstadt)

For me, someone who still has a potent recollection of Goethe's grand personality and of many of his specific pronouncements; for me, someone who received some of his most powerful impulses and stimuli from Goethe's intellect *[Geist]*; for me, someone who already several years ago dedicated a treatise to the task of making it possible for my contemporaries to arrive at a better understanding of his intellect[15]—for me, the inducements to participate in this general event [in the celebration of Goethe's hundredth birthday] were so great that, despite my many other arduous undertakings, and despite the violent upheavals of the present day, I could not help but demonstrate my engagement for this celebration by composing the present work. (v–vi)

Carus explains here the deeply personal sentiment that motivated him to write this treatise, but he is also careful to establish his own authority as an interpreter and mediator of Goethe's thought. Implicit in his introductory remarks is the assumption that the arguments about the natural, God-given inequality of the different human races, which he is about to unroll, are consistent with the worldview of Goethe himself, the great human being and intellectual whose memory this essay is intended to celebrate. Carus thereby consciously transforms Goethe, the guiding spirit of the humanitarian culture of German Classicism, into the intellectual forerunner of a decidedly chauvinistic attitude that establishes the relative worth and natural abilities of the distinct human races—an attitude to which Goethe himself would most likely never have subscribed. But the role Goethe plays as the impulse behind this treatise goes well beyond his invocation as the intellectual precursor of the ideas Carus will present; indeed, Goethe himself serves as a paradigmatic example that testifies in support of Carus's thesis that the Europeans, but above all the Germanic peoples, exhibit a natural intellectual superiority over the other peoples and races of the earth. In other words, Goethe's undeniable greatness and genius are no longer viewed as characteristics peculiar to him as individual; they are abstracted from his personality, universalized, and held up as traits that distinguish the Germanic peoples as a whole. For Carus, Goethe's "individuality," as he unambiguously writes, represents "a consummate prototype of the daylight peoples [this is Carus's designation for the "Caucasian" race], a prototype, moreover, drawn from one of its most noble branches, from the branch of the Germanic peoples" (*Über ungleiche Befähigung* 101). Goethe, in short, becomes "living" proof of the racial and genetic superiority of the Germanic peoples.

One of the primary points of departure for Carus's arguments is a fundamental questioning of one central proposition of humanist thought, a position stridently defended in the tradition of Goethean Classicism: the belief in the basic equality of all human beings. Thus already very early in his essay Carus asserts "that anyone who presumes that humanity is an . . . aggregate of individual intellects with equal capacities and equal competencies has fallen prey to a gross fallacy" (*Ungleiche Befähigung* 2).

It is important to recognize that with this proclamation Carus not only argues for the inequality of individuals, but also for the natural superiority of particular races over other races, and that he does so fully four years before the publication of Count Arthur Gobineau's infamous *Essai sur l'inégalité des races humaines.*[16] Especially interesting in the present context is that Carus justifies his presupposition of a basic human inequality by appealing to the same theory of the organic totality that forms the basis of his physiognomics. In *Ungleiche Befähigung,* however, this conception of the necessary harmony of parts to the whole in all organic structures is extrapolated from the category of the individual and applied at the level of the species in general: "humanity" itself, as an organic aggregate, obeys the "natural" laws of the organic totality. What is more, in this larger context Carus stresses not so much the symmetry of this totality as he does the necessary differences and "inequalities" that exist among its various parts. He expresses this relationship among unequally weighted components, which he takes to be inherent in the structure of an organic whole, in the form of a universal law: "we can now express as a universal and significant law, *that the greatest possible manifoldness*—that is to say, INEQUALITY—*of the parts, accompanied by the most consummate unity at the level of the totality, can always be taken as an indication and as a standard for the greater consummateness of any particular organism*" (4). With nothing but a rhetorical sleight of hand, Carus transforms the basic principal of organicism, which asserts that all organic totalities are constituted out of harmonious manifoldness, into the proposition that organic unities are in fact grounded in hierarchically ordered inequalities. This semantic displacement, as small as it may at first seem, takes on critical importance. For it is only by replacing the word "manifoldness" with "inequality" that this conception assumes a hierarchical dimension, containing the implication that some of the individual components in an organic totality are simply more important than others, and hence that those less significant parts can legitimately be subordinated to those that play a more fundamental role. Carus ignores the fact that this implicit hierarchization threatens to call into question the entire notion of organic unity: he no longer emphasizes the indispensability of each and every integral part for the perfect operation of the organic structure, but rather the idea that some constituents are, as it were, less dispensable than others.

This subtle semantic displacement only makes sense in view of Carus's desire to portray humanity as a unity that is constituted by the necessary interaction of principally unequal parts: it paves the way, in other words, for Carus's ultimate conclusion that the natural inequality of the different human races has a higher, indeed, a divine meaning, and that this inequality is justified by the inscrutability of this divine purpose. Carus summarizes his hypothesis in the following way:

> The mysterious bond that unifies humanity into a great totality is not predicated on equality, but rather on inequality; and this inequality is not evidence that hatred and injustice are ordained in God's creation, but instead it is the sign of a profound love and supreme justice, because this was the only way in which consummateness could be achieved at the more general level. It should be obvious, moreover, that such an inequality must necessarily reveal itself in everything, not merely in the external form and the internal structure of the organism, but also in the internal sensibility and the lesser or greater capacities of individuals for the realization of supreme intellectual development. (*Ungleiche Befähigung* 5–6)

What Carus presents here is a kind of racial theodicy, one that does not set about trying to explain the existence of evil in divine creation, but that instead seeks to legitimate the thesis of human inequality by establishing it as a divinely ordained, and hence necessary "fact" of nature. The only justification Carus provides for this "fact" is derived from his conception, schooled on the thought of his teacher Schelling, that the world, as divine creation, is structured as an organic totality. Even humanity, Carus would have us believe, must be conceived as a conglomerate of human races, and as such it cannot simply be composed of "manifold" human types, but rather precisely of "unequal" ones. For Carus, this theological perspective defines the "justness" of this relationship of inequality: it is legitimated by the higher purpose of the consummate development of the human race as a whole. These are arguments, of course, that have exact parallels in the philosophy of racial superiority widely propagated in Germany several decades later. In their scientific manifestation, these ideas culminated at the turn of the century in the natural philosophy and "monism" of Ernst Haeckel (1834–1919), whose works were widely read and exerted a profound influence on the proponents of racial anthropology (see Poliakov 319–25).

No doubt, those human beings who are privileged and who profit from a particular system, social condition, or an existing inequality have always declared this condition to be "just" or "divinely ordained," just as those who are underprivileged and who suffer under this system are adamant about its injustice. In this regard, Carus is no exception. And it probably is not a coincidence that he wrote this treatise immediately subsequent to the political rebellions that rocked Europe in March of 1848—these are, most certainly, the "violent upheavals of the present day" to which he ominously refers in the preface to *Ungleiche Befähigung* (vi). We are tempted to surmise that in his justification of the unequal constitution of the divergent human races as something ordained in nature, he was probably also alluding to the common belief that the social, economic, and political inequalities that incited the revolution were natural and unalterable conditions. Viewed in this way, it would be possible to read Carus's essay in commemoration of Goethe as a defense of the socioeconomic and political status quo in prerevolutionary Germany, enciphered into the discourse of natural history. For ultimately Carus's theory of the harmonious cooperation of *unequal* constituents is formulated in such general terms that it can be applied to *any* structure capable of being comprehended in terms of an organic totality—hence to the political state, in its Romantic conception, as well. It is certain, at any rate, that in this treatise Carus exhibits the tendency to treat socially determined conditions as natural and immutable states of affairs—a proclivity that makes itself widely manifest in the history of racism.[17]

In the above-cited quotation in which Carus makes a plea for the role of inequality among the constituent parts of an organic entity, the deep-seated connection between his physiognomic theories and his racial thought also comes to the fore. Here he declares with blithe confidence that the naturally determined inequality of the diverse human races must inevitably manifest itself in the "external form" as well as in the "internal structure" of the individual human specimens who represent the primary human races. Thus cranioscopic measurements of a small set of skulls will ultimately provide him with the "objective" scientific data for determining the relative intellectual capacities of the different races. What is more, he anticipates the general methodology he will practice four years later in *Symbolik der menschlichen Gestalt.* Already, in this commemorative essay, he treats the outward physical appearance of the human races as symbolic symptoms for their internal—more specifically, for their intellectual—constitution. This is reflected in the designations he gives to the four major races he identifies: instead of using the terms "Caucasians," "Negroes," "Orientals," and so on, the common terminology of Carus's day, he invents the designations "daylight peoples" *(Tagvölker)* for the Europeans, "nocturnal peoples" *(Nachtvölker)* for Africans, "Eastern twilight peoples" *(östliche Dämmerungsvölker)* for Asians, and "Western twilight peoples" *(westliche Dämmerungsvölker)* for the indigenous populations of North and South America. Carus stresses that this "great *division of humanity into four parts*" is conditioned by the "four-fold modalities of the planet" on which they live: day, night, morning twilight, evening twilight (*Ungleiche Befähigung* 13). As evidence for this geographically oriented racism, he appends to his treatise a map that illustrates the distribution of these four races across the globe. (Fig. 19)

These designations do not refer to the geographical locations in which these peoples have their indigenous homes, in analogy to the German terms for Occident and Orient, *Abendland* (literally: evening land) and *Morgenland* (morning land). For although the relative position of the earth in relation to the sun seems to supply Carus with his terminology, it does not, in fact, define the relevance of these names for the human races to which they are applied. On the contrary, here a different form of symbolism is called upon. This is how Carus explains the way he arrived at this terminology: as the basis of his categorization he sought "ethnic peoples, who correspond to a dearth of light—the *night of the planet;* . . . peoples who correspond to the illumination—the *daylight of the planet;* peoples who portray the *twilight of ascent* in humanity"; and finally, an ethnic population

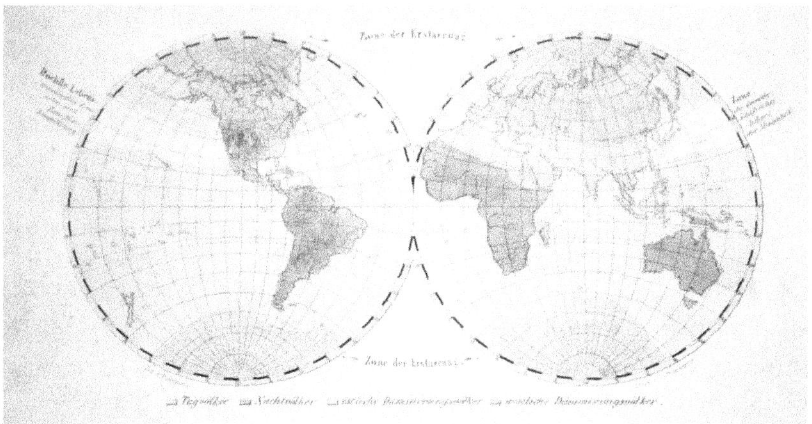

Fig. 19. Map of the world with the distribution of the four human races, from Carl Gustav Carus, *Über ungleiche Befähigung,* 1849. (Courtesy of the Hessische Landesbibliothek, Darmstadt.)

"that corresponds to the twilight of decline" (*Ungleiche Befähigung* 14–15). Once again, these designations do not allude to environmental factors, for example, to the relative degree of sunlight or to the climatic conditions in the geographical regions in which these races are found. Viewed in this way, it would be the Africans who deserve to be called the daylight people, due to the persistent sunshine to which they are exposed, whereas the Europeans, because of the harsh coldness and cloudiness of their northern climate, would more appropriately be termed the nocturnal peoples. But that is obviously not Carus's perspective. Far from viewing the designations daylight, nocturnal, and twilight as concrete environmental descriptions, he employs them—in the tradition of Hegel's philosophy of history—in a metaphorical, "symbolic" sense as designations for the relative historical-evolutionary development of each race. In accordance with this assumption, he argues that no other race can be associated with the nighttime of the planet "than the physically and intellectually inferior Negroes . . . —they are the NOCTURNAL PEOPLES—identified as such by their dark, often thoroughly *black* complexion" (14). It should be obvious that Carus's logic operates here according to the principle of the vicious circle, for the conclusion his study is supposed to prove—namely, the relative intellectual inferiority of the Africans and other non-European peoples—is already presupposed in the peculiar "symbolism" that forms the basis of his methodology. Ultimately, it is nothing other than Africans' dark skin color that serves as an unequivocal sign—a fundamentally *physiognomic* sign—for the innately "black" sensibility and intellectual "darkness" of the peoples who live on the African continent. The logic of Carus's racial typology is as simple as it is simple-minded: light skin equals intellectual enlightenment equals daylight peoples; dark skin equals benighted intellect equals nocturnal peoples, and so on.

According to Albert Memmi, the historian of race, "racism begins at the moment in which we start to interpret differences" (quoted in Claussen 20). Following this definition, Carus's attempt to draw distinctions among the various "races" of the world transmogrifies into a form of racism as soon as he seeks to interpret *physical* distinctions in terms of his physiognomically grounded symbolism. For in the process of this symbolic hermeneutics evaluative judgments and prejudices—unwittingly or wittingly?—creep into his categories. This becomes most apparent when one examines the manner in which Carus establishes his racial hierarchy and the philosophic-historical, evolutionary worldview out of which it emerges. Carus is forced by the logic of his own symbolism to admit that the "Eastern twilight peoples," those who first saw, as it were, the light of day, are also those people in whom "the higher light of intellect was first ignited" (*Ungleiche Befähigung* 54). But despite this recognition, Carus refuses to acknowledge the possibility that these peoples might in fact have intellectual potentials superior to those of the Europeans. To be sure, he concedes that they exhibit superlative achievements in the primary domains of cultural productivity, which he takes as the measure for the possibility of superior intellectual development: they have produced a well ordered political state, they cultivate the literary arts, have created highly developed technological products and a sophisticated written language. Yet he criticizes in them the absence of "the incessant striving . . . that contributes so much toward maintaining the freshness and vitality of the intellect" (64). This is how Carus explains why, as he believes, the Asian peoples, contrary to the Europeans, ceased to make further intellectual and developmental progress after a certain historical point was reached.

Here, at last, we can discern the strict Eurocentrism, even Germanocentrism, of Carus's position. What this Goethe-admirer demands above all from all human cultures, if they want to be numbered among the productive subgroup of the human population, is the Faustian quality of eternal striving. The central principle of this philosophy is articulated by the Angels near the conclusion of *Faust, Part Two:* "Whoever engages in eternal striving merits our redemption" ("Wer immer strebend sich bemüht, / Den können wir erlösen"; verses 11937–11938, *Gedenkausgabe* 5: 520). In Carus's world-historical translation: Only those races who struggle and strive incessantly are redeemed by superior intellectual development and hence by cultural history. Here, as well, Goethe, Carus's prototype of the "daylight peoples," informs in a profound manner the thought of this commemorative essay. All the other peoples of the world are measured by this Goethean standard and found to fall far short of this ideal. But at least the merits of the "Eastern twilight peoples" are sufficient to assure them of second place in Carus's racial hierarchy. In the case of the "Western twilight peoples," love of freedom and the resistance to slavery also constitute signs of certain intellectual capacities, and this, in Carus's understanding, sets them far above the level of the "nocturnal peoples." On the other hand, these indigenous peoples of the Americas do not, according to Carus, develop well organized political structures, nor do they invent a written language. Moreover, he maintains, they are incapable of comprehending the concept of number. All of this testifies for him to their reduced capacity for intellectual development. Above all, they cannot grasp the notion of infinity, which gives rise to the comment: "And how impoverished the human intellect must remain without this notion!" (*Ungleiche Befähigung* 51). But how much more impoverished, according to Carus's way of thinking, are the nocturnal peoples of Africa, who constitute the lowest form of humanity: they have no organized state, no literature, no written language, and no high art. What is worse, they have succumbed to slavery. And yet Carus admits, in a moment of higher illumination—of which he, as a representative of the Goethean daylight peoples, is perfectly capable—that "the fact of slavery" has determined and conditioned the fate of the African peoples in significant ways (22–23). With this statement Carus approaches the recognition that the external conditions of economic and political power, created by European colonialism, are at least partially responsible for the subordinate, deprivileged status of the African peoples. But he immediately closes his mind's eye to this inchoate insight by asserting that slavery would never have had such a profound impact on the African "race" "if its intellectual capacity had not from the outset been of a lower degree than that of all other races" (23). Carus concludes this line of argumentation by citing Friedrich von Schiller's statement that "world history is the tribunal of the world" ("Die Weltgeschichte ist das Weltgericht"),[18] applying it to the fate of the four primary human races (23). Perhaps it would be more correct to maintain that abstract intelligence is the tribunal of the world, or at least that it determines the fate of every human culture? For the conclusion at which Carus ultimately arrives is that the degree to which any race or nation develops the inherent intellectual potential of the divine human being has a definitive influence on its history and its destiny. This legitimates the economic, cultural, and political superiority of the European nations as a fact indelibly inscribed into *natural* history, and hence into the evolutionary development of the species homo sapiens. In other words, the conditions of European colonialism are interpreted as the unavoidable historical consequence of the higher intellectual capabilities of the "daylight peoples." This explains why Carus can accept and explain away the ever-advancing suppression of the indigenous populations in North and South America by the colonial Europeans as an irrevocable and necessary development in the divinely prescribed development of humanity (17). With Carus's theories we begin to comprehend the profound role that physiognomics played in the justification of the institution of slavery and of European colonialism.[19]

By now it should be clear just how circular and fundamentally chauvinistic Carus's value judgments are. One might, of course, try to relativize these prejudices by claiming they were indicative of Carus's European contemporaries, and hence his only fault is his assumption of the values that saturated his own cultural heritage. But this argument carries less weight in Carus's case, since one of the principles he attempts to establish for the physiognomic judgments derived from an application of his symbolic method is that these evaluations can never be established by holding the object of study up to alien standards. In the realm of somatic investigation, this principle leads Carus to introduce the "module" as a measure that can be derived from each individual human specimen. This unit becomes the standard by which one can calculate the relative proportionality of any individual human body, since all the separate parts can be measured in comparative terms based on the "module" unit extrapolated from the length of its particular backbone. The module has the benefit of allowing both comparative analyses from one body to another, but it also functions as an internal norm for the measure of other parts of a single body. In his *cultural* evaluation, however, Carus does not develop such a sophisticated set of norms; and in his judgments of other races it is almost solely cultural standards—political organization, language, art, literature—according to which he measures the relative value of the different races he identifies. But instead of reaching these assessments by applying a set of norms derived from the culture under examination itself, Carus takes his measures exclusively from the achievements of European civilization. Is it any wonder that his evaluations end up affirming the abstract intelligence of the Europeans and deprecating the intellectual capacities of the non-European peoples? This manner of thought, which takes the norms of its own cultural attitudes and applies them to others in order to demonstrate their inferiority, is characteristic of racism in all its manifestations.

Wherever one set of *cultural* values—one's own—are hypostatized as universally valid laws of *nature,* it also becomes necessary to launch a strategic offensive against the idea of cultural relativism. Carus, too, finds himself obliged to bend to this necessity. When he attempts, for example, to prove that sensitivity for beauty can be established as a universal standard by which one can measure the degree of "intellectual energy" inherent in a given people (*Ungleiche Befähigung* 68), he is forced to reject the relativistic idea that beauty can only be assessed in terms of the taste and particular norms of the culture under examination. "Anyone who could really believe that a statue by Phidias, a Madonna by Raphael, or a Mozart symphony is only beautiful because it is pleasing *to us* . . . would also have to assume, in order to be logically consistent, that mathematics is only true because it appears to us as though it is" (72). This comparison, however, is an inappropriate one, for the simple reason that it elides the distinction between cultural values—beauty—and rational laws—mathematics. Similar attacks on cultural relativism are typical of the racial fictions promulgated by the Nazi ideologues, for whom all the zeniths in human cultural achievement can be attributed to the impact and influence of a single "master" race, constituted by the "Nordic" or "Aryan" peoples.[20]

In Carus's case this chauvinism forms the basis for legitimizing the colonial empowerment of the Europeans over other nations and peoples of the earth. After summarizing the merits that, to his mind, set the Europeans apart from other human beings, Carus arrives unabashedly at the following self-aggrandizing conclusion: "All of this gives the race of the daylight peoples the right to view itself as the true pinnacle of humanity, and this in turn lays upon it the duty to be not only a guiding light for those peoples who are in many respects weaker and less favored, but also to stand by them and lend them assistance whenever necessary" (*Ungleiche Befähigung* 84–85). The preeminence of the Europeans, in other words, endows them with a kind of paternal responsibility toward the other races of the world: as exemplary human beings, they must point the way that less privileged peoples should follow, encouraging them to emulate this most perfected model of the human being. Because of their divinely and naturally ordained superiority over the other nations of the world, the Europeans have an absolute duty to lend these inferior peoples aid and assistance. Such arguments have the function of simultaneously disguising and justifying the economic and political mastery the European colonial powers exercise over those peoples they economically exploit. This self-righteously patronizing attitude toward other human beings was—and is still today—the distinctive mark of colonialism in all its forms: it transforms the vice of economic exploitation into the virtue of developmental assistance.

It is characteristic of Carus's intellectual orientation that the only attempt to support his cultural value judgments with objective, "scientifically" derived data lies in his employment of cranioscopic measurements. Carus was—this needs to be stressed—one of the primary representatives of a scientific cranioscopy in the nineteenth century, and his writings on this subject were widely held to be the leading work in this field.[21] (Fig. 20) In this regard, Carus relies directly on the thought of his influential predecessors Lavater and Gall; like them, he takes it to be self-evident "that the infinitely distinct skull structure of the human being, which at times points to a stronger, at other times to a weaker development of the brain, must be considered one of the most significant physiognomic signs for intellectual predispositions" (*Ungleiche Befähigung* 18). In accordance with this belief, he presents a table with data based on cranioscopic measurements in which the superior intellectual capacity of the "daylight peoples" is graphically illustrated. The findings Carus relates here demonstrate that the cranial dimensions of the European peoples are fundamentally greater than those of other races, and that the cranium of Africans—in keeping with Carus's assessment of their relative intellectual inferiority—is the smallest. Not surprisingly, and again confirming Carus's subjective evaluation, the skulls of the Eastern and Western "twilight peoples" fall somewhere in between those of the Europeans and the Africans in terms of size. Although Carus insists that these figures have been arrived at "with absolute exactitude and great impartiality" (19), he ignores the fact that the number of skulls from which these data were derived is statistically insignificant. For example, his figures about the cranial dimensions of the "typical" African are based on the measurements of only twenty-nine specimens. But even if we set aside the statistical irrelevance of this extremely small sample, there is no scientifically persuasive reason for equating skull size with intellectual capacity. Here, again, it is a matter of a purely symbolic relation, mental "greatness" being comprehended somewhat arbitrarily in analogy to the "greatness"—that is, the presumed size—of the brain. With this Carus, like Lavater and Gall before him, reduces the *qualitative* value of higher intelligence to a purely *quantitative* sum.[22]

Carus's treatise in commemoration of Goethe's hundredth birthday represents one of the first racial histories with a

NEUER ATLAS

DER

CRANIOSKOPIE

ENTHALTEND

DREISSIG TAFELN ABBILDUNGEN

MERKWÜRDIGER TODTENMASKEN UND SCHÄDEL

VON

DR. CARL GUSTAV CARUS.

LEIPZIG:

F. A. BROCKHAUS.

1864.

Fig. 20. Title page, Carl Gustav Carus, *Neuer Atlas der Cranioskopie,* 1864. (Courtesy of the Hessische Landesbibliothek, Darmstadt)

physiognomic grounding written in the German language.[23] Carus's racial typology takes on an exemplary character not only because of the manner of argumentation it pursues, but also—and perhaps above all—because it was composed by a highly respected scientist with strong credentials as a leading humanist and humanitarian. This treatise finds many imitators in the early decades of the twentieth century, above all in the racial typologies developed by the representatives of the Nordic Movement and the ideologues of Nazi racial theory. Especially noteworthy in this connection is the style of Carus's thought and the characteristics of his discourse, especially the peculiar mixture of natural-scientific "proof" with a mode of analogical, symbolic reflection that is passed off as ironclad logic. This same discursive and argumentative style is characteristic of the writings of people like Hans F. K. Günther or Ludwig Ferdinand Clauss, not

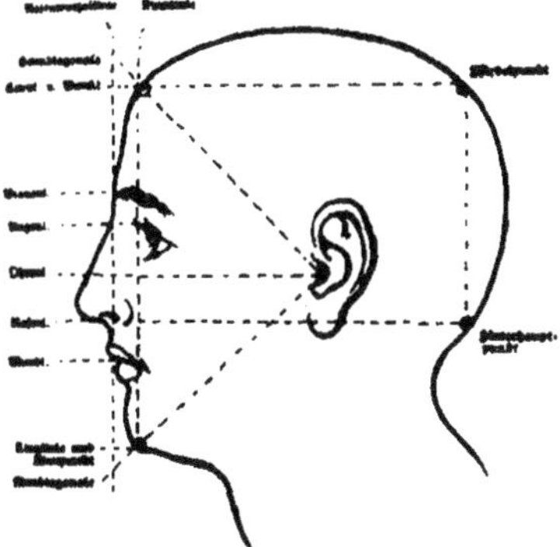

Fig. 21. Sketch of ideal cranial form, with proportional lines, from Robert Burger-Villingen, *Das Geheimnis der Menschenform,* 1912.

to mention the works of less capable and less influential racial physiognomists of the early twentieth century such as Robert Burger-Villingen (b. 1865) (Fig. 21), Friedrich Märker (b. 1893), or Bruno K. Schultz (1892–1942).

Carus's role as a link between the German physiognomic tradition as represented by Lavater and the racial anthropology generated during the period of the Weimar Republic and under Nazi rule can also be approached from the perspective of his reception and influence. A few examples will have to suffice here as a way of documenting the wide resonance Carus and his physiognomic theories enjoyed in the early decades of the twentieth century. Exemplary in this regard is a book by the characterologist Wilhelm Böhle, who in 1929 celebrated the rebirth of scientific physiognomics that he saw taking place in Germany and who situated Carus in a physiognomic tradition that begins with Lavater, moves through Gall's phrenology, and culminates in the characterological theories of Ludwig Klages and the racial anthropology of Hans F. K. Günther (Böhle 1–15). Böhle calls Carus's *Symbolik der menschlichen Gestalt* "the best work on physiognomics to date," and he stresses Klages's role in initiating the rediscovery of Carus and his thought that took place in the years immediately prior to the publication of his own work in 1929 (7). In fact, Ludwig Klages was one of the first to recognize and acknowledge not only the importance of Carus's theories for modern characterology, but the writings of Lavater, as well. Already in 1901 he published an essay with the telling title "Prinzipielles bei Lavater" (Principal recognitions in Lavater), in which he sought to establish Lavater's role as significant precursor of modern characterology. In 1925 Christoph Bernoulli published a book that examined Carus's psychological theories and their intellectual-historical significance, and one year later Klages himself was responsible for reprinting Carus's *Psyche;* this edition included an introduction, authored by Klages, praising the significance of Carus's thought for modern psychological theories.[24] Moreover, one of Klages's students, Hans Kern, published in the same year the first significant scholarly monograph that surveyed and examined Carus's work in its entirety. Not coincidentally, one of the sections of this scholarly appreciation bears the title "Racial Psychology," and summarizes the ideas Carus laid out in *Über ungleiche Befähigung.*[25]

One recognizes in the example of Ludwig Schemann (1852–1938), the German translator of Gobineau and a popularizer of racist doctrines, that the reception of Carus and Lavater was transpiring at this time in the emerging discipline of racial anthropology as well as in the fields of characterology and psychology. In his anthology-like review of the intellectual roots of racial thought, *Die Rassenfrage im Schrifttum der Neuzeit* (The racial question in modern scholarship), published in 1931 as volume three of his monumental *Die Rasse in den Geisteswissenschaften* (Race in the human sciences), Schemann not only refers to Carus's *Symbolik* and *Über ungleiche Befähigung,* he also draws an explicit connection between Carus's thoughts on race and the section entitled "National Physiognomies" in volume four of Lavater's *Physiognomische Fragmente* (Schemann 206–7). The centrality of Carus's position as a theoretician of race is evident in the title of Erich Voegelin's history of racial thought, *Die Rassenidee in der Geistesgeschichte von Ray bis Carus* (The idea of race in intellectual history from Ray to Carus), published in 1933.[26] The growing interest in Carus and his thought beginning in the 1920s is also manifest in the increasing number of dissertations dedicated to him and his works beginning at this time,[27] as well as in the frequency and regularity with which new editions of selected works, especially the *Symbolik,* appeared.[28]

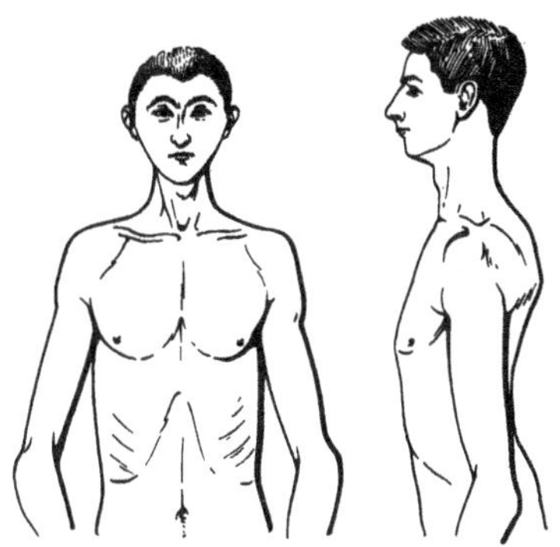

Fig. 22. Schematic drawing of the leptosomatic type, from Ernst Kretschmer, *Körperbau und Charakter*, 1948.

Perhaps even more telling is the fact that a new edition of Carus's complete works, beginning in 1938 with the publication of *Symbolik*, was planned and partially realized between 1938 and 1944, despite the disruptions and shortages caused by the war.[29] In this edition, a volume containing Carus's commemorative essay on Goethe was published as early as 1938, and reprinted in 1943.[30] There can be little doubt that the publication of *Über ungleiche Befähigung* in this historical context was intended to help legitimize the racial politics of National Socialism and the racially grounded myth of the Germans' claim to world mastery.

All too often the history of physiognomics has been treated as no more than a footnote to the history of racism in Germany.[31] Even in contemporary research on physiognomics one discovers the tendency either to view the racially tainted forms of physiognomics as an exception to the rule or to separate racist ideas from physiognomics as a mode of thought sui generis.[32] I hope to have taken steps here toward counteracting this tendency by giving initial indications of the complex and subtle ways in which physiognomics and racism are historically intertwined. The revival of physiognomics in Germany during the 1920s and 1930s is fueled in fundamental ways by the fact that intellectuals at this time could look back on a physiognomic tradition with venerable historical roots and which guaranteed its relevance by associating its methodology with that of the positivistic empirical sciences. Moreover, as I have tried to demonstrate here, this physiognomic tradition itself already contained important points of contact with the modern theory of race. The racial theoreticians of the Weimar Republic and the Third Reich were able to turn to this tradition in order to lend their own ideas the semblance of scientific truth and humanistic orthodoxy. In addition, this emergence of racial physiognomics ran parallel with the rediscovery of physiognomics by a cadre of influential conservative humanists. One need only think of Oswald Spengler's or Rudolf Kassner's evocation of a "physiognomic worldview" as appropriate to the state of modern culture,[33] of Ludwig Klages's physiognomically based characterology,[34] or of the medical typology developed by Ernst Kretschmer in *Körperbau und Charakter* (Physique and character), which was founded on a physiognomics of bodily form. (Fig. 22) Carrying on the tradition initiated by Lavater and Carus, Spengler and Kassner demonstrate the deep-rootedness of this physiognomic renaissance in the modern reception of Goethe and his age, an issue that constitutes the subject of the next chapter. In this diverse landscape of physiognomic theories it was relatively easy for racially defined variants of physiognomics to gain credence and legitimacy. Indeed, it is no overstatement to assert that the dissemination of racial thought in scientific circles, but also among the general populace in the early decades of the twentieth century in Germany, is closely connected with the fact that these racial thinkers could point to and rely upon the "venerable" tradition of German physiognomics, with its scientific and assertively humanistic self-understanding. It is certain, at any rate, that this tradition helped give racial physiognomics the legitimacy and popular appeal that allowed it, in the first half of the twentieth century, to be accepted and practiced in drawing rooms throughout German civil society.

4

Goethe as Found(l)ing Father of Modern German Physiognomics

The Founding Father as Foundling Father

In matters of intellectual paternity almost no other German has fathered as many illegitimate intellectual children as Johann Wolfgang von Goethe (1749–1832). Whereas today in the United States political or business leaders tend to be the most popular targets for paternity suits, during the nineteenth and early twentieth century Goethe was the preferred defendant in questionable matters of intellectual paternity. It is apparently the unavoidable fate of outstanding artistic and intellectual minds of this kind to be conjured up and cited as ultimate, unquestioned authorities. Anyone (or anything) who can claim to be an intellectual descendent of Goethe will always have sufficient authority reserves to fend off effortlessly any critical attack.

In the case of the graphologist, characterologist, and psychologist Ludwig Klages (1872–1956), we are dealing with just such a specious paternity suit. In an essay entitled "Stammväter der Seelenkunde" (Founding fathers of psychology), which first appeared in 1930, Klages names only two men whom he recognizes as intellectual forebears of his anti-Freudian, philosophically based *Seelenkunde,* Klages's alternative Germanized designation for the Latinate term *Psychologie:* one is none other than Goethe himself, and the other is the Romantic scientist and landscape painter Carl Gustav Carus (Klages 4: 568–78). We have grown accustomed to the fact that the ingenious polyhistorian Goethe is regarded as the founding father of myriad literary, artistic, philosophical, and even scientific movements; nonetheless it is surprising to find him identified as the founding father of Klages's empirical psychology, since Goethe would certainly never have seen himself in such a role. Goethe authored practically no "psychological" treatises in the narrow sense—if one disregards the psychological portrayals of his literary characters and his limited contributions to Lavater's *Physiognomische Fragmente* (see von der Hellen, *Goethes Anteil*). Only the latter, which constitute an extremely small body of material, could perhaps be viewed as prolegomena for an empirical psychology. In the essay in which Goethe's ancestry is claimed, Klages does not mention a single work of Goethe's by name. The same is true for those essays Klages collected in the book *Goethe als Seelenforscher* (Goethe as psychologist), where we find at most scattered quotations from Goethe, without citation of any explicit works that decisively establish Goethe's significance for, and his contributions to, the field of psychology (see Klages 5: 218–59; cf. also 4: 564–67). Klages's claim of intellectual descent from Goethe thus appears to be based on rather vague intellectual and methodological affinities rather than on any concrete and elaborated theories propounded by Goethe himself. If that is the case, then the phrase "founding father" appears to contain a strategic exaggeration. Indeed, the supposed ancestry of Goethe for Klages's version of psychology is a largely fictitious paternity line, and as such Goethe's position with regard to Klages's psychology is more that of a found*ling* father—an adopted and arbitrarily identified ancestor—than that of a found*ing* father.

If Klages's case were only an isolated phenomenon, it would hardly be worthy of consideration. But especially from the middle of the nineteenth century up through the 1930s, when, in Germany, physiognomic thought underwent a phenomenal boom, Goethe served in general as an important intellectual found(l)ing father whose authority was exploited in order to rehabilitate physiognomic views that had otherwise fallen into disrepute. In the nineteenth century it was above all Carl Gustav Carus—whom Klages, not coincidentally, named, along with Goethe, as the other founding father of his *Seelenkunde*—whose physiognomic theories appealed to forms of reasoning based largely in Goethean thought. During the time of the Weimar Republic a physiognomic renaissance took place in Germany (Campe and Schneider 9),[1] in which, aside from Klages, influential thinkers such as Oswald Spengler and Rudolf Kassner developed complex physiognomic theories that appealed to scientific and poetic principles attributed to Goethe. That Goethe of all people should be regarded as the intellectual ancestor of these extremely diverse physiognomic theories is more than just curious; if there is one name indelibly linked to the concept of physiognomics in the German-speaking world, it is without doubt that of Johann Caspar Lavater. Yet surprisingly, not one of the modern physiognomic theorists mentioned here relies upon Lavater's authority in these matters. Quite the opposite: Lavater functions as a kind of specter that must be banished at all costs in order to insure the credibility of their own physiognomic theories.[2] The historical reason for this is the notorious quarrel Lavater waged with the Göttingen physicist Georg Christoph Lichtenberg about physiognomic questions, in which Lavater came away the clear loser. Lavater's theories were, and still are, regarded as having been thoroughly ridiculed and ultimately dismissed altogether by the enlightener Lichtenberg, so that in 1798 Immanuel Kant could already claim, in his *Anthropologie in pragmatischer Hinsicht* (Anthropology from a pragmatic point of view), that physiognomics was "no longer in demand, and nothing has remained of it" (649). And yet, in spite of Immanuel Kant, any rumors about the death of physiognomics are premature and exaggerated: Lavater, the bearer of the physiognomic message, was executed in effigy, but the physiognomic message itself survived the attack of Enlightenment science. In the absence of a definitive "founding father" who possessed unquestioned authority concerning questions of physiognomics, Goethe was adopted as the found(l)ing father for modern German theoreticians dealing with issues of physiognomy.

Goethe as Physiognomist and Morphologist

Originally Goethe reacted with enthusiasm to Lavater's full-scale physiognomic project, not only contributing numerous articles to the first volumes of the *Physiognomische Fragmente,* but even mediating between Lavater and the Weidmann publishing house in Leipzig, which ultimately printed the *Fragmente* (Loewenberg, "Der Streit um die Physiognomik" 19). To this extent he played a crucial role—more that of a midwife than of a founding father—in the publication of this central work of physiognomics. Goethe also allowed his portrait, with an appropriate physiognomic interpretation, to appear in the third volume of the *Fragmente,* implicitly lending credibility and support to this project. (Fig. 23) However, it did not take long before his skepticism regarding Lavater's methods and rhetoric became apparent. As early as 20 February 1776, Goethe noted his negative reaction to the second volume of the *Fragmente* in a letter to Lavater: "I hope and feel that the tone of your third part [that is, the third volume of the *Physiognomische Fragmente*] will be less effusive and excited. I wanted to delete all of that. But if you were able to write it, then it might as well be published" (*Gedenkausgabe* 18: 312). Goethe is alluding to the fact that Lavater gave him the liberty to edit, as he saw fit, the manuscript of volume 2, which Lavater had sent to him. Goethe's refusal to alter Lavater's overly emotional style demonstrates not only his frustration with Lavater himself, but also his resignation concerning this physiognomic project in its entirety. A few months later, in a letter to Lavater dated 8 January 1777, Goethe mixed his praise for the second volume of the *Fragmente* with explicit criticism of the tone of Lavater's writing: "There are magnificent things in [these fragments], I thoroughly enjoyed them. If only the good impression had not been spoiled by your 'Lavaterianism' with its breathlessness, constant emphasis, abuse, hair-splitting, and the battles with paper tigers" (*Gedenkausgabe* 18: 355).

If the exaggerated "Lavaterianism" spoiled Goethe's appetite for Lavater's physiognomic project, this does not mean that Goethe's interest in physiognomics itself was diminished. His disappointment with the way Lavater developed and articulated his physiognomic theories only intensified Goethe's resolve to pursue his own physiognomic ideas. To be sure, physiognomics gained such a bad reputation due to Lavater and his ebullient raptures that Goethe was actually on the verge of turning away from it altogether. He makes this quite clear in a letter to Johann Heinrich Merck dated 14 November 1781: "At the same time, I treat the bones as a text to which I can attach all that is vital and human. . . . I have decided completely to avoid using the words physiognomics and physiognomy, and instead to let the awareness of their relevance emerge for every reader over the entire course of my exposition. Perhaps I can subsequently

Fig. 23. Portrait of Johann Wolfgang von Goethe by Heinrich Lips, from volume 3 of Johann Caspar Lavater, *Physiognomische Fragmente,* 1777.

make a useful contribution to your work with some of my thoughts derived from a closer examination of the animal economy" (*Goethes Briefe* 1: 373–74). Goethe's explicit refusal to use the terms "physiognomics" and "physiognomy" for his osteological studies expresses a clear rejection of Lavater's physiognomic views. We need to recall here that the main idea—and at the same time the most controversial theory—presented in Lavater's physiognomic treatises was the claim that bones or the so-called "firm parts" of the body are the sole bearers of genuine physiognomic significance. If for Lavater, then, physiognomics was essentially osteology, Goethe, by contrast, seeks to suspend all physiognomic questions in his osteological studies. As Goethe's later scientific work shows, especially his research on the intermaxillary bone, he was interested exclusively in anatomical, not characterological or physiognomic issues. Although the word "morphology" is not mentioned in Goethe's 1781 letter to Merck—Goethe will not use it for the first time until fifteen years later, in a journal entry from 1796 (*Gedenkausgabe* 17: 995)—the shift in Goethe's interest from physiognomic to morphological issues already looms large in the 1780s. His talk of bones as "a text to which I can attach all that is vital and human" already points ahead to his subsequent typological studies. Lavater's metaphor of legibility is retained in this image of the bones as a text; but whereas Lavater's reading of bones serves as a basis for deciphering the characteristics of the individual, Goethe's concern is with more general issues related to the definition of particular species or the nature of mammals as such. When in the essay "Bildung und Umbildung organischer Naturen" (Formation and transformation of organic nature) Goethe maintains that "the decisive character of every form is preserved for us definitively and for all time in the skeleton" (17: 20), he does not use the word "character" in the morphopsychological sense common to Lavater, but alludes instead to the character of the species, to the idiosyncratic form or "structure" *(Gestalt)* of a specific animal type. For this reason Goethe remarks shortly thereafter in the same essay that his osteological studies awakened in him the desire "to establish a type according to which all mammals would be able to be examined for their similarities and differences." He goes on to cite the connection between this task and his botanical studies: "and as I had searched previously for the primordial plant *[Urpflanze]*, I now sought to find the primordial animal *[Urtier]*, which ultimately means: the very concept, the idea of the animal as such" (17: 21).

As is generally known, it was this search for the unified osteological type that motivated Goethe's work on the intermaxillary bone: if humans were missing such a bone, then the whole concept of a primordial animal—and hence of the primordial plant, as well—would have to be abandoned. Goethe's holistic concept of nature therefore would be threatened in toto if no evidence for the existence of the intermaxillary bone in human beings could be found. Confirming the importance of this research, Goethe noted in a late essay, "Das Schädelgerüst aus sechs Wirbelknochen auferbaut" (The skull as composed of six vertebrae), written in 1824: "The recognition that the intermaxillary bone also played a role for humankind was of such tremendous importance because it simultaneously confirmed the conclusion that all animal forms were based on one osteological type" (*Gedenkausgabe* 17: 346). Goethe's osteological research thus culminated—in contrast to Lavater's physiognomic endeavors—in issues of comparative anatomy; indeed, one suspects that Goethe's interests in anatomy were spurred on and expanded by his critical involvement with Lavater's physiognomic project (Brednow, "Symbol und Symbolik in der Biologie Goethes" 244).

In his attempt to segregate morphology from physiognomics, Goethe emphasizes above all the much broader view inherent in his morphologic conception. He already suggests the basic relationship that obtains between physiognomics and morphology when he asserts in the "Fragmente zur vergleichenden Anatomie" (Fragments on comparative anatomy) that morphology rests on the conviction "that everything that exists must also allude to and reveal itself" (*Gedenkausgabe* 17: 415). This definition overlaps completely with the principle that motivated Lavater's interest in physiognomics. But Goethe immediately takes this farther than Lavater, who remains faithful to the physiognomic tradition as passed down from Greek antiquity and thus largely restricts his physiognomics to the human form. By contrast, for Goethe the principle that all living things must reveal themselves is operational "from the first physical and chemical elements on up to the intellectual expressions of the human being" (17: 415). Similarly, although somewhat more emphatically, Goethe writes in his scientific fragments: "to claim that a thing does not reveal what it is, is tantamount to saying that it is not what it is, or that the human mind is not capable of grasping a faithful concept of it" (17: 702).

The fundamental principle that links Lavater's physiognomics and Goethe's morphological and scientific studies is this belief in an identity between the inner substance and the phenomenal appearance of every living creature. Goethe's argument for this identity reads almost like a product of Lavater's pen: anyone who dares to doubt this identity calls into question the human capacity to conceptualize as such. On the other hand, Goethe and Lavater conceive the nature of this identity and the relation between inner and outer in completely different ways. For Lavater they stand in a semiotic, that is, in a semantic relation to each other, whereby the sensible phenomenon is treated as the sign of a transcendental content. For Goethe, inner and outer relate to each other syntactically, so that the object perceived by the senses is understood as a constitutive element in a hypothetical unity and alludes indirectly to the supersensible elements of the entity as a whole. To state it another way:

Lavater works with a relatively simple referential system, an "alphabet," as he calls it (*Physiognomische Fragmente* 1: "Vorrede" [unpaginated]), in which a body part, like a linguistic lexeme, refers to a distinct meaning. Goethe, by contrast, operates with a complicated hermeneutics—in the narrow sense of that word—in which the systematic meaning of every element stands in a dialectical and mutually determining relationship with a hypothetical conception of the whole. The theories of the primordial plant in his botanical studies and of the primordial animal in the osteological works play precisely the role of such hypothetical conceptions of the holistic idea that lend meaning to the perceivable outer form of any specific organic entity.

The difference between these two strategies already implies the fundamentally broader view taken by Goethe's morphology as compared to Lavater's physiognomics. In the "Fragmente zur vergleichenden Anatomie" Goethe treats morphology as a superordinate view of nature that adopts and exploits certain insights or methodologies from various disciplines, such as natural history, anatomy, chemistry, and so on. He also places among these subdisciplines the study of physiognomics, which he describes in the following way: "Physiognomics. Observes form *[Gestalt]* insofar as it alludes to certain characteristics; one could divide it into semiotics, which deals with the physical aspect, and into true physiognomics, which would concern itself with the intellectual and moral aspects" (*Gedenkausgabe* 17: 416). Goethe emphasizes shortly thereafter the proximity of morphology and physiognomics, or semiotics, and identifies the concrete points at which these disciplines overlap.

> The semiotician and the physiognomist are closest to the morphologist. The form *[Gestalt]* is comprehended by means of visual perception, and all three deal mainly with the form *[Gestalt]* and its significance; they are only distinct in the scope of their investigations and the ends they pursue. . . . [F]rom the former [the semiotician], the morphologist learns to pay attention to the most subtle changes in organic nature, not only in the form *[Gestalt]*, but also in the color; from the physiognomist he learns to pay attention to the infinitely determined, both lasting and ephemeral effect of intellectual *[geistiger]* changes on physical organs. (17: 417–18)

It is already obvious in Goethe's description that he understands physiognomics in an essentially different manner than Lavater.

Whereas the latter fixes physiognomics as the unconditional relation between physical characteristics and intellectual-moral qualities, Goethe consciously separates these two realms from one another and relegates physical concerns to the semiotician and intellectual-moral questions to the more narrowly conceived physiognomist. In addition, Goethe limits physiognomics exclusively to the effect of the intellect on the body—that is, to the formative influence that the intellectual sphere exercises over the somatic realm. It was exactly this intellectuality, understood as the human ability to exercise arbitrary will and transcend its own nature, whose influence Lavater sought to eliminate with his theory that only the "firm features" of the body, not the flesh and muscles subject to human control, carry genuine physiognomic significance. Ultimately, Goethe's conception is much more dynamic than is Lavater's: semiotics deals with "*changes* in organic nature," not with unalterable givens, and the more narrowly conceived physiognomist is concerned with the effect of "intellectual *changes* on physical organs." This explicitly dynamic conception marks a further decisive difference between Goethe's morphology and Lavater's physiognomics.

As noted in chapter 1, Goethe's more dynamic conception of physiognomics already found its way into the first volume of Lavater's *Physiognomische Fragmente,* in the "Addendum" to the fragment "Von der Physiognomik überhaupt" (Concerning physiognomics in general), which Goethe authored. We must examine Goethe's addendum once again in the present context, since it can be read as a direct objection and contradiction to Lavater's static, almost mechanistic approach to physiognomics.

> One will often not be able to refrain from using the words physiognomy and physiognomics in an extremely broad sense. This science draws conclusions about the internal based on the external. But what exactly constitutes the external side of the human being? Certainly not his or her naked form *[Gestalt],* unconscious gestures that designate his or her inner energies and their interaction! Class, habit, possessions, clothing, they all modify him, disguise him. It appears extremely difficult, even impossible, to penetrate all of these veils to a person's innermost being. . . . But take heart! The things that surround human beings do not only have an impact on them; they also have an influence on these things, and at the same time as people let themselves be modified by these things, they also make their own modifications in their immediate environment. As a result, we can

> draw sure conclusions about a man's character from his clothes and household effects. Nature forms human beings, but they in turn transform themselves, and these transformations are once again natural. (*Gedenkausgabe* 13: 33; cf. Lavater, *Physiognomische Fragmente* 1: 15)

In the present context we can disregard the fact that, in his conception of what is physiognomically significant, Goethe includes culture as a second nature deriving from a dialectic with nature itself, although this principle also marks a fundamental discrepancy between his and Lavater's physiognomic theories.[3] Central to the present discussion is the metamorphosis the human being undergoes in the reciprocal interaction of nature and culture. The focal concepts of "formation" and "transformation," which Goethe will later associate closely with his morphology, are already employed in this addendum. "Nature forms *[bildet]* human beings, but they in turn transform themselves *[bilden sich um]*, and these transformations are once again natural": this is Goethe's formula. And it is precisely this fundamentally *artistic* process of formation and transformation that characterizes his later definition of morphology. He writes, for example, in the essay "Vorarbeiten zu einer Physiologie der Pflanzen" (Preliminary studies of plant physiology): "Morphology should encompass the theory of form *[Gestalt]*, formation and transformation of organic bodies, and it hence is part of the natural sciences" (*Gedenkausgabe* 17: 115; cf. also 17: 416). It is no coincidence that one of Goethe's most fundamental morphological essays bears the title "Bildung und Umbildung organischer Naturen" (Formation and transformation of organic nature). In this work, written in 1807, Goethe gives a kind of epistemological summary of his understanding of the natural sciences.[4]

> However, if we examine all forms *[Gestalten]*, especially organic ones, we find there is nothing that simply persists, nothing that is at rest or complete; rather, everything is in a state of constant flux. . . . If we want to introduce a type of morphology, then we must not speak of form *[Gestalt]*, but rather when we use this word, we must associate it only with the idea, the concept, or with something that can be held fast, as an empirical phenomenon, only for a moment. What is formed is immediately transformed, and we must remain just as mobile and plastic if we want to attain a living intuition *[lebende Anschauung]* of nature, following the example with which nature provides us. (17: 14)

From the irrepressible "flux" of nature—to allude to the Hericlitean heritage of this conception—Goethe draws consequences not only for the morphologist's use of language, but also for his scientific methodology. The word "Gestalt," as a firm, static concept, threatens to mislead the researcher about the perpetual metamorphosis of genuine living forms; therefore, one must never forget that this word is only a useful construct, an idea that attempts to grasp what is essentially mobile and ungraspable. Moreover, Goethe describes the morphologist's preferred cognitive state as one of epistemological fluidity that imitates the dynamism exemplified in nature. Only this mimesis of what is principally fluid and changing guarantees what Goethe calls *lebende Anschauung*, "living intuition" of nature, a conceptualization that remains true to nature's essence and does not force upon it preconceived, mechanical, static, or dogmatic notions.

With this a further discrepancy between Lavater's physiognomic views and Goethe's morphology becomes manifest: Whereas Lavater always conceived of *Gestalt* as a fixed form or an immutable structure, Goethe sees it as something fundamentally mutable. He expresses this unequivocally in the "Fragmente zur vergleichenden Anatomie": "Form *[Gestalt]* is something dynamic, something that evolves, that perishes. Morphology is the theory of metamorphosis, and the theory of metamorphosis is the key to all the signs of nature" (*Gedenkausgabe* 17: 415). The term *Gestalt* signifies the seminal idea that in vital nature such metamorphoses are not indicative of a loss of identity: although a living creature does not remain the selfsame being, it nonetheless still retains self-identity as long as its transformations are expressions of its original "idea," of its guiding principle. Because of this cognizance of the mutability inherent in the phenomenal appearance of his object of investigation, the morphologist in particular must be aware that his task is threatened by the paradox that he "must treat something that in nature is always in motion as though it were still and stationary; that [he] is supposed to reduce something in nature that is eternally changing to a visible and, as it were, tangible law" (17: 131–32). The insight into this problematic is what motivates Goethe's methodological resistance to the analytical procedure of the empirical sciences. The natural scientist's goal must be "to rescue himself from the limitless multiplicity, fragmentation, and intricacies of the modern theory of nature and escape back into something simple" (17: 758), that is, to find a way back to the holistic conception that he designates with the term *Anschauung,* or intuition.

This leads us to the final criterion that distinguishes Goethe's morphological studies from Lavater's physiognomic theories: their wholly contrary methodological points of departure. For despite his enthusiastic rhetoric and his pietistic, religious perspective, Lavater, as we saw in chapter 1, was completely committed to the analytic-mathematical models of Enlightenment science. A passage from a letter Lavater addressed to Goethe on 18 March 1780 illuminates especially clearly the discrepancy in the approaches manifest in their studies of nature, despite any affinity in their scientific goals. Here Lavater writes: "I am about to make a new and highly important physiognomic discovery—a wholly *simple* portrayal of the gradations of animals up to the most childlike human being, one that will allow me, as I suspect, to demonstrate at the same time the inner and eternally untranscendable boundary between humans and animals on the basis of this medial line alone" (*Goethe und Lavater* 106). Lavater was concerned with determining the face's "medial line," an idea derived from Petrus Camper's *linea facialis,* or "facial line." This line, constructed mathematically out of the geometry of the face, was intended to serve as the key to the anatomical segregation of humans from the higher forms of animals. The conformity of the larger outlines of this undertaking with Goethe's anatomical interests, especially with his search for the human intermaxillary bone as a connecting link between humans and animals, is obvious. Lavater's interest in determining specific gradations among mammals also reminds one of Goethe's osteological and morphological studies. But Lavater's need to determine this medial line *mathematically* could only meet with Goethe's disapproval, since such mathematical and systematic procedures ran contrary to Goethe's view that all living creatures possess dynamic, ever changing forms. This, as is well known, is precisely what called forth Goethe's opposition to Carl Linné's (1707–1778) systematization of the natural world (see Kuhn 201).

As opposed to the analytic, fragmenting, empirical method that depended on causal relationships and operated on the basis of induction, Goethe's scientific approach was based in subjective experience guided by "living intuition," and it operated according to a kind of analogic reasoning rather than with analytical tools. In his *Maximen und Reflexionen* (Maxims and reflections), Goethe writes about this analogic approach: "There is nothing wrong with thinking according to analogies: analogy has the advantage that it does not bring closure and does not seek a final position; by contrast, induction is disastrous when it has a preconceived purpose in mind and works toward it, carrying both truth and falsehood along in its current" (*Gedenkausgabe* 9: 567; cf. 17: 732–33). Here it is the inductive method that assumes the role of analogy's evil opposite; in other contexts Goethe juxtaposes analogy with analysis, as for example in his summary of the dispute between Geoffroy de Saint-Hillaire (1805–1861) and Georg Leopold Cuvier (1769–1832) that was waged in 1830 at the French Academy (see 17: 380–414). Goethe recognizes in this dispute a "conflict between two schools of thought that have long divided the scientific world" (17: 381): a conflict between those, like Cuvier, who operate analytically, draw distinctions, and proceed inductively on the basis of empirical facts, and those analogic thinkers, represented by Saint-Hillaire, who take an idea as their point of departure, attend to the totality rather than its distinct parts, derive individual phenomena from the whole on the basis of deductive reasoning, and are guided by analogic relations. Analogic reasoning is thereby hypostatized as a fundamental manner of establishing truth and contrasted with analytic thought. Goethe clearly takes the side of analogic thought in this dispute.

The role discrimination plays in the analytic system is occupied in analogic thought by the imagination or "fantasy" of the researcher. Imagination must be at work in order for analogic connections between singular phenomena to be drawn at all. Goethe asserted the pertinence of the artistic quality of imagination for scientific research in one of his scientific fragments. "Fantasy *[Phantasie]* is much closer to nature than sensuality, for the latter is in nature and the former hovers *[schwebt]* above it. Fantasy measures up to nature, but sensuality is ruled by nature" (*Gedenkausgabe* 17: 699). The word sensuality refers here to the insistence of the empirical researcher on what can be perceived by the senses, and on the facts arrived at by means of sensual perception. According to Goethe, these phenomena are subordinated to nature, while the imagination or fantasy has the advantage of "hovering" above it. The verb *schweben* is important, since it suggests the free and liberated quality of this kind of imagination. In another context, Goethe writes of "an exact sensual imagination *[Phantasie]*" (17: 779), which is always at work in art, but is not acknowledged by the exact sciences. Goethe is concerned with just this "exact sensory imagination" in his scientific research; it represents a kind of synthesis of the exact, sensual perspective of empirical, positivistic science and the creative imagination of the artist. Moreover, the analogic, imaginative way of thinking does not conceive of nature as a separate world of objects, but instead asserts the dialectical bond that joins the objective and the subjective spheres. "The phenomenon is not detached from the observer," Goethe writes in one of his scientific fragments, "rather it is intertwined and entangled in its very individuality" (17: 752). This dialectical interwovenness of the empirical phenomenon and the observer constitutes the essence of the scientific attitude that Goethe calls "living intuition" or "pure intuition of the outer and inner" (9: 567). In Goethe's understanding, *Anschauen* means not only "to observe" in the concrete sense, but also "intuition" in the broader sense, as subjective insight. *Anschauen* thus implies an occupation with the active, dynamic intersection between subject and object, the sensible and the supersensible.

Such emphasis on the subjective, imaginative element in the observation of nature locates Goethe's views once again in proximity to Lavater's physiognomic thought. After all, it was the subjective element, the arbitrariness of Lavater's physiognomic judgments, that evoked many contemporaries' disapproval. But what distinguishes Goethe's scientific, morphological thinking is his effort to banish all subjective fancy from his imaginative approach. This is exactly what he means by "exact sensual imagination": the imagination is kept in check by precision and the serious regard for sensually perceptible phenomena. The role imagination plays in this dialectical system is to project a concept of unity that is not strictly limited by the transitory details of the natural world. In this respect, Goethe develops a complex, conscientiously dialectical method for his contemplation of nature, one that might serve as the yardstick by which one could measure the methodological sensitivity of his physiognomic successors.

It seems appropriate to summarize briefly the attributes of Goethe's "physiognomic" or "morphological" thought outlined here, so that we can recognize the extent to which, and exactly where, his physiognomic stepchildren rely on his principles. In the first place, Goethe is interested almost exclusively in anatomical, not characterological matters; related to this is the fact that rather than concentrating on individuals, his outlook ranges from focusing on broader questions of species and genus to unifying theories of the "primordial plant" and "primordial animal." Furthermore, Goethe emphasizes the living—that is, the dynamic and constantly changing—aspects of nature and draws from this recognition certain conclusions about the methodology of the natural scientist: if one wants to conceive of dynamic nature adequately, one cannot force it into static systems; rather one must imitate in one's methods the dynamism and transmutability of the natural world itself. Goethe hence supports a hermeneutics that interprets individual phenomena in the context of a hypothetical concept of the totality. Ultimately this hermeneutics operates according to the logic of analogy and is supported by creative fantasy, the imaginative power of the researcher.

Carl Gustav Carus: Symbolism and Racism

Of all Goethe's physiognomic descendants, Carl Gustav Carus (1789–1869) is the closest to him personally and historically. As early as 1818, Carus began a scientific exchange with Goethe that continued until the latter's death (Carus, *Goethe* 5). In 1821 the two men met in Weimar to discuss their scientific ideas, and Goethe formed an exceptionally positive opinion of Carus and his abilities. In one of his scientific fragments Goethe describes his admiration for Carus's work, claiming that Carus succeeded in "sketching all the traces of development from the simplest to the most variegated form of life" and "placing the great mystery before our eyes in words and images" (*Gedenkausgabe* 17: 766).

Yet it is doubtful that he would have had similar praise for Carus's physiognomic and cranioscopic works, which were only published after Goethe's death. It was not until 1853 that Carus's major physiognomic work, his *Symbolik der menschlichen Gestalt* (Symbolism of the human form), appeared; yet already the title of this work carries an obvious allusion to Goethe's thought. To be sure, Carus had already formulated the central theses of *Symbolik* in 1846 in his constitutive psychological work, *Psyche: Zur Entwicklungsgeschichte der Seele* (Psyche: On the developmental history of the soul). Here he defines the body as a "manifestation of the soul itself" (32), and he uses the symbolic relation between the somatic and the psychic dimensions as the basis for elaborating the unconscious foundation of human beings. According to Carus, who in this regard is following the ideas of his primary teacher, Friedrich Wilhelm Joseph von Schelling (1775–1854), every human being evolves out of a "primordial image" or "idea" to which his or her entire essence and character, as well as his or her physical appearance, can be reduced. Symbolism is thus defined as the "science governing the meaning of outer human form *[Bildung]* for inner psychological and intellectual life" (Carus, *Symbolik* vi).

Although Carus attempts to distinguish his own "symbolic" method from Lavater's ill-reputed physiognomics (*Symbolik* 5), his approach is, in fact, much closer to Lavater's pragmatic, materialistic orientation than it is to Goethe's morphological methodology. This is best illuminated by the fact that Carus mistakenly attributes to Lavater Goethe's "Addendum" to the fragment entitled "Concerning Physiognomics in General" from the *Physiognomische Fragmente*, which we examined above, and then proceeds to distinguish his own theory from Lavater's on this basis (*Symbolik* 6). Thus Carus unwittingly negates the strategic extension Goethe wanted to introduce into Lavater's narrow physiognomic conceptions, and this instance can be taken as representative of a general retreat in Carus's *Symbolik* from Goethe's more subtle and complex views to the simple, often even simple-minded methods of Lavater. Of central importance here is Carus's defection from Goethe's fundamentally dynamic conception of form, or *Gestalt*. For Carus the human form once again has the static, even deterministic element that was already present in Lavater's theories. He writes, for example, that the physiognomist has the task of "deriving from the symbols manifest in the external appearance of human beings a clear image of their actual essence, the *idea,* the image of their Being that exists *prior to* their Being" (*Symbolik* 356). The idea of a primordial "Being" that precedes and predetermines phenomenological existence is starkly reminiscent of the deterministic metaphysics of Lavater and Franz Joseph Gall (1758–1828), which Hegel so convincingly criticized in his *Phänomenologie des Geistes* (233–62). Indeed, Carus's anatomical studies have a pronounced materialistic bias that shares a great deal with Gall's phrenology. Due above all to his cranioscopic theories, Carus was, and still is, regarded as having revived and extended Gall's phrenology (see Volrad Deneke 95). In his 1841 study *Grundzüge einer neuen und wissenschaftlich begründeten Cranioscopie (Schädellehre)* (Fundamentals of a new and scientifically based cranioscopy [phrenology]), Carus claims, for example, "that the form and development of the head, as the structure that is determined by the brain and contains the brain as its most essential component, has a particular and very evocative relationship to the specific individuality of the person and *necessarily* represents this individuality" (1; emphasis added). The reference to the "necessity" of this principally semiotic relationship essentially repeats the strategy by which Lavater and Gall legitimated their characterological interpretations: without this purportedly irrefutable, causal connection, which can only be asserted and never proven, there could be no "symbolism" of the human form. Of course, instead of the twenty-seven "brain organs" and the significant "bulges" with which they correlate in Gall's phrenological system, Carus recognizes only three significant parts of the brain: the frontal, middle, and anterior lobes. But this simplification is not tantamount to a refinement of Gall's system.

Carus's symbolism shares with Lavater's physiognomics and Gall's phrenology this referential system, this orientation toward the *semantic* significance of somatic characteristics as contrasted to the syntactic reference system that Goethe stressed. However, Carus does pay lip service to Goethe's syntactic, context-oriented hermeneutics by strongly emphasizing the proportionality of the body, that is, the harmonious relationship among the parts of the individual organism. In his "Symbolische Rhapsodien" (Symbolic rhapsodies) Carus formulates a concise definition of symbolism that reduces it to this proportional theory: every true understanding of human form, he writes, must be based on "the correct interpretation and judgment of the relation of all the individual parts to the whole and vice versa—in a word, on its symbolism" (103). But this conception of a holistic totality, which views the human body as an aesthetic construct and forces onto it the classicist dogmatism of harmony and proportion, has little to do with the subtle, dialectical hermeneutics of Goethe's morphological views.

Carus's methodology, which derives its scientific claims from mathematics, numbers, and body measurements, also runs counter to Goethe's anti-analytic, anti-mechanistic, nonquantitative tendencies. It is above all the act of measuring that Carus emphasizes when he wishes to distinguish the scientific validity of his own procedure from the insufficient disciplinarity of his predecessors Lavater and Gall. In the *Symbolik der menschlichen Gestalt,* for example, he criticizes Lavater's "divinatory gaze" and claims that, in contrast to this, one must "compare and measure" if one wants to practice a "scientific symbolism" (5). And in his *Cranioscopie* he regards the impossibility of exact measurements as the most glaring flaw in Gall's phrenological theory (14–15). In contrast to this, Goethe voiced his vehement opposition to the measurement of living creatures, and in his "Studie nach Spinoza" (Study based on Spinoza) he expressed this in unequivocal terms: "The measurement of a thing is a crude act, which can only be applied to living creatures in a highly imperfect manner. A living, existing thing cannot be measured by anything that exists outside of itself; if such measurement is to take place at all, then this creature must provide the standard for itself. This standard is, however, highly intellectual and cannot be discovered by the senses" (*Gedenkausgabe* 16: 841–42). What Goethe designates as a "crude act" and an imperfect practice, Carus glorifies as the principal criterion of his scientific symbolism. In a certain sense, to be sure, Carus does agree with Goethe's qualification that the standard of measurement for living things must be found in the creature under examination. Carus's theory of the human "module," which he defines as a third of the length of the spine, serves as a relative gauge for his measurements on humans (see *Symbolik* 52–54). However, Goethe conceived of this standard as something "highly intellectual," and not as a concrete, quantifiable part of the body. But Carus did not, in fact, carry out his measurements on living objects; instead, he studied and measured corpses, the skeletons and skulls of the deceased. This occupation with corpses reveals the reification and mortification of the human body that is part and parcel of Carus's symbolic methodology,[5] a tendency that stands in stark contrast to Goethe's sensitivity to the vitalism and dynamism of life.

Although Carus understands his symbolism as the interpretation of individuality, one would search his works in vain for characterological interpretations of individual personalities like those familiar to us from Lavater's *Physiognomische Fragmente.* Instead, Carus's physiognomics culminates in general typologies that anticipate some of the qualities of Ernst Kretschmer's psychosomatic theory of constitution (Kloos 54). In this sense he gravitates toward Goethe's concept of type, with the important difference that Goethe's type remains an idea and a speculative hypothesis, whereas Carus's human types take on concrete form. Carus's materialistic view of the typological system already makes itself manifest in the fact that he, like Gall, takes as his starting point the physiology of the brain. Orienting his theory around the three cerebral lobes, Carus distinguishes three fundamental human types. The frontal lobe he identifies with cognitive ability, the medial cranium with the emotions, and the anterior section, or occiput, with volition and will (*Cranioscopie* 5–9). Depending on which part of the brain dominates the individual, a person will either tend toward intelligence, emotionality, or strong will and powerful desire. Carus not only grounds gender differences in this theory (men = frontal lobe = abstract intelligence; women = medial section = emotionality), but also develops a racial typology that clearly indicates his role as a precursor for the proto-fascist race theorists of the Weimar period.[6]

Ironically, it is the centennial celebration of Goethe's birth in 1849 that Carus takes as the occasion to further develop this incipient racial typology. His "Denkschrift zum hundertjährigen

Geburtsfeste Goethe's" (Essay in commemoration of Goethe's hundredth birthday) carries the title *Über ungleiche Befähigung der verschiedenen Menschheitsstämme für höhere geistige Entwickelung* (On the unequal capacities of the different human races for higher intellectual development). Since we examined the materialistic and Eurocentric thrust of Carus's symbolic interpretations of race in the previous chapter, we need not expound on them here. One supplemental point does, however, need to be made. This is that Carus underwrites his racial typological distinction of the "daylight," "twilight," and "nocturnal" peoples by arguing for the predominance of one specific cranial lobe as the determining factor for each type. His cranial measurements of diverse human types demonstrate, he claims, that for the "daylight peoples" of Europe the frontal lobe (the seat of intelligence) predominates, whereas the "twilight peoples"—those of Asia and the natives of North and South America—manifest a larger medial brain (the locus of the emotions), and the "nocturnal peoples," the African blacks, provide evidence for the primacy of the occiput (the domain of desire and will). The conclusion he then will draw from these "findings" is easy to surmise: Carus's applied physiognomic logic is, after all, a coercive, syllogistic logic. The daylight peoples have the greatest intellectual capacities, since the frontal lobe of the brain dominates their physiognomy; the nocturnal peoples have the most meager intellectual capabilities and are controlled by desires and instincts; the twilight peoples have an average intellectual ability and tend to be ruled more by emotion (*Über ungleiche Befähigung* 18–22). In other words, the symbolism of the human form, which took Goethe's complex idea of analogical thought as its point of departure, is collapsed into a reductive analogic reasoning that serves as an ideological instrument to justify the superiority of Europeans over other human beings. It is but a small a step from these views, as I argued in chapter 3, to the physiognomic race theories of the Weimar Republic. This small step also marks the discrepancy between Goethe's morphological model and the scurrility of Carus's racist symbolism.

Since Carus's essay *Über ungleiche Befähigung* was conceived in commemoration of Goethe, it seems justified to ask what possible connection this fundamentally antihumanistic attitude has with Goethe at all. I have already given an answer to this question by alluding to the dependence of Carus's symbolism on the scientific method—or at least on the natural-scientific discourse—of Goethe's analogic-anatomical views. But Carus's symbolism is at best a perversion of Goethe's reasoning. Carus himself points to another connection between Goethe and this racial theory. In the introduction to *Über ungleiche Befähigung* he claims that the course of his arguments will make us understand "how an individual as powerful as . . . our *Goethe* could be descended from a people that already manifests higher intelligence as such and for that reason promises in general that its representatives will possess a more powerful intellectual development than any other peoples" (7). In other words, Goethe's genius provides the final proof of the intellectual superiority of the Western Europeans, which Carus is at pains to portray in this essay (see 99). It is not merely Goethe's scientific method that suffers abuse for ideological purposes; Goethe the man must himself serve as the figurehead for a racial theory that exploits traditional prejudices so as to valorize one human group and debase all others. If Goethe, the "found(l)ing" father, were still alive in 1849, he most certainly would have sought to have his "symbolic" and self-adopted stepson Carus intellectually disowned.

Ludwig Klages: Metamorphosis as the Adversary of Stasis

If Carus puts a materialist spin on Goethe's physiognomics, Ludwig Klages's appropriation of Goethe's thought runs in an entirely different direction. Here it is once again the strategic role Goethe the man assumes in Klages's worldview and not so much Goethe's thought itself that is the decisive factor. Goethe represents for Klages an ideal human being who fuses the capacity for sensual intuition with the capability for intellectual structuration, an ideal that serves, in his view, as an antidote to the exaggerated intellectualization and mechanization of modern humanity. The ostensible characterological essence of "Goethe" the human being thus becomes the touchstone for the viability of Klages's philosophy of life, in which, as he declares in the title of his primary work, *Der Geist als Widersacher der Seele* (Mind as adversary of the soul; 1929–1933), intellect is interpreted negatively as the hyper-cerebral enemy of the creative soul. In the almost proverbial "harmony" of Goethe's character Klages recognizes the "portrayal of a *successful* balance, if not to say the lasting armistice between two inimical camps," as he states in *Goethe als Seelenforscher* (Goethe as psychologist), the extended, book-length version of the essay with the same name (Klages, *Sämtliche Werke* 5: 241). We will return shortly to the importance of Goethe as an intellectual-historical *phenomenon,* since in this instance he is once again exploited as a legitimating figure who serves to validate Klages's vitalistic ideology of life. But first I want to lay out in schematic fashion the common ground that Goethe's physiognomic-morphologic thought and Klages's psychology share.

In the first chapter of his *Prinzipien der Charakterologie* (Principles of characterology)—first published in 1910 and subsequently included as an appendix to the later editions of this work, which appeared under the revised title *Die Grundlagen der Charakterkunde* (Foundations of the study of character)—Klages hints at the significance of Goethe's scientific thought for his psychological theories. After providing a long explanation as to why the "meaning" of psychology lies in "viewing the phenomenon *symbolically*" (4: 422), Klages claims: "with this turn [that is, to symbolism] we return once more to the importance for psychology of the visual point of departure. As defined here, psychology is understood primarily as morphology, a theory about the form of the psychic 'organization'" (4: 423). Klages's version of empirical psychology is thereby understood as a continuation, or at least a subset, of Goethe's morphological teachings. But if Goethe had already recognized the affinity between morphology and physiognomics, this is also true for Klages, who almost immediately following his identification of psychology with morphology appends the remark: "We do not regard the psychological viewpoint to be merely related to the physiognomic view, rather we see them as identical in their deep structure. The new insight . . . always has its source in the expansion of relations for the semiotics of the physical world or in the progressive intellectual appropriation of previously unknown physiognomies" (4: 423). Thus psychology in Klages's sense subsumes characterology, graphology, and the science of expression as distinct subdisciplines, and in its broader conception it is identical with physiognomics, understood as the "semiotics of the physical world." Already the proximity of the concepts "morphology," "physiognomics," and "semiotics" in Klages's argument hints at Goethe's influence, since, as we have seen, the latter had already articulated the close connection among these three disciplines (see Goethe, *Gedenkausgabe* 17: 416). But Klages also resists reducing physiognomics to the narrow idea of a stable construct or static structure that it had for Lavater; instead, he understands physiognomics in the broader sense with which Goethe imbued the term. Hence he writes in his *Grundlegung der Wissenschaft vom Ausdruck* (Foundation of the science of expression) that physiognomics should always be equated with "kinetic physiognomics" *(Bewegungsphysiognomik)* or "pathognomy," and he differentiates it explicitly from the conceptions of Lavater and Gall, both of whom confine themselves to solid forms and whose approach he calls "organic physiognomics" *(Organphysiognomik)* (Klages, *Sämtliche Werke* 6: 546). Where the body-soul relation is concerned, Klages states simply and emphatically that "*the body is the manifestation of the soul, the soul is the meaning of the somatic manifestation,*" and he calls the relationship between body and soul, outer and inner, a "primordial connection" (6: 397). In another context he describes body and soul as "the two inseparably fused poles of one and the same being" (4: 327). What ultimately guarantees the "primordial connection" of these two poles—and here Carus's influence becomes apparent—is their symbolic relationship: following the classic physiognomic conception, Klages views the body as the medium through which the soul attains self-expression.

The body as communicative medium of the soul—that is one of the founding ideas of physiognomics, and Klages emphatically shares it. The fundamental difference lies in Klages's understanding of the soul itself, and here once again Goethe's morphological theories are of principal importance. For Klages the soul, the "character," is not a preordained unity—not predetermined by the bones or firm and unchanging parts of the body. Rather, it is an entelechy, a bundle of dispositions that in their interaction with the life world can pass through different, even unanticipated developmental phases. Thus when Klages describes his psychology as morphology—that is, as a *Gestaltlehre,* a theory of form—he conceives the word *Gestalt* in the same dynamic way Goethe understood it. His "theory about the form of the psychic 'organization'" is conceived as a morphology in the style of Goethe, except that, contrary to Goethe, it consciously restricts itself to the realm of human expression.

The key idea informing this morphology could be called, borrowing a phrase from Goethe, *Dauer im Wechsel,* "permanence in change." Similar to Goethe, Klages notes that the words "character," "essence," or "soul" disguise the fundamentally dynamic quality of the psychic formations to which they refer, and he insists that each of these entities "is ultimately a kind of dynamic event, albeit with a fixed center, comparable to a whirlpool that continually renews itself at a certain point in a river in forms that are always similar to one another" (*Sämtliche Werke* 6: 400). The soul is thus not a "thing," but rather a series of events or occurrences whose dynamic structural changes evince formal consistency in relation to a certain fixed point, a controlling nucleus, or regulative idea, as it were. In Goethe's osteological morphology this regulative idea was called the "primordial plant" or "primordial animal": in Klages's theory the human soul is likewise determined by just such a regulative form that constitutes the source for all individual transformations of character. He calls this regulative structural principle an individual's personal "Leitbild," his or her exemplary or guiding image (6: 596). To be sure, although for Klages character is an "*act*uality of nature" ("Natur*tat*sache," 4: 218; emphasis added), the stress lies more on the "act" it executes than on the nature that determines it. For Klages, then, the soul is an "experience of transformation"; but this transformation becomes "a kinetic experience by means of its *translation into the language of the body*" (6: 439). The transformations of the soul, which obey a specific formal or structural law, correlate to the movements of the body as their faithful "translation." Klages sees the task of empirical psychology as the reversal of this translation, that is, the de-translation of the kinetic language of the body back into the transformative events that transpire in the psyche. This explains why Klages conceives of psychology as a theory of appearances, or as a phenomenology (5: 231–34). The transformations of the soul are in no way willful or arbitrary; they correspond to a particular, individual law of transmutation that, as "characteristic" of a specific being, constitutes the permanent and inalterable element of this being's psychic attitude. This characteristic law of transformation could be compared with the peculiar "style" of a soul, or, as Klages says, with its "type" (cf. 4: 247). In other words, no random, temporally determined manifestation of a particular transformational psychic phase constitutes and codifies character; rather, the *rule* governing this structural transformation determines what is "characteristic" or "typical" in this and every other manifestation of the psyche. As in Goethe's theories, it is nothing other than the transmutations a living organism or human being undergoes that are fraught with significance. The fact that these transmutations of an individual psyche always take place according to a form peculiar to that individual accounts for characterological permanence, which is always permanence in change and the permanence of change according to a characteristic pattern.

These are the principal features of Klages's psychology that can be attributed to Goethe's morphologic-physiognomic conceptions; whether they suffice to define Goethe as a "founding father" of Klages's psychology is a judgment call and need not be answered definitively here. What is certain is that the significance Klages accords to Goethe in *Goethe als Seelenforscher* goes well beyond these methodological and conceptual affinities. Several themes that Klages follows in this work make this especially clear, above all the aforementioned belief that Goethe, as *individual,* exemplifies an ideal balance between the "adversaries" of *Geist* and *Seele,* intellect and soul. The entire structure of Klages's writings on Goethe is guided by this dualistic understanding of the poet-scientist and his proverbial "two souls": Goethe is for Klages a fundamentally androgynous being who fuses the "sensibility for reality" (that is, the intuitive capacity and the "passivity") characteristic of woman with the "factual sensibility" (that is, the ability to shape and lend something form, as well as the power of abstraction) typical of man (*Sämtliche Werke* 4: 564–65). These two poles of being, which represent "psyche" (or "soul") and "intellect" respectively in

Klages's system of thought, are then developed in the construction of his image of Goethe, whereby it is significant that the attributes aligned with the psyche have priority and are accordingly discussed first. Owing to his intuitive capacity, Goethe is anointed as the first "scientist of phenomena," or the first "phenomenologist," who seeks access to the inner essence via the medium of the phenomenal appearance (5: 232–33).[7] Moreover, Klages regards Goethe as the discoverer of the unconscious, or, more specifically, as the first person to appreciate the *priority* of the unconscious over the conscious mind, and Klages sees this trait in connection with Goethe's feminine "sensibility for reality" (5: 235–36). In an argument that can only be read as an ideological short circuit, Klages equates the unconscious with Goethe's concept of the demonic and portrays the representative of Weimar Classicism as a proto-Nietzschean thinker, claiming Goethe recognized "that in relation to perpetually unconscious *life,* consciousness can only be understood as a *disruption* of life" (5: 236). Here he makes Goethe out to be the forerunner of a philosophy of life that conforms to Klages's conceptual model, whereby consciousness—that is, abstract thought or the "intellect" in general—is regarded only as a "disruption" of the genuine mode of "life" instantiated in unconscious existence. This, in turn, is tied to Klages's belief that Goethe as characterologist acknowledged the "primacy of willing over knowing" (5: 249). Goethe thereby becomes not only a representative of the pessimistic Schopenhauerian worldview, a philosophy that profoundly shaped Klages's thought, but also the forebear of a principle, already articulated in the *Grundlagen der Charakterkunde,* that is of vital importance in Klages's characterological system: the primacy of the will as the fundamental determining element of the human being.

Klages associates above all Goethe's "creative nature," his "moral inclination," with the intellectual aspect of his personality, that is, with his so-called "masculine" side. This trait defines Goethe's creative capacity, the power that permits him to set certain limitations on the passive principle of intuition (*Sämtliche Werke* 5: 243–44). Yet Klages sees Goethe's intellectuality through the pessimistic lens of post-Schopenhauerian philosophy, which views intellectual "perspicacity" only "as the sign of a *fundamental* skeptic and doubter . . . , whose skepticism is not even surpassed by the likes of Montaigne, Larochefoucald, Schopenhauer, Stirner, Nietzsche" (5: 240–41). In other words, Klages projects onto Goethe the role of a pioneering advocate of a philosophy of life that conjures up the unconscious, the will, and skepticism toward abstract rationality as its defining principles. He is thereby portrayed as the champion of a life-affirming vitalism and an irrationalism that struggles against the lifelessness, abstraction, and mechanistic viewpoint of sterile rationality. Ultimately Klages's invocation of Goethe stands for a revitalization of the "soul," for its revolt against the oppressive, abstract-mechanical, positivistic intellect. This very same antirationalistic attitude—which glorifies intuition as a mode of prerational truth and opposes the modern, empiricistic, and scientistic understanding of natural science—also has a determining influence on the image of Goethe promoted by two further representatives of physiognomics in the time of the Weimar Republic: Oswald Spengler and Rudolf Kassner. However, these two additional stepchildren of Goethe develop this emphasis on the intuitive element of physiognomic thought in different and distinctive ways.

Oswald Spengler: Physiognomics as Anti-Systematics

"Anyone who tries to drum up 'predecessors' from the last twenty years seems not to have any inkling whatsoever that all these thoughts . . . were already contained in Goethe's prose writings and letters" (Spengler, as quoted in Koktanek xx). So wrote Oswald Spengler in a letter to Oskar Beck dated 18 December 1921, three years after the publication of the first volume of his primary work, *Der Untergang des Abendlandes: Umrisse einer Morphologie der Weltgeschichte* (The decline of the West: Outlines of a morphology of world history). Spengler penned these words in reaction to critics who sought influences on his thought in his immediate temporal and intellectual environment. In the "Foreword" to the revised first volume of *Untergang,* published in 1923, Spengler likewise acknowledged Goethe's significance for the development of his ideas (ix). Yet anyone who takes seriously the word "morphology," which appears in Spengler's subtitle, will already suspect that Spengler's ideas are based on Goethe's morphologic-physiognomic conceptions. Indeed, the critic Fritz Gräntz recognized this as early as 1921. In December of that year—and hence at the same time Spengler acknowledged Goethe as a precursor in his letter to Oskar Beck—Gräntz published an essay entitled "Spengler und Goethe" in which he designated Goethe's "living nature" as the "wellspring" out of which Spengler derived his ideas (325). Today it has become a scholarly truism that Spengler transferred Goethe's morphological conceptions from the domain of nature to that of cultural history. But the fact that, in the process, Spengler contributed to the affirmation of a physiognomic tradition that was increasingly being deployed in strategic defense of dubious political and ideological purposes has not yet been sufficiently acknowledged by scholars of intellectual and cultural history.[8]

"Physiognomik und Systematik" (Physiognomics and systematics) is the title of a subchapter in the first volume of *Untergang des Abendlandes* in which Spengler provides his reader with a kind of discourse on his method (125–52). Here Spengler sets his own procedure, called "physiognomics," apart from the "systematic" approach of the mechanistic sciences: "*the morphology of the mechanical world, of the world of spatial extension, a science that discovers and orders laws of nature and causal relations, is called systematics. The morphology of the organic world, of history and of life, of everything that bears within itself direction and destiny, is called physiognomics*" (135). Systematics and physiognomics are distinguished above all with regard to their object of analysis: while the former studies lifeless, static entities, the latter deals with living and organic beings or structures. Moreover, systematics attempts to discover eternal laws and causal relationships among its objects; physiognomics views the *Gestalt* of a dynamic being and "perceives" the metamorphoses this form undergoes (see *Untergang* 130). Instead of working according to principles of causality as does systematics, physiognomics functions on the basis of an analogic reasoning that is grounded in a symbolic connection between inner and outer, body and soul. Spengler expresses this fundamental physiognomic principle in his posthumously published collection of fragments, *Urfragen* (Primordial questions), when he writes: "The body forms itself from the inside out according to an idea—the *soul.* Its structure corresponds to that of the soul.

The soul is the idea of this structure. . . . The body is the *phenomenal* soul (as perceived by the senses in its becoming)" (162). Similar to Goethe, as well as to Klages, who followed Goethe in this respect, Spengler seeks the somatic expression of the soul in the process of dynamic becoming, in the metamorphosis of the body: for him, soul is "*that* which is unified in its becoming" (*Untergang* 386). Soul is, in short, Goethean *Gestalt,* "permanence in change." As was the case for Goethe, as well, the soul is an entelechy that originates in a certain "primordial image" or "primordial symbol"—both these concepts are derived semantically from Goethe's "primordial plant" or his "primordial phenomenon"—which determines and structures the metamorphoses the body undergoes. For Spengler, physiognomics attempts to track down this "primordial symbol," the deep structure of any particular cultural formation, on the basis of its phenomenological manifestations, striving subsequently to recreate it.

This interpretative procedure is based, on the one hand, on Goethe's theory of the symbol, and, on the other hand, on a conception of intuitive perception that likewise is derived from Goethe's scientific thought: "Everything that has *evolved,* everything that phenomenally occurs, is a symbol, is the expression of a soul. It wants to be viewed by the eye of the adept of human beings *[Menschenkenner]*; it does not want to be subjected to laws, it wants to be sensed in all its significance. And thus my investigation ascends to the ultimate and highest certainty: *All that is transitory is just a symbol*" (*Untergang* 136–37). The Goethean formulation, in which this passage culminates, becomes the guiding maxim that Spengler follows in the historical approach and methodology applied in *Der Untergang des Abendlandes.* Manifestations of the soul cannot be analyzed or examined, nor can they be systematically or mechanically explained; they can only be perceived intuitively and experienced. Spengler consciously returns here to an old theme of physiognomics: the innate talent of the physiognomic genius whose pronouncements cannot be explained rationally. He terms this talent "physiognomic tact," whereby the word "tact" indicates not only a particular kind of refined sensitivity, but also alludes to a rhythmic element. "*Physiognomic tact:* that is the decision of the *blood,* the knowledge of human nature extended into the past and the future, the innate eye for people and situations, for every event, for everything that was necessary" (611). Spengler's combination of the idea of a genius-like physiognomic intuition with the "blood and soil" rhetoric of German nationalism is especially ominous here. This nationalistic tone is in no way accidental; in his foreword to *Der Untergang des Abendlandes* Spengler explicitly claims to offer *"a German philosophy"* (ix), and he ultimately regards his own physiognomic method as the culmination of "Faustian" culture (209).

Similar to Klages, Spengler believes that the Goethean heritage of physiognomics is firmly anchored in the tradition of German *Lebensphilosophie,* the philosophy of life. One suspects that Wilhelm Dilthey (1833–1911) was the immediate transmitter of this image of Goethe, just as he also supplied the distinction between the factually based natural sciences and the hermeneutically oriented humanities, a distinction that was critical to the further development of German *Lebensphilosophie.* At any rate, Spengler, too, utilizes physiognomics strategically as a countercurrent to, and adversary of, the hyperrational intellect. He claims that the "skepticism of the West," which relativizes, and thereby places in question, the absolute knowledge arrived at by the mathematical, scientific approach, proceeds "physiognomically" (*Untergang* 64). In *Jahre der Entscheidung* (Years of decision, 1933) he describes this physiognomic skepticism as a "fundamental doubt about the meaning and value of theoretical contemplation, doubt about its ability to grasp anything critically and conceptually or achieve any practical end" (9). This leads to a valorization of "experience," of intuitive perception over rational cognition and theoretical reflection. In accordance with this, Spengler claims in *Der Untergang des Abendlandes:* "There is a difference—a difference that is rarely truly acknowledged—between *lived experience* and *abstract knowledge,* between the immediate certainty provided by the forms of intuition . . . , and the results of reasoned empiricism and experimental techniques" (75). In Spengler's theories Goethe functions as the model for this glorified intuition grounded in lived experience, a form of intuition with immediate access to "certainties" that completely escape the grasp of theoretical reason. Spengler cites Goethe's scientific studies as exemplary for this intuitive methodology, with which Spengler identifies his own physiognomic procedure: "what historiography *truly* is—namely, pure physiognomics—is nowhere as clearly in evidence as in the development of Goethe's studies of nature" (205). "Pure physiognomics" is the designation Spengler gives to this pre-rational intuitive perception, concretized in Goethe's natural-scientific method. In contrast to abstract, theoretical reason, which functions according to the laws of causality, this intuitive procedure fathoms at a glance, and on the basis of analogic thinking, the primordial image and truth of any phenomenon. Goethe thus becomes the exemplar of an essentially subjectivist mode of comprehension that—in spite of, or perhaps precisely *because of* its subjectivism—can lay claim to deciphering with absolute "certainty" particular facts that cannot be derived or verified by rational means. Spengler connects physiognomics as instinctual understanding with the power of the imagination and with fantasy (see *Urfragen* 195). Indeed, as early as 1904, in his study of Heraclitus, he associated this intuitive "orientation toward forms *[Gestalten]* and thoughts, as opposed to the abstract conclusions, concepts, and laws derived from them," with Goethe's theory of an "exact sensual imagination" ("Heraclitus" 1). Symbolism, analogy, *Gestalt,* intuitive apprehension, life, dynamism, idea, the primordial image: these are the basic concepts, borrowed from Goethe and modified to suit his purposes, that underpin the theoretical edifice of Spengler's physiognomics, a physiognomics that intuitively ferrets out trans-rational truth.

Rudolf Kassner: Unquantifiable Face

One of the dichotomies Spengler incorporates into his heuristic opposition between systematics and physiognomics is that between number and function. "In the number, as the *sign of consummate boundedness,* lies . . . the *essence* of everything that is real, that has evolved, is discerned and delimited at once" (*Untergang* 77). Number—that is, whatever is quantifiable—corresponds to existing things that are finite, complete, no longer evolving. Only what exists in stable form can be the object of knowledge and of causal-mechanical reasoning for Spengler, which automatically excludes all living things. Organic entities are always involved in the process of becoming and evolving; they are unbounded, incomplete, and therefore not quantifiable in terms of number. Only "function," understood as "pure relation" (101), can allude to the absoluteness of evolving life as something relative. Static, mathematical, absolute number is opposed to the dynamic function that is defined in terms of relationality. Just one year after the initial publication of the first volume of *Der Untergang des Abendlandes,* in 1919, the first physiognomic work by another significant modern German physiognomist and admirer of Goethe appeared: Rudolf Kassner's *Zahl und Gesicht* (Number and face), with an introduction entitled "Der Umriß einer universalen Physiognomik" (Outline of a universal physiognomics). As the title of Kassner's work demonstrates, his physiognomic worldview is predicated on a distinction between "number" and "face" that bears many similarities to Spengler's opposition of number and function.

Zahl und Gesicht begins dialectically with a fictitious dialogue between a biologist, the representative of number, and a physiognomist, the advocate of face. Like Spengler's systematist, Kassner's biologist seeks the "purpose" and "meaning" of finite, static objects (Kassner, *Sämtliche Werke* 3: 188). Such objects are subject to the law of identity, A = A, and can therefore be expressed in numerical relations. To the principle of identity the physiognomist opposes the hypothesis of the non-identical, of the fundamentally meaningful, of all that is dynamic and points beyond its own limited existence. Furthermore, he counters the principle of identity by postulating "the great paradox of every physiognomics," which states "that the human being only is the way he looks, because he does not look the way he is" (3: 192). Kassner thus seems to break with an essential principle of the entire physiognomic tradition: the identification of the external and the internal, the theory that the body is the expressive medium of the soul. But Kassner's physiognomic paradox does not, in fact, make such a radical break with this tradition; it simply problematizes the signifying relationship that obtains between the external and the internal realms. For Kassner, this relationship is no longer one of identity, as is the case, he believes, in every "superficial" physiognomic theory—for instance in Lavater (3: 197)—but rather one of non-identity. The analogical reasoning proposed by Goethe or Spengler is transmogrified here into the category of non-identity, which has the potential advantage of greater specificity. But unlike Spengler, Kassner does not so much define physiognomics as a specifiable position or a determinable method; he conceives it purely in terms of negation, as the dialectical antipode of identity. "Physiognomics is at play everywhere the law of identity is invalid, or better yet: where it does not arise, where we go beyond it. . . . It [the law of identity] constitutes the content of all logic and the cornerstone of mathematics. Everything that is built on mathematics and logic refers back to it: all science, all technology, etc." (3: 197). As in Klages's and Spengler's theories, physiognomic thought eludes all logic, systematics, mathematics, causality, even "science" as such. In other words, it transcends rational knowledge in toto. Kassner's physiognomist attempts to enlighten his interlocutor, the biologist, about the virtues of non-identity: "The more you lose the ability to apply, with total consciousness, the principle [of identity], the more intimately what we call significance will merge for you with form *[Gestalt]*" (3: 197). Here the Goethean themes in Kassner's physiognomics are already suggested: for Kassner, as for Goethe, physiognomics is a theory of form or *Gestalt,* which grasps, by means of an act of intuitive perception, a profound significance that could never be arrived at by following the path of logic and causality. But in the case of Kassner the pre-rational and intuitive element of physiognomic perception is exaggerated to the point of becoming anti-logical, even mystical: in the realm of Kassner's physiognomics, only the "universal unity of nature" *(All-Einheit der Natur)* is capable of functioning as a hypothesis that produces meaning and significance (3: 200; cf. 5: 10). Kassner sees this alogical, mystical element as essential to physiognomics. "Physiognomics is arational," he writes in the 1930 essay "Das Menschengesicht" (The human face), "insofar as the face—that is, what is objective, be it significant or insignificant—could not exist without the seer, or without the seer's subjectivity" (6: 266). Here the subjective element, which is inherent in physiognomic thought from the outset and which leads to Klages's and Spengler's glorification of intuitive reasoning, is radicalized and legitimized as wholly unrestrained speculation. With this move, physiognomics ultimately reverts back to the rhetoric of unfathomable "genius" and the effusive "fanaticism" that critics like Goethe and Lichtenberg so feverishly opposed in the works of Lavater. Where then are the concrete points of intersection between Kassner's radically subjectivist conception of physiognomy, which is elevated into the ethereal realm of the mystical and paradoxical, and Goethe's morphologic-physiognomic thought?

The criticism of measurement and of applying quantitative techniques in the study of organic entities can be attributed to Goethe: his diatribe against measurement as a procedure that kills all living things has already been cited (*Gedenkausgabe* 16: 841–42). Beyond this, in an aphorism from his *Maximen und Reflexionen,* he defines the mathematician as someone who is dependent "on the quantitative, . . . on everything that can be determined by number and measurement, and therefore to a certain degree on the externally perceptible universe" (9: 661). However, whatever is qualitative, divine, what is "absolutely immeasurable," is excluded by definition from the realm of the quantifiable and of number (9: 662). Kassner refers to this quasi-religious distinction when he juxtaposes number and face. In Kassner's physiognomic theory this religious perspective, which was so prominent in Lavater and was banned from physiognomics, or at least radically secularized in Goethe, Carus, Klages, and Spengler, enters the scene once more. This brings Kassner's physiognomic theory—despite his vehement attack on Lavater's approach and methods—back into proximity with Lavater's "fanatical" physiognomics.

When Kassner speaks of his physiognomic predecessors—which occurs seldom enough—it is almost always Goethe whom he mentions as a positive model. In a conversation with Alfons Clemens Kensik he states simply: "*Goethe* is the only one [among all the physiognomists] whom I accept entirely; his completely fragmentary and sporadic physiognomics is universal, all the others are sectarians" ("Gespräche" 220). Kassner is concerned, like Goethe, with an expansion of physiognomics into the universal—that is, with a physiognomics that can pass for a general theory of intuition. It is consistent with this extension, as well as with Goethe's remarks in his "Addendum" to Lavater's fragment "Von der Physiognomik überhaupt" (On physiognomics in general), when Kassner claims "that clothes reveal people to us, or that people incorporate and embrace their clothes, their tools, their household effects, their weapons" (*Sämtliche Werke* 4: 40). Indeed, the similarities in expression lead to the assumption that Kassner is alluding, consciously or unconsciously, to the arguments Goethe made in his "Addendum." But whenever Kassner refers directly and specifically to Goethe's significance for his physiognomics, he emphasizes the dynamic element in Goethe's physiognomic views, which also had such a profound influence on Klages and Spengler. In *Das physiognomische Weltbild* (The physiognomic worldview, 1930), for example, he describes Goethe's physiognomic works as a turning point in the history of physiognomics—a turn that leads directly to Kassner's own physiognomic conceptions: "It is not until the exceptional fragments on physiognomics that we have from Goethe that a turn becomes apparent, the turn from the rational or static attitude toward what we call the dynamic view, to a physiognomics of the animated human being like that advocated in my works" (4: 382). Kassner overlooks the fact that this turn was already initiated in Lichtenberg's criticism of Lavater, and that the lineage of those who champion a dynamic physiognomics extends from Hegel through to his contemporaries Klages and Spengler.

In *Zahl und Gesicht* Kassner attempts to discriminate in a similar way between "old" and "new" physiognomics, and in doing so he invokes Goethe's distinction between allegory and symbol. Here he maintains "that the old, static physiognomics is allegorical, whereas the new, dynamic one is symbolic," and he goes on to equate allegory with "identity" and symbol with "individuality" (*Sämtliche Werke* 3: 317). For Goethe "genuine symbolism" was at work "where the particular represents the universal, not as a dream or shadow, but as a living, momentary revelation of the inscrutable" (*Gedenkausgabe* 9: 532). Kassner conceives of his physiognomic hermeneutics in exactly this sense, as the grasping of a symbolic meaning that, in a momentary flash, illuminates or reveals something universal in the somatic particularity of a given individual. But the motor behind this symbolic illumination is the imagination of the interpreter, of the physiognomic observer himself. The imagination is for Kassner the glue, as it were, that fuses the internal and external into an inseparable unity: "for what is significant is that the internal cannot simply be connected with the external (without being instituted by decree or through magic), but rather that the imagination *[Einbildungskraft]* must step between them so that this union can take place and be valid" (*Sämtliche Werke* 4: 425). In the imagination—which he at times also equates with the concept of fantasy (*Phantasie;* see 6: 425)—Kassner discovers the mysterious link that can bridge the gap between internal and the external. And yet the subjectivist dimension of this theory remains somewhat problematic; for if it is only the observer's imagination that is important, then nothing stands in the way of a completely speculative projection of the observer's ideas onto the human being under examination. We are then no longer dealing with the "speaking body"—to use the terminology suggested by a contemporary philosopher (Küchenhoff 169)—but rather with the "inscribed body," which is determined and defined externally in the very act in which it is placed under physiognomic scrutiny.

This problem is never completely resolved in Kassner's physiognomics. The theory that is supposed to serve this end is once again borrowed from Goethe. In "Bildung und Umbildung organischer Naturen," as we have seen, Goethe argues that the thought and vocabulary of the morphologist must be just as dynamic and fluid as the constantly transforming object he or she studies. This mimesis of what is fundamentally mobile demands a dialectical rapprochement of the observing subject with the observed object, a rapprochement in which the metamorphoses of the object are more or less imitated by the investigative subject. Kassner would also like to see the discovery of physiognomic significance structured according to just such a dialectic. For him this dialectic is concretized in the multifaceted significance of the word *Gesicht,* meaning "face" or "countenance," which functions as a cipher for his entire physiognomic worldview. In a note to *Zahl und Gesicht* he describes the significance of this word for his physiognomic theory: "Because human beings only arrive at content by means of intuitive perception, by means of *Gesicht* (vision), physiognomics must remain something thoroughly irrational. This is why a human *Gesicht* (visage, figure) cannot be dissolved, cannot be fixed—in contrast to a mask—but rather is something mobile, something that can only be interpreted in motion, something infinite. . . . We should note the ambiguity of the word *Gesicht,* as something that both observes and is observed" (*Sämtliche Werke* 3: 346). The face, *Gesicht,* represents for Kassner not only "visage" in the ordinary sense, but also sight and vision; the word thus circumscribes for him all the tensions and discrepancies inherent in the act of viewing a living, dynamic being. In his physiognomic worldview there is—ideally—no abyss between the subject and the object. Indeed, there is no subject—object relation in the classic sense, but only the irrational, infinite, paradoxical unity of the *Gesicht,* the face as visage and vision. It is typical of Kassner's style of argumentation that he falls back on word plays when explanations are in order. Perhaps this dialectic of the *Gesicht* could be characterized as a kind of "empathy," which human imagination employs in order to approach the individuality of another living entity. But this must remain hermeneutical speculation, since Kassner refuses to dissolve the mysterious, paradoxical, and purely evocative elements associated with the concept of *Gesicht.*

Although Kassner positions *Gesicht* and, accordingly, his physiognomic paradox, in relation to human individuality, this should not be taken to imply that individuality is a positive term in his worldview. Already Goethe, in his fragments on comparative anatomy, voiced his opposition to the use of the concept of individuality in the study of organic beings: "The concept of individuality hinders the recognition of organic beings. It is a trivial concept" (*Gedenkausgabe* 17: 421). Goethe was particularly interested in the typical, understood as the reference to the "type," to the common "idea" of a species. Kassner shares with Goethe this preference for the type, but with the significant difference that whereas for Goethe this concept only refers to an idea, or an archetype in the Platonic sense, for Kassner the word "type" still has a concrete meaning and application. Types represent for Kassner a lost human ideal that has been suppressed due to the obsession with individuality. He makes this clear in a passage from his *Grundlagen der Physiognomik* (Fundamentals of physiognomics; 1922), in which he glorifies distinct types as the building blocks of a strong nation.

> The richer a society, a race, a Volk, an age is in types, the more unequivocal human beings are: they are deeper, more decided and decisive in their actions and aptitudes. The wealth of types defines their distinctness. And the more distinct the types, the more the actions of

> a Volk are also a form of knowledge, the expression of an inner clarity. To strip a Volk of this potential to form types is to turn it into a mass, to emasculate it. Such a Volk will also no longer produce rulers from its own ranks and will therefore remain subjected to foreign rulers. With this assertion I merely want to point to the fact that types and masters belong together, the ability to form types constitutes the ability to attain mastery. (*Sämtliche Werke* 4: 39)

The formation or existence of types promotes "clarity," "distinctness," and "mastery" of one people over others. Individuals, by contrast, are ambiguous, unstable, unclear, and threaten a people with debasement to a faceless mass that lacks an identifiable unity. Kassner is aware of the coherence of this view with fascist thought. In *Das physiognomische Weltbild* he writes the following about the desire for the formation of types among the fascist ideologues: "It appears to us as if fascism represents an attempt—a very violent one—to try to reach new virtues of typology by progressing from the actor to the personality and thereby to a new world of types" (4: 493). Yet Kassner believes that this attempt must fail because "the available material is no longer suitable to fend off, as it were, the victory of all-encompassing mediocrity" (4: 493). Here Kassner expresses a potent cultural pessimism, one that envisions no possibility for salvation from the curse of individualism, not even in the radical "solutions" proposed by German fascism. With this Kassner articulates an important theoretical strand of modern German physiognomics that radically diverges from the views of Goethe, the eternal optimist. This cultural pessimism permeates the intellectual skepticism and the critique of modernity voiced by Klages and Spengler, and it extends back, via Schopenhauer, to the attack on human arbitrariness that forms the central motivation of Lavater's physiognomics.[9] Ultimately it is this embeddedness in a worldview steeped in a profound cultural pessimism that distinguishes the physiognomic theories of Goethe's modern stepchildren most poignantly from the views of Goethe himself, the putative founding father of their physiognomic conceptions.

Concluding Intellectual-Historical Remarks

I would like to close this schematic analysis of the points of intersection between Goethe's morphologic-physiognomic views and the theories of Carus, Klages, Spengler, and Kassner with a few general intellectual-historical remarks. The physiognomic dispute that raged between Lavater and Lichtenberg in the 1770s does not by any means sound the death knell for German physiognomic thought, nor does it introduce a decisive break in the German physiognomic tradition. Nonetheless, Goethe channels German physiognomic theory into new directions. Above all, like Lichtenberg and Hegel before him, Goethe refutes the static, materialistic approach of Lavater, which is grounded in a logic of identity. This provides at least a partial explanation for the "Sonderweg," the special path, followed by modern German physiognomics (Schmölders, *Das Vorurteil im Leib* 16). While in the Romance countries—one thinks, for example, of Cesare Lombroso (1835–1909), Guillaume Duchenne (1806–1875), and Alphonse Bertillon (1853–1914)—and in the Anglo-Saxon world—Charles Bell (1763–1820), Charles Darwin (1809–1882), and Francis Galton (1822–1911), for example—physiognomics clearly pursues a materialist course, this direction remains relatively underdeveloped in the German-speaking world, despite the broad popularity of Lavater's work and of Gall's phrenology. Only Carus ventures down this path, and he does so, ironically, while invoking Goethe as his exemplar. In the early twentieth century the German theoreticians of race will take up this materialistic path with a vengeance, and the theories of Carus provide them with a link to Goethe's morphological studies that will lend their theories the veneer of scientific legitimation. Independent of this, the vitalistic physiognomics that emerges out of the marriage of physiognomics and German *Lebensphilosophie* also traces its descent from Goethe. Taking as its starting point Goethe's critique of analytical rationality and his valorization of intuitive perception, this strain of physiognomics glorifies the irrational certainty of the intuitive soul and debases the cerebrality of the intellect, finally culminating with Kassner in an unbridled subjectivistic mysticism. This line of physiognomic thought is steeped in a cultural pessimism that was completely foreign to its "foundling" father Goethe. In the Germany of the Weimar Republic, these two physiognomic lineages complement each other at certain critical junctures—for example, in their valorization of pre-rational and subjective judgments. Only the fusion and reciprocal promotion of these two distinct physiognomic worldviews in the time between the two World Wars explains the preeminence and popularity of physiognomics among German thinkers and writers at this time. Significantly, the linchpin of this fusion, their common point of intersection, is their purported derivation from Goethe. Thus the pre-fascist, often proto-fascist renaissance of modern German physiognomics can ultimately be traced back to an irony in the reception of Goethe and his scientific theories: the unwilling "foundling father" of these morphological doctrines is anointed as the vital founding father of modern German physiognomics, an act that breathes new life and intellectual vitality into an otherwise discredited intellectual pursuit.

5

The Emergence of the "Physiognomic Worldview" in Weimar Germany

Oswald Spengler and Rudolf Kassner

The Physiognomic Boom in Weimar Germany

The cultural atmosphere in German-speaking Europe in the early decades of the twentieth century is marked by an unusual and seldom recognized intellectual-historical constellation. Taking a cue from Rudolf Kassner (1873–1959), we can call this constellation, for lack of a better term, the "physiognomic worldview." It was under this title, *Das physiognomische Weltbild,* that in 1930 Kassner published one of the many treatises on physiognomics that constitute a major segment of his collected works. The relevance of the phrase "physiognomic worldview" to describe a marked intellectual attitude is suggested by the truly phenomenal resurgence of physiognomic theories in diverse yet discrete domains across the German intellectual landscape during this period.[1] In the realm of psychology, Ludwig Klages (1872–1956) championed a brand of characterology and a theory of expression *(Ausdruckskunde)* that presented a physiognomically based alternative to Freudian archaeologies of the individual. Instead of relying on the interpretation of dreams and other deep-level psychic material, Klages's psychological analyses were based on empirical evidence such as body structure, gestures or facial expressions, and handwriting. However, the complexity of his thought and the difficulty of his language, especially his sometimes willful and overly abstract terminology, prevented Klages's thought from extending very far beyond narrow academic and scholarly circles.[2] Simultaneous with the emergence of Klages's work, physiognomic theories were being resuscitated in other scholarly disciplines as well. In the realm of medical diagnostics, for example,

Ernst Kretschmer (1888–1964) tied physiognomic body types to predispositions for certain mental illnesses. (See Fig. 22 in chapter 4) Kretschmer's groundbreaking and widely influential book *Körperbau und Charakter* (Physique and character), which first appeared in 1922, is still published today and has achieved the status of a scholarly classic. In the area of film studies, Béla Balázs, under the influence of the prominent role facial expression and gesture played as a communicative dimension of silent film, theorized the importance of physiognomics for the emerging art of cinema in his 1924 book *Der sichtbare Mensch oder Die Kultur des Films* (The visible human being, or The culture of film).[3] Most notable and perhaps most infamous is the role physiognomic theories played in the racial anthropology of the proto-fascist thinker Hans F. K. Günther (1891–1968), also known as "Rassen-Günther," or "Race-Günther." One of the earliest and most articulate advocates of the Nordic Movement in Germany, Günther practiced a rather crude form of materialist physiognomics that aligned certain intellectual, cultural, and spiritual traits with specific physical features such as blue eyes, blonde hair, skull form, and the shape of the nose. These pseudo-scientific banalities, as we know, found in the Nazi movement the fertile soil necessary for their ideological incubation. Finally one thinks of Ludwig Ferdinand Clauss (1892–1974), who represents a kind of disciplinary crossbreeding between Klages's *Seelenkunde* and Günther's racial ethnology. A student of the phenomenological philosopher Edmund Husserl (1859–1938), Clauss sought to develop the discipline of *Rassenseelenkunde,* or racial psychology. His aim was to apply Husserl's phenomenological method to the discrimination of racial types: as a result, Husserlian *Wesenserschauung,* the perception of essence, was tainted by the ideas of racial typologies so prevalent in German-speaking Europe at this time. (Fig. 24) The works of Günther and Clauss fueled an upsurge of popularizing physiognomic typologies with explicit or implicit racial overtones that continued through to the end of the Second World War. (Fig. 25) Surprisingly, this tendency spilled over into the postwar years, as well.[4]

This list presents only the most prominent representatives of the physiognomic revival of the period; one can supplement it with myriad other names of more obscure figures, people

Fig. 24. Dust jacket, Ludwig Ferdinand Clauss, *Rasse und Seele*, 1937.

such as Robert Burger-Villingen (b. 1865), Wilhelm Böhle, Norbert Glas, Willy Hellpach (1877–1955), Leo Herland, Walther Jaensch (b. 1889), Otto Kroh, Hermann Krukenberg (1863–1935), Fritz Lange, Philipp Lersch (1898–1972), Friedrich Märker (b. 1893), Karl Noghe, Bruno Petermann (1898–1941), Ottmar Rutz (b. 1881), Bruno K. Schultz (1892–1942) . . . and the list could go on. What is perhaps most fascinating about physiognomics in this period is its wide-ranging, truly multi-disciplinary intellectual spread.[5] Several intellectual-historical threads intertwine in the early decades of the twentieth century in Germany and substantially nourish this physiognomic renaissance. One of these is the tradition of German *Lebensphilosophie,* the philosophy of life, first propounded by Wilhelm Dilthey (1833–1911), but lent

Fig. 25. Caricature of Jewish physiognomy, from Ernst Rittershaus, *Die Rassenseele des deutschen Volkes,* 1937. (Courtesy of the Hessische Landesbibliothek, Darmstadt)

philosophical resonance by the works of the young Friedrich Nietzsche (1844–1900). *Lebensphilosophie* valorized instinctual, pre-rational forms of understanding over abstract, reasoned thought, and it opposed to the positivistic, quantifying methodology of the natural sciences what it called the "interpretive" method of the human sciences, or the sciences of the mind *(Geisteswissenschaften).* A second line unifying diverse physiognomic theoreticians is the natural scientific thought of Johann Wolfgang von Goethe, who, as we saw in the previous chapter, stands as a kind of spiritual godfather for many of the prominent physiognomists of the Weimar period—including Spengler and Kassner. Central here are Goethe's morphological studies, which came to represent a kind of ideal fusion between intuitive, imaginative insight and empirical evidence: a perfect marriage, if you will, between idealist and materialist modes of science. A third feature of physiognomic theories of this period—and one that seems to stand in stark contrast to their Goethean inheritance—is their tendency to absorb and reflect the virulent antimodernism and cultural pessimism so prevalent in German-speaking Europe in the early decades of the century.

Because its roots spread so diversely throughout the cultural soil of Weimar Germany, physiognomics was singularly well adapted to thrive even in this chilly, often chilling, intellectual climate. Indeed, physiognomics takes on the character of a super-discipline. It is hypostatized as a universal theory of knowledge, perception, and instinctual understanding that presents a powerful counter-model to the Enlightenment narrative of a rationally endowed, historically progressive humanity. I will cite just one example of this universalization of physiognomic insight as a fundamental sub- or pre-rational—hence purportedly originary—mode of comprehension. It is drawn from Heinz Werner's *Einführung in die Entwicklungspsychologie* (Introduction to developmental psychology), first published in 1926.

> Only certain objects of knowledge are physiognomically accessible to cultured human beings of today: the faces and bodies of human beings themselves. But we should never forget that this kind of experience, restricted today to a tiny part of the objective world, grows out of an originary mode of comprehension in which the entire world was expressively, facially alive. The primordial world is given as a physiognomic phenomenon; and this is true not because of some anthropomorphic animation of nature, because of an analogical transference of living character onto a lifeless environment, but rather because the physiognomic gaze is the truly primordial manner of perception as such, in which a distinction between lifeless and living world has not yet been drawn. (45–46)

This passage evokes several motifs typical for the conception of physiognomics in German-speaking Europe in the interwar period. Fundamental here is Werner's assertion that physiognomics is based not on anthropomorphic projections, but that instead it constitutes a fundamental mode of human intuition. As such, it is endemic to all human beings, a claim that arises in various forms throughout the writings on physiognomics of all ages. Lavater, for example, appealed to the human being's reliance on physiognomic judgments in practical matters such as the selection of fruits, the purchase of commodities, or the choice of friends, and his deliberations culminated in the statement that all of nature is structured around physiognomic relations (*Physiognomische Fragmente* 1: 47–49). Similarly, Carus cited the half-conscious physiognomic judgments of primitive peoples as proof for the universality and validity of physiognomic perception (*Symbolik* 3–4). But Heinz Werner's premise that physiognomics is *the* primordial mode of human perception is formulated in a far more apodictic and comprehensive manner than the claims made by Lavater and Carus. Werner's assertion that "physiognomic perception" represents an originary, instinctual, and universal manner of seeing is typical of the physiognomic worldview of this period. Equally important, however, is his implicit critique of contemporary civilized human beings for their diminished or limited physiognomic faculty when compared to that of primitive peoples. This nuance positions Werner's arguments in the antimodernist, anti-civilizationist mythos of Weimar intellectuals. This belief is closely tied to a prominent cultural-ideological program: If the hyper-rationality of modern "civilized" human beings represents a developmental regression from the omnipresence of intuitive perception characteristic of primitive peoples, then the cultivation of physiognomics becomes one of the primary avenues by which modern human beings can re-attain this valorized pre-rational intuition. This positive evaluation of physiognomics both plays into, and plays out, one of the central themes of German *Lebensphilosophie:* the belief that the dynamism of vital life-structures resists comprehension by means of abstract rationalistic constructs and reflective understanding and must hence be approached by a descriptive, interpretive, and intuitive mode of perception. This stress on intuitive knowledge is one of the most prominent themes in the physiognomic literature of this period. Indeed, it is no exaggeration to maintain that in the interwar years physiognomic thought becomes a kind of standard bearer or universally valid test case for the superiority of intuitive over rational forms of cognition.

Physiognomics and Cultural Morphology in Oswald Spengler's *Untergang des Abendlandes*

These two motifs, the "decadence" of twentieth-century civilized Europeans, and the expedience of intuitive perception in comparison with abstract, systematic knowledge, figure prominently in the "cultural morphology" Oswald Spengler presents in *Der Untergang des Abendlandes* (The decline of the West). It is no coincidence that Spengler explicitly identifies the historical methodology he pursues in this treatise with physiognomic practice, contrasting it with systematic, rational procedures (*Untergang* 135). The systematic procedure Spengler identifies with the natural sciences, which deal with mechanical laws governing objects in space. These laws, Spengler claims, are structured according to causal relations, and in this sense systematics is a mode of cognition that relies on causality. Physiognomic methodology, by contrast, deals with living organisms that develop out of their own center over time. As vital structures, these organisms bear their own teleology, their own "destiny," within them; they are entelechies that cannot be adequately comprehended by subjecting them to the external laws of nature or by viewing them in terms of causal factors. In Spengler's definition, then, physiognomics is restricted to the world of becoming, of emerging, constantly changing entities that stand over against the static, "lifeless" matter that is the object of scientific thought per se. Its pertinence for the understanding of dynamic entities that change over time is what makes the physiognomic method germane for Spengler as a model for historical understanding. "The consummate system of a mechanical view of nature," Spengler categorically remarks, "is, however, not physiognomics, but rather *system,* that is, pure spatial extension, ordered logically and quantitatively; nothing living, but rather something that has become and is lifeless" (498). Systematics is concerned with dead objects in space to which logic and mathematical order are appropriate, physiognomics with living entities whose medium is time, history. In this sense his distinction between systematics and physiognomics is consistent with Wilhelm Dilthey's segregation of the mode of comprehension practiced in the natural sciences from the hermeneutic method appropriate to the human and historical sciences.[6] Indeed, Dilthey's famous statement "Die Natur erklären wir, das Seelenleben verstehen wir,"—"We explain nature, but we understand the life of the soul" (144)—seems to inform Spengler's opposition between systematics and physiognomics. Spengler alludes to Dilthey's terminology in the introduction to *Untergang des Abendlandes* when he writes: "The means for comprehending *[erkennen]* lifeless forms is mathematical law. The means for understanding *[verstehen]* living forms is analogy" (4). This discrimination between rational explanation and descriptive-analogical understanding stands as the watchword that legitimates a wide variety of physiognomic theories throughout this period.

Spengler's association of physiognomics with nonscientific, nonrational, or—better, perhaps—pre-rational thought stands in a complex relationship of continuity and discontinuity with the German physiognomic tradition from Lavater to Carus. Physiognomic judgment was perennially viewed as a form of understanding that was illogical, intuitive, and nonscientific; thus physiognomics, especially in the pre-Lavaterian tradition, was closely associated with astrology, prophecy, chiromancy, and other forms of divination. Insofar as Spengler views his physiognomic history as predictive and prophetic (*Untergang* 3), he re-invokes the divinatory aspect of traditional physiognomics. What is new in Spengler's understanding, however, is the unfettered glorification of this intuitive and pre-rational moment. Whereas Lavater, for example, went to great lengths to free physiognomics from this association with nonrational, non-systematizable forms of divination and avidly sought to found physiognomics as a respectable—that is, positivistic and empirical—scientific discipline, Spengler valorizes this nonrational moment as a creative, authentic sensibility that he terms "physiognomic tact" (611).

Although he consciously distanced his own physiognomic theories from those of Lavater, Carl Gustav Carus's *Symbolik der menschlichen Gestalt* in many ways represents the fulfillment of Lavater's project for a scientific physiognomics. Objecting to Lavater's reliance on his "visionary gaze" *(Seherblick),* Carus insisted that he would approach physiognomics in a strictly scientific manner, applying a method that relied on anatomical measurement and systematic comparison. He called this procedure a *"scientific symbolics"* (*Symbolik* 5). For Spengler, the very notion of a scientific symbolism would be impossibly contradictory. While he subscribes to the belief in the symbolic character of the life world and sees his physiognomic world history as a comprehensive symbolism, a "metaphysics for which *everything,* no matter what it is, possesses the significance of a *symbol*" (*Untergang* 211), he specifically opposes this physiognomic understanding to the scientific conception of the world. In his critique of physiognomics and phrenology Hegel, as we have seen, had already pointed to the paradox that identifying the individuality of any living, developing creature with the immutable structure of its physical being, with its skull, is to treat it as dead matter. This paradox inheres in Carus's attempt to define the symbolic significance of human individuals on the basis of anatomical or cranioscopic measurements.

Spengler's physiognomic theory stands in strict opposition to the anatomical and scientific turn German physiognomic thought took with Carus. Like Hegel before him, Spengler protests against the application of quantitative methodologies in the treatment of living things. He unequivocally writes: "Only lifeless things—and living things only insofar as one ignores their vital substance—can be counted, measured, dissected" (*Untergang* 128). This conception of physiognomics as a form of understanding that is diametrically opposed to mathematics, number, and all forms of quantification is one of the primary innovative features of Spengler's theory. It is an aspect shared with the physiognomic program of Spengler's Austrian contemporary, Rudolf Kassner. In Spengler's case this resistance to quantification derives from his sense that living, organic beings exist in a constant state of change and development: they are dynamic entities and hence can only be reduced to static structures at the price of stripping them of all vitality, treating them, as Spengler says, as lifeless things. Here again Spengler stands in stark contrast to the physiognomic tradition initiated by Lavater. Lavater's identification of physiognomics with the a priori given, stable, and static human features leads directly to Franz Josef Gall's (1758–1828) phrenological theories and ultimately to the racial anthropologies of the early twentieth century, which likewise stress the unalterable and naturally or genetically given—hence untranscendable—features that define and condition every human being. Spengler is adamant about his disagreements with this materialistic bias in much of the racial theory of his age. In a posthumously published note he unequivocally remarks: "*Race:* The fundamental error from which all racial research still suffers today is the error of the time that gave birth to it, of the middle of the nineteenth century: materialism. Racial research took as its point of departure the crassly material, what one could see and touch; instead of viewing this materiality as expression, as a symbol in the Goethean sense, it saw it as the essence of what it investigated and what it was looking for" (*Frühzeit der Weltgeschichte* 131). Spengler was decidedly wrong in identifying contemporary racial theory solely with this materialistic bias. To do so is to ignore an influential branch of proto-fascist racial theory, the racial psychology founded by Ludwig Ferdinand Clauss. Nonetheless, Spenglerian physiognomics breaks with the materialist line of physiognomic thought represented by Lavater, Gall, and Carus because Spengler's worldview is grounded in an entirely different conception of the human being and the life world in general. For Lavater, character is divinely ordained and hence exists as given in nature, prior to all the conscious acts and activities of the individual. Spengler, by contrast, defines the character of any living creature as the sum of its activities, in terms of a dynamic process of transformation and self-transformation over time. "We measure what a human being is," he apodictically maintains, "by its *activity,* which can be directed both inwardly and outwardly; and we evaluate all individual intentions, reasons, energies, convictions, habits solely on the basis of this direction. We designate this aspect with the word *character*" (*Untergang* 402). For Spengler, as for Hegel, character is not a predetermined, static construct, but rather a dynamic process of interaction with both the external and the internal world. Activity, not passive stasis, is the operative term in this conception, which views the human being as an actor on the stage of history, one who can intervene both in the dramatic events and in the substance of his or her own being, his or her own "character." To be a living creature, a vital being, is, in short, to transform oneself and the world, and character resides solely in the consistent *direction* this transformation takes.

If Spengler's physiognomic theory departs from Carus's "scientific symbolism" insofar as it denies the possibility of codifying symbolic relations in a quantitative, scientific system, it is consistent with Carus's theories to the extent that it stresses the symbolic nature of physiognomic expression. However, Carus's and Spengler's conceptions of the symbol are ultimately quite distinct, even though they derive in part from the same source, namely from Goethe. Carus, who was strongly influenced by the philosophy of nature propagated by his mentor, the

Romantic philosopher Friedrich Wilhelm Joseph Schelling (1775–1854), viewed the human soul as a divine "idea," which then received its material realization in the human body. "The human being in his wondrous anatomical edifice," Carus states in the opening pages of his *Symbolik der menschlichen Gestalt,* "is *the first creation of the soul,* or rather of the idea . . . ; we therefore justifiably view this edifice as the highest sign, as *the most characteristic symbol of this idea*" (3). If the human body is the symbol of the soul it houses, or the perfect expression of the idea it embodies, then the goal of Carus's physiognomics is to develop an anatomical hermeneutics that reverses this creative process, moving not from idea to body, but from body back to its formative idea. Following Goethe's definition of the symbol, Carus interprets the body-soul duality as the revelation of the universal (the "idea") in the particular (the body). "True symbolics," Goethe noted in his *Maximen und Reflexionen,* "exists where the particular represents the universal, not as a dream or shadow, but as a vital-momentary revelation of the inscrutable" (*Gedenkausgabe* 9: 532).[7]

Spengler, too, as he himself admits, has a Goethean conception of the symbol in mind when he develops the significance of symbolic representation for his cultural morphology: "Everything that has *evolved,*" he maintains, "everything that phenomenally occurs, is the expression of a soul. It does not want to be subjected to laws, it wants to be sensed in all its significance. And thus my investigation ascends to the ultimate certainty: *All that is transitory is just a symbol*" (*Untergang* 137). This ultimate recognition, of course, is taken from the closing words of Goethe's *Faust.* Although Carus and Spengler both insist on the centrality of symbolic relations, their conceptions of the symbol are distinct on three counts. First, Carus's notion of the symbol represses the dynamic, vitalistic aspect that is inherent in the Goethean conception, whereas Spengler explicitly plays up this dimension. In this respect Carus's debt to his teacher Schelling becomes apparent. The second distinction is also related to Carus's reliance on Schelling: his notion of the symbol still has the overtones of a religious conception in which the soul represents a *divine* idea, the idea of the creator, which makes itself manifest in the human body. Spengler's "soul," by contrast, is wholly secularized: it is a human creation; its expressions are not divinely instituted signs, but rather human—that is, *cultural*—products. This is closely related to the third point: Spengler's insistence on the *historical* nature of these expressions of the human soul. That is what he implies when he insists that these expressions have *"evolved" (geworden),* have "emerged," have been created, and are subject to the element of time. This historical dimension is also evoked in the quotation from Goethe's *Faust* in which the passage culminates: everything *transitory* is a symbol. Here again we perceive the dynamism inherent in Spengler's conception of the cultural world; it contrasts starkly with the static world of "Being" evident in Carus's worldview: because of its static, stable nature the human body can be subjected to measurement and mathematical quantification. For Spengler, on the other hand, not only the human body, but all cultural products, dynamic and vital by their very nature, resist this reduction to static spatial objects.

Gesetz, or "natural law," is one of Spengler's key terms. It is burdened with the negative connotations of abstract knowledge, scientific thinking, and empirical evidence, all of which stand for him in opposition to the "physiognomic" method of the cultural historian. Spengler calls his preferred mode of understanding *Erleben,* "lived experience"—one of the central terms of Diltheyan *Lebensphilosophie*—and he opposes it, in this regard again similar to Dilthey, to *Erkennen,* or "abstract knowing." "There is a difference—a difference that is rarely truly acknowledged—between *lived experience* and *abstract knowledge,* between the immediate certainty provided by the forms of intuition, and the results of reasoned empiricism and experimental techniques. In the first instance simile, image, symbol are the means of communication, in the latter instance formula, law, schematic tables" (*Untergang* 75). What is striking about Spengler's program is the strict consistency between theory and methodology: if the objects of the historico-cultural world are distinct from those of the natural world, they must also be subject to a mode of understanding appropriate to their own constitution, and the cultural historian, in turn, must communicate his derived insights by means of tools appropriate to this mode of understanding. One gains access to historical, dynamic cultural expressions by means of lived experience and communicates the "certainty" of this experience through similes, images, symbols. One approaches static natural phenomena with "reasoned empiricism and experimental techniques" and communicates the results of this abstract understanding in formulas, laws, and schematic tables. The former is "physiognomic" understanding, the latter "systematic." By and large, Spengler's methodology and language are informed by this distinction; only when he succumbs to the drive to organize the vast material of world history into schematic tables does he fall back into "systematic" portrayal.[8] This methodological regression stems from a demand placed upon Spengler by his own cyclical theory of history, his argument that each culture is a windowless monad that passes through the same structural phases. This is, to be sure, the most controversial aspect of Spengler's view of history, and perhaps its least influential tenet. On the other hand, Spengler's insistence on the aptness of an intuitive, experiential, "physiognomic" approach to historical phenomena, and his translation of this theory into his own methodological practice, is arguably the most innovative, significant, and influential aspect of his cultural morphology.

One of the most powerful dimensions of Spengler's project in *Untergang des Abendlandes* is his ability to appropriate the central theses of German *Lebensphilosophie*—dynamism, vitalism, pre-rational intuitiveness, lived experience—and actualize them for his own historical theory. He accomplishes this primarily by identifying them with the mode of perception and thought common to physiognomic experience and by subsuming them under what he broadly defines as a physiognomic mode of understanding. More important, perhaps, is that Spengler then transfers this conception of physiognomic perception and understanding to the study of history.

> The visible foreground of all history has the same significance as the external appearance of the human being, such as physique, facial expression, posture, gait; not what is spoken, but the speaking; not what is written, but the handwriting. All of this is present for an adept of human beings *[Menschenkenner]*. The body with all its effects, everything that is delimited, has evolved, is *transitory:* all of this is an expression of the soul. But to be a true adept of human beings also

> means to be adept at understanding those large-scale human organisms that I call cultures, to grasp their facial expression, their language, their actions, just as one grasps those of an individual human being. (*Untergang* 136)

Just as the experienced physiognomist intuitively recognizes the character of an individual on the basis of body, facial expression, handwriting, and so on, the cultural historian intuits the essence of a particular cultural phenomenon on the basis of its expressions, its actions, its formal characteristics. This transference of the principles of physiognomic expression to the understanding of history and culture is made possible by the presupposition, expressed in this passage, that cultural constructs are themselves human organisms—that is, human expressions that exist in a relationship of physiognomic meaningfulness with the human community that produces them. They are subconsciously guided by what Spengler calls their *Ursymbol,* their "primordial symbol," the "soul," the organizing idea of their cultural community (226–27). What is valid for the individual, in short, is also valid for any tightly woven cultural community.

> Each of our emotions expresses itself, every emotion of another person makes an impression, and thus everything of which we are conscious, regardless of the form it takes, . . . has for us a profound meaning; and the sole and utmost means for making this incomprehensible element comprehensible resides in a kind of metaphysics for which *everything,* regardless of what it is, bears the meaning of a *symbol.* A symbol is a feature of reality that signifies something with immediate inherent certainty to discerning human beings, something that cannot be communicated in rational terms. (210–11)

The legibility of human expressions theorized by physiognomics is inflated here into a vast metaphysics of the symbolic significance of human cultures. For Theodor Adorno it is precisely this Spenglerian mythology of the cultural soul that anticipates the *völkisch* ideology of the Third Reich. According to Adorno, Spengler is guilty of "mythologizing cultural souls, which leads to the relativistic delusion that reason is exhausted in the collective-psychological expressions of individual national groups. From here it is only a small step to the *völkisch*-political anthropologies that flourish in the Third Reich" ("Wird Spengler recht behalten?" 147). Adorno's association of the metaphysical and irrational element in Spengler's physiognomics of cultural expression with the racial mania of Nazi ideology is perhaps somewhat exaggerated. Important for the current argument, however, is the recognition that traditional physiognomics served as an important model for Spengler because it exemplified precisely that intuitive, experiential understanding of the human world that he advocates as the proper stance of the cultural historian. Physiognomics becomes for Spengler a generalized worldview, a mode of experience based on the rationally unfathomable signifying power of the symbol. Physiognomic experience represents a way of comprehending the incomprehensible; the appeal to physiognomics as a traditionally recognized domain in which this intuitive understanding is effectively practiced serves to corroborate Spengler's arguments for the validity of this pre-rational manner of comprehension.

Spengler constantly insists on the absolute "certainty" *(Gewißheit)* of these intuitive physiognomic judgments; he thereby defends these insights against the potential criticism that they are wholly arbitrary or subjective. Lavater, too, insisted, of course, on the absolute truth of his physiognomic intuitions; and he legitimated the exclusiveness of his ability to accurately decipher character with the claim that physiognomic abilities are based on a special and rare talent (*Physiognomische Fragmente* 1: 170). Spengler repeats this elitist, ultimately self-aggrandizing view when he writes: "One can be taught the facility to understand nature, but the adept of history *[Geschichtskenner]* is *born*" (*Untergang* 137). His description of the historian's innate skills—strong feelings, spontaneity, intuitiveness—read much like the qualities Lavater attributes to the born physiognomist (see *Physiognomische Fragmente* 1: 170–79). Thus to all those who claim they do not understand his ideas or share his judgments, Spengler retorts that they have not been bestowed with the necessary talents for historical understanding. This elitism is part and parcel of Spengler's own self-understanding, and he transfers it to his physiognomic worldview.

The first volume of Spengler's *Untergang des Abendlandes,* which appeared in 1918, shortly after the German defeat in the First World War, exploded onto the intellectual scene in

Weimar Germany like an incendiary bomb: there was probably no work that was as widely read and as hotly debated as this "outline of a cultural morphology of world history," as the subtitle of the book reads.[9] The reasons for the book's popularity—and sometimes infamy—have been frequently discussed and need not be reiterated here.[10] What is significant, however, is that with this work Spengler popularized a vision of a physiognomic worldview that justified subjective historical and cultural interpretations as absolutely "certain" judgments whose validity could not be called into question. His valorization of physiognomic tact as a mode of intuitive knowledge that could legitimately be applied to the understanding of historical and cultural phenomena clearly helped fuel the boom in physiognomic theories characteristic of Weimar Germany. Indeed, Spengler even suggests that his physiognomic world view will be the central philosophy of the immediate future: "The physiognomic [view of the world] still has its age of greatness ahead of it" (*Untergang* 135); and he implicitly identifies this physiognomic worldview as characteristic of the late phase of Western civilization, whose culmination, as we know, Spengler saw in the Prussian state. In this sense he explicitly argues for a "physiognomization" of German thought as appropriate to the current state of German cultural history. Moreover, the advocates of racial physiognomics could find grist for their misanthropic mills in Spengler's text. The second volume of *Untergang* contains an entire section entitled "Nations, Races, Languages," in which one can read, among other things: "But what are the perceptible, above all visible features that will allow us to recognize and distinguish races? There can be no doubt that this belongs to the domain of physiognomics, just as the classification of languages is a part of systematics" (703). Despite Spengler's distaste for the materialist form racial physiognomics later took, it is hard to imagine stronger words of encouragement for this direction of physiognomic thought. Regardless of how one views this particular instance, however, it is undeniable that Spengler's work helped disseminate a positive image of physiognomic perception as a valid mode of pre-rational, intuitive understanding that stood over against the negative representation of abstract rationality, systematic science, and the conceptualist bias of "enlightened" human beings.

Rudolf Kassner and Physiognomic Imagination

Spengler was not the only intellectual in German-speaking Europe at this time who was concerned with the development of a universalizing physiognomic worldview. In 1919, just a year after the first volume of *Untergang des Abendlandes* appeared, the Austrian essayist Rudolf Kassner published *Zahl und Gesicht* (Number and face), the first in a long series of physiognomic treatises that would constitute the primary direction of his life work. This book begins with an extensive introduction entitled "Outline of a Universal Physiognomics," which sketches the major tenets of Kassner's physiognomic theories. The phrase "universal physiognomics" gives a first indication of the connection to Spengler's physiognomic project: both Spengler and Kassner seek to break with the limited physiognomic tradition, represented in particular by Lavater, that reduces physiognomic interpretation to the realm of the human face. For Kassner as for Spengler, physiognomics becomes a more fundamental philosophy, a principal worldview that governs one's entire mode of perception and thought. This broader scope manifests itself in the title of one of Kassner's later physiognomic works, *Das physiognomicshe Weltbild,* published in 1930. By the same token, it is incorrect to claim, as one critic has, that Kassner is "the creator of universal physiognomics" (Bock 719), since credit for this accomplishment—if it deserves credit at all—should by rights fall to Spengler. At the same time, Kassner's contribution to the theorization and dissemination of this universal physiognomics should not be underestimated. It is at least theoretically possible that Kassner read the first volume of Spengler's *Untergang* before publishing *Zahl und Gesicht;* yet it seems more probable that these two thinkers developed their physiognomic philosophies independently of one another. Kassner, at least, does not mention Spengler until 1930, and nowhere does Spengler refer to Kassner or his works, despite the fact that the latter published his major writings on physiognomics well before Spengler's death in 1936. In his discussions with Alfons Kensik, Kassner claims that the idea to write a book on physiognomics occurred to him suddenly one afternoon in 1913 while riding on a streetcar ("Gespräche" 219). The actual structure of *Zahl und Gesicht,* he later maintains, came to him during a stay in Munich in winter 1916–1917. As far as can be discerned, it is merely serendipitous that Kassner and Spengler developed their physiognomic outlooks in the same city, Munich, at precisely the same time; but serendipity can also make strange bedfellows, and in this case it highlights the similarities in Spengler's and Kassner's physiognomic theories.

If Spengler developed his own "intuitive" physiognomic mode of thinking and methodology by distinguishing it from the rational systematism of natural science, Kassner's juxtaposition of "number" and "face" serves a similar function. It is already telling in this regard that his introductory sketch of a universal physiognomics is structured as a dialogue—a dialectic following the Platonic model[11]—between a biologist, who represents number, and a physiognomist (Kassner himself), who defends the significance of face. The juxtaposition of the physiognomist with a biologist gives a first indication that Kassner, like Spengler, seeks to contrast physiognomic perception with the thought and methodology of the natural sciences. Throughout his works, the opposition of "number" and "face" remains the central constant of Kassner's physiognomic outlook, and it spawns a long list of related dialectical pairs: identity/non-identity; equation/metaphor; concept/form; essence/transformation; being/signifying; finitude/infinity. The first term in each of these dualities is aligned with "number," the second with "face."

Kassner's physiognomics is predicated on a radical break with the principle of identity, which he views as the dominant theorem of the natural and mathematical sciences. He unequivocally asserts in *Zahl und Gesicht:*

> The principle of identity is invalid in physiognomics. We can also turn this statement around and say: physiognomics exists everywhere where the principle of identity is invalid; or even better: where it does not arise, where we go beyond it. Whenever physiognomics has shown itself to be false, frivolous, or even just incidentally correct, as is often, if not always true in the case of Lavater, the principle of identity has been smuggled in without being noticed. You are aware of its formula: A = A or 1 = 1. It constitutes the entire content of logic and the fundamental principle of mathematics. (*Sämtliche Werke* 3: 197)

Kassner defines the realm of physiognomics *ex negativo,* as it were, as the realm in which the principle of identity does *not* apply—or cannot be validly applied. In this sense Kassner's physiognomic domain overlaps with what his contemporary Austrian Ludwig Wittgenstein (1889–1951), whose *Tractatus logico-philosophicus* was written at approximately the same time as *Zahl und Gesicht,* defines as the realm of the "metaphysical" or the "mystical": the sphere that falls outside of strict logic and that hence, for Wittgenstein, represents what is ineffable, unsayable (Wittgenstein 115). Kassner deviates from Wittgenstein, however, insofar as he defines this trans-logical realm as precisely the "sayable"—that is, as something that belongs specifically to the realm of language as a discursive form that stands over against the formulaic discourse of mathematics. "The depth of the earth is number, the depth of the human being is language," Kassner maintains in *Zahl und Gesicht* (*Sämtliche Werke* 3: 240), implicitly orienting physiognomics, as the evocation of what lies in the depths of the human being, in the space of nonlogical, *poetic* language. He goes on to develop a metaphysics of human language that is strikingly reminiscent of Martin Heidegger's (1899–1976) ontological perspective: "Without language the human being would not be deep; that is why it is senseless to maintain that anything lies deeper, or is deeper than language. It is not God, but only a numerical being who lies deeper, ever deeper, no matter how far down we dig. Or perhaps God after all, at least insofar as human beings have made him into a numerical being. The human being is not deep due to analogy, but due to his very Being *[aus Sein tief];* he is deep because he *is*" (3: 240–41). Physiognomics for Kassner thus becomes the name for a specifically metaphysical understanding of the human being as an entity that exists in and through the medium of language.

It is difficult to imagine a more radical break with the German physiognomic tradition since Lavater than that proposed by Kassner. To be sure, from Lavater through Carus to the racial anthropologists of Weimar and Nazi Germany, physiognomics is, as I have argued, a metaphysics, an attempt to transcend the human body as physical reality so as to penetrate into its transphysical—its characterological, its moral, its racial—essence. But for Lavater, Carus, and racial physiognomists like Hans F. K. Günther or Bruno K. Schultz, physiognomics becomes a discipline that pursues metaphysics with the tools and methodologies of *empirical* science, studying the human being solely on the basis of physical data organized into schematic tables. Witness the cranioscopic bent of physiognomics beginning with Lavater's "Stirnmaaß," proceeding to Gall's phrenology, through Carus's cranioscopic studies, to the *Taschenbuch der rassenkundlichen Meßtechnik,* the methodological handbook for racial measurement of the human body published by Bruno K. Schultz. (See Fig. 61 in the conclusion below) In this respect, at least, Kassner's physiognomic theories represent an explicit protest against the scientific, mathematical tendency Lavater introduced into the study of physiognomics. Lavater, after all, claimed that, correctly practiced, physiognomics would most definitely become "a science definable in mathematical terms" (*Physiognomische Fragmente* 4: 481). By contrast, in *Das physiognomische Weltbild* Kassner states without qualification "that physiognomics, as we understand it, is not a science, and neither can nor should ever be one. Every science operates by trying to explain by means of concepts. Physiognomics does not explain, it interprets. . . . And the deeper physiognomics digs, the more it sees image, the more it sees structure *[Gestalt]*" (*Sämtliche Werke* 4: 377). Kassner's juxtapositions of explanation and interpretation, concept and *Gestalt,* are reminiscent of Spengler's distinctions; they also invoke Dilthey's segregation of the natural sciences, which describe and explain, from the human sciences, which "understand" and interpret.

Kassner's conception of physiognomics as a mode of understanding that runs counter to the logic of identity is concretized in his famous physiognomic paradox, first expressed in *Zahl und Gesicht,* but reiterated throughout his texts on physiognomics. It is "the great paradox of all physiognomics," Kassner asserts, "that the human being only is the way he looks, because he does not look the way he is." Mathematical or geometric figures, on the other hand, "are exactly the way they look; the paradox is not applicable to them" (*Sämtliche Werke* 3: 192). In place of the absolute logical junction of identity between appearance and essence that governs traditional physiognomics, Kassner substitutes the absolute logical disjunction of the paradox. What is it about the human being that ruptures the principle of identity and introduces paradox in its stead? It is what

Kassner calls individuality, or freedom. "What we call freedom is definitely the meaning, the rectification—to use a term drawn from the realm of analysis—of this paradox. The world of freedom—I could also call it the infinite world" (3: 192). Physiognomics applies only to the infinite world of human freedom, the domain in which identity, quantification, and number do not hold sway. The finite world, by contrast, is that of static, unchanging objects that can be quantified and measured. "Only in a finite world," Kassner states in his *Grundlagen der Physiognomik* (Fundamentals of physiognomics), "in a world in which word and thing coincide, could there be such simple numerical relations. Wouldn't geometry then be the unity of nature and art, and number be the entire content of the world? Wouldn't nature then be full of angles? Already interpreted before it was created? Predetermined? Mute, dead?" (4: 36). Kassner's language indicates the proximity of his own physiognomic conceptions to Spengler's argument that physiognomic intuition is appropriate to the immeasurable, unquantifiable world of human cultural products. Kassner goes beyond Spengler, of course, in his specific identification of this vital human realm with the sphere of creative language, which stands over against the identical world of geometrical figures and lifeless objects. But more significant is his opposition to the determinist aspect of traditional physiognomics that is contained in his evocation of human freedom and his turn away from a world that is wholly preordained.

Kassner resists not only the predetermination of traditional physiognomics, but also the static, mechanical method by which it operates. Thus in *Zahl und Gesicht* he distinguishes his own dynamic methodology from that of Aristotle: "In contrast to the static physiognomics of Aristotle, the new physiognomics will be dynamic. It will interpret things in motion" (*Sämtliche Werke* 3: 317). This dynamism, of course, is closely related to the vitalism championed by Spengler, and it represents a significant departure from traditional physiognomic theories. To the "constructive" physiognomic method of Lavater or Aristotle, in which a single physical feature is assigned to a particular characterological or moral trait—say, a protruding nose to greed—Kassner opposes what he calls a "differential" physiognomics.

He elucidates this conception in *Grundlagen der Physiognomik:* "Anyone who looks at the face in this second, differential manner (in contrast to the first, constructive manner), who looks, that is, at its expression, sees the fluidity, the motion, and he is forced to look for the transitions, for the bridges, for the seams and rifts of this being" (4: 20). To the extent that it is physiognomically interpretable, the human face manifests a mobility and mutability that defies definition in static, stable terms. As was true for Spengler's physiognomics as well, one of Kassner's central terms is *Ausdruck,* "expression." For Kassner, however, the dynamism of human expressivity is concretized in rifts and discontinuities: the human face does not represent a coherent whole; rather it is, as he says in *Zahl und Gesicht, gespalten,* "split," and divided into disjunctive parts (3: 202).[12] The task of the physiognomist does not consist, then, in identifying a single feature with a specific trait—to do so would be to succumb to the logic of identity—but rather in reading the face in terms of the differences, the tensions that arise among two or more features. "When viewing a face," Kassner claims in *Das physiognomische Weltbild,* "we must above all concentrate on its tensions: between forehead and chin, forehead and mouth, profile and frontal view, neck or back and the entire front as it approaches us, if we want to grasp its drama" (4: 456). The "drama" of the face: this is another fundamental concept in Kassner's physiognomic worldview. The physiognomically significant face is characterized by drama, by the dynamic interaction of diverse traits, just as the human being is constituted not by identity, not by the dominance of one single characteristic, but by the complex interplay of many characteristics. This does not mean that character cannot somehow be delimited, even named; however, it can never be deciphered as a stable, stationary given, but only as tendency, direction, process—just as a drama, while portraying the complex interaction of several characters, can have a definable plot and direction. In other words, Kassner views the human face, like the human being, not as a geographic map in which some traits stand out and others recede into the background, but rather as a constantly changing network, a vortex of dynamic characterological forces. This facial mutability is the visible complement to human freedom, which constitutes the individual's potential for his or her own constant redefinition and redetermination. Individuality, in short, becomes subject to the Heraclitean notion of flux: as for Spengler, who saw direction and "destiny" as the essence of vital cultural entities, for Kassner, too, physiognomics becomes a fundamentally historical discipline to the extent that it takes account of self-transformation over time.

If the physiognomic text of the human face is always changing as a function of freedom, then how, we might ask, is it ever possible to arrive at an interpretation? Kassner's answer seems as straightforward as it is mysterious: by applying the power of human imagination *(Einbildungskraft).* To be sure, unbridled subjectivism, the passing off of imaginative correlations between face and character as incontestable facts, has always been one of the most virulent critiques voiced against physiognomics. Kassner is aware of this, and he seeks to disarm criticism by appropriating precisely this creative subjectivism as the keystone of his own physiognomic theory. In the introductory pages of his *Physiognomik,* first published in 1932, he writes: "The most common objection to physiognomics brought by those who want to know what is behind it, is that we project into the face or its individual traits something that is, so to speak, not in it. This objection becomes invalid as soon as we have applied the correct notion of imagination *[Einbildungskraft].* It is upon this notion . . . that the most lucid and the most encompassing concept of physiognomics rests" (*Sämtliche Werke* 5: 9). This notion of *Einbildungskraft,* of the power of the "imagination," which, like most of his central terms, Kassner tends to employ more in a mystical, evocative manner than as a firm concept with defined significance, is difficult to grasp. Indeed, Kassner himself seems to lend it varying significance throughout his works. In a passage from *Das physiognomische Weltbild,* however, he comes closest to specifying its function in his physiognomic worldview. Here he defines the physiognomically significant human being as "the unity of inner and outer by means of imagination *[Einbildungskraft];* for what is significant is that inner is not simply outer (by means of decree or magic), but rather that imagination must intervene so that their union can occur and be valid" (4: 425). Imagination takes the place of freedom as the basis of the physiognomic paradox: imagination is, as it were, a refracting lens that mediates between inner and outer but does not establish a relationship of identity between them. A passage from Kassner's *Physiognomik* amplifies this notion of imagination as a mediating term: "Between inner and outer, between content and form, there is not simply nothing; rather, imagination *[Einbildungskraft]* resides between them. That is why we cannot see form *[Gestalt]* without imagination, and it is precisely this type of seeing that constitutes the sole object of physiognomics" (5: 68–9). Whereas the first passage locates imagination in the physiognomic object, in the human being subjected to physiognomic interpretation, the second passage posits imagination as the instrument of the physiognomic interpreter, the physiognomic "seer" who by applying the power of imagination is able to perceive the inherent *Gestalt,* the form or meaningful structure, of the observed human subject.

Taken by itself, this conception of imagination as the interpretive tool of the physiognomist could scarcely be used as a defense against unbridled subjectivism, since this physiognomic imagination could still be accused of projecting into the interpreted face something that is not inherently there. When read in conjunction with the first passage, however, we begin to realize that for Kassner imagination is the shared force or competence that unites physiognomic interpreter and interpretand. Imaginative power is at work in what is physiognomically "seen" as well as in the physiognomic "seer" who is doing the "seeing."[13] Imagination thus names the dimension that constitutes the ontological difference of the human being. Both the subject and object of physiognomic sight share this capacity, which makes it the basis for a kind of empathy, a melding of subject and object, interpreter and interpretand, that lends credence and validity to physiognomic interpretations. Kassner thus attempts to use imagination as a bridge across the subject-object dichotomy. Indeed, the transcendence of this dichotomy is a fundamental aim of Kassner's physiognomic worldview. "Anyone who wants to grasp the ultimate thought of physiognomics," he notes in *Das physiognomische Weltbild,* "should know that the segregation of the objective and the subjective realms, as practiced by the eighteenth century, its rationalism and individualism, no longer holds" (*Sämtliche Werke* 4: 443–44). Modern physiognomics for Kassner represents the paradigmatic instance of a mode of perception and understanding that escapes the hierarchy of subject and object: seer and seen are brought onto the same plane by their shared power of imagination, a force that also forges the link between outer and inner in the individual human being.

In a passage from his *Physiognomik* Kassner directly theorizes imagination as the bond between human seer and human seen. "Imagination *[Einbildungskraft]* means that the seer belongs to the face, or that even if someone is not identical to the way he looks, then this occurs by following the princely detour that we call imagination" (*Sämtliche Werke* 5: 103). Characteristic of the texture of Kassner's writings is the way in which one central notion, in this instance the concept of imagination, displaces other principal terms, here freedom and individuality, without ever being directly identified with them.[14] Their association is evoked by their parallel function in the explanation of the physiognomic paradox. Ultimately, then, it is the creative, the poetic dimension of imagination-freedom-individuality that both ruptures the modern human being—causing the disjunction between inner and outer, profile and face—and transcends this disjunction in the act of physiognomic seeing. That is why Kassner insists on the significance of the word *Gesicht* (face) in his own physiognomic theories rather than on the term *Antlitz* (countenance), which dominates the earlier physiognomic tradition and has powerful Christian implications. In a promotional piece for *Zahl und Gesicht* he highlights the ambiguity of the term *Gesicht*, claiming that this word is unique and untranslatable because it fuses the seeing and the seen, visage and vision.[15] This union of physiognomic interpreter and physiognomic interpretand, of seer and seen by means of a shared power of imagination, forms the foundation of an empathy that validates the act of physiognomic hermeneutics. It supplies Kassner's physiognomics with the philosophical underpinnings necessary for a legitimization of its subjectivism, and circumvents the criticism that it falsifies and hermeneutically masters the interpretand by enforcing upon it arbitrary and willful constructions. This subtle dialectic, which merges perceiving subject and perceived object, powered by the mediation of human imagination, is the defining trait of Kassner's physiognomic theories, lending them, as it were, their own theoretical physiognomy. The word *Gesicht,* with its double meaning of "visage" and "vision," is the emblem of this complex dialectic.

Spengler, Kassner, and the Ideological Complicity of Humanistic and Racial Physiognomics

If one concentrates solely on an internal understanding of Kassner's physiognomic worldview, especially on its key concepts—freedom, imagination, individuality, the dynamic transmutability of personality—it is tempting to interpret his physiognomic thought as a liberal philosophy, one that could then be viewed as an intellectual bulwark against the burgeoning antiliberalism of the interwar years. The construction of such an intellectual rampart in the sphere of physiognomic thought could then be interpreted as a brilliant strategic move for a first defense against the racial physiognomics that became one of the powerful forces of antimodernist, antiliberal thinking in the period leading up to the Nazi seizure of power. Seen in this way, Kassner's physiognomics would not only represent a break with traditional physiognomic thought and its logic of identity, but would also constitute a line of defense against the misuse of physiognomics in the service of racial and political mastery. However, such a reading, tempting as it is, is too optimistic and highlights only one side of Kassner's physiognomic theories. There is another side to this physiognomic worldview, an underside, if you will, that is distinctly antiliberal, anti-individualist, conservative, and antimodern. It is on this broader plane, beyond the realm of theoretical details, that Kassner's and Spengler's physiognomic worldviews are most closely related. Both participate in a cultural pessimism or cultural nostalgia that views modern, twentieth-century European culture, society, and technology as a state of historical decline, a moment of regression and degeneration that one can bemoan, but cannot correct. In this sense, both Spengler and Kassner are fatalists: indeed, it is no exaggeration to classify them both, applying the phrase Thomas Mann coined for Spengler, as "defeatists of humanity" ("Über die Lehre Spenglers" 174). To be sure, Spengler, in this regard a true Nietzschean, subscribes to the notion of *amor fati* and embraces this historical decline as "destiny," as he calls it. He accomplishes this, of course, by subscribing to the theory of decadence current at the turn of the century, which dialectically coupled physical decline with cultural and intellectual ascendancy. This allows Spengler to interpret "Faustian" culture both as historical end point and as cultural high point of Western civilization. He makes this argument most forcefully in the essay "Pessimismus?," first published in 1921 as a rebuttal of the critiques directed at *Untergang des Abendlandes.* Here he claims that the word *Untergang,* "decline," in his understanding does not imply catastrophe, like the sinking of an ocean liner, but instead suggests "consummation," a coming to absolute fruition (63–64). By contrast, Kassner's view of historical development is not tinged with Spengler's notion of "destiny" as *amor fati,* and as a result his antimodernism is considerably more nostalgic—I am consciously avoiding the word "pessimistic" here—than is Spengler's, but for that not less fatalistic.

Although Kassner's physiognomic theory seems to valorize individualism as a force responsible for human nonidentity, there are signs that ultimately he is reluctant to affirm the very nonidentity that generates his physiognomic paradox. It is thus an oversimplification to regard Kassnerian physiognomics as an attempt to restore lost identity, as Werner Bock has claimed (715). On the contrary, in Kassner's physiognomic worldview individuality as nonidentity appears as a degenerate historical form that supercedes the world of types, a world that was more cohesive and comprehensible because it was structured by strict social and class hierarchies. In a passage from his *Grundlagen der Physiognomik,* for example, Kassner expresses his approbation of human types as the building blocks of a strong nation:

> The richer a society, a race, a Volk, an age is in types, the more unequivocal human beings are: they are deeper, more decided and decisive in their actions and aptitudes. The wealth of types defines their distinctness. And the more distinct the types, the more the actions of a Volk are also a form of knowledge, the expression of an inner clarity. To strip a Volk of this potential to form types is to turn it into a mass, to emasculate it. Such a Volk will also no longer produce rulers from

> its own ranks and will therefore remain subjected to foreign rulers. With this assertion I merely want to point to the fact that types and masters belong together, the ability to form types constitutes the ability to attain mastery. (*Sämtliche Werke* 4: 39)

One easily perceives in Kassner's remarks the anxiety of uncertainty, the fear of a social texture that lacks absolute clarity. Individuals are ambiguous, whereas types are unambiguous; the worst fate that could befall any Volk would be degeneration into a faceless mass that lacks all distinctions, all moments of "clarity." The gravitation of Kassner's thought in the direction of *völkisch,* even fascist ideology is evident not only in his implicit identification of nation with race, but also in his thesis that the power to generate types—not individuals—is prerequisite for the emergence of true political rulers, *Herrscher.* The reason for this is easy to discern: types are more static, more predictable, and hence easier to govern. Individuals, by contrast, are dynamic, mutable, and constituted by the paradox that inner and outer being are always disjunct. The type, as Kassner's ideal,[16] stands somewhere between the masses, those with neither individual nor typical features, and the individual, who is pure paradox and hence resists all categorization. Consistent with the anti-cosmopolitanism of the early twentieth century, Kassner identifies the masses with the indistinct, easily shepherded hordes of the European metropolis (see *Sämtliche Werke* 4: 41). A society of individuals, on the other hand, would be wholly ungovernable because it would by nature erupt into total anarchy. The curse of the modern world, for Kassner, is its lack of human types, the absence of something akin to class, estate, or social station in premodern society.

In his *Physiognomik* Kassner gives a working definition of what he calls the *Ständegesicht,* the "socially determined face." "The socially determined face means that the physician, the scholar, the schoolteacher, the tailor, the interior decorator, the painter, the Count, the Baron, the accountant, that each of these figures also has the peculiar face befitting his social class, the socially apt face" (*Sämtliche Werke* 5: 29). He then goes on to identify this socially determined face with typology and reiterates his lament about the loss of types in the modern world: "If we replace the concept of class or station with that of type, then we can undoubtedly connect the decrease in types, their impoverishment in our day and age, and the resulting lack of clarity, with the often cited 'victory of technology'" (5: 29–30). The industrial revolution, with its technological innovation, its factory products, its division of labor, its quickening tempo, and its cosmopolitan masses has stripped the human being of all that is "typical," of everything that defines him or her as belonging to a specified and stable social order. Kassner's physiognomic theory emerges, in other words, out of fear of the nameless, classless indistinction of modern cosmopolitan human beings. It is this same fear, of course, that produced typological inventories such as August Sander's (1876–1964) monumental photographic inventory *Antlitz der Zeit* (Face of the time, 1929), and nourished *völkisch* ideologies in this same period, giving rise to the clarity—to the false and misanthropic clarity—of racial physiognomics.

It is no coincidence that the periods of concentrated interest in physiognomic theories in German-speaking Europe, the final three decades of the eighteenth century and the years from 1918 to 1945, are also times of tremendous social cataclysm. Physiognomics evolves in the eighteenth century, on the one hand, as an ideological instrument in the struggle of emerging civil society to differentiate itself from the aristocratic state and its system of stable estates: it endows the civil subject with a morally and characterologically profound inner self, while jettisoning the formalism and conventionality of aristocratic self-understanding. On the other hand, as a mechanism for discovering hidden internal traits, it contributes to a social reorientation and regrouping based not so much on social status as on identification and empathy with another person's internal character. In this sense physiognomics plays a role in the development of the new sentimentalism of the eighteenth century, one that is similar to the function of the diary and the letter as forms of intimate expression that reveal the internal individual. In the years of the Weimar Republic it is a new social rupture, the decline of the civil subject and the emergence of the "faceless" masses of the industrial cities, that calls forth a new crisis of social disorientation. Once again physiognomics emerges as a theoretical domain that can offer new forms of reorientation and social bonding. The most crass form this physiognomic identification took was the proto-fascist racial anthropologies of the 1920s and 1930s, which sought to draw distinct lines of racial kinship and clearly segregate the unified racial community from the racial Other. Hans F. K. Günther's *Rassenkunde des deutschen Volkes* (Racial ethnology of the German people), which divides the Germans into four physically and psychologically recognizable racial types, the "Nordic," "Western," "Dinarian," and "Eastern" races, provided a well defined grid that allowed each and every German to situate himself or herself in a carefully charted racial landscape. (Fig. 26)

Rudolf Kassner, for his part, was keenly aware of this close relationship between social disorientation and the resurgence of physiognomic theories in Weimar Germany. In a passage from *Das physiognomische Weltbild* he reflects specifically on this connection between the dissolution of social bonds and the emergence of the new physiognomic worldview:

> Physiognomics thus stands in a specific relation to social theory, which is why it is no coincidence that it necessarily occupies the human spirit once more in an epoch in which all social bonds are beginning to dissolve and new ones beginning to evolve. For it is not merely a matter of physiognomics in the strict sense, but also of the fact that science (theory of relativity), historiography and the theory of nature (abandonment of the concept of progress, of evolution), as well as literature have become physiognomic. (*Sämtliche Werke* 4: 435)

Kassner's reference here to a new physiognomic historiography, with its rejection of the notion of progress, is possibly an allusion to Spengler. The breadth of his own view of physiognomics is expressed in his inclusion of the theory of relativity and modern literature in this new physiognomic outlook. Two years later, in his *Physiognomik,* he also includes the emergence of racial physiognomics as a further symptom of the universality of the modern physiognomic world view (5: 78). Kassner assigns his own physiognomic philosophy a fundamentally conservative, conservational role in the reorientation that must take place in response to the modernist rupture: although physiognomics cannot possibly return us to a historically antedated cultural phase by reinstituting human types, it can at least be shaped into an instrument that can be employed against the most nefarious tendency of the modern world, the drive to translate the qualitative into the quantitative, to reduce face to number, human beings to anonymous masses. In *Das physiognomische Weltbild* he thus gives the following metacommentary on his physiognomic project:

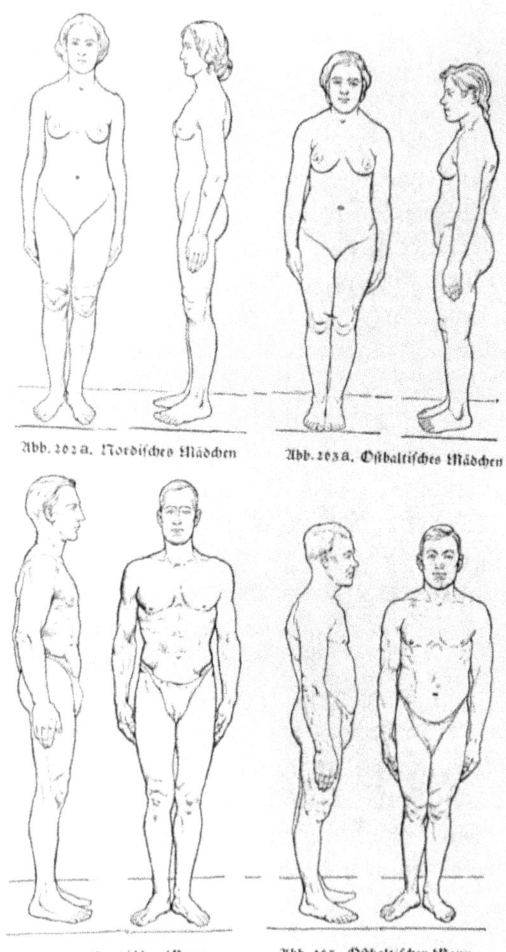

Fig. 26. Contrastive sketches of the East Baltic and Nordic types, from Hans F. K. Günther, *Rassenkunde des deutschen Volkes*, 1939.

Physiognomics as we want to conceive it . . . is supposed to teach us to transform quantity into quality, or to see what is qualitative in the quantitative; it is supposed to teach us to see as such. The types of the old world have disappeared. This loss is commonly attributed to what we call the mechanization or atomization of the world. Physiognomics is just as incapable of creating new types in the sense of an exhausted world as it is of creating new classes. But it is capable of putting an end to quantification by, as I have said, transforming the quantitative into

> something qualitative and by thereby positing a world whose ultimate meaning is the assertion of its opposition to the world of number, of atoms, etc. (4: 492–93)

The advocacy of physiognomics becomes a compromise position between the ideal but unrecoverable typology of the premodern world and the hegemony of pure number, the merely quantifiable, in the world of modern technology. Physiognomics is the last bastion against a modernism that threatens to jettison the very notion of substance, replacing it with the superficiality and abstraction of pure number, of mathematics, of the nameless masses. In this sense Kassner's physiognomic worldview attempts, as does Spengler's, to offer a kind of antidote to the abstraction and rationalism of the modern world. The cultivated antirationalism and subjectivism of Kassner's texts represent the stylistic manifestation of this antimodern worldview, and it has its parallel in Spengler's consciously analogical methodology.

To the extent that Spengler and Kassner rebel against the "scientific" and "quantifying" tradition inherent in traditional physiognomics, their physiognomic theories also represent a kind of preemptive strike against the reductive, pseudo-scientific strategies characteristic of most proto-fascist and fascist racial physiognomics. By the same token, as Kassner himself points out, their physiognomic worldviews and those of the racial anthropologists have certain intellectual-historical affinities, not least of which is their inherently conservative antimodernism and the nostalgia for a clearly defined and hierarchical social order. But even on the level of methodology and argument Spengler's and Kassner's physiognomic theories play into certain aspects of racial physiognomics. Most significant here is their unabashed glorification of the subjectivism that underpins their physiognomic hermeneutics. Kassner, as we saw, defends subjectivistic interpretation of the face as a form of empathy via the medium of imagination. But there was certainly a great deal of imagination invested in the development and application of Günther's racial types. Indeed, the inherent problem with Kassner's appeal to imaginative power is precisely its lack of definition: it remains a mystical, indefinable concept, and this vagueness permits it to be appropriated as a tool for the legitimization of every and any "imaginative" interpretation of other human beings. Spengler goes even farther insofar as he turns this subjectivism into a programmatic element of physiognomics: "The most profound knowledge of human beings does not prevent one's insights from displaying the color of those who have these insights, rather it encourages it," he baldly asserts (*Untergang* 584). If the most profound physiognomic judgments are tainted by the "color" of the person passing judgment, then what prevents the prejudices of the racial bigot from exhibiting the "color" of his or her bigotry? In this sense the exuberance for the pre-rational, intuitive, even mystical quality of physiognomic interpretation, shared by Spengler and Kassner, could not help but lend moral and philosophical support to racial physiognomists, who sought a guise of intellectual legitimacy to cover the arbitrariness of their ideologically tainted interpretations. If this intellectual affinity is a sin, it is a sin of omission, not one of commission: both Spengler and Kassner can be faulted for not vigorously and clearly distinguishing their own subjectivistic physiognomic philosophies from the popularized subjectivist physiognomics of racial hatred. Indeed, their general failure publicly to exploit their positions as recognized physiognomic "experts" so as to denounce racial physiognomics in all its forms threatens to push their positions across the fine line that distinguishes sins of omission from silent complicity.

The case for ideological complicity between Spengler's physiognomic worldview and proto-fascist political and racial theory is, of course, much clearer than the one that can be made for Kassner. Most significant in this regard is the coherence of Spengler's ideas and vocabulary with the discourse of the Nordic Movement and with fascist political propaganda. Above all his evocation of a new "Caesarism" that would emerge on German soil, and his identification of this political autocracy with "the formative powers of the blood" and against the "rationalism of the great metropolises" (*Untergang* 1143) reads like a page out of *Mein Kampf.* To be sure, Spengler attempted to voice his opposition to the materialist bias that characterized a large segment of German racial physiognomics, but only by insisting that race is a spiritual rather than a physical quality. In a posthumously published fragment dealing with the issue of race he notes: "It is not the *somatic* type that is important (object of anatomy), but rather the psychic; physiognomics" (*Urfragen* 154).[17] Implicit in this remark is Spengler's belief that physiognomics is certainly relevant to racial psychology, if not to racial anatomy. This is confirmed by another posthumous note in which he stresses: "*Race is the sum of the vital-physical expressions in the life of the psyche,* a kind of materialized expression" (*Urfragen* 161). Race does manifest itself in the material of the human body, in other words, but only as dynamic expression, not as static bodily form. Here again we see Spengler's departure from the Lavaterian physiognomic tradition that sought character in the firm, stable features. But Spengler does not abandon the concepts of race or of racial physiognomics in toto, and in this sense he contributes to a broadening of racial physiognomics into the realm of the psychological. He thereby lends implicit credence to *Rassenseelenkunde,* the branch of physiognomics that called itself "racial psychology" and was developed most fully and articulately by Ludwig Ferdinand Clauss. A critical analysis of Clauss's theories, as we will recognize in a later chapter, reveals similarities not only with Spengler's physiognomic philosophy, but with that of Rudolf Kassner as well.

Spengler's discourse certainly participates more directly in the *völkisch* ideology of the 1920s and 1930s than does Kassner's, of course. It is Spengler, after all, not Houston Stewart Chamberlain or Adolf Hitler, who writes: "Throughout history, wherever a small band victoriously invades an expansive territory, it is regularly the call of the blood, the yearning for a great destiny, the heroism of genuinely racial human beings that motivates them" (*Untergang* 751–52). To recognize this is not to identify Spengler as an unabashed racist in the Nazi fashion. Quite to the contrary, we know that he objected to the fascist conception of race as something to which one belongs, juxtaposing it to a quality of race that one possesses, much like one possesses—or does not possess—aristocratic mannerisms or an aristocratic pedigree (see *Jahre der Entscheidung* 161). But these criticisms begin to look like minor intra-ideological skirmishes in the context of Spengler's overall discourse, which is rife with the catchphrases of racial and political conservatism that won the hearts and minds of so many Germans in the years of the Weimar Republic. In this important respect, *Der Untergang des Abendlandes* could not help but underwrite an association between the newly proclaimed physiognomic worldview and the principles of racism and *Blut und Boden* politics, the ideology of "blood and soil."

Although the case of Rudolf Kassner is not nearly so clear as that of Spengler, even he cannot be declared wholly innocent of a certain intellectual collaboration with *völkisch* and fascist ideologies. We have already examined the pessimism and cultural nostalgia his physiognomic theories shared with the conservative antimodernism inherent in the fascist world outlook. But the affinities run deeper than this. Although the word "race" is not as prevalent in Kassner's physiognomics as it is in Spengler's, it occurs often enough, and usually with positive connotations. Already in *Zahl und Gesicht,* for example, he remarks: "The more a Volk is a Volk, the more a race a race, the closer it comes to the mystery of identity and the happier it is" (*Sämtliche Werke* 3: 325). If the world of individuality, of the physiognomic paradox, represents a stage of historical degeneracy vis-à-vis the world of types, then the identity of race, the awareness of belonging to a racial community, evokes a longed for, but seemingly unattainable, utopian condition. Kassner astutely diagnoses the malaise that motivated Nazi racial politics: racial identity relieves the modern human being both of the painful paradox of individuality and the amorphous indistinction of the masses. Kassner repeats this thought in a similar formulation three years later in *Die Grundlagen der Physiognomik:* "The more the individual human being feels that he is bound up with his race, the more this virtue becomes happiness, and the more this happiness (success, joy, energy) becomes virtue" (4: 44). To be sure, Kassner does not employ the word "race" in the openly belligerent, ideology-strategic manner in which it functioned in fascist propaganda; but the positive connotations he lends the term are already enough to cast a shadow on his theories. In actuality, Kassner saw his own physiognomic worldview as an alternative to fascism, which he interpreted as an attempt to reinstitute a world of types. "It appears to us," he comments in *Das physiognomische Weltbild,* "as if fascism represents an attempt—a very violent one— . . . to arrive at a new world of types, and, what is inherently connected with it, at new virtues for life lived as type," and he goes on to predict that this experiment must necessarily fail (4: 493). But the only alternative Kassner can offer to the psychologically compelling and politically effective program of active racial "hygienics" is the vague and abstract program of a physiognomics that resists the encroaching mechanization and quantification of the world by appealing to human imagination.

There are other elements in Kassner's works that seem to reflect aspects of the racial ideology so dominant in the interwar years. His remark in *Das physiognomische Weltbild*, for example, that identifies Jews with "schlemiels" who have no racial traits invokes the insidious "assimilationist" quality for which Jews were attacked in contemporary racial propaganda (see *Sämtliche Werke* 4: 471–72). Echoes of anti-Semitic discourse also ring in an anecdote Kassner relates in a footnote to *Die Grundlagen der Physiognomik* about an assimilated Jew, unaware of his Jewish heritage, whose typical Jewish physiognomy slowly reemerges as he matures and ages (4: 57–58). Kassner makes matters worse when he takes this anecdote as an occasion, later in the same footnote, to offer comments on the "physiognomics of racial intermingling" between Germanic and Jewish blood (4: 58). Once one has recognized this tendency in Kassner to assimilate certain axioms of anti-Semitic prejudice, one cannot help but wonder whether his identification of the human nose as the physiognomic mark of race is not also a subtle, if perhaps unwitting, allusion to the purportedly characteristic "Jewish" nose,[18] exploited so viciously in Nazi propaganda. (Fig. 27)

If these recognitions suggest that Kassner's thought was influenced by the racial ideology current at the time, then an incident from 1942, when the Nazi state was at the pinnacle of its power, marks the point at which silent affinity crosses over either into strategic collaboration with the ruling Nazi ideology, or exploitation of that ideology for the purpose of opportunistic self-interest. In this year Kassner was approached by the publishing house Atlantis about contributing an introductory essay to an illustrated volume that would bear the title *Das deutsche Antlitz in fünf Jahrhunderten deutscher Malerei* (The German face in five centuries of German painting). Kassner was given a

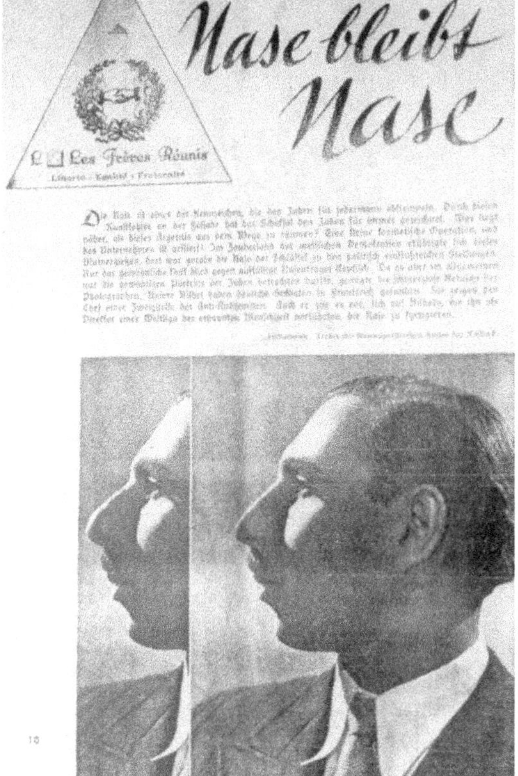

Fig. 27. Racial propaganda piece, "Nose Remains Nose," from *Neues Volk*, 1934. (Courtesy of the Bundesarchiv, Coblenz)

great deal of freedom with regard to the composition of this volume, to the extent that he had significant input into the selection of portraits that would be reproduced.[19] Given the rampant misappropriation of German art by the advocates of a Nordic racial ideology, in particular the frequent reproduction of the Bamberg Rider and the sculptures of the Naumburg cathedral as representative of Nordic physique and physiognomy (Fig. 28), Kassner should have been immediately aware that any publication seeking to illustrate the characteristics of the "German face" could not help but play into and implicitly buttress Nazi racial theories. Moreover, the culture of everyday life in Nazi

Fig. 28. The Bamberg Rider as example of Nordic nobility, from Paul Schultze-Naumburg, *Nordische Schönheit im Leben und in der Kunst,* 1937.

Germany was flooded with a stream of illustrated books and magazines of precisely this type that glorified the "German" face as beautiful, heroic, and so on.[20] Nonetheless, Kassner agreed to lend his name to this project, composed the requested introduction for the volume, and submitted it to the publisher. Because of the shortages brought on by the worsening war situation, the book could not be published during the Third Reich. However, it ultimately appeared, almost ten years after the war, in 1954, under the same title as planned in 1942. (Fig. 29) This volume includes Kassner's original introduction, which bears the title "Zur Physiognomik des Porträts" (On the physiognomy of the portrait).[21] Kassner's active participation in this project, which is so clearly ideologically tainted, cannot simply be excused, as Claudia Schmölders suggests (*Das Vorurteil im Leib* 36), by Kassner's lack of political tact. Political tact is, after all, something that most intelligent Germans learned from the experiences of the Nazi excesses. On the contrary, his participation in this project indicates that Kassner, whose works were not overtly

Fig. 29. Dust jacket, Rudolf Kassner, *Das deutsche Antlitz,* 1954.

banned during the Third Reich but who suffered under drastically waning popularity, was prepared to exploit the prominence of racial physiognomics in Nazi Germany in order to gain a wider audience for himself and his physiognomic worldview. Kassner took advantage of the opportunity to write the introduction to this illustrated volume, which promised to be a popular bestseller, as a vehicle through which he could disseminate, by means of his introductory essay, the central ideas of his physiognomic theories—the significance of types, for example (*Sämtliche Werke* 10: 387), or the differential methodology characteristic of his physiognomic procedure (10: 402–3). But Kassner also suggests that there is a smooth interface between his own ideas and the mythology of a racially Germanic physiognomy when he characterizes some of the portraits reproduced in this

Fig. 30. Example of an "Exceedingly German Face": Albrecht Dürer, self-portrait (1500), from Rudolf Kassner, *Das deutsche Antlitz*, 1954.

volume as "exceedingly German faces" (10: 398). (Fig. 30) This is enough to indicate that Kassner was willing at least to flirt with Nazi racial ideology if it was a matter of lending credence to, and gaining popularity for, his own views on physiognomics. This complicity has a reverse side, of course, since the association of Kassner's name with racial physiognomics could also serve to lend credibility among intellectuals to the latter. What is clear, at least, is that Kassner did not exploit *Das deutsche Antlitz* as a medium for voicing direct opposition with Nazi racial ideology, something that would have been a praiseworthy venture. One can only be surprised that he agreed to the publication of this work after the war: an indication that even in retrospect he remained insensitive to the questionable ideological collaboration manifest in his initial participation in this project.

With the clarity of historical hindsight it seems almost inevitable that the physiognomic worldviews of Oswald Spengler and Rudolf Kassner would nourish and legitimate that other physiognomic worldview, the philosophy of racial superiority, hatred, and demonization of the racial Other, that took center stage in German political and cultural life during the Weimar

Republic and the ensuing Nazi years. Perhaps the will to power over one's fellow human beings, which is inherent in proto-fascist and fascist physiognomic theory and practice, is part and parcel of every physiognomics, of every attempt to interpret and judge other individuals, other nations, other "races." A certain violence toward the physiognomic Other is implicit, at any rate, in the metaphors with which Kassner describes his physiognomic hermeneutics. On the opening page of his *Physiognomik* he asserts the importance of analyzing "living faces," claiming that only they are "authentic and made to be . . . seized and penetrated by the seeing eye" (*Sämtliche Werke* 5: 7). The metaphorical violence of this passage, the seizure and penetration of the perceived human face by the physiognomist's gaze, can perhaps be read as a symptom of a subliminal drive to mastery that informs all physiognomic judgments. This violence, at any rate, is quite explicit in Spengler's view of physiognomics. In a posthumous note that employs language strikingly similar to Kassner's, Spengler describes the sense of power and domination over the interpreted human object that physiognomic interpretations afford the interpreter: "The adept of human beings *[Menschenkenner]* seizes the alien psyche by comprehending it. That is power, superiority of the person who comprehends over the person who is comprehended" (*Urfragen* 69).[22] In the final two chapters I will examine how this drive for superiority motivated the racial physiognomics of the Nazi era, and in particular how the dissemination of applied physiognomics among the German populace in this period infused the common person, charged with passing physiognomic judgments on a day-to-day basis, with this powerful sense of superiority and mastery over others.

6

Constructing Race

Hans F. K. Günther's Ethnological Physiognomics

> Racial politics is not natural science; rather, it is the political application of natural-scientific knowledge.
>
> Walter Gross, Head of the Nazi Office for Racial Politics (Weingart et al. 405)

The Fusion of Racial Ethnology and Physiognomics

In his exploration of the relationship between the modern metropolis and modern literature in "Das Paris des Second Empire bei Baudelaire," Walter Benjamin remarks on the prominence around 1840 of the literary genre of the "physiologies," which sought to expose and describe the diverse types of human beings who populated modern Paris. Noting the heritage that ties this literary fad to the physiognomic practices of the eighteenth century, Benjamin identifies the superiority of these older physiognomists as their grounding in empirical observation.

> [The views represented in the physiologies] hark back to the physiognomists of the eighteenth century. To be sure, they have no connection whatsoever with the more substantial views of these earlier thinkers. In the instances of Lavater and Gall genuine empiricism, not merely speculation and fanaticism, was at work. The physiologies lived off of their credit, without providing any of their own capital. They assured people that everyone, unburdened by disciplinary expertise, was capable of reading occupation, character, origin, and lifestyle out of the faces of passers-by. For them this gift takes on the semblance of an inherent ability with which good fairies endow all city dwellers while they are still in the cradle. (Benjamin 1.2: 541)

Benjamin's praise of the empirical foundation in Lavater's and Gall's physiognomics is interesting as a reflection on the reception these founders of modern German physiognomics enjoyed in the early decades of the twentieth century. It is noteworthy that even as perspicacious a critic of modern culture as Benjamin failed to see the connection between Enlightenment physiognomics and its modern racial variant, even though by 1938—when he completed this essay—physiognomics had long-since taken its racial turn in Germany. His comments not only affirm the "credit" accorded such figures as Lavater and Gall in the Paris of the 1840s; they also exemplify the persistence of this "credit" into the Germany of the first half of the twentieth century. Benjamin explicitly argues that the writers of the "physiologies" exploited the credence people like Lavater enjoyed in order to lend legitimacy to their own interpretations of character. If Lavater and Gall, in his view, at least underwrote their speculations and their fanaticism with empirical evidence, the physiologists, lacking empirical data, relied solely on unfounded conjectures. However, his ironic critique of the physiologists' appeal to a talent mysteriously given at birth is actually doubly ironic: as we have seen, beginning with Lavater this appeal to "genius," innate physiognomic talent, and scientifically unsupportable intuition is a persistent part of the discourse with which physiognomic judgments are authorized and validated. It is, in fact, precisely the intertwining of practices drawn from the empirical sciences with unfettered speculation and prejudice that both characterizes post-Lavaterian physiognomics and underwrites its—oftentimes insidious—dissemination.

If, as Benjamin's example demonstrates, the authority of physiognomic conceptions in the early twentieth century stood in direct proportion to the degree of empirical evidence on which they relied, then it comes as no surprise that the theories of Hans F. K. Günther (1891–1968)—known in Germany as "Rassen-Günther" (Race-Günther)—would represent the leading edge of an academic boom in physiognomics that took place during the Weimar Republic and the Nazi regime. (Fig. 31) Günther's meteoric rise to fame and popularity in Weimar and Nazi Germany directly mirrors the upsurge in racially rooted ideologies, and he is a pivotal figure insofar as he both rode the crest of this wave of interest in racial issues and contributed in seminal ways to its popularity both inside and outside the boundaries of strict acad-

Fig. 31. Photograph of Hans F. K. Günther, from an advertising brochure.

emic discourse. Heavily influenced by Arthur Gobineau's (1816–1882) theories of human inequality and Houston Stewart Chamberlain's (1855–1927) belief that the Teutonic race is the sole culturally productive human species (see Chamberlain 7–8), Günther became a proponent of the so-called *Nordischer Gedanke,* the Nordic Idea, an ideology that identified superior Nordic "blood" as the unifying trait of all Germans and argued for the racial and cultural enrichment of the German people and the German nation based on a policy of selective breeding. Günther was one of the primary ideologues of the *Nordische Bewegung,* the organized Nordic Movement that consciously promoted this racial ideology.[1]

In 1925 Günther published a book with the title *Der nordische Gedanke unter den Deutschen* (The Nordic Idea among the Germans) that was destined to become the bible of this movement. As the basis of its ideology he articulated an idea that formed the core of his entire racial philosophy: the belief that race manifests itself as "a unitary somatic-psychic image" in all its representatives (*Der Nordische Gedanke* 31). The absolute identity or one-to-one correspondence between somatic and psychological traits, which formed the basis of Lavater's physiognomic "alphabet" a century and a half earlier, is reiterated here. What has changed, of course, is the mediative power that ensures this identity: whereas for Lavater this was guaranteed by the Christian divinity and the reflection of the divine idea in the individual human being, for Günther this bond is fused by the emergent genetic and hereditary sciences. The "scientific" impulse that propelled even Lavater's physiognomics thus reaches a kind of ironic culmination in Günther's racial physiognomics.

It is not surprising that Günther became the lodestar of Nazi racial ideology. Already in 1930 he was appointed professor for racial anthropology at the University of Jena, and present in the audience for his inaugural lecture were none other than Adolf Hitler (1889–1945) and Hermann Göring (1893–1946). They had employed their political clout to press for Günther's appointment by Wilhelm Frick (1877–1927), who as representative of Hitler's National Socialist Party was serving as *Volksbildungsminister,* minister for popular education, in the state of Thuringia (Weingart et al. 453; Hau and Ash 19). The rector and the faculty senate of Jena University, recognizing that Günther's selection was motivated purely by politics, voiced unanimous and unequivocal protest against his appointment, citing his "lack of disciplinary qualifications" and an absence of any "original scholarly contributions" (Hedler 57–58). Their protest fell on deaf ears, however, and the *Sächsischer Beobachter,* the local newspaper of the National Socialist Party in the state of Saxony, would subsequently celebrate Günther's ascendance to this academic post, calling it a "professorship for Jew-baiting" (Hedler 58). Günther's role as one of the primary ideologues of Nazi anti-Semitism and racial doctrine was eminently clear to his academic colleagues. His career advancements after the Nazi seizure of power to highly visible professorships in Berlin (1934), and ultimately in his native Freiburg im Breisgau (1939), confirm his prominent status within the Nazi hierarchy. Indeed, in 1935 Günther received the backing to found the *Anstalt für Rassenkunde, Völkerbiologie und ländliche Soziologie* (Institute for Racial Ethnology, National Biology, and Rural Sociology) in Berlin-Dahlem (Ash and Geuter 177), an institute whose research program, as its name clearly indicates, was keyed to Günther's own interests and pursuits. Moreover, in the same year he was granted the first award for science given by the National Socialist Party, and in 1941, on his fiftieth birthday, he was awarded the prestigious Goethe Medal for excellence in arts and sciences (Weingart et al. 455). Yet paradoxically—and in apparent confirmation of the belief that postwar Western Germany did not make energetic efforts to overcome its Nazi past—Günther received only minor punishment after the war for his role in the Nazi terror. Although he was suspended from his university post and sentenced to three years imprisonment, he was officially declared to be nothing but a *Minderbelasteter*, a "minor offender," and he was permitted to continue publishing and republishing his books up until his death in 1968. Günther's role as one of the primary racial ideologues for the Nazi movement was also quickly forgotten—if it was ever fully acknowledged—in international scientific circles, and as early as 1953 he was elected corresponding member of the American Society of Human Genetics (Weingart et al. 455). This is perhaps indicative of a tendency among some scientists to distinguish all too simplistically what they recognize as "good" scientific information from the "bad" political ends in whose service it is sometimes placed.

In his numerous books on race and the races of Europe, Günther consistently based his theories on diverse forms of empirically derived evidence. His most influential book, the *Rassenkunde des deutschen Volkes* (Racial ethnology of the German people), first published in 1922, went through numerous editions and reached a circulation of 124,000 by 1942 (Weingart et al. 452). (Fig. 32) In the preface to the sixteenth edition, published in 1933, shortly after the Nazi seizure of power, Günther credits his book with having brought racial ethnology, in the brief span of eleven years since its first publication, from a veritably unknown discipline to one that has become a required area of study in the German schools (*Rassenkunde* iii). This claim is as self-congratulatory as it is true: Günther was largely responsible for the repute this discipline had gained, and his books were commonly used as textbooks in schools throughout the Third Reich (Burleigh and Wippermann 213). Indeed, his *Kleine Rassenkunde des deutschen Volkes*—the so-called "Volks-Günther," a greatly abridged and popularizing, nonacademic version of his *Rassenkunde des deutschen Volkes*, which was first published in 1929—became

Fig. 32. Dust jacket, Hans F. K. Günther, *Rassenkunde des deutschen Volkes,* 1939.

required reading in all German schools during the Third Reich (Breitling 55).

Günther unequivocally lays out the empirical, positivistic foundation of his investigations in the opening pages of his *Rassenkunde des deutschen Volkes.* Here he stresses that racial ethnology is concerned first and foremost with the human body (6), and he specifically aligns the notion of race with the modern natural sciences, above all with the nascent field of human genetics: "The concept 'race' is above all a concept borrowed from the natural sciences. . . . Just as natural science begins by describing the somatic features that, taken together, define a particular species or generic type, racial ethnology proceeds in the exact same way: the purely measurable, quantifiable physical features that can be expressed in numeric terms form the unequivocal and certain basis of its body of knowledge" (7). We are reminded here of Lavater's assertion that physiognomics would "certainly become a science definable in mathematical terms" (*Physiognomische Fragmente* 4: 481), as well as of the debate about the relative importance of *Zahl* and *Gesicht,* "number" and "face," that raged in the theories of the Weimar physiognomists. Günther, for his part, explicitly treated physiognomics as a subdiscipline of physical anthropology, and his theories were largely based on the study of human remains, on skull measurements, and on the interpretation of human artifacts. He considered, for example, the measurement of skulls to be one of the most important criteria for the determination of race (*Rassenkunde* 29), and his fourth chapter, devoted to anthropometrics, concentrates almost exclusively on measurements of the head and face (28–37). Günther describes the instruments ethnologists employ to arrive at their statistical evidence, and he explains how the cephalic index and the facial index, used to compare different anatomical remains, are derived (31–35). (Fig. 33) He will later use the measurement and proportions of the skull as the primary distinguishing characteristic of the European races he identifies, associating above all the long and narrow (dolichocephalic) skull with the "Nordic" race his cultural theory valorizes, and which he identifies with a cross section of modern Germans (42–46). (Fig. 34) He contrasts this skull form with the short and broad (brachycephalic) skull associated with what he terms the "Eastern" *(ostische)* race, above all the Slavic peoples of eastern Central Europe. (Fig. 35) Bone and body size, hair color, eye color, and so on also play central roles in Günther's classifications. But his primary reliance on skull and bone measurements allows him to infuse his studies with a historical dimension: bones tell a story of race that extends back to prehistoric times. (Fig. 36) In order to supplement this data with more ephemeral qualities such as hair and eye color, he turns to cultural evidence such as, in the case of the Germanic peoples, the descriptions Tacitus (ca. 55–120) provides in his *Germania.*

When he sets about tracing the intellectual lineage of his racial ethnology, Günther goes back, significantly, to the anthropologists of the German Enlightenment, whose theories

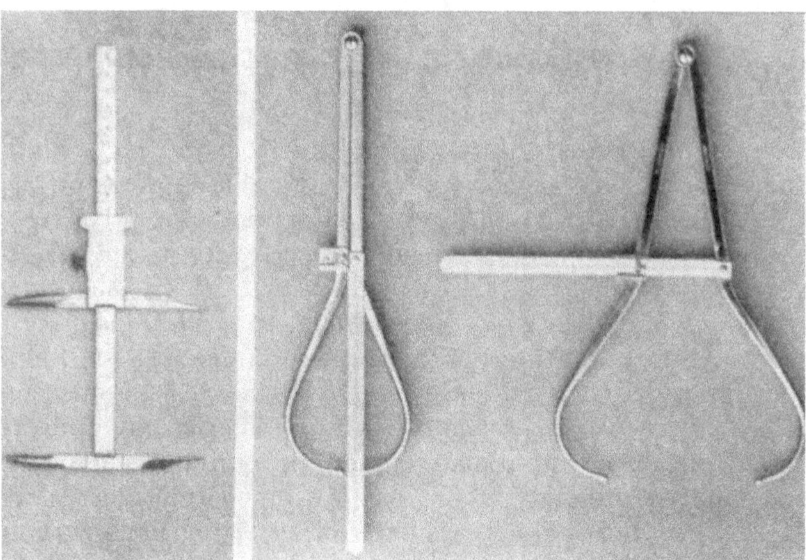

Fig. 33. Tools for anthropological measurements, from Hans F. K. Günther, *Rassenkunde des deutschen Volkes,* 1939.

Fig. 34. Portraits of Nordic individuals, from Hans F. K. Günther, *Rassenkunde Europas,* 1929.

Fig. 35. Portraits of Eastern individuals, from Hans F. K. Günther, *Rassenkunde Europas,* 1929.

developed largely parallel to, and in partial conjunction with, Lavater's physiognomics. In the *Rassenkunde des deutschen Volkes* he names Johann Friedrich Blumenbach (1752–1840) as the father of modern racial ethnology. Blumenbach, a highly respected professor of medicine at the University of Göttingen, was one of the first researchers to attempt to reconstruct a history of humankind and develop a taxonomy of the different human races on the basis of anatomical investigations (Muckermann 10).

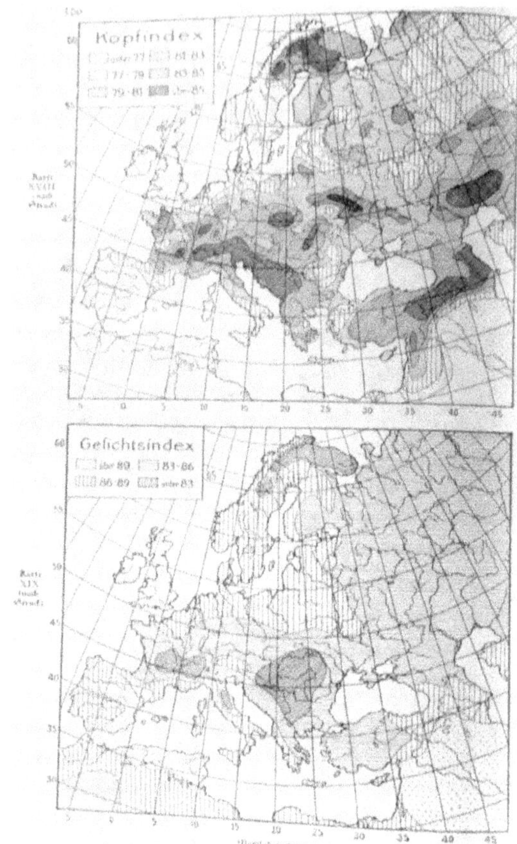

Fig. 36. Maps of distribution of cranial and facial index across Europe, from Hans F. K. Günther, *Rassenkunde des deutschen Volkes*, 1939.

Significantly, Blumenbach's studies were based on the relatively small sample of skulls—ten, to be exact—from different parts of the world available in the collection of the Königliche Societät der Wissenschaften (Royal society of science) in Göttingen; yet he used this evidence to reconstruct the entire skeletal structure of every identifiable human species based on extrapolations from the proportions of the skull alone (Dougherty 98). Blumenbach's anatomical method and his extrapolative speculations called forth the protest of his colleague Christoph Meiners (1747–1810), triggering a scholarly debate in which Blumenbach represented the position of hard, empirical science, and Meiners the intellectual, reasoned speculation of someone whose evidence derived solely from book knowledge (see Dougherty 89–94). Günther was clearly aware of Blumenbach's reputation as someone who sought to define race by strictly empirical means, and this explains his eagerness to identify Blumenbach as his intellectual and methodological predecessor.

In addition to Blumenbach, Günther names as a precursor Immanuel Kant, who, in the essay "Von den verschiedenen Rassen der Menschen" (On the different races of humankind; 1775), sought to distinguish four principal human races (*Rassenkunde* 14). Kant is important not only because of his intellectual pedigree, but also because he was the first to segregate physical anthropology from what he termed "pragmatic" (or cultural) anthropology, and to identify specifically the theory of race as belonging to the domain of the former (Malter 114). Günther also mentions Petrus Camper (1722–1789), the Dutch anatomist who discovered the *linea facialis,* the so-called "facial angle," formed by the intersection of two lines, one drawn from the base of the nose to the base of the skull, the other from the nose to the most prominent part of the forehead. Camper interpreted the facial angle as an objective criterion for determining racial distinctions, and as early as 1770 he lectured on the different facial features that identified human beings as belonging to particular geographical regions (Visser 325; Meijer 5). Over the course of the eighteenth and nineteenth centuries, Camper's *linea facialis* became the foremost material criterion for human racial classification. The facial angle harked back to one of the central tenets of physiognomics since the *Physiognomica* of (pseudo-)Aristotle, the anatomical comparison of humans with animals. For Camper this comparative anatomy was based on the relation of the facial angle in human beings and lower primates (Fig. 37), and Camper sought to establish that the facial angle of Africans approached that found in apes, which was taken by subsequent thinkers as confirmation of their lower evolutionary status.[2] The German physician and anthropologist Samuel Thomas Soemmerring (1755–1830) adopted Camper's facial angle and used it as the basis for establishing a racial hierarchy (Visser 331). Indeed, in 1784 Soemmerring published a treatise entitled *Über die körperliche Verschiedenheit des Mohren vom Europäer* (On

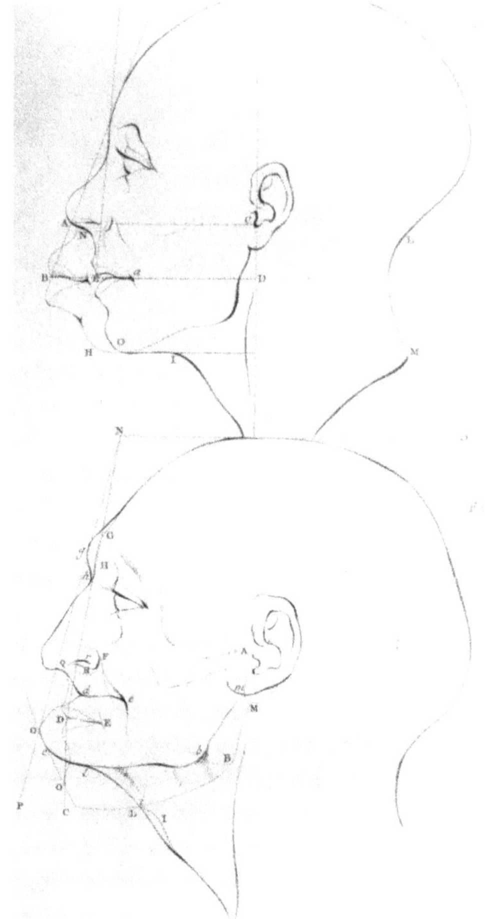

Fig. 37. Facial angle of Negro superimposed on that of a European, from Petrus Camper, *Dissertation physique, sur les différences réelles que présentent les traits du visage chez les hommes de différents pays et de différents âges,* 1791. (Courtesy of Special Collections, University of Washington Libraries)

the anatomical differences distinguishing the Moor from the European), in which anatomical evidence was used to defend the belief, widely held among Europeans, that they were generally superior to the blacks in Africa.[3] Camper's theory of the facial angle was so influential, in fact, that even as late as 1850 it was employed as a means to prove the racial superiority of Europeans over other peoples (Visser 332). Camper thus came to be seen as one of the founders of a scientific racism based on "objective," anatomical evidence (Meijer 172), and this again explains why

Günther makes a point of placing himself in Camper's intellectual heritage.

The intellectual genealogy Günther sketches in his *Rassenkunde des deutschen Volkes* does not include the physiognomics of Lavater and Gall, but the connection to them is made implicitly through Günther's emphasis on figures who focused on anatomical studies, especially the measurement and examination of the skull. We should recall here that Lavater devoted a lengthy section of his *Physiognomische Fragmente* to the discussion of animal and human skulls (2: 139–73), and that he was one of the first to invent an instrument specifically designed to measure the dimensions of the skull, his so-called "Stirnmaaß" (4: 237–46). Moreover, as we have seen, Lavater insisted on the physiognomic significance of the firm and enduring features, valorizing their reliability as definitive signs of character above "pathognomics," the changing forms of facial expression, gesture, and so on. Likewise, Gall's phrenology concentrated exclusively on the human cranium, and it unleashed a veritable rage throughout Europe for the collection and study of the skulls of famous individuals (Lesky 10). The common denominator of all these theories, then, is their materialist, classificatory approach to the body, and Günther clearly understands himself as the modern heir to this anatomical focus in anthropology and physiognomics.

In a passage from his *Kleine Rassenkunde des deutschen Volkes*, Günther makes explicit mention of his connection to the German physiognomic tradition, especially to Lavater and Gall:

> All people unconsciously perceive their fellow human beings to have a distinct racial-psychological predisposition. From a thin, narrow-faced individual one generally expects a different demeanor, behavior, and sensibility than from a heavyset person with a broad face; from someone with a flat nose a different demeanor than from a person with a narrow, long nose; from someone with protruding, bulging eyes and an unpronounced chin a different demeanor than from a person with concave, more deep-set eyes and a pronounced chin; from someone with black hair a different demeanor than from a person with blonde hair; indeed, from someone with short fingers a different demeanor than from a person with long fingers, etc. Over a hundred years ago so-called phrenology sought to determine the psychological nature of a person based on the structural features of the skull; in the ancient

> Greek writers and those of the Italian Renaissance, and subsequently, above all in the works of Lavater and those of his contemporaries inspired by him, we find attempts to derive information about the psychological constitution of human beings from the interpretation of somatic features as a whole, especially of the face. Today such attempts to establish physiognomics . . . have once again gained a great deal of attention. (58)

It is no coincidence that Günther concludes this reflection on the venerable physiognomic tradition by pointing to the resurgence of physiognomic theories in his own day. This testifies to his awareness of the prominent place physiognomic thought assumed in German scientific discourse of the period. It also indicates, however, Günther's attempt to harness the popularity and credibility of physiognomics in order to ensure the success of his own endeavor.

The logic of Günther's argument, which defends attributions of race based solely on the identification of physical traits, has intimate affinities with the appeal to a "natural physiognomics," an unconscious but purportedly omnipresent mechanism in human nature, which is part and parcel of the evidence brought in support of physiognomics at least since Lavater.[4] In the first volume of the *Physiognomische Fragmente,* for example, in an entry entitled "Von der Wahrheit der Physiognomik" (On the truth of physiognomics), Lavater writes: "All human beings (this cannot be denied) judge, all, all, all things according to their physiognomy, their external appearance, their existing surface. From this they continually—every day, every moment—draw conclusions about their internal constitution" (1: 47). After citing examples of how the merchant, the farmer, the physician, the painter, and the traveler continually rely on spontaneous physiognomic judgments, Lavater summarizes his thoughts in typical generalizations, supported by overwrought rhetoric:

> Isn't all of nature physiognomy? Surface and depth? Body and spirit? External effect and inner energy? Invisible beginning, visible end? Is there any bit of knowledge the human being eternally possesses that is not based on external appearance, on character, on the relationship of the visible to the invisible, the perceptible to the imperceptible?— Physiognomics, understood in its wider but more precise meaning, is

> the spirit that animates all human judgments, desires, actions, expectations, fears, hopes, all pleasant and unpleasant sensations caused by things external to us. (1: 49)

For Lavater, physiognomics names human perception in its entirety; every act of seeing is at base an act of physiognomic judgment, a conclusion about internal traits based on external characteristics. Hans F. K. Günther simply transfers the universality of this physiognomic gaze to the domain of race.

Günther exploits the intuitive "truth" of this natural and universal physiognomics to underwrite the anatomical racial taxonomies he establishes in his various books. Thus hair and eye color, the shape of the nose, the prominence of the chin, the placement of the eyes, and even the shape and size of the fingers become indicators of one's racial constitution. But more important, perhaps, is that for Günther these physiognomic attributions are always mediated by criteria of race; if we react negatively to people with dark hair, say, or to someone with a pointed nose, then this is because our "blood"—to speak from within Günther's own discourse—intuits the racial difference that separates "us" from these Others. The goal of his racial anthropology thus is a relatively simple one: to raise this unconsciously practiced racial judgment to the level of conscious decision making and to develop tools that will help train and shape it into a systematic and disciplining physiognomic gaze. In this sense, his project is no different from Lavater's, who likewise sought to promote a systematized, scientifically directed mode of physiognomic perception. Günther's major contribution to this tradition is the specific localization of the criteria for these judgments in matters of racial or genetic constitution.

Günther was not the only promoter of proto-fascist racial ideologies who recognized the connection of these conceptions to Lavater's physiognomics. In his *Die Rassenfrage im Schrifttum der Neuzeit* (The racial question in modern scholarship), volume three of his monumental three-volume collection documenting the historical antecedents to modern racial ideology, *Die Rasse in den Geisteswissenschaften: Studien zur Geschichte des Rassengedankens* (Race in the human sciences: Studies in the history of racial thought), Ludwig Schemann (1852–1938) calls Lavater "a man who came very close to formulating the idea of race, indeed, one who perhaps unconsciously nourished this idea." He continues: "It was none other than Lavater, this amazing person, who treated the issue of national physiognomies in the fourth volume of his *Physiognomische Fragmente.* He quite correctly senses that these nationalities are based on race, and that is why he quotes longer passages from the works of Buffon, Kant, Blumenbach, and others" (206). Significantly, Schemann draws an explicit link leading directly from Lavater's fragment on national physiognomies to the racial physiognomics of the early twentieth century, even claiming that Lavater himself was aware of the racial impetus behind these attributions of national character. Schemann, in short, interprets Lavater as a significant precursor to the racially founded physiognomics promoted above all by Günther. But Schemann could just as well have referred back to (pseudo-)Aristotle, the father of Western physiognomics, in whose *Physiognomica* racial pursuits are named as one of the three primary directions of this science (Aristotle 1: 1237; see Armstrong 53–55).

Schemann was not the sole contemporary of Günther who drew this connection to Lavater. In his important and ideologically balanced book on physiognomics, *Die Körperform als Spiegel der Seele* (Body form as mirror of the soul; 1929) (Fig. 38), Wilhelm Böhle traces the intellectual lineage of contemporary physiognomics back to the writings of the Swiss pastor (Böhle 2–4). Moreover, Böhle notes that, although Günther himself does not specifically identify himself with this physiognomic tradition, he nevertheless "deserves to be awarded one of the most prominent places in the literature on physiognomics" (14). Böhle's opinion is especially significant because he openly opposes the ideological tendencies of Günther's theories and attacks the representatives of the Nordic Idea for presenting a prejudiced apotheosis of their own—the Nordic—race and belittling all others. Despite this ideological objection, however, Böhle acknowledges "the great contribution of Günther's work to the science of physiognomics" as his "detailed portrayal of the physical features . . . and the characterological traits peculiar to the human racial types" (14). For Böhle, Günther's significance lies in the fact that he provides a taxonomy according to which

Fig. 38. Dust jacket, Wilhelm Böhle, *Die Körperform als Spiegel der Seele,* 1929. (Courtesy of the Hessische Landesbibliothek, Darmstadt)

other researchers can measure the correctness of their physiognomic rules (15). Thus even for ideologically neutral advocates of scientific physiognomics, the catalogues of physical and psychic characteristics Günther establishes for the different European races become the standards against which all other investigators must measure their own insights and discoveries. Nothing could speak more clearly for the determining influence Günther's racially tainted physiognomics had at a time when physiognomic theories were attaining intellectual prominence. The wake he created was clearly strong enough to pull the bulk of contemporary German physiognomic theories along in the direction of racial research.

Günther's Racial Physiognomics and the Physiognomic Tradition

In the opening pages of his *Rassenkunde des deutschen Volkes,* Günther articulates his belief that with the beginning of the twentieth century, a new thought-paradigm—the paradigm of race—asserts its dominance in Western culture. The terms in which he formulates this intellectual transition give keys to the principles around which his own theories have crystallized.

> If I am not mistaken, since about 1900 we have been experiencing a historical turning point, which, in contrast to the vanishing historical, indeed, historicizing epoch, in contrast to the age that stressed the influence of milieu, an age that everywhere discovered development, determination, dependence, and becoming—in contrast to all these obsolete views our new age has turned to the *essence [Wesen]* itself, to the historyless Being *[Sein]* of things. . . . If I am not mistaken, we are living in an age in which peoples no longer seek to grasp what is unique in their history, but rather what is characteristic, what is not time bound, so as to elevate the energies to which they owe their greatness from the level of the unconscious to that of consciousness. The will to accomplish, on the basis of clear recognitions and through one's own free will, what is vitally inherent in a people seems to me to be characteristic of the present day; more than that, it is a sign and an omen of the future. Connected with this is a turn from *Doing [Tun]* to *Being [Sein],* a turn to those unverifiable, innate views that are given as a conviction of the blood; connected with this, finally, is a turn to the specific racial makeup of every people. (*Rassenkunde* 3)

Günther's juxtaposition of the "vanishing" age of the nineteenth century, dominated by the liberalist and rationalist doctrines of the French Revolution, with the dawning age of the twentieth century, characterized by the nobility of "blood" and a reliance on pre-rational intuition, sounds an ideological refrain common in this period. It is articulated most vociferously in Alfred Rosenberg's (1893–1946) *Der Mythus des 20. Jahrhunderts* (The myth of the twentieth century), in which the birth of the new century marks the emergence of a new faith. "Today," Rosenberg writes, "a *new* faith is awakening: the myth of the blood, the faith that by defending one's blood one is also defending the divine essence of the human being as such. This faith is embodied in the most lucid knowledge that our Nordic blood represents the arcanum that replaces and overcomes the old sacraments" (114). Günther's racial ethnology lends a scientific face to this new mysticism that defends the significance of Nordic blood. This new myth is defined for Günther above all by its resistance to the Hegelian worldview of the nineteenth century, with its emphasis on change, productive development, the influence of and the adaptation to environmental factors. The enlightened belief in universal adaptability, Günther realizes, is the motor behind the doctrine of equality that he, following Gobineau and Chamberlain, so vehemently decries. To this notion of progressive human development he opposes what he calls *der heldische Gedanke,* "the heroic idea" that all individuals must face and resolve certain existential tasks on their own. Life is thus viewed as a challenge to which each individual must respond according to his or her own strength, will, and character (*Ritter, Tod und Teufel* 33). Günther sees the potential to rise to the challenges presented by existence, however, as genetically or racially determined: in his view, these qualities are programmed to a proportionately larger degree into the "blood" of the Nordic race in particular.

To the Hegelian notion of development, to Darwinian principles of adaptation, and to the milieu theory that stresses the role of external conditions in the formation of personality and character, Günther opposes the predominance of a primordially given Being, a *Sein* that transcends, antedates, and preempts any acquired, learned, or appropriated characteristics. In *Adel und Rasse* he expresses this distinction between action and primordial essence, *Tun* and *Sein,* in its most absolutistic terms: "All that is noble does not reside in *deeds,* but rather in *Being [Sein]* alone, and this Being forms our innate constitution, it is given in the blood" (75). In contradistinction to the economically determined notion of the "self-made man," Günther valorizes a pseudo-aristocratic notion of nobility as inborn and transmitted by bloodlines. In fact, his overriding argument in *Adel und Rasse* is that throughout the centuries, all the noble clans and lineages of every nation have been defined by their Nordic blood (see esp. 72–74). He even presents a pseudo-physiognomic argument to support this identification of nobility and Nordic race: "blue blood," as the traditional sign of nobility—so this legitimating argument runs—only makes sense in the context of the pale white skin characteristic of the Nordic race, through which this blue blood becomes visible (*Rassenkunde des deutschen Volkes* 56). Hence for Günther this designation for aristocratic lineage alludes to the preponderance of Nordic blood in all the great, noble families of Europe. Similarly, he maintains that all conceptions of human beauty, beginning with the ancient Greeks, are unconscious representations of the physical features that, from time immemorial, have consistently been manifest in, and hence associated with, persons of noble character (*Adel und Rasse* 57). Moreover, he asserts that the composite image of all nobility and beauty approaches precisely those physical traits characteristic of the Nordic race: blue eyes, blonde hair, muscular build, harmonious physical proportions, a long and narrow face, and so on.[5] Thus in *Adel und Rasse* he argues: "Unconsciously we have, as it were, combined the physical build, facial features, demeanor, and expression of those who appear to us as 'noble,' as 'nobility,' as superior, into *one single* composite image of the beautiful and noble master: and this image approximates, or is identical to, the image of the Nordic human being" (59). Günther seeks confirmation of this thesis in the beautiful and noble countenances and bodies depicted in Germanic art. (Fig. 39) The question, of course, is whether Günther's Nordic race simply reflects these qualities of beauty and nobility, or whether he has not rather *constructed* his vision of the Nordic ideal around those traits traditionally associated with the aristocratic classes. Indeed, Günther's definition of the Nordic race is clearly produced by the impulse anthropologists call "pseudo-speciation," the assumption that the clan or group with which an individual identifies has exclusive claim to those qualities considered grand, noble, or specifically "human" (see Sennett 308). This impulse characterizes much of the racial doctrine of this period, from Gobineau, through Chamberlain, to Rosenberg and Nazi ideology; but Günther exaggerates it to the extreme. Indeed, he even expresses the belief that people of Nordic blood will rise to the top of any group, regardless of how it is defined, like the "cream" of society, to take over the leadership roles for which they are "genetically" programmed (*Kleine Rassenkunde* 94–95).

What is especially noteworthy about Günther's opposition between innate being and deeds, *Sein* and *Tun,* is that it reit-

Fig. 39. Expression of beauty of the Nordic race in art, from Hans F. K. Günther, *Adel und Rasse,* 1926.

erates the very same dichotomy, even the very same terms, around which the debate over physiognomics was waged more than a century earlier. We recall that Lichtenberg criticized Lavater's notion of physiognomics for its deterministic aspect, its projection of character into the unalterable forms and solid features of the body. To Lavater's notion of physiognomics as the deciphering of this primordially given Being he opposed the idea of pathognomics as the reading of affects and deeds, as "signs of transitory actions" ("Über Physiognomik" 278). Lichtenberg stresses precisely the ephemerality both of these pathognomic signs and of the actions to which they relate, since for him the human being is not a static construct, but a dynamic entity that changes in reaction to impulses received from the outside world. Thus he emphasizes the liminal position of the body as the interface between the internal and the external world. "Our body stands," Lichtenberg maintains, "mid-way between the soul and the rest of the world, and it reflects the effects of both spheres; it not only tells the story of all our dispositions and abilities, but also of the blows of fate, climate, illness, nourishment, and a thousand afflictions" (266). Hegel's critique of the anatomical physiognomics of Lavater and Gall was even more explicit and excoriating than Lichtenberg's, and in Hegel's formulations it is the very opposition between deed and stable Being, *Tun* and *Sein*, that comes to the fore. Thus he unequivocally asserts: "The *true Being [Sein]* of the human being is rather *his deed;* in this deed his individuality is *real*" (*Phänomenologie* 242). Being for Hegel is not some predetermined, a priori set of physical or psychical traits, but rather the translation of any such traits into deed and action. Instead of defining human character as stable Being, Hegel views it as a process of becoming that expresses itself in actions registering the response of the individual to external circumstances and needs.

Günther's racial physiognomics conjures up the terms of this century-old debate in order to take sides against the developmental theories of Lichtenberg and Hegel, which for him represent nothing other than liberalist-egalitarian hogwash, and to throw his weight behind the deterministic conceptions of Lavater and Gall. This is the fundamental sense in which Günther's racial theories manifest a significant reiteration of the physiognomic doctrines articulated in the eighteenth and nineteenth centuries. The human being for Günther, as for Lavater and Gall, is not a self-fashioning entity, but rather a physical-psychical construct whose nature has been preordained from the moment of birth. To be sure, in its Güntherian iteration this older physiognomics has been radically secularized; it is no longer an omniscient and wise deity who oversees and controls this ordination of character, but rather the more anonymous, biologically grounded entities of "genes" and "blood." Traditional religion, in effect, has been displaced by a theology of race. This points to a further transformation that Lavaterian physiognomics undergoes with Günther: although he retains its fundamentally materialist bent, Günther shifts the emphasis away from the individual, who stood in the forefront of Lavater's and Gall's physiognomic conceptions, to trans-individual groups he calls "races" or "peoples." Physiognomics for Günther no longer has the task of identifying the peculiar distinguishing traits of a specific person; instead, its aim is to subordinate the individual under the rubric of a certain specified type. This orientation away from the individual toward typologies is a common feature of many twentieth-century physiognomic theories (see Hake 484; Lalvani 43). Its most obvious manifestation occurs, aside from in Günther's racial typology, in Ernst Kretschmer's alignment, in *Körperbau und Charakter* (Physique and character), of bodily physique with the proclivity for certain psychological pathologies. We recall, as well, that even the ostensibly "humanist" physiognomic theory of Rudolf Kassner attacks the individual as a symptom of a degenerate modernism and glorifies the development of types.[6] Günther's racial physiognomics thus is anti-individualistic—and this is one of the things that made it so compatible with Nazi ideology—in that it valorizes in the individual only those qualities that make it representative of a larger group, of the "Nordic" or "Western" race, or of one of the other races whose typical features he lays out in a clear taxonomy.

It would be wrong, of course, to understand Günther's insistence on innate Being and immutable essence as simply an anachronistic fallback on antiquated positions represented by the likes of Lavater and Gall. Indeed, both Günther's ideas and his language have peculiar affinities with central tenets of a major philosophical system emerging in Germany at this time: Edmund Husserl's (1859–1938) phenomenology. In the first book of his *Ideen zu einer reinen Phänomenologie und phänomenologischen Philosophie* (Ideas for a pure phenomenology and phenomenological philosophy), for example, Husserl explicitly calls phenomenologists "'Platonizing realists,' [who] hypostatize ideas or essences as objects and attribute to them, as to other objects, real (true) Being *[Sein]*" (47). This is precisely what Günther seeks to accomplish with his definitions of racial types. It is perhaps no coincidence that when he describes the notion of the pure racial type—"the *pure image* of a particular race," as he calls it—he explicitly refers to it as an "idea in the Platonic sense" (*Rassenkunde des deutschen Volkes* 12). But like Husserl's phenomenologist, Günther, too, wants to attribute "real (true) Being" to this purely Platonic idea of race; he does so by cataloging the anatomical traits that "correspond" to the characteristics constitutive of the "pure image" of any given race. Another feature Günther's theory of race shares with the phenomenological study of essences is its fundamentally transhistorical nature: race represents a Being beyond time, even outside of time, and clearly beyond the everyday existence of real individuals. It is not surprising, then, that in a philosophical climate in which "ideas" were being accorded reality by phenomenological researchers, the archetype of race as propagated by Günther and others would be able to lay credible claim to substantial Being, especially since it could derive additional evidence from the natural-scientific sphere of genetics, on which it also heavily relied.

There is one further principal idea that Günther's racial physiognomics shares with Husserlian phenomenology: the belief that the human being is constituted as a psychosomatic entity in which there are clear, if generally unspecifiable, connections between the psychical and anatomical domains. In the second book of his *Ideen zu einer reinen Phänomenologie und phänomenologischen Philosophie,* Husserl makes claims about the connection of body and "spirit/mind" *(Geist)* that ring similar to the assertions of many advocates of physiognomics. He writes, for example: "The body is not merely a thing among others, rather it is the expression of the spirit/mind *[Geist], and it is simultaneously the organ of spirit/mind*" (96).[7] Later in the same treatise he concentrates on specifying the nature of the interrelations between body and soul, postulating a "functional interconnection" between these two domains: "The flow of psychic life has its own internal unity; and if the 'soul' that corresponds to a particular body stands in a relationship to this body based on a functional interconnection of reciprocal dependency, then the soul has its own durable psychic characteristics that are expressions of certain regulated *dependencies of the psychic matter upon the body.* The soul is something existent *[Seiendes]* that stands in a conditional relation to bodily circumstances, to circumstances of physical nature" (*Ideen II* 132). What is important here is that Husserl attributes an inherent unity to the "flow" of psychic existence; this would be what we call "character." But nothing in his definition prevents us from identifying this stable element with some other unity such as race. Moreover, Husserl maintains that the "soul" is something inherently existent *(Seiendes)* that stands in a condition of mutual dependence or reciprocal interrelation with a specific body. The relation between body and soul in the human being, as psychosomatic entity, is hence not coincidental, but rather physiognomically significant. Husserlian phenomenology could easily be read as a legitimation of general physiognomic propositions. In fact, one of Husserl's students, Ludwig Ferdinand Clauss (1892–1974), did just this; what is more, he gave this phenomenological physiognomics a decidedly racist bent.

Clauss and his theories are the subject of the following chapter and need not be discussed any further here. He is important in the present context because he helps demonstrate the inherent affinities that relate racial physiognomics to the phenomenological psychology developed in the early decades of the twentieth century in Germany. For Hans F. K. Günther, not surprisingly, the body-soul integrity that Husserl views as a "functional interconnection of reciprocal dependency" is circumscribed more generally as a function of race. In *Rassenkunde des deutschen Volkes* he defines race, his central concept, in the following way: "*A race manifests itself in a group of human beings who are distinct, based on their unifying amalgamation of somatic features and psychic characteristics, from every other group of human beings (defined in the same way) and who always only produce individuals of the same type*" (14). Every race possesses its own characteristic interconnection of physical and psychic traits, and one of the primary tasks of Günther's book is to describe and categorize these sets of interrelated features for the six primary racial groups present, as he believes, in the German population of his day. While it does not specifically address the trans-historicity of race, this definition does imply that race is an immutable Being that underlies, and remains constant throughout, the historical progression of generations. The only thing that threatens this "permanence," of course, is racial intermixture; only under the condition that race retains its "purity," that it is not infiltrated or diluted by "foreign" blood, can the constant propagation of the same be guaranteed. Günther's theory, in other words, recognizes neither internal mutations nor external influences, other than the introduction of "foreign" blood. A race can, so to speak, step out of history and achieve a state of absolute constancy, without decline and degeneration, but also without progression and improvement (such improvement is not necessary for the Nordic race, since for Günther it embodies near perfection!). Racial genes are windowless monads, just like the individual entelechies described in Leibniz's *Monadologie.* The marriage of racial likes, so Günther's definition goes, always produces racial likes. At the same time, in such an ideological context, racial intermarriage becomes tantamount to undermining the pure, originarily given, and ahistoric Being of racial type.

Clearly, the discourse of race generated in part and propagated in Günther's theories profited greatly from its almost uncanny ability to conjure up interrelationships with past and present philosophical and scientific discourses that enjoyed wide credibility. For if in its materialist manifestation Günther's racial ethnology fed off an appropriation of genetic theory and the science of heredity, in its philosophical underpinnings it was parasitic on many of the central concepts of German idealism, not least of which was the idea, revived by Husserl, of an indelible and transhistorical essence. Perhaps it is easier to comprehend—although certainly not to legitimize or even forgive—the power this racial discourse wielded over intellectuals in the 1920s and 1930s in Germany when we recognize the manner in which it strategically appropriated the terminology of this philosophical heritage.

Günther's Conception of Cultural History

Given his drive to identify immutable Being with the indelible characteristics of race, it is easy to understand why Günther, despite his attack on the "historicizing" tendency of the nineteenth century, himself approaches his racial theories on the basis of cultural-historical studies. The aim of his method, which he terms *rassenkundliche Gesittungsforschung,* or the "racial-ethnological investigation of culture" (*Rasse und Stil* 128), is not to document the changes and transformations that particular historical epochs undergo, but rather to extract from cultural history nothing other than the unchanging, permanent structures and motives that can be interpreted as the expressions of a constant, non-transitory racial Being. Alfred Rosenberg alludes to this practice of what we might call a physiognomic historiography when, in *Der Mythus des 20. Jahrhunderts,* he calls history *Charakterdeutung,* the "interpretation of character," whose aim is the "portrayal of an essence in its struggle to realize its most authentic ego" (40). However, history as a form of characterology is not concerned, either in the case of Rosenberg or in that of Günther, with great individuals as such, but only with these individuals as representatives of a specific, racially and "genetically" defined group. Cultural achievement, in other words, is never the product of an individual with unique traits; it is generated by the highest, most representative, most "perfected" specimen of a certain racial type. Not only does race make the man, so to speak, it also shapes culture in its entirety.

Comte Joseph Arthur Gobineau, in his *Essai sur l'inégalité des races humaines* (1853–1855), was the first to propagate the myth that a single unified race, which he called the "Teutons," was responsible for every cultural high-water mark ever achieved in the Western world, from Greek civilization, to ancient Rome, to Celtic culture and the Italian Renaissance. The major ideologues of the Nordic Idea—including Houston Stewart Chamberlain, Alfred Rosenberg, and, of course, Hans F. K. Günther—appropriate and expand on this one-sided and perverse racial historiography. They also adopt from Gobineau the idea that the decline of great civilizations results from the intermingling of this master race with the inferior races it conquers and subdues. For Gobineau, as for Günther and the other spokespersons of the Nordic Movement, history is a cyclical, not a progressively developmental phenomenon. Its cycles are generated by the repeated self-assertion and ultimate degeneration of a culture-bearing class derived from what Günther calls the "Nordic" race, but which Chamberlain, following Gobineau, refers to as the "Teutonic" race. This cyclical idea of history becomes especially prominent in Germany during the Weimar period, and it manifests itself most visibly, perhaps, in Oswald Spengler's monumental and highly influential *Untergang des Abendlandes.* The fatalism implicit in Spengler's theory of history, which discerns a set and stable pattern of rise and decline in every world culture, is also inherent in Gobineau's view. For the latter, decline is inscribed, as it were, into the very characterological essence of the ruling race. Although it is driven by an absolute will to conquer inferior peoples, this very act of conquest ultimately brings with it the demise of this group of Nordic conquerors through racial mixture with the "inferior" conquered people. History, for Gobineau, thus follows the ebb and flow of genetically superior blood, its geographical and cultural expansionism when present in its "pure" forms, its decline and regression when it is diluted due to racial intermixture. In the language of Günther and the advocates of the Nordic Movement, this process of decline is identified as *Entnordung*, "de-Nordification," or the watering-down of the culturally productive elements contained in Nordic blood.[8]

In his *Kleine Rassenkunde des deutschen Volkes* Günther details three primary waves that mark the historic ebb and flow of Nordic culture: classical Greece, ancient Rome, and Celtic civilization. But this pattern transfers, he claims, to every civilization produced by the peoples represented by the Indogermanic language, which he broadly identifies with the Nordic race. Each of these historical waves follows a pattern consisting of four epochs, which Günther terms "antiquity" *(Altertum)*, the "medieval period" *(Mittelalter)*, the "end phase" *(Spätzeit)*, and ultimate decline *(Untergang)*. He describes the cycle of these historical epochs in the following way:

> The significant cultural formations of the individual Indogermanic peoples . . . [are] characterized by an "antiquity" and "medieval period" in which the Nordic spirit inherent in the individual upper classes has a constructive impact; following this, due to increasing *de-Nordification*—that is, the extinction of the predominantly Nordic segment of the population—and *degeneration*—that is, an increase in inferior genetic material in all the races represented in that particular people—an "end phase" ensues, which ultimately leads to the "decline" of this specific culture, and in most instances also to the waning of the political power wielded by these Indogermanic peoples. (114)

"Antiquity" and "medieval period" designate times of cultural ascendancy, in which the Nordic blood of the ruling classes has a beneficent influence and expresses itself in productive cultural accomplishments. However, once a zenith has been achieved, de-Nordification inevitably sets in, accompanied by an increase in "inferior" genetic predispositions throughout the population, and this in turn calls forth the "end phase" of this civilization and its ultimate disappearance. In Günther's historical logbook, the last of these waves of Nordic culture-building began around 120 A.D. with the first migration of the Germanic tribes, continued through the conquests of the Vikings and the Normans, was weakened by the flourishing of the Christian church, and reached its end phase in post-World War One Europe (*Kleine Rassenkunde* 124–38). This generally pessimistic view of the contemporary age conforms, of course, with the other antimodernist dogmas that flourished throughout the Weimar Republic in Germany. However, as opposed to those "fatalists" who, like Spengler, embraced the idea of historical decline with a kind of Nietzschean *amor fati,* or the leftist intellectuals who sought salvation from the problems of modernism in socioeconomic restructuring, Günther and the advocates of the Nordic Idea look elsewhere for redemption: to the emerging fields of eugenics and racial hygiene.

If civilizations emerge and rise due to a preponderance of Nordic blood in their population, and decline and disappear when this Nordic blood is diluted through intermingling with "inferior" races, then eugenics and racial hygiene offer clear antidotes that will permit this final wave of Nordic "conquerors" to break the seemingly inevitable historical cycle of emergence and decline. It is certainly no coincidence that Günther's two most popular books, his *Rassenkunde des deutschen Volkes* and its abridgement, the *Kleine Rassenkunde des deutschen Volkes,* detail the historical cycles of past Nordic civilizations and paint a devastating picture of the contemporary state of German society—the embodiment of the final Nordic civilization—only to conclude in each instance with an upbeat chapter that challenges the German people, to whom the books are addressed, to intervene in their fate and take actions to prevent their racial degeneration. Hence at the outset of the final chapter in his *Rassenkunde des deutschen Volkes,* which bears the telling title "Die Aufgabe" (The task), Günther asserts: "*Degeneration* (that is, a powerful increase in inferior genetic material) and *de-Nordification* (that is, a decrease in the purely Nordic segment of the population) have led to the 'decline' of every Indogermanic people; an increase in the productive, healthy genetic material and an increase in the proportion of Nordic blood must accordingly lead to a new ascent" (462). The logic is as simple as it is potentially deadly. If decline is brought on by the dilution of Nordic blood and the spread throughout the German population of non-Nordic, hence "inferior," genetic material, this process of degeneration can be suspended and even reversed by means of specific racial-hygienic measures. One tactic is so-called "negative" eugenics, the eradication of "tainted" bloodlines, such as those that manifest hereditary diseases or represent especially threatening racial mixtures. Another is to consciously implement strategies of selective breeding, so-called "positive" eugenics, in order to effect a renewed concentration of Nordic blood in certain segments of the population, thereby ensuring a strain of racial "purity." To this process Günther applies the term *Aufnordung,* or "re-Nordification," which is constructed as the semantic opposite of *Entnordung,* "de-Nordification."

The entire ideological program of the Nordic Movement is driven, for Günther, by this eugenic aim. In the treatise that defends this movement against its detractors and summarizes the articles of faith that define it ideologically, *Der Nordische Gedanke unter den Deutschen* (The Nordic Idea among the Germans; 1925), Günther defines its central belief as "the idea that the Nordic human being is the model for selective breeding among those peoples with a Nordic heritage" (4). A few pages later he refines this definition somewhat, adding the qualifier "healthy" to modify "Nordic people" and specifying the *German* populace, not the Nordic people in general, as the group it addresses: "the idea that the healthy Nordic human being is the model for selective breeding among the German populace" (30). The Nordic race is taken as exemplary—that is, the race with the highest, most vital, most noble qualities—among those racial groups represented in the German population, and hence held up as the proper genetic material for planned *Auslese,* "selective breeding." The entire thrust behind the Nordic Movement is thus this program of positive eugenics, a program that was partially realized in "breeding institutions" for the generation of pure Nordic children instituted under Nazi rule (see Mosse, *Crisis of German Ideology* 113–14).

In the final chapter of *Kleine Rassenkunde,* which bears the title "Der Nordische Gedanke" (The Nordic Idea), Günther describes the tasks of the Nordic Movement as the "increase in the Nordic element in all the German lineages *[Stämme]*" and the "re-Nordification of the German people" with the purpose of "bringing about the genetic improvement of this population" (141). Günther seeks to justify this emphasis on the eugenic aims of the Nordic Movement and the significance of eugenic practices for the Nordic race in particular by turning to a (pseudo-)historical argument. In his *Herkunft und Rassengeschichte der Germanen* (Origin and racial history of the Germanic tribes; 1935), for example, he maintains that a special awareness of the holiness of race is part and parcel of ancient Indogermanic culture:

> The Nordic element of every Indogermanic people, which transmitted all beliefs, culture, and language and laid the foundation for the state, demonstrates throughout the history of these peoples that it constitutes the *genetic material of a master race,* which exhibits a conscious and pronounced joy in the *productive breeding of new generations.* The outstanding trait of the Indogermanic peoples, their affirmation of all that is supremely human, all that is wholly human, of *humanitas* . . . exerted its influence even by fostering the purity of new generations by adherence to selective breeding practices and the elimination of unfit specimens. Even in their pursuit of selective breeding, the Germanic tribes, like every other Indogermanic people, strive to approach the *ideal image of the noble person,* and every clan wants to see this ideal image realized in its own individuals. (141–42)

This passage pulls together a number of leitmotifs that run throughout Günther's celebration of the Nordic race. From a historical perspective, he views the Nordic element in every Indogermanic people as the font of all religious faith, social mores, language, and governmental structure. In short, the genetic substance of the Nordic race accounts for the purported cultural mastery of these civilizations. But beyond this, the representatives of Nordic blood within these cultures were aware of, and consciously affirmed, according to Günther, their own genetic superiority: they were, in the truest sense, Nietzschean *Übermenschen* who guiltlessly and self-assuredly lorded over more "inferior" peoples and races in the self-assurance of their own ascendancy. This self-awareness of their superiority expressed itself, among other things, in their commitment to a kind of natural eugenics, the extermination of unfit specimens in their own racial-genetic pool, and the conscious promotion of selective breeding as a way of ensuring and enhancing this genetically determined preeminence. Günther wants to instill this Nietzschean self-consciousness and self-affirmation of their rightful place as the cultural aristocracy of Europe, if not of the world, in his contemporary Germans. The didactic message of all his writings amounts to a plea for the establishment of a new Nordic nobility, modeled on the aristocratic classes that generated the great Nordic civilizations of the past. In *Adel und Rasse* he identifies the Nordic Movement as the (re-)awakening of a will to establish just such a new nobility. "The conscious will to found a New Nobility has awakened, a Nobility constituted by the innate equality of those who have equal portions of Nordic blood" (98). He goes on to define this "innate equality" *(Ebenbürtigkeit)* in more specific terms as including "all the healthy genetic, genetically productive, genetically intelligent people who have equally pure Nordic blood" (104). Günther's mission, then—and the rhetoric of these final citations testifies clearly to his sense of mission—is to raise the Germans' unconscious, unacknowledged sense of their racial "difference" to a heightened level of consciousness and self-certainty.

He laid out this mission in its most proselytizing form in a series of lectures given between February 1933, just prior to the Nazi seizure of power, and June 1936, after the promulgation of the Nuremberg Laws in 1935 had already begun to transform some aspects of Günther's eugenic reform into a legislative program. These lectures were ultimately published together as a book under the telling and nearly untranslatable title *Führeradel durch Sippenpflege* (Noble leadership through the cultivation of clans). This work gives the most detailed exposition of Günther's ideas for the salvation of the Nordic race by means of well organized eugenic practices. What his missionary rhetoric reveals is that Günther saw his contemporary Germans—or at least some of them, namely, those with identifiably high proportions of Nordic blood in their veins—as a bridge between modern human beings and the *Übermensch.* The allusion to Nietzschean terminology and phraseology is appropriate here, since Günther's language is informed throughout by Nietzschean rhetoric, and never more so than when he dons his robe of racial proselyte.[9]

The Ethics of Existential Decisionism

In its ethical or existentialist dimension Günther's discourse most clearly appropriates elements of a racially construed Nietzschean philosophy of the *Übermensch.* Günther's call to his fellow Germans to consciously implement a eugenic turn in their ways of thinking and living rests upon two decidedly Nietzschean pillars: an appeal to the Germans' will to self-empowerment; and an invocation of their willingness to intervene in their everyday existence and make a conscious existential decision for a new way of living that highlights eugenics and genetic health. On the most general level the ongoing theme of Günther's ethics is the Nietzschean motif of self-overcoming. Near the conclusion of *Kleine Rassenkunde des deutschen Volkes,* Günther himself draws this connection to a—to be sure, banalized—Nietzschean philosophy when he notes that every advocate of the Nordic Idea will "always, or at least for the next few centuries, [possess] the ability to think beyond himself and his own genetic disposition, the ability to conceive of himself—as Nietzsche demanded—as a 'transition and decline,' the ability to seek out the 'land of his children'" (147). The final sentence of this treatise conjures up a spirit of "self-overcoming" that is rewarded for its self-sacrifice by the consciousness of contributing to a more vital human spirit (148). It is consistent with Günther's overweening glorification of the Nordic race that this quality of self-overcoming—the turning-inward and self-application, as it were, of the Nordic race's endemic will to overpower and conquer others—is interpreted as a characterological peculiarity of Nordic human beings.

Günther expressed the categorical imperative of his racial ethics already in 1920, in one of his first books, named after a famous painting by Albrecht Dürer (1471–1528), *Ritter, Tod und Teufel: Der heldische Gedanke* (Knight, death, and the devil: The heroic idea). Consciously structured in analogy to Kant's famous categorical imperative, to which Günther explicitly refers, this racially updated version of Kantian ethics reads: "*Act in such a manner that you will always be able to conceive the direction of your will as the basic direction of a legislation carried out in the spirit of the Nordic race*" (191). Individual actions should no longer be guided by what is deemed appropriate and beneficial for human beings as a whole, but only according to the demands exacted by a self-awareness of racial (self-)enhancement. For the German populace this means that *all* Germans, regardless of their individual racial constitution, must work to foster and promote the Nordic components in their own blood. This requirement turns on an existential decisionism, an *Entscheidung*, a conscious and willful option for the values presumably represented by the Nordic race. Günther expresses this existential demand near the conclusion of *Rassenkunde des deutschen Volkes*: "Whether regarded physically or psychically, almost every human being today has become a crossbreed *and hence is faced with a decision*—based on an awareness of racial issues, especially if a racial renewal is to occur. This *decision regarding our attitudes* will have to be a characteristic of what is to come" (474). Recognizing that the Germans, like all modern Europeans, are composed of a racial mixture, and hence are, by his standards, racially degenerate "crossbreeds," Günther calls for a conscious decision on the part of all Germans to promote their "Nordic" traits in order to ensure the viability of the Volk and resist the tendency toward racial-historical decline. He sees this categorical imperative as a rallying cry that will unify the German people behind a mission whose aim is the promotion of their own most vital characteristics, contained in the proportion of Nordic blood—however small that might be in some instances—that flows in their veins. For Günther this Nordic blood represents the sole common bond that ties all contemporary Germans into a unified people. "The only thing that Germans of *all* races have *in common* is their Nordic blood, *so that the turn toward an emphasis on the Nordic race can become an expression of the Germans' striving to recognize what binds all of them together*" (474; cf. *Der nordische Gedanke* 42). All Germans, in short, are faced with the existential decision of opting for or against a eugenic program that promotes the development of the Nordic race (see *Nordische Gedanke* 41). Since, according to Günther, decisiveness and the ability to make tough choices are inherent in the Nordic character (*Rassenkunde* 76), the Germans' willingness to line up in support of his categorical imperative becomes a test case of their inherent Nordic "health," their potential—more, their deservingness—of racial advancement. We recognize in this decisionistic program an essential, indeed, a fateful element of Nazi ideology, one that prolonged the Second World War and increased the destruction and death toll by demanding of the German populace that it either prove its "Nordic superiority" or be utterly exterminated.

In chapter 4 I investigated the paradoxical, almost ironic role that Goethe, both as morphologist and exemplary intellectual figurehead, played in the history of modern German physiognomics in general, but more specifically in the history of its racial turn in the thought of Carl Gustav Carus. It is significant that Günther, too, invokes the example of Goethe when he seeks to present his readers with a model for the kind of decisionism and self-overcoming advocated in his racial ideology. In *Der nordische Gedanke* Günther refers to Goethe in order to defend his demand that the Germans focus their energies on furthering their Nordic traits, countering the objection by his critics that this amounts to self-falsification and the brutal suppression of other racial components in one's genetic constitution.

> What is important is the *direction* that emerges from the struggle of distinct racial souls in one and the same breast. It seems to me that Goethe, who was a racial crossbreed (his facial features betray Nordic-Dinaric traits, while his physique testifies to Eastern influences), is a good example of a human being who affirms himself with all his genetic dispositions, who does not practice "self-abnegation" in any form. . . . He exemplifies how such a self-affirming person can bundle all his internal conflicts and channel their energy in a specific direction. The "Faustian element," which defines the Nordic soul as such, constantly determined the direction Goethe took. He placed the non-Nordic, and even the questionable aspects of his own psychic constitution in the service of progression in this chosen direction. (63)

The famous "two souls" who struggle against one another in the hero of Goethe's *Faust* have now become *racial* souls, and the Faustian personality, as in Spengler's characterization of the soul of modern Europe, stands as the icon for a heroic struggle that transpires within every Nordic individual and is reflected in the macrocosm of cultural expression. Goethe himself as individual is elided with this racially interpreted Faust-figure, and for Günther he comes to represent above all the successful channeling of non-Nordic racial proclivities into directions that ultimately serve the ends of Nordic self-realization. Goethe is important because his example is intended to demonstrate that the subjugation of one's non-Nordic racial tendencies does not amount to self-abnegation. Goethe's example shows how these other racial streams can be redirected in such a manner as to flow into and support the current that is driven by one's Nordic genes. Even the "questionable" racial features that are part of one's inherent constitution can be rechanneled and made productive if they are given decisive direction in the service of this greater Nordic program. The challenge that faces Günther's contemporary Germans, then, is to harness the antagonisms inherent in their status as racially "mixed" individuals and invest this energy into the realization of goals consistent with the demands of their Nordic blood. The upshot of this would be, of course, given Günther's emphasis on strategic eugenics, that primarily non-Nordic people would have to decide willingly to avoid marriages with predominantly Nordic individuals, to have fewer or no children, and so on, while those with a strong Nordic heritage would have to marry like-gened individuals and produce as many children as possible. In order to accomplish this, of course, one would first need to distinguish, as Günther himself argues, between the value of the individual qua individual, and the value of a particular human specimen as breeding stock for the generation of relatively pure Nordic children for future generations, and hence for the vitality of the Volk as a whole (*Der nordische Gedanke* 47).

From Theory to Practice: Günther's Applied Physiognomics

Implicit in the idea that for purposes of selective breeding, individuals with a higher percentage of Nordic blood must be segregated from the rest of the population is the belief that one can establish objective criteria for identifying every individual's exact racial composition. In other words, those people with relative racial purity must somehow be recognized, as must those who contain high proportions of racially "tainted" blood. There was not during Günther's day, nor will there—thankfully!—ever be, a simple "blood test" to calibrate the "Nordic" or "Eastern" or any other racial component of a person's blood. The question then becomes: On what basis does Günther propose to distinguish individuals who belong to the different racial types that make up the German populace? His answer is, of course, on the basis of *physiognomics,* by interpreting the anatomical features of individual human beings as indicative of racial type and hence as symptoms of specific psychological or characterological traits peculiar to that racial type. Physiognomic hermeneutics plays an absolutely crucial role in the structure of Günther's ideological program because it is solely on this basis that the *theory* of eugenic purification and genetic health can be turned into a concrete *practice* that deploys specific eugenic instruments in select instances. Physiognomics thereby becomes the indispensable tool by which Günther will classify and segregate human subjects into particular racial categories.

The structure of *Rassenkunde des deutschen Volkes* already gives an indication of the prominence that physiognomic examination will play in Günther's theory. The first four chapters define race, present a history of racial thought, identify the primary races present in contemporary Europe, introduce the importance of anthropometric methods, and stress the role of physical traits such as eye and hair color for the determination of racial constitution. (Fig. 40) Günther devotes one chapter each (chapters 5 through 10) to descriptions of the anatomical features that, in his view, are characteristic of the six major races represented in the German populace: the Nordic; Western (or Mediterranean); Dinaric (named after its supposed origin in the Dinaric Alps); Eastern (called "Alpine" by other contemporary racial anthropologists); East Baltic; and Phalian (whose name derives from an association with the geography of the German province of Westphalia; this group was referred to as "Dalian" by other racial researchers of the time). In each instance Günther provides detailed descriptions of the typical skull form, the cranial index, the size and proportions of the body, the general texture of the fleshy parts of the face, as well as eye, hair, and skin color. What is most significant about Günther's presentation of these racial

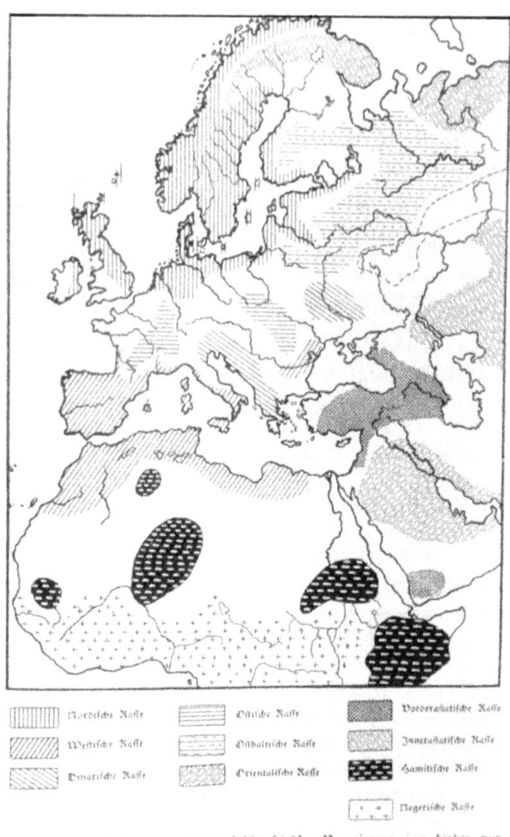

Fig. 40. Map of distribution of races across Europe, from Hans F. K. Günther, *Rassenkunde des deutschen Volkes*, 1939.

types, however, is the profuse number of photographs, depicting either historical personalities or contemporaries whom he considers especially representative of a particular racial type, to illustrate the specific features he aligns with each racial category. (Fig. 41) There can be no doubt that these illustrations help to account largely for Günther's success in proliferating his typology throughout wide segments of the German population. Indeed, Lehmann Verlag, the publisher of Günther's books, made representative illustrations available both as photographic sets that could be purchased or borrowed for use in demonstrations

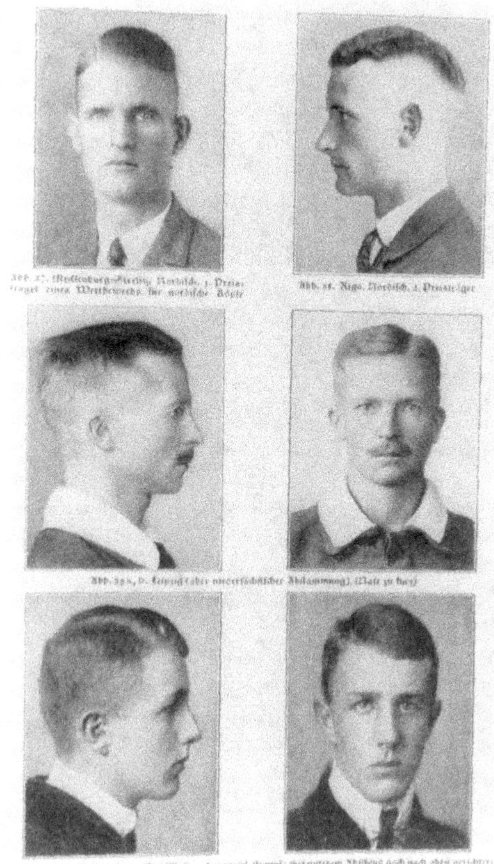

Fig. 41. Portraits of Nordic individuals, from Hans F. K. Günther, *Rassenkunde des deutschen Volkes,* 1939.

of racial anthropology, and as wall posters that were particularly adapted for use in schools to support lessons on racial ethnology.[10] (Fig. 42)

Only *after* he has portrayed the physical characteristics of these six races does Günther turn to their psychological or characterological features, again committing a separate chapter to the description of each type. The Nordic race is characterized, according to Günther, by boldness, a powerful will, a strong sense of justice, a heroic sensibility, and exemplary qualities of leadership. Nordic people tend to be cool and reserved; they have

Fig. 42. Racial instruction in a German elementary school during the Third Reich, from *Neues Volk,* 1934. (Courtesy of the Bundesarchiv, Coblenz)

a powerful imagination, are generally creative, technologically astute, and display a strong inclination toward truthfulness (*Rassenkunde* 190–214; *Kleine Rassenkunde* 59–61). The Western race, which is approximately congruous with the Romance peoples, is especially passionate and excitable, strives for enjoyment and pleasure, has strong rhetorical abilities and a proclivity for theatricality, tends to be disorganized, and frequently displays signs of sadism (*Rassenkunde* 215–22; *Kleine Rassenkunde* 61–62). The Dinaric race, which Günther locates in the southeastern Alpine region of Germany, is marked by physical strength and honesty; Dinaric people live for the present, are easily enraged, and have a special talent for music. Criminality, especially crime involving bodily harm, is relatively high among Dinaric people (*Rassenkunde* 223–27; *Kleine Rassenkunde*

62–64). The Eastern race, which approximates the Slavic population of Eastern Europe, is characterized by the love of comfort and the avoidance of all competition, tends toward mediocrity, and succumbs easily to the force of habit—even to the extent of feeling hatred toward individuals with superior capabilities and talents—and lives in close, but closed, family circles (*Rassenkunde* 228–35; *Kleine Rassenkunde* 64–66). The East Baltic race, which populates areas of Eastern Prussia, Poland, and Silesia, comes away worst in Günther's depiction. They are described as coarse, deceptive human beings who tend to display the mentality of the masses and want only to be led, never to lead. They have a strong proclivity toward serious crime, especially bodily harm and theft, and their character is marked by sudden oscillations between emotional extremes (*Rassenkunde* 236–40; *Kleine Rassenkunde* 66–68). The Phalian race, by contrast, fares relatively well in Günther's evaluation, coming closest in both physical and psychological features to the Nordic race. Phalian human beings are resolute, decisive, and calm, with a tendency to take life extremely seriously, often to the point of brooding. The Phalian, like the Nordic race, is typified by perseverance and strong-willed stubbornness (*Rassenkunde* 241–43; *Kleine Rassenkunde* 68–69).

What especially stands out in Günther's characterizations is that, primarily in the cases of races like the Western and Eastern, which are more or less identifiable as the Romance and Slavic peoples, his catalogue of features reads like a list of the common prejudices middle-class Germans of this time would have held about these nationalities in any case. Günther's descriptions thus serve to confirm long-held prejudices and transform them from cultural to racial—that is, genetically innate and unalterable—characteristics.

The Jewish people, whom Günther identifies as the Near Eastern race, are not specifically treated in the *Rassenkunde des deutschen Volkes* or in the *Kleine Rassenkunde* because, unlike the races whose features he catalogues here, they are not endemic to Europe. The Jews, like the African blacks, the Mongols, and the Romanies, represent "foreign elements" when they infiltrate the German population, and this, according to Günther, makes them especially insidious. In Günther's Eurocentric taxonomy, these extra-European races are lower than the low, so to speak, and they must be kept out of the gene pool of the German populace at any price. Indeed, what makes the Jews and the Romanies especially threatening is that they have already begun to infiltrate the German population and have become the primary vehicles of degenerate Otherness (*Kleine Rassenkunde* 51). In general, the picture of the Jews Günther paints in his *Rassenkunde des jüdischen Volkes* (Racial ethnology of the Jewish people) again confirms and expands upon the anti-Semitic prejudices that festered in the thinking of most representatives of the Nordic Movement at this time. Indeed, the obverse side of the ideological coin, on whose face was minted the glorification of Nordic virtues, was stamped with the images of Jewish defamation. Modeling his ideas about the Jewish people in many fundamental ways on the vehement anti-Semitism expressed in Karl Eugen Dühring's (1833–1921) infamous *Die Judenfrage als Frage der Raçenschädlichkeit für Existence, Sitte und Cultur der Völker* (The Jewish question as a question regarding racial perniciousness for the existence, morality, and culture of all peoples), first published in 1880,[11] Günther insists, first of all, that the Jews constitute a race, or a specific racial conglomerate, not merely a religious community (*Kleine Rassenkunde* 55). Once Jewishness is defined as an innate racial characteristic instead of a cultural or religious sensibility, of course, the only possible way for eradicating its attributes is to eradicate the Jews themselves. The definition of the Jews as race, in short, drives the logic of the Final Solution. But Günther, again similar in may ways to Dühring, goes even farther than this: he identifies the Jews as the only other "race" that possesses the will, the capital, and the power to compete with the Nordic race for world dominion. In *Der nordische Gedanke* he notes: "In the present age there are only two races that compete for mastery over the earth: the *Near Eastern race* (by dint of the capital controlled by Jewish banks and the dissemination of Bolshevist propaganda among all the nations of the earth); and the *Nordic race* (by dint of the productive capital of all those peoples who speak Germanic languages). One of these two races will eventually rule the earth—assuming that both do not perish from their mutual competition" (131). The confrontation between the Near Eastern (that is, the Jewish) and the Nordic races is formulated here as a fight to the finish, the ultimate racial shoot-out at the OK Corral, in which only one race will emerge as victor and hence as ruler of the entire world. Günther thus hypostatizes a deep-seated inimicality between the Nordic Germans and the Jews, representing the Jews as the Germans' natural enemies. If Günther's anti-Semitic rhetoric was less vitriolic and less charged than that of many other Nazi ideologues, this perhaps helped make it more palatable to ideological moderates in the German populace. Moreover, consistent with his philosophy of race in general, Günther believes that Jewishness could be identified by physiognomic means based on specific anatomical features. (Fig. 43) Here again, the somatic racial traits he identifies as peculiarly Jewish affirm traditional prejudices, and the illustrations of Jews included in his books tend to approach the typical caricatures of the Jewish physiognomy found in propagandistic anti-Semitic sheets of the day like Julius Streicher's (1885–1946) *Der Stürmer.* (Fig. 44)

Günther's physiognomic ethnology faces most of the theoretical quagmires that confront traditional physiognomics, above all the issue of precisely how to conceive the interrelation between physical and psychological traits. Where Lavater, for example, turned to semiotics to solve this problem, and Carus to the Romantic philosophy of the symbol, Günther relies on a rather unrefined notion of genetics and heredity. Just as Lavater's turn to semiotics does not solve the inherent problem, neither does Günther's appeal to genetics: in both cases these "solutions" paste over or divert attention away from the underlying issue by assuming the guise, and thus purloining the credibility, of current scientific theory.[12] Günther is fully aware that genetics does not provide an answer to the problem of mediation between physical and psychical traits, especially since genetics expressly addresses the important distinction between phenotype, the genetic potentials actually realized in any individual, and genotype, the unactualized, "invisible" genetic material that also constitutes this same individual "behind the scenes," as it were. In other words, there is no good reason why the *psychic* characteristics of a "Nordic" human being would have to express themselves in terms of particular *physical* traits such as blue eyes and blonde hair. Barring such a one-to-one identification,

Fig. 43. Portraits of Jews, from Hans F. K. Günther, *Rassenkunde Europas,* 1929.

however, the entire edifice of Günther's ethnological physiognomics, whose foundation is built upon the study of somatic features and the extrapolation of psychic qualities from these anatomical traits, collapses like a house of cards.

Günther is aware of this problem, as a passage from his *Rassenkunde des deutschen Volkes* clearly indicates, and it is instructive to see precisely what tactics he deploys to avoid its consequences.

> One question for which investigators have still presented no conclusive answers is the question about the racial-genetic transmission of

Fig. 44. "For Blind People," racial propaganda piece from Julius Streicher's anti-Semitic journal *Der Stürmer,* 1934. The ironically intended subscript reads, "All creatures with a human face are equal." (Courtesy of the Bundesarchiv, Coblenz)

> psychological qualities. For example, do the laws of genetic transmission allow for the possibility that predominantly Nordic psychological traits can be combined with a predominantly Eastern body in one and the same human being? We will perhaps have to assume that this is possible. Does the genetic transmission of psychological qualities operate so autonomously that a purely Nordic spirit could reside in a purely Eastern body? This most extreme of all possible cases of intermeshing seems to me to be very improbable. At any rate, given the current state of research on this matter, we can say very little today about the racial-genetic transmission of psychological qualities. No doubt, somatic-psychological combinations of a contradictory sort are possible, even if extremely infrequent. What is most likely is that, in general, the human being does indeed "appear to be what he actually is" (Schopenhauer). (262)

Günther takes the most extreme example possible, the psychosomatic fusion of Eastern and Nordic traits, which in his typology are diametrically opposed, in order to address this problem. This already represents a rhetorical strategy, since his readers are least likely, having read to this point in his book, to view such an interconnection as plausible. An appeal to scientific evidence, he claims, cannot be made because, as the formula goes, the proper studies have not yet been undertaken. Given the inability to support the principle that somatic and psychic traits are genetically transmitted in some necessary interconnection, Günther turns instead to other forms of legitimation. The first is common sense: although it may be possible that "contradictory" body-soul combinations can occur, the likelihood and frequency of such contradictions are extremely small (since, we are led to presume, nature does not operate in terms of contradiction, but rather on the basis of harmony). The second is philosophical authority. He appeals to a statement by Arthur Schopenhauer (1788–1860), drawn from the essay "Zur Physiognomik" (On physiognomics) in his *Parerga und Paralipomena,* which asserts an absolute identity between Being and appearance. The fact that this philosophical observation essentially elides the scientific distinction between phenotype and genotype—a distinction on which Günther otherwise insists—is a fact that, for good reason, Günther fails to mention here.[13]

Günther had in fact already cited this statement by Schopenhauer, at somewhat greater length, earlier in his book, in a section that similarly touched on the problem of legitimizing the parallel between physical and psychical dimensions of the human being. Here he turns to a strategy that is standard fare for nearly all physiognomic theorists: the invocation of the intuitive awareness with which all human beings operate, an "unconscious," or a "natural" and "innate" physiognomic judgment.

> The fact that particular psychological traits usually appear in conjunction with specific somatic features represents a certitude that almost every human being arrives at "subconsciously," just as every human being is unconsciously or consciously convinced that psychological traits can be genetically transmitted. Almost every human being also arrives at judgments about other human beings based on an unconsciously developed "science of facial expression," as one might call it. "All people secretly operate with the hypothesis that everyone appears to be what he actually is. This hypothesis is indeed correct; but the difficulty arrives when one attempts to apply it, since this ability is partially innate, partially acquired on the basis of experience." This is the opinion of *Schopenhauer.* (190)

If in the previously cited passage Günther approached the body-soul connection from the negative position of scientific skepticism, here he broaches it from the positive perspective of commonsense affirmation. The inherent relation between somatic and psychic traits is hypostatized as an unconscious "certitude," an intuitive and experiential truth that no one would dare call into question. This unconsciously formed "science of facial expression," on which every individual relies, becomes the ultimate legitimation for Günther's physiognomic ethnology and his practice of interpreting racial-characterological traits out of anatomical features. Schopenhauer, again, is the authority he names in order to justify this practice. Günther has good reason to invoke his name, since in his magnum opus, *Die Welt als Wille und Vorstellung* (The world as will and representation; 1819), Schopenhauer blithely asserted that the human body is "sichtbar gewordene Wille," the will made visible (cited in Kloos 68). Günther goes on, however, to cite other "authorities," from Shakespeare, to modern-day caricaturists and advertisers whose cartoons and drawings, to Günther's mind, confirm his general typological interrelation of physical and psychical features, to the statements of other contemporary physiognomists (*Rassenkunde* 190–91). But the citation from Schopenhauer is the most central one because, aside from asserting the intuitively founded identity of Being and appearance, it also points to the difficulties inherent in the application and *practice* of physiognomic interpretation.

This pragmatic dimension plays a fundamental role in Günther's entire ethno-physiognomic program, where it expresses itself as an explicit didactic intention. The aim of Günther's project is none other than to train the German populace to be more observant and more astute in the extrapolation of racial information out of physical indices, to "teach the eye to recognize valuable blood," in Günther's own words (*Der nordische Gedanke* 113). His aim, in short, is to transform everyday Germans into amateur racial ethnologists who will practice physiognomics according to the methodologies and typologies he himself has laid out. Already in 1920, in the book *Ritter, Tod und Teufel,* Günther expressed the need to train the eye of his contemporary Germans to practice a disciplinary gaze that discerns in physical features the underlying qualities of race.

> In contemporary Europeans the ability to observe racial features has been completely lost, has become totally atrophied. Above all the

> Germans—who have a special difficulty in training their eyes to accommodate plastic observation—these unplastic Germans meander through the streets of their cities without reading anything out of the build, skull shape, skin color, or gestures of the people they encounter, without ever having even an inkling that this or that wrinkle in the eye lid, this particular form of the cheekbone, skin color, hair color, soft or coarse hair texture, this or that gesture—gestures are always expressions of the racially-determined structure of the bones and the muscles—without ever having an inkling that these things provide one with a glimpse into the natural history of the Occidental human being. . . . Among us [Germans] a lamentable lack of knowledge prevails about things concerning the racial differences and the racial composition of the German populace. We lack the ability to see in fresh ways; all our perceptions are clouded by an absence of creative observation, something that is characteristic of an age like ours that relies so heavily on calculation. . . . Our age, which is often noted for its accomplishments in the natural sciences, has brought us to the point—due to its solely calculative procedure, due to its epistemological methodology, which necessarily translates everything that appears immediately to our senses into a numerical expression—this age has brought us to the point that our senses themselves have been enfeebled, that the structuring powers of our empirical perception have dissipated. (166–67)

Of all Europeans, contemporary Germans, according to Günther, are the most oblivious to the physiognomic and racial features of those around them, and they are ignorant of an entire dimension of empirical knowledge that would give them insight into their own history and the history of Europe in general. Instead, they have been seduced by the more theoretical, more abstract epistemological practices of the modernist age and have lost their natural ability to interpret empirical facts. Especially noteworthy here, once again, is Günther's implicit opposition between *Zahl* and *Gesicht,* number and face, the very same dichotomy played out in Rudolf Kassner's first physiognomic treatise—which appeared, as we recall, in 1919, one year before the publication of Günther's *Ritter, Tod und Teufel.* Günther's lament that the Germans have sold their souls, as it were, to the devils of calculative reason and abstract thought rings strikingly similar to the outcries voiced by Kassner and Oswald Spengler. As in their cases, for Günther, too, physiognomic study appears as the antidote that will cure this modern illness: it will teach the Germans to *see* again with "untainted" eyes.

It is no coincidence that this call for greater powers of observation, for a training of the gaze, is already present in Lavater's physiognomic program. In the second volume of the *Physiognomische Fragmente,* for example, Lavater voiced an attack on his own age that seems to resound in Günther's critique of the modern German's lack of empirical vision. "Oh, you weak, frail, pale, fragile century—who will be capable of endowing your gaze with fortitude, your gait with courage, your hand with audacity, your works with—confidence and determination; that is—who will give you eyes that you may see?—*Powers of observation*?" (2: 23). To be sure, what Günther wants his contemporary Germans to be able to perceive is something quite different from what Lavater had in mind; what Günther will try to teach them to observe, of course, is nothing other than racial difference.

Günther leaves no doubt about the pedagogical project he pursues in his *Rassenkunde des deutschen Volkes:* the task of teaching his fellow Germans to absorb a prescribed mode of physiognomic seeing. "Our gaze can be trained," he categorically declares at the start of this treatise, "or at the very least: we can develop the power to see and grasp the body as meaningful" (1). The modification in his rhetoric is significant: one teaches people something they do not yet know, but one facilitates in the training of faculties they inherently possess. And this is Günther's basic position: the Germans, like all human beings, are in possession of an innate ethno-physiognomic ability that needs to be properly cultivated. His books are intended to provide the instruments for this cultivation. If the number of printed copies of his central works, their implementation in the schools, and the production of didactic materials based on his ideas are any indication, Günther was extraordinarily successful in this pedagogical project.[14] There are other ways to measure his influence, of course. One is the credit he accrued from his contemporaries for having trained many an amateur physiognomist (see Weidenreich, "Das Problem der jüdischen Rasse" 79). Another is the sheer number of racial physiognomists and racial geneticists, people like Wilhelm Böhle, Robert Burger-Villingen (b. 1865), Ludwig Ferdinand Clauss (1892–1974), Norbert Glas, Jakob Graf (b. 1891), Willy Hellpach (1877–1955), Carl Helm, Fritz Lange,

Friedrich Märker (b. 1893), Erich Murr, Eduard Ortner, Bruno Petermann (1898–1941), Bruno K. Schultz (1892–1942), and Gerhard Venzmer (b. 1893), who emerged in his wake. A further symptom is the vehemence of the attacks launched against Günther and his theories, manifest most notably in Friedrich Merkenschlager's *Götter, Helden und Günther: Eine Abwehr der Güntherschen Rassenkunde* (Gods, heroes, and Günther: A repudiation of Günther's racial ethnology) and Adolf Hedler's *Rassenkunde und Rassenwahn: Wissenschaft gegen demagogischen Dilettantismus* (Racial ethnology and racial mania: Science against demagogic dilettantism). Popular magazines of the day also published scorching parodies of the racial typologies Günther and his followers disseminated. A 1923 cartoon from the widely distributed weekly *Simplicissimus,* for example, satirizes these types by asking "What does Hitler look like?," and offering a panoply of physiognomic caricatures in answer to this. (Fig. 45) A similar piece published in the same journal a year later, entitled "New Types: Racial Man," parodies both the prominent faith in racial typologies and the specious utopianism with which racial ethnology identified the production of pure racial types with a healthy Nietzschean *Übermensch,* the "new" human being. (Fig. 46) To be sure, these excoriating critiques were published before the Nazi seizure of power, at a time when criticism of Günther's position and of racial ideology in general was still possible.

Günther's influence on Nazi policy and practice can be seen in the fact that his racial categories and the physical attributes associated with each were ultimately standardized in the "Richtlinien zur Rassenbestimmung," the guidelines for determining racial constitution formulated by the *Rasse- und Siedlunghauptsamt SS,* the Nazi agency charged with the racial evaluation of indigenous populations in the territories under German occupation.[15] But a press release by the National Socialist Office for Racial Politics, dated 28 November 1935, gives perhaps the best evidence that Günther succeeded in introducing a wave of popular racial physiognomics and that, given the context of Nazi racial ideology, many people were attempting to turn the popularity of this activity to their own profit. The press release names a certain Reinhold Kohlhardt, who resides in Berlin and

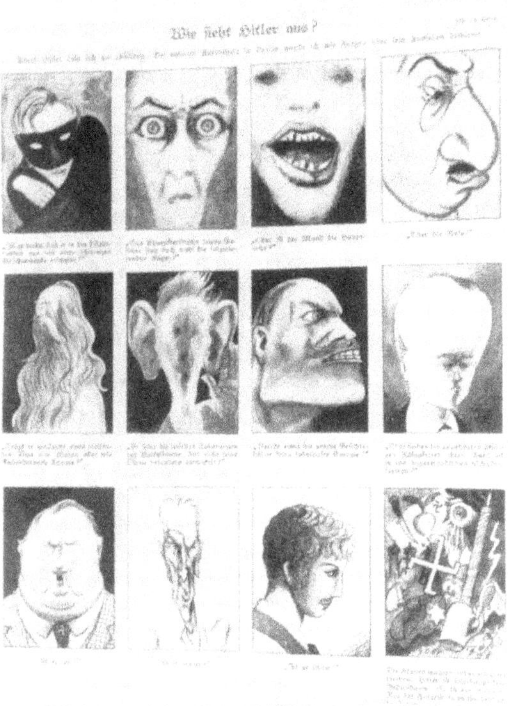

Fig. 45. Parody of Nazi racial typologies, "What Does Hitler Look Like," by Thomas Theodor Heine, from *Simplicissimus*, 1923. © 2003 Artist Rights Society (ARS), New York / VG Bild-Kunst, Bonn. Reprinted with permission from *Simplicissimus: Eine satirische Zeitschrift, München 1896–1944* (Munich: Haus der Kunst, 1977).

calls himself a professional phrenologist and characterologist, who has plastered the city with posters promising, for a small fee, to identify the race to which people belong. He also includes advertisements for his "well reviewed" pamphlets, "Du bist erkannt" (You are exposed) and "Dein Schädel verrät dich" (Your skull betrays you), both of which can also be obtained for a small price. The press release goes on to report that Mr. Kohlhardt's posters have been removed and that he is being sought by the authorities. Moreover, it concludes by warning people about the proliferation of such imposters and quacksalvers: "Kohlhardt is not the only one of this ilk; there are numerous other prophets who seek to pursue racial investigations in a similar way. We intend to take drastic actions against all these imposters."[16] Günther and the Nazi racial ideologues had let the genie of racial

Fig. 46. Caricature of racial typologies, "New Types: Racial Man," by Karl Arnold, from *Simplicissimus,* 1924. © 2003 Artist Rights Society (ARS), New York / VG Bild-Kunst, Bonn.

physiognomics out of the bottle, but they themselves, obviously, became concerned at a very early date that they no longer had this genie under their control. Even Otto Reche, one of the noted German scientists who supported Nazi racial ideology, concluded a lecture on the "Rassebild des deutschen Volkes" (The racial image of the German Volk) with the warning: "I want to conclude this description of the races with a warning against participation in a sport that, unfortunately, is already widely practiced: I mean the sport of analyzing one's fellow human beings to discover their racial constitution, in the belief that one can determine with absolute exactitude and from bodily features alone what percentage a given individual has of this race and what percentage he has of another or of several other races" (39). Günther's project of training the Germans to acquire an ethno-physiognomic gaze was clearly so successful that it unleashed and promoted this "sport," against which even prominent Nazi authorities felt they had to take preventive measures. Günther contributed in major ways to transforming Nazi society into a kind of racial panopticon, in which every citizen could feel intimidated and potentially exposed by the discerning ethnophysiognomic gaze of his or her contemporaries. This penetrating panopticism ultimately reached such proportions that the Nazi leadership itself began to perceive it as potentially dangerous and divisive.

Conclusion

Günther's racial physiognomics is of special significance because it represents a kind of intellectual-historical nodal point in which several traditions merge and congeal into a powerful and popular ideology. We have already examined two of these lineages, the marriage of the materialist physiognomics of Lavater, Gall, and Carus with the racial thought of Gobineau, Chamberlain, and others. To this mix Günther adds the dimension presented by the newly evolving sciences of genetics and eugenics. But there is yet one more intellectual heritage that Günther actively engages, and it is this that perhaps best accounts for the success and wide dissemination of his theories. We have already alluded to this line of thought in our discussion of the Nietzschean elements in Günther's ethics and his proximity to Husserlian phenomenology: the tradition of German *Lebensphilosophie,* life philosophy, from Goethe to Schopenhauer and Nietzsche, the same intellectual thread that lent vitality to the humanistic physiognomics of people like Spengler, Kassner, and Klages. In the lecture "Volk und Staat in ihrer Stellung zu Vererbung und Auslese" (The relation of Volk and state to heredity and selective breeding; first delivered in February 1933), Günther himself acknowledges the importance of this intellectual heritage in affirming the unified body-soul conception that informs the racial research of his day.

> At any rate, what has been called "*Lebensphilosophie*" more or less bypasses the school of German Idealism, moves from Goethe and some of the impulses derived from Romanticism's so-called philosophy of nature, via Schopenhauer to Nietzsche and, as many people believe,

> ultimately to Ludwig Klages. We recognize in all of these thinkers a certain Darwinism, an emphasis on what is innate and genetically transmitted, as well as an inkling of, or even a firm belief in, the very body-soul unity that was prevalent in the thought of the ancient Indogermanic peoples, a unity that is also confirmed by present-day biology. (*Führeradel durch Sippenpflege* 28–29)

Günther traces the derivation of the psychosomatic conception articulated in genetics and in his racial-physiognomic ethnology from conceptions held by the ancient Indogermanic peoples, from which his Nordic race is purportedly descended. The crucial intellectual-historical link between these two is forged by the tradition of German *Lebensphilosophie.* It is no coincidence that this lineage bypasses German Idealism, above all the philosophy of Hegel. This is wholly in keeping with intellectual trends in Germany at the time, as well as with Günther's own ideological resistance to Hegel's developmental, nonessentialist thinking. The vitalism of German *Lebensphilosophie* contributed in major ways to the resurgence of physiognomic theories of all sorts during this period—including Günther's racial physiognomics. More than anything else, it is Günther's almost uncanny ability to fuse these diverse intellectual traditions into a coherent theoretical system with practical existential implications that accounts for the tremendous influence his ideas exerted during the Weimar Republic and the years of Nazi rule. But what Günther assembles in his diverse books, under the guise of scientific knowledge about race, is, in fact, nothing but a well-knit ideological construction. His racial physiognomics exemplifies the thesis propounded by David Theo Goldberg that "[r]acial knowledge is not just information about the racial Other, but its very creation, its fabrication" (*Racist Culture* 184). However, as Günther's example clearly demonstrates, this fabrication of the racial Other is inseparable from a construction of the racial "self" as an integral unit belonging to some definable, clearly circumscribable group. There is, apparently, no better way to define this line between self and Other than on the basis of physical appearance. The trick—and the reason why physiognomics is called into play here—is to make a case for these outward differences as infallible signs of inner, psychic, and characterological disparities. Günther was clearly more adept at this than any other racial theoretician.

7

Learning to See (Race)

Ludwig Ferdinand Clauss's Racial Psychology as Applied Phenomenology

Modernism and the Physiognomic Gaze

The eponymous protagonist of Rainer Maria Rilke's (1875–1926) modernist classic *Die Aufzeichnungen des Malte Laurids Brigge* (The notebooks of Malte Laurids Brigge) repeatedly describes his self-imposed task as "learning to see": "Ich lerne sehen" (8–9). The gaze Malte practices, however, is not trained on the empirical world of appearances; rather it penetrates this surface into what Malte experiences as the existential horror underlying the phenomenal world. Relating a phantasmagoric episode in which a woman who rests her face in her hands suddenly withdraws her head, peeling away the face that mysteriously adheres to her palms, Malte comments: "I was horrified to see a face from the inside" (10). Malte's experience can stand as a kind of parable for the emergence of the piercing physiognomic vision that was one of the theoretical fixations of German modernist intellectuals. His horror at seeing "a face from the inside" can be read as a premonition of the mortification this mode of modernist vision, with whose cultivation Malte, a true representative of modernism, is obsessed, represents when it is applied in the domain of human subjects.

This penetrating gaze assumes two distinct forms, both of which are actualized in the history of German physiognomics. One is the materialist, positivist mode of empirical observation that tends to predominate in the theories of Lavater, Gall, Carus, and, most concretely and perniciously, in the ideas of Hans F. K. Günther. A second, no less discriminating, but more ideational model of seeing is advocated by the line of humanistic physiognomists from Goethe to Klages, Spengler, and Kassner. The German word *Anschauung,* which means both "observation" and "intuition," becomes the focal term in this metaphysical physiognomics that joins the concrete act of visual perception with a kind of visionary imagination. These two modes for studying the body-soul relationship correlate with differing conceptions of the somatic dimension as communicative medium. The first, which reads anatomical traits as a priori signs of stable character, sees the body as always already inscribed with an unalterable text; the second, which views the body as a medium of the emotions, treats it as an active generator or translator of meaning, the mouthpiece, as it were, of a discourse composed by the psyche. In this conception, the body is—to use a different but related metaphor—the paper upon which the text of passion is written.[1] What is curious and noteworthy about German racial theory during the Weimar Republic and the Third Reich is that it was able to appropriate and put into productive practice both of these, oftentimes antithetical, physiognomic models.

Somatology versus Psychology: The Methodological Breach in Fascist Racial Ideology

Fascist racial theory is often thought of as a monolithic ideology in which all the primary players marched in lockstep, like a well-trained SS corps. In fact, however, the racial physiognomics that formed the core of this ideology was ruptured by a major theoretical rift, one side of which was represented by the natural-scientific orientation of Hans F. K. Günther, the other by the human-scientific, psychological direction pursued by Ludwig Ferdinand Clauss (1892–1974). To be sure, Clauss had a great deal in common with Günther, who was just one year his senior, and with whom he initially enjoyed a close friendship (Weingart 14). Above all, both shared an obsession with the notion of race as the most basic, formative layer of human personality and cultural community. In a 1934 essay about the racial constitution of the German people, for example, Clauss maintains: "The individual human being is not simply determined by racial type; rather, he or she is also shaped by other types. He or she is, for example, also a typical farmer, a typical man or typical woman, a typical female artist, et cetera. But all of these types, such as social role, are ultimately permeated by the typology of race" ("Der germanische Mensch" 8). According to Clauss, race does not simply represent one type among many. It is, so to speak, a super-type that determines and shapes all other typologies, social, professional, gender-bound, and so on, which also play a role in the constitution of individual character. Similarly, in a 1925 essay outlining the pedagogical methodologies appropriate for the introduction of racial anthropology in the classroom, Clauss defines race as a "formative power" that is the source of all culture and history ("Rassenkunde im Unterricht" 91). As was the case for Günther, for Clauss, too, race forms the ineradicable substrate of the individual and of every human culture.

Clauss, again like Günther, traced his intellectual roots back to the racial thought of Gobineau and Chamberlain (*Rasse und Seele* [1926] 27), and along with Günther he was one of the principal leaders and spokespersons of the Nordic Movement in Germany. In 1934, after the Nazi seizure of power, Clauss and Günther became the cofounders and principal editors of the periodical *Rasse* (Race), which bore the subtitle "Monatsschrift der Nordischen Bewegung" (Monthly magazine of the Nordic Movement). (Fig. 47) This journal quickly advanced to the status of one of the leading German-language venues for the publication of research into issues of race, eugenics, and racial psychology. Consistent with these ties to racial thought and the ideas of the Nordic Movement is Clauss's vehement opposition to the modern world, which, true to the tenets of German antimodernist sentiment of the time, he believed had been perverted by the democratizing principles of equality, liberalism, and rationality. In the essay "Der germanische Mensch," in which Clauss attempts to define the racial characteristics that distinguish the German people from other nations of Europe, he attacks the principles of the French Revolution as devious strategies aimed at bringing the Germans into political submission—the allusion, of course, is to the terms of the Treaty of Versailles—by diverting them from their natural drive for mastery: "[F]or years now, people have preached to us [Germans] the virtues of 'reason' and 'humanity' so as to enslave us. But we know that the call of the

Rasse

Monatsschrift der Nordischen Bewegung

Herausgegeben im Auftrage des Nordischen Ringes
von
R. v. Hoff
in Verbindung mit
L. F. Clauß und H. F. K. Günther

Schriftleiter: M. Hesch

Erster Jahrgang 1934

Verlag und Druck von B. G. Teubner in Leipzig und Berlin

Fig. 47. Title page, *Rasse: Journal of the Nordic Movement,* edited by Ludwig Ferdinand Clauss and Hans F. K. Günther, 1934. (Courtesy of the Hessische Landesbibliothek, Darmstadt)

blood contains more wisdom than all reason could ever express" (19). The pseudo-Nietzschean pathos of a master race "enslaved" by the shrewd abstractions of "reason" and "humanity" is typical of Clauss's writings composed prior to 1937, and his vitriolic rhetoric, especially his evocation of the "call of the blood," is reminiscent of that employed by the likes of Chamberlain, Rosenberg, and Hitler.

Clauss's most important book, *Rasse und Seele* (Race and soul), went through seventeen editions between 1926, the year of its first appearance, and 1941 (Weingart 37).[2] With 116,000 printed copies over these fifteen years, this book was a close competitor in terms of circulation with Günther's *Rassenkunde des deutschen Volkes*—although it could not come close to matching the tremendous popular appeal of the "Volks-Günther," the *Kleine Rassenkunde.* In the "Introduction" to the first edition of

Rasse und Seele, Clauss unambiguously expresses his ideological investment in the Nordic Movement, which he calls *"a second Protestantism,"* praising it above all for standing up against "the excesses of the faith in a common humanity" (3). At the same time, however, he voices a strident admonition against the degeneration of this movement into blind and chauvinistic dogmatism: "It strikes one as strange to see all kinds of new 'sciences' emerging out of the Nordic Movement, sciences that teach us to believe that all the great deeds and creations of the world were produced by Nordic people, that the Nordic human being constitutes the sole creative force. Here we witness a dangerous misuse of the standard [manifest in the Nordic human being], its encroachment into evaluative domains in which it is a foreign element. Here we witness the incipient proliferation of a new dogma" (*Rasse und Seele* [1926] 3). Clauss protests specifically against the process of pseudo-speciation, the valorization of the Nordic spirit at the expense of all other races, which was practiced by Chamberlain, Günther, and others, and which would ultimately shape Nazi ideology. There can be little doubt that the barb against those new "sciences" that assume such a position is directed against Günther, and here we get a first inkling of the theoretical divide that would later separate these two primary protagonists of the racial idea in Germany. To Clauss's credit it should be noted that he never ceased to defend the notion of racial relativity, the belief that each race must be held to and measured by *its own* standards, rather than to measures derived from some ostensible super-race (see, for example, *Rasse und Seele* [1926] 80–81; *Rasse und Seele* [1937] 169–71; *Rasse und Charakter* 85).

To be sure, Nazi racial propaganda also paid lip service to this idea of racial relativity,[3] yet this never prevented Nazi ideologues from evaluating the Germans as a "master race" destined to rule the world. The same critique holds in many ways for Clauss, as well. Despite his campaign for acknowledging the individual value of each race, it is obvious that the psychic characteristics he attributes to the various racial types are strikingly similar, oftentimes identical, to those Günther ascribes to his racial categories. Indeed, these qualities themselves imply a hierarchy coherent with the one openly defended by Günther. The Nordic and Phalian races, which for Clauss, as for Günther, provide the primary genetic components of the German population ("Der germanische Mensch" 10; *Die nordische Seele* [1932] 54–60), possess generally noble characteristics, while the other races descend from this pinnacle, with the Eastern race, or Slavic peoples, assuming the lowest position among the Europeans. Thus the Nordic "soul"—the term Clauss prefers to use—is marked above all by *Leistung,* a drive for achievement and accomplishment. Nordic human beings are motivated by an instinct for mastery, for controlling and manipulating the raw materials of nature. As a result, they have a tendency toward brutality, they operate alone and like to be loners, and they approach others and the world with distance and coldness (*Rasse und Seele* [1926] 40–79). (Fig. 48) The Phalian race has most of these same features, with the addition of one more central characteristic: perseverance and steadfastness (*Rasse und Seele* [1937] 33). The "Mediterranean" race—called "Western" in Günther's terminology and, once again, identifiable with the Romance peoples—displays a proclivity for play and playfulness. Mediterranean people exist for others, and their life is one of constant showmanship, as though they were always on stage. They live only in the present, and although they generate uncommon beauty and are noted for their grace and graciousness, they are incapable of producing a *powerful* culture of mastery, in contrast to the Nordic peoples. (*Rasse und Seele* [1926] 80–99). Representatives of the Mediterranean race are, in Clauss's words, "accomplished do-nothings *[Meister des Nichts-Tuns]*" (99), whom he identifies with predominantly "feminine" features, as opposed to the overtly "masculine" Nordic individual (88). As with Günther's categorization, this classification is clearly based on—and confirms—the common Germanic prejudices about the Romance character. The same is true for Clauss's assessment of the "Eastern" race, who in his view is characterized by indolence and a love of comfort. As opposed to the cool remoteness of the Nordic individual, the "Eastern" human being knows no distance, relies on community—especially the family—is a natural servant, and displays a generally pacifist attitude (*Rasse und Seele* [1926] 108–23).

It is indicative of Clauss's method that, in contrast to Günther, psychological features take precedence over somatological traits. Whereas Günther began by introducing the physi-

Fig. 48. Nordic type or person of achievement, from Ludwig Ferdinand Clauss, *Die nordische Seele,* 1932.

cal characteristics of each race and only subsequently addressed the psychological traits that correspond with these anatomical features, Clauss gives priority to the psychic qualities, attributing to physical traits a decidedly secondary place. Hence he develops his own designations for each racial type, based on what he believes to be the most prominent psychological feature: the Nordic individual he calls the *Leistungsmensch,* the "person of achievement" (*Rasse und Seele* [1937] 13–30); the Phalian becomes the *Verharrungsmensch,* the "person of perseverance" (31–45); the Mediterranean is the *Darbietungsmensch,* the "person of performance" (45–56); and the Eastern individual he calls the *Enthebungsmensch,* the "person who seeks release from all responsibilities" (99–112). Consistent with this psychological orientation are Clauss's repeated assaults on the materialist and statistical method employed by other racial theoreticians, and there can be little doubt that, once more, this critique is directed above all at his friend and colleague Hans F. K. Günther. Already in the early essay "Rassenkunde im Unterricht an Mittelschulen" (Racial studies in the middle-school classroom), for example, Clauss vigorously maintains: "a one-sided somatological treatment of the doctrine of race would be more harmful than productive; for it could all too easily nourish the weeds of a bleak cognitive materialism and a fatalistic attitude" (94).

What is especially interesting here is that Clauss raises the same accusations against Günther and his anatomically based racial physiognomy that Lichtenberg and Hegel invoked in their fight against Lavaterian physiognomics and Gall's phrenology more than a hundred years earlier: the specters of materialism and fatalism. In fact, the theoretical and methodological gulf that increasingly separates Günther and Clauss repeats down to specific details the terms of the debate on physiognomics that raged at the end of the eighteenth and beginning of the nineteenth centuries in Germany. Whereas Günther represents "physiognomics," an insistence on the "primordiality" of the body, a focus on a priori Being, and the (pre-)determination of the human being on the basis of natural—here, genetic—predispositions, Clauss stresses "pathognomics," the priority of the psyche and the emotions over the body as natural phenomenon, the expression of the inner personality in actions and deeds, and the mutability of character beyond any anatomically or genetically conditioned primordiality.

Clauss's insistence on race as a primarily *psychological* factor, while it stands in diametrical opposition to Günther's practice, is not a renegade idea. Indeed, it is consistent with certain lines of Nazi ideology. In the opening pages of *Der Mythus des 20. Jahrhunderts* (The mythos of the twentieth century), for example, Alfred Rosenberg makes the apodictic assertion: "*However, soul is nothing other than race seen from the inside. And vice versa, race is the external aspect of a soul*" (2). The virtual identity between race and "soul"—that is, between racial character and the psychological constitution of the individual—is one of the pillars on which Rosenberg's ideology rests. He explores this relationship later in this treatise, claiming: "Every race has its constitutive soul, every soul its constitutive race, its own internal and external architectonics, its characteristic phenomenal form and expression of its lifestyle, a relationship between the powers of the will and reason that is all its own" (116). While affirming the priority of the soul over the body, Rosenberg implies that the somatic substrate of the human being is shaped and determined by the expressions of the psyche. This idea of the body as the expressive medium of the soul is one of Clauss's primary theses. His idea of a racial psychology, the notion that every race displays its own typical psychic traits and that these internal characteristics take precedence over anatomical forms, could appeal to the authority of Rosenberg, one of the principal Nazi ideologues of race. To be sure, Clauss formulated his theory of racial psychology well before Rosenberg recorded his ideas, and it is certainly possible that the latter's emphasis on the racial soul bespeaks Clauss's direct or indirect influence.[4]

Rosenberg, like Clauss, was also outspokenly skeptical about the identification of racial constitution based purely on anatomical features or anthropometric measurements. In *Mythus des 20. Jahrhunderts* he contends:

> Nothing would be more superficial than to try to approach questions about the value of an individual human being with a measuring stick and data about the cephalic index. On the contrary, in such matters the first criterion must be how one stands up to the test of life, one's service to the nation, which, to be sure, must go hand in hand with the cultivation of an ideal of beauty grounded in the Nordic race. The new nobility must, in other words, be both a nobility of blood *and* a nobility of accomplishment *[Leistungsadel]*. (596)

Rosenberg, clearly, does not want to deny the role of anatomy in the determination of race; but he sets actions and deeds on an equal footing with the manifestations of "blood" and implies that these two directions run on parallel, if inherently unconnected, tracks. It is certainly no coincidence that the term he uses to designate the internal, psychic dimension of the Nordic race is *Leistung,* accomplishment or achievement, the very word Clauss employs to name the central psychological feature of this race. Of course, the Nazi leadership was more or less forced to embrace a trans-anatomical, literally metaphysical notion of racial constitution: on the basis of the physical criteria for the Nordic race established by Günther, many of the Nazi leaders—including Rosenberg and Hitler themselves—could scarcely lay claim to Nordic heritage. This also helps explain why the Nazi propagandists invested so much energy in publicizing Hitler's *Ahnentafel*—his family tree, which served to demonstrate his roots in Austrian peasant stock, believed to possess the purest bloodlines—and playing up the racial and cultural coherence of his ancestors. (Fig. 49)

The methodological and ideological split that separated Günther and Clauss is interesting not merely because it reiterates the terms of the eighteenth-century debate on physiognomics, but also because it marks an ideological rift in the theory of race and its expressions within the thought of the Nazi Party itself. The tensions between Günther and Clauss mounted early on, and already in 1937, just four years after its founding, Clauss resigned from the editorial board of the journal *Rasse,* citing as his reasons both deep-seated scholarly differences and unnamed ideological issues (Weingart 38). Clauss's departure can be viewed as a symptom that his "pathognomic" approach to race was losing the ideological battle against Günther and the materialistically oriented representatives of racial "physiognomics." Clauss himself identified his opposition to the Nordic chauvinism of people like Günther as the primary point of ideological conflict. In a note to the 1937 edition of *Rasse und Seele,* for example, he points to this problem, claiming—with undue optimism, as it will turn out—that his point of view has been embraced as the official doctrine of the Nazi Party.

> A distinction in psychological type (race) clearly implies a distinction in the values that are realized by one race or another; it implies a distinction in the *kind* of values, not in their *magnitude.* . . . This insight, which I have defended for more than twelve years, has earned me nothing but disparagement and defamation from the fanatical devotees of the belief in the sole worth of the Nordic race—even though I enjoyed the assent of those men and women who, along with me, assumed leadership roles in championing the cause of the Nordic Idea. Increasingly, my view came to predominate among those scholars who also thought in political terms. . . . Today it is the view represented by the rulers of the [National Socialist] state. (182–83)

As we have seen, Clauss did indeed adamantly defend this relativistic view of racial worth throughout his works (see *Rasse und Stil* [1926] 80–81; *Rasse und Stil* [1937] 170; *Rasse und Charakter* 85). The unnamed ideological conflict he cites as one of his motivations for leaving the editorial board of *Rasse* certainly turns on this issue. But Clauss's assertion that his view was gaining ascen-

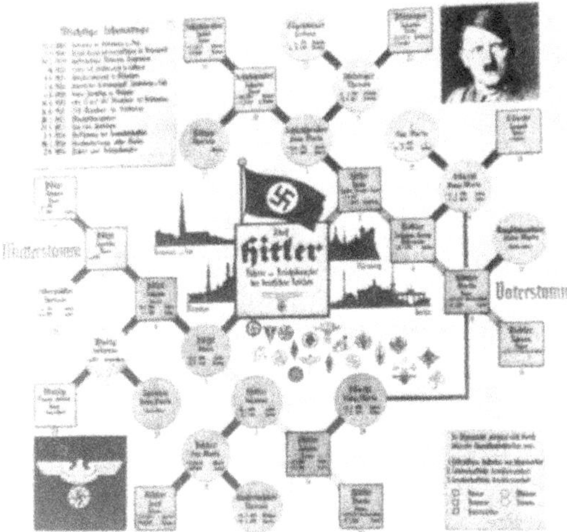

Fig. 49. "Hitler's Family Tree," from *Neues Volk*, 1937. (Courtesy of the Bundesarchiv, Coblenz)

dancy over the position of those fanatics who saw the Nordic race as the only one responsible for the great cultural achievements of humankind was certainly mere wishful thinking.

Clauss would pay a dear price for his political naiveté and undue optimism several years later. One of the figures Clauss names as having taken his side on this issue of racial value is Walter Gross (1904–1945), the head of the *Rassenpolitisches Amt der NSDAP,* the Nazi Office for Racial Politics, who, along with Alfred Rosenberg, was the final authority in all questions of race during the Third Reich. However, this same Walter Gross would later initiate a veritable vendetta against Clauss that would ultimately lead to Clauss's expulsion from the Nazi Party in 1943, which he had joined immediately after Hitler's assumption of power in 1933. The note in the informational flyer from the Office of Racial Politics reporting Clauss's expulsion states laconically that this act was motivated by Clauss's long-time association with a Jewess, his assistant Margarete Landé, whom, moreover, he hid from the authorities and whose Jewish background he had helped conceal. The report further comments that while Clauss's books are not to be removed from libraries, the previously implemented policy that bans them from pedagogical use in the schools is still in force.[5] Gross initiated a formal intra-Party proceeding against Clauss as early as 1941, after Clauss was denounced by his estranged second wife for the protection of Landé.[6] Two other important Nazi officials joined Gross in the move to ostracize Clauss: Alfred Rosenberg and Alfred Baeumler (1887–1968), a leading professor and Nazi supporter from the university in Berlin where Clauss had held an instructorship since 1936.

Although the proceedings against Clauss were initially founded on purely personal infractions, it was ultimately Clauss's method, not Clauss himself—or only Clauss insofar as he was the founder and spokesperson of that method—that was put on trial. In part, this was Clauss's own fault, since his defense against the Party proceedings was based largely on claims about the significance of his contributions to the Nazis' ideological position on matters of race. In a long affidavit addressed to the Party tribunal charged with the Clauss case, Gross made a point of denying the purported influence of Clauss's racial psychology on the racial ideology of the Nazi Party.

> This [Clauss's] portrayal of the political significance [of his doctrines] is in need of being corrected. It must be noted that in terms of content, Clauss's works did not contribute anything new to the tools already implemented in the political struggle of the NSDAP. . . . There is absolutely no basis for assuming a fundamental influence on the part of Dr. Clauss. This could never have been possible, since none of Clauss's works presents either new knowledge or principal developments of other positions; instead, they merely offer psychological elaborations of basic racial truths. . . . In sum, it must be said that the ideology of the NSDAP with regard to racial science and racial policy would still be complete and exist in its present form if none of Clauss's works had ever been published—although the same claim cannot be made about Günther's works. (Quoted in Weingart 145)

Gross insists on the marginality of Clauss's theories with regard to Nazi racial policy; he points instead, significantly, to the importance Günther's works played in the formulation of the Party's racial thought. Gross wounds Clauss, as it were, at his most vulnerable spot: he disputes his originality as a scholar and the general importance of his research, something Clauss dedicated his life to ascertaining and defending.

But Gross's opinion alone was not enough to seal Clauss's fate; an independent scholar, the psychology professor Kurt Gottschaldt (b. 1902) from the University of Berlin—who, incidentally, was not a member of the Nazi Party—was asked to supply a formal, independent scholarly evaluation of Clauss's work. This evaluation calls into question both Clauss's theoretical positions and his methodology, and it concludes by accusing Clauss of having for years viciously attacked and belittled "the renowned representatives of German racial science and their methodologies, which are both admired and imitated throughout the world" (quoted in Weingart 84). Clauss's assault on the materialist presuppositions of German racial research is singled out as an especially egregious sin, since this attack seemed to ally Clauss with the Nazis' ideological opponents, who also used the materialist foundations of Nazi racial theory as their primary argument against fascist race doctrine.

Clauss clearly lost the ideological battle with Günther for ascendancy in the discipline of Nazi racial thought, and his defeat marks the victory of a sterile racial physiognomics over the more subtle, more thoughtful, and certainly more complex—if no less ideologically questionable—racial pathognomics represented by Clauss. Contrary to Walter Gross's protestations of its insignificance and the belittling evaluation composed by Gottschaldt, Clauss's racial psychology enjoyed a generally positive reception in Germany, especially in the scholarly community. Fritz Lenz (1887–1976), one of the authors of the highly influential scholarly reference work on race and eugenics, the two-volume *Menschliche Erblehre und Rassenhygiene* (Human genetics and racial hygiene), explicitly praised Clauss for his investigations into the racial content of bodily and facial expression (Baur, Fischer, Lenz 1: 761). And a significant follower and promoter of Clauss and his method emerged in the person of Bruno Petermann (1898–1941), whose book *Das Problem der Rassenseele* (The problem of the racial psyche) openly acknowledges the importance of Clauss's contributions to the field of racial psychology (61–102). Furthermore, Erich Voegelin (b. 1901), unquestionably the most expert and impartial investigator of the racial question in the intellectual atmosphere of the Weimar Republic, particularly lauded the unusually high quality of Clauss's ideas and his research (*Rasse und Staat* 12–13; 92–104). Indeed, it may have been precisely the scholarly acclaim that Clauss and his theories were beginning to reap that helped motivate Gross's campaign against him. At any rate, it is certainly the case that the purging of Clauss and his ideas represents the *Gleichschaltung,* the forced standardization, of Nazi racial policy along the lines of the simplistic and materialistic racial physiognomics represented by Hans F. K. Günther.

Although Clauss protested against his expulsion from the Party and objected to the unfair and unjust treatment he felt was accorded him, this rejection was ultimately a blessing in disguise. After the Second World War Clauss could legitimately, if somewhat mendaciously, claim that he had been an opponent of the Nazis and their racial practices. Indeed, the postwar investigation into his possible complicity with the National Socialist regime concluded with his full exoneration; his rescue of Margarete Landé even brought him the honor of having a tree planted in his name on the Avenue of the Righteous in Jerusalem (Weingart 247). Yet Clauss did not abandon his racial psychology after the war; instead, he recast and republished it in 1958, in a form that not only expunged most of its allusions to Nazi ideology, but actually shifted to the strategy of open critique of the Nazi's political "misuse" of racial theory (*Die Seele des Andern* 14, 163, 184, 227).

Clauss's "Racial Psychology" as Stylistics of Character

From the standpoint of Nazi racial ideology, Walter Gross—head of the Office for Racial Politics, and, as such, the person responsible for the coherence of Nazi racial theory and practice—had good reason to be skeptical of Clauss's position. Indeed, anyone who read Clauss's writings carefully, as Gross clearly had, was likely to stumble over certain ideas or formulations that could not help but strike one as, from the Nazi standpoint, downright heretical. Take, for instance, the definition of race Clauss proffered in *Rasse und Charakter,* a book published in 1936, three years after the foundation of the Nazi state and one year after the promulgation of the Nuremberg racial laws. "For *race* is not," Clauss proclaims here, in open opposition to the theory of race propounded by the Gobineau—Chamberlain—Günther line, "as lay people still often assume today, a clump of genetically transmitted characteristics . . . , but rather a *genetically transmitted structural law,* which expresses itself in all the characteristics a given individual possesses and which lends them a certain *style.* One does not recognize the race of a human being based on the possession of specific characteristics, but rather in the style in which these characteristics are expressed" (82). It is difficult to imagine a more strident contradiction of Günther's racial physiognomics and its eugenic program—a critique that, nonetheless, remains within the terminological field of racial ideology itself. What is more, by implication Clauss accuses Günther, and any others who are so naive as to understand race as a "clump" of inherited genetic characteristics, of being amateurs incapable of comprehending the concept of race in all its scholarly and scientific ramifications. What Clauss essentially does is displace the entire conception of race from the domain of content, from issues of physical and psychic substance, into the realm of *form:* race expresses itself not in the *substance* of one's body or personality, but rather in the *style* in which one articulates these psychosomatic givens. Clauss could, of course, appeal, in defense of this position, to the "expertise" of a certain Adolf Hitler on the issue of race and its stylistic expression. In a speech before the Nazi Party convention in 1933, for example, Hitler insisted on the stylistic discernibility of race in the products of culture, claiming that every race has its own "handwriting in the book of art" (quoted in Claussen 100).[7] Clauss, however, applies the concept of style not simply to artistic products, but to the psychological pattern, the *Gestalt,* that defines the racial type of every individual. This is one of his central principles, which in the 1926 edition of *Rasse und Seele* he succinctly defines in the following way: "We have chosen to call a stylistic law that holds sway over the manner in which a given soul experiences things and thereby lends it a specific form *[Gestalt],* the *racial law [Artgesetz]* of this soul" (11). Clauss implicitly compares the task of the racial psychologist with that of the art historian, who sifts through the diverse artistic creations of a certain historical period in order to discover the stylistic laws they share, thereby identifying their common historical character (8–10). His procedure, then, is diametrically opposed to Günther's. If the latter gave priority to establishing the anatomical features of the individual races, then moved on to the psychic content that conforms with these physical traits, Clauss begins with the psychological content, the entire set of character traits that are part of the human domain, and attempts to extrapolate from this psychological content racial typologies based not on specific subsets of these characterological traits themselves, but on the styles that govern their articulation. It is not the *possession* of the characteristic "courage," for example, that defines someone as racially "Nordic," "Eastern," "Mediterranean," and so on, for this trait itself is not peculiar to any given race. However, the *manner* in which this quality is actualized, the style or form according to which it is structured, is, for Clauss, race-specific: Nordic individuals will display a different *form* or *style* of courage than will, say, Mediterranean people.

Clauss expresses this distinction most clearly in the text of the photographic lecture, *Rassenseele und Einzelmensch* (Racial soul and individual human being), which he frequently delivered to youth groups such as the *Hitlerjugend* during the Third Reich.

> Characteristics relate to the individual human being; one person has certain characteristics, another does not. These traits distinguish individual character, not race. Race is not determined by the existence of characteristics, but rather by *the manner* in which these characteristics influence the human being *when and if* they are present. We call this manner *the style* according to which this individual experiences things, or the style of its soul. This style constitutes the essence of all racial-psychological features, and it is at work in everything, in our most base and most lofty experiences, as well as in our everyday habits. (8)

Later in this text Clauss calls this racial style "hereditary form *[vererbbare Gestalt]*" (28), indicating that it is precisely this style, not any specific characterological or anatomical content, that is genetically determined and transmitted. Moreover, this style expresses itself in everything the individual person is and does, from one's manner of thought down to the most banal actions, presumably even in the way one reads a newspaper or combs one's hair. Modern individuals, as racial bastards, can be the product of multiple racial styles, and each style will express itself in different ways and in differing contexts. (Fig. 50)

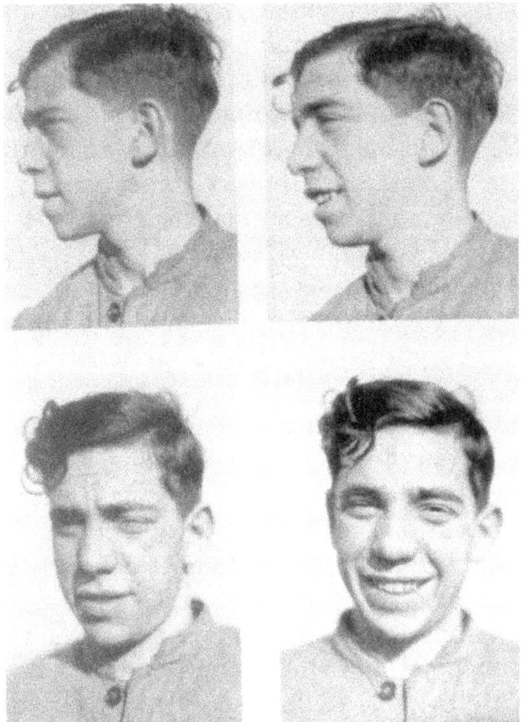

Fig. 50. Differing racial styles in different expressive contexts, from Ludwig Ferdinand Clauss, *Rasse und Seele*, 1937.

With this stress on the omnipresence of racial style Clauss brings a significant variation on a theme endemic to physiognomic thought since Lavater: the nonarbitrary nature of physiognomic (or pathognomic) symptoms, the inevitability with which they betray, to the person who understands how to read them, the most profound essence (in Clauss's case, the "racial" essence) of the individual under scrutiny. What Clauss has managed, however, is the transference of this quality of inevitability from the material-anatomical domain, where it is located for Lavater, Gall, and Günther, to the realm of pathognomics. We recall that Lavater rejected pathognomics as indicative of the essential person because he believed the signs of these emotions could be imitated or feigned, as they are by actors on stage; Clauss circumvents this problem by arguing that each personal expression bears a stylistic stamp, as it were, a peculiar form into which it is cast. This *Gestalt* is not shaped by one's individuality, but rather by one's race, and its inevitable presence in everything we say and do perpetually betrays our racial constitution.

There is something especially insidious in this theory, something that makes it perhaps even more ominous than Günther's racial-anatomical physiognomics: this is the inexorability of *racial* self-expression, since for Clauss racial style is all-pervasive. One can, presumably, abandon particular character traits or assume new ones; what one can never do, however, is escape the particular style or form in which these traits will be articulated. Race is, ultimately, the most fundamental dimension of one's personality and the only dimension that can never be disguised or hidden. Clauss's racial psychology, once fine-tuned into a standardized methodology and promulgated among trained practitioners, would hence be able to lay claim to a high degree of accuracy in the determination of race. The "style" of one's experience, in short, would become the absolute litmus test of one's racial constitution.

Clauss's racial stylistics approaches the formalism inherent in the humanist strain of German physiognomics: his stylistic law has certain affinities both with Goethe's morphology as well as with Ludwig Klages's conception of the *Leitidee,* the dominant idea, the underlying unifying structure that informs all the typical expressions of an individual's character.[8] To be sure, Clauss gives this morphological conception a racial turn, taking up a middle position, as it were, between Goethe's notion of the *Urtier,* the primordial animal form that serves as the morphological basis of all animal species, and Klages's more individualistic conception of the *Leitidee* as the formal trait common to all the expressions of any particular individual. In the thought of Goethe, Klages, and Clauss, the constant that defines identity has shifted away from matter itself, which is recognized as mutable, to the principle that structures in a regular and discernible pattern the mutations this matter undergoes. For Clauss, this structuring principle is racial style, which he views as an absolute given, an a priori and intransgressible law much like the laws of geometry (see *Rasse und Seele* [1926] 127). Clauss's racial stylistics plays a role in his theoretical edifice similar to that assumed by genetic and eugenic principles in Günther's racial physiognomics; each represents those constants that signal the immutable and insurmountable expression of race. Without doubt, this marks Clauss's most audacious and most consequential departure from accepted Nazi racial policy: his summary rejection of its belief in eugenic practices. Clauss was, to be sure, much too intelligent to voice this repudiation openly, but it is clearly implied in his theory of racial stylistics. And the manner in which he avoids the mention of eugenics throughout his writings—at a time when eugenic theory was de rigeur in treatises on racial topics—is symptomatic of his rejection of it.

Nowhere is this critical divergence from the standard Nazi platform, represented with such unquestioning dogmatism in Günther's position, more obvious than in Clauss's conception of the idea of *Aufnordung* or re-Nordification. According to Günther, it is Clauss who deserves credit for having invented this conception in the first place (*Rassenkunde* 459). Günther, as we recall, lent this idea a decidedly eugenic cast, using the term to designate a program for the development of genetically more "desirable"—that is, of course, more "Nordic"—traits in the German population as a whole. For Clauss, by contrast, the idea of re-Nordification has none of these eugenic undertones; instead, it names a process of self-overcoming that begins and ends with every individual himself or herself: re-Nordification is nothing other than an exercise in self-discipline and self-education.

> It is not possible to discern who is Nordic by examining their hair, but only by studying the attitude of their soul. Anyone who can step outside himself, freely look himself in the face and accomplish something with himself as though this self were an object—such an individual *is* Nordic in this one decisive trait. Based on this attitude he can shape and conquer himself. Re-Nordification does not begin with people trying to change things in others, rather it begins as the solitary achievement of the individual in shaping himself. Only by following the path of solitude can one arrive at Nordic community. Re-Nordification means that every individual must reenact upon himself the act of Nordic conquest through which the German Volk first emerged on German soil. ("Der germanische Mensch" 20)

Clauss begins with his trademark objection to Günther's anatomical criteria for racial constitution and insists that race expresses itself instead in style or attitude. But he also implies a larger objection to Günther's racial-physiognomic program: its judgmental nature—that is, its outwardly directed concern with deciphering the racial composition of *others* and introducing programmatic measures for the reform of this racial constitution. One of Günther's most adamant critics correctly diagnosed his program as a kind of eugenic self-colonization of the German people (Merkenschlager 64), the attempt to resettle, as it were, the genetic territory of the Germans by introducing new conquering waves of Nordic blood into the gene pool of the populace and gradually reducing or eliminating other racial-genetic types.

At the heart of the entire racial-materialist ideology represented by Günther there lies, of course, an inherent paradox—one similar to the paradox that marks Lavater's physiognomics. Beginning with Gobineau, thc history of race is characterized by a profound cultural pessimism, the implicit belief, underwritten by historical argument, that every phase of racial ascendancy is followed by a retrograde phase of racial decline. In the theories propagated by the advocates of race, there is no historical precedent for stemming or even reversing such decline. While Günther's eugenic program provides an answer in theory, in practice this process of re-Nordification, if it were successful, would only bear fruit untold generations into the future. The uncertainty of success and the vast time frame, which greatly exceeds the lifetime of individuals, not only lends this position a kind of mythic dimension—re-Nordification as Wagnerian *Gesamtkunstwerk*, as it were—but also makes the stringent eugenic measures Günther demands seem like a rather bitter pill, one that it would certainly be difficult to bring large proportions of the populace to swallow willingly. Clauss, on the other hand, offers a more immediate solution, one that promises tangible results that every individual can experience in her or his own lifetime: a program of psychological self-fashioning based on the valorization of one's Nordic traits and the subordination of other racial characteristics to this Nordic "style."

As we have seen, Günther made a similar argument for a kind of Nordic decisionism, an ethics of Nordic self-assertion and self-mastery. But this ethics of existential choice runs counter to his deterministic, materialistic view of race and the eugenic program it engenders. What stands out about Clauss's theory is that it is not fractured by this inconsistency: the ethical demand that one re-Nordify oneself by making an existential decision to cultivate and foster the psychological "style" of the Nordic race is consistent both with his racial-psychological theory and with the program of immediate racial improvement. Clauss counters the cultural pessimism of racial decline with a strong disciplinary regimen that each individual can opt to pursue, and this program for re-Nordification is coherent with the Nazi call for the self-improvement and self-discipline of the German nation from the ground (the individual) up. A process of colonization is still taking place, to be sure; but it is a process of *self*-colonization, as it were, the submission of one's individual characterological traits to a *stylistic* regimen dictated by the psychological *Gestalt* Clauss identifies as typical of the Nordic race. He invokes the central features of this Nordic style in the above quotation: the spirit for mastery (here given a self-reflective turn toward self-mastery), the instinct for accomplishment and achievement, and the drive to fashion and shape the material and matter that confronts one or enters into one's life world. For Clauss the training of the eye to see racial difference is not so much a method for exposing the Other as other, rather it is a process that helps the individual accomplish self-understanding and disciplined self-mastery.

In his preface to *Semiten der Wüste unter sich* (Desert Semites among themselves), in which he attempts to justify to his German readers—in 1937!—his interest in studying Bedouin peoples and their culture, Clauss makes the general claim: "We purify ourselves when we learn to recognize what is foreign *as* foreign" (5). Understanding the Other, or at least recognizing it in its otherness, ultimately serves the ends of self-awareness. While this constitutes one of Clauss's primary points of disagreement with Günther, it should not be interpreted to mean that Clauss does not perceive certain other races as threats; he clearly does. In fact, the story he tells in *Semiten der Wüste unter sich* relates the self-alienation of the Bedouin people through their adaptation to, and adoption of, a foreign manner and style: they have abandoned their racial-stylistic "purity" by assuming the stylistic principle, the *Gestalt,* of the Near Eastern race. We know from our examination of Günther's theories that in the racial discourse of the time, "Near Eastern" was a code word for the Jews, used to lend anti-Semitic sentiments the guise of racial-scientific objectivity. In this sense, Clauss's book about the decline of the Bedouin lifestyle serves as a kind of historical parable for the Germans themselves: it tells by way of example what will happen to the Germans if they, too, let their character be shaped and formed by a "foreign" racial style, indeed, by the very same "Near Eastern" racial *Gestalt* that caused the Bedouins' undoing. It is no coincidence that Clauss begins this book with the Biblical parable of David and Goliath, which in his retelling undergoes a Nietzschean trans-valuation (*Semiten der Wüste* 7–17): Goliath becomes the symbolic incarnation of the Nordic human being who, despite his physical strength and his superiority, is brought down by the cunning and trickery of the "Jew" David. Clauss depicts this confrontation as a conflict of styles: the Germanic values of integrity, fair play, and honorable engagement in battle succumb to the values of guile, opportunism, and malice.[9] The lesson Clauss wants to present is that an *understanding* of racial styles and their differences, in particular the strengths and weaknesses of one's own racial predispositions vis-à-vis those of other races, can bring an individual and a race an important strategic advantage in a world threatened by racial intermingling. This is, in essence, Clauss's sales pitch for his theory and his method of racial psychology.

The difference between the racial programs of Günther and Clauss can best be articulated, perhaps, by aligning them along the nature—nurture divide. Günther was clearly an advocate of nature; indeed, following Chamberlain, Hitler, and others, he openly attacked what was branded in this period as "Lamarckism," the theory propounded by the French naturalist Chevalier de Lamarck (1744–1829) that environmental influences could have an impact on genetic makeup and that acquired traits could be genetically inherited. As a result of his anti-Lamarckism, Günther rejected any idea of pedagogical reform—except the training of the gaze to recognize in certain physical features the indelible signs of race. Clauss, by contrast, is a definitive advocate of a nurture theory of race, and this manifests itself in the ethical-pedagogical program he outlines both for individuals and for the German Volk as a whole. Thus in the 1934 essay "Der germanische Mensch," Clauss discusses certain foreign influences, above all the "Near Eastern" style that was imported when the Germans embraced Christianity, and the "Mediterranean" style that, according to Clauss, has gained in influence in the modern age (following the French Revolution). Each of these brings with it, according to Clauss, a "transformation" in the German soul. However, he insists that this mutation should not be understood in terms of blood, but only in terms of the models the Germans themselves have chosen to adopt and follow: "[it is] a transformation that does not imply a change of race, a change of one's racial law, nor even of one's genetic makeup; but it does indeed imply a change in the *model* one follows: a change in the image according to which the Germanic human being conceives both itself and its mission" (10). In other words, for Clauss, racial purity is not a matter of one's genetic constitution or one's nature; rather it is a function of *lifestyle,* of the way one lives. Racial purity means, above all, *choosing* and *following* a lifestyle consistent with one's own psychological nature, with the style typically manifest in one's race. To be racially "pure," in short, is nothing other than living a life of racial-psychological authenticity. One accomplishes this above all by choosing exemplars, on whose model one can pattern one's own life, who are consistent with one's own inherent racial style. This explains, for example, the total rejection of non-Germanic words in Clauss's writing, a trait he shares with Günther and other proponents of the Nordic Idea. Such imported foreign words, according to Clauss, inject an alien element into the indigenous style of the speakers of a language (*Die nordische Seele* [1923] 86–87). The requirement Clauss places on the German people, as he maintains in the essay "Der germanische Mensch," is nothing less than the demand that they choose to cultivate the "Nordic" attitude of achievement, mastery, and control, and that they subordinate to this Nordic style any other tendencies they might harbor. He calls this "the task that is constantly present in the Germanic nature: unifying, through an act of self-structuring, those forces in oneself that tend to move in divergent directions" (18). Conscious self-fashioning, practiced at the level of the individual, has replaced Günther's eugenic program for the re-Nordification of the German people. The racial reform of the Volk,

Clauss believes, must be based on the racial-psychological re-formation of every individual member of the German populace. What is more, the very ability to perform such self-fashioning lies at the racial core of the Nordic individual. If achievement, control, and creative shaping form the heart of the Nordic psyche, the Nordic individual must simply train this psychological energy upon himself or herself. The result will be a self-disciplined, self-mastering human being who manifests a consistent Nordic "style" marked by achievement and accomplishment.

In *Rasse und Charakter* Clauss invokes, in Nietzschean manner, the engagement of one's own volition as the decisive factor in this process of racial-psychological reconstitution: "The racially authentic *[artrechte]* human being is not something that falls from the sky, nor does it grow out of the soil: whatever falls or grows is merely the stuff that must be fashioned by exerting one's 'own' will. Whether a racially authentic human being emerges in all its purity from this naturally-given, indigenous ground is a function of whether its 'own' will is directed at racially authentic *values*" (79). One must, in essence, display a will to racial purity; it "is not something that falls from the sky" or emerges like a native plant from its indigenous soil. With this Clauss invokes a theme that was paramount in Nazi ideology: the "triumph of the will," a theme brilliantly articulated and cast into images in Leni Riefenstahl's (b. 1907) infamous propaganda film of the same name. Clauss cleverly adapts this ideological theme for the purposes of his racial psychology. Indeed, in the above-cited passage volition becomes indistinguishable from the racial law of style that shapes and forms the characterological matter given in nature. Implicit in all of this is the casting of Clauss's own theory of racial psychology as the leading player in the drama of self-realization. It is only on the basis of Clauss's method that the stylistic-psychological laws governing the attitudes of particular races can be discerned. The knowledge of that stylistic law to which one, as Nordic individual—or, for that matter, as representative of any other race—must adhere, is prerequisite for structuring one's life in a racially authentic manner. Simply stated, I must know the psychological laws of my race before I can structure my life in accordance with them. Clauss's theory of the "Nordic soul," laid out in great detail in his first book, *Die nordische Seele* (The Nordic soul; first published 1923), would become the compulsory blueprint for the racial self-fashioning of the German Volk. (Fig. 51)

If there is a hidden irony in the ideological dispute that rages between Günther and Clauss over the definition and constitution of racial physiognomics, it is that although they begin at diametrically opposed positions, their theories ultimately merge and overlap at one crucial juncture: their invocation of a Nietzschean ethics of the will to self-overcoming. The influence of Nietzsche, especially the Nietzsche of *Also sprach Zarathustra,* is evident in the rhetoric and pathos of both Günther's and Clauss's texts, especially in their early writings.[10] Like Günther, Clauss invokes the spirit of Nietzschean *amor fati*—appropriating it, of course, as the domain of the Nordic individual—when in the first edition of *Die nordische Seele* he remarks: "One of the essential features of the *Nordic* soul . . . is the affirmation of its fate" ([1923] 212). As was the case with Günther, Clauss's theory of racial psychology culminates in a form of existential decisionism: threatened with their own demise due to the influence of racial mixing—not of blood or genes, as in Günther's instance, but the adaptation of inappropriate racial styles and models—the Germans are admonished to "be themselves" and affirm the Nordic racial—that is, "stylistic"—constitution endemic to their nature. The Germans must embrace the stylistic law dictated by their Nordic heritage and employ it to conquer all the foreign influences that have perverted the purity of their racial "souls" (see 152–55).

Clauss saw himself as the founder of the new science of racial psychology, *Rassenseelenforschung,* as he called it (*Semiten* 113). What is more, he believed the emergence of this science was grounded specifically in the special talents and facilities of the Nordic soul. In *Rasse und Charakter,* for example, he writes: "However, racial psychology—as a form of research appropriate to the Nordic style—must attempt to discover objectively the racial standard specific to every particular race, so as to fathom what is racially authentic *[artrecht]* for each race in its own terms" (101). Despite his arguments about the relative value of each race, to which Clauss alludes in this passage, the understanding of racial psychology as a specifically *Nordic* science

Fig. 51. Dust jacket, Ludwig Ferdinand Clauss, *Die nordische Seele,* 1932.

accords Nordic human beings a privileged position: in Clauss's understanding, only they are truly capable of racial psychology, of studying all races "objectively" and determining which standards can appropriately be applied to them. Clauss does not explain here why the Nordic race in particular should enjoy this privileged position. Indeed, his assertion that Nordic individuals possess peculiar evaluative abilities—abilities, moreover, that are grounded in a special *physiognomic* sensibility—seems inconsistent with some of the characteristics both Clauss and Günther ascribe to the Nordic type, above all its haughtiness and proclivity for isolation and loneliness. These do not at first blush appear to form an auspicious basis for what the Germans call *Menschenkenntnis,* special insight into the minds and characters of other human beings. In fact, Günther, for his part, insists that Nordic people lack *Einfühlung,* the capacity to identify and empathize with others (*Rassenkunde* 195; *Rasse und Stil* 24). Clauss seems to be alluding to this view when he maintains: "Genuine, selfless goodness is not often a gift bestowed upon Nordic human beings, for they live too much out of themselves and for themselves to be able to pass judgments based on true understanding, on internal empathy with the needs of others" (*Die nordische Seele* [1932] 38). Nordic people are so self-involved, according to Clauss, that they rarely have the capacity for true interpersonal understanding, or even for displaying a genuine interest in other individuals. If the Nordic race inherently lacks this will to participate in the life of others, to experience things as others experience them, we are justified in asking: How can racial psychology be explicitly defined as a science that requires a Nordic sensibility? This is an especially crucial question for Clauss and his racial psychology, since he defines this "Nordic" science according to what he terms a "mimic" methodology that demands nothing less than the racial researcher's close identification with the subjects he or she is studying.

The only place Clauss gives an answer to this critical question is in an explanatory note appended to the third edition of *Rasse und Seele,* in which he defends his "mimic" methodology against the criticism that it constitutes a form of pre-rational empathy.

> Those who are not well versed in these matters sometimes designate our mimic methodology as a "method based on *empathy.*" People usually understand under this term a prescientific procedure, and this has nothing whatsoever to do with our mode of operation. Our research direction is based on empirical experience *[Erfahren]* in the strict sense of this word: we must ex-perience *[er-fahren]* the alien world in an organized manner and thereby also construct the foreign life-role. This is only possible on the basis of a Nordic attitude in which the distance that separates one human being from another can never disappear. For ultimately it is only this always present distance that establishes for us the possibility of processing what we have experienced in a scientific manner—at the end of this journey. (*Rasse und Seele* [1937] 180).

Clauss's mimic method, which he at times calls *Mitleben,* or "participation" in the life of the Other, amounts to dramatic role-playing in which the racial psychologist attempts to assume the attitude and sensibility of the individual he wants to scrutinize. This procedure entails a kind of transference in which the scientist "mimics" the life of the person under investigation and thereby comes, as it were, to an internal understanding of what it means to live and experience the world from that person's point of view (see *Rasse und Seele* [1937] 113–24; *Die Seele des Andern* 173–89). Clauss practiced this method most completely in the years 1927 to 1931, when he traveled to the Middle East, abandoned his outward identity as a European, and assumed the life of a nomadic sheik. The product of this research experience was the book *Als Beduine unter Beduinen* (A Bedouin among Bedouins), later republished in revised form under the title *Semiten der Wüste unter sich* (Desert Semites among themselves).

As the above quotation demonstrates, Clauss was intent on distinguishing his "participatory" or "mimic" method from nonscientific, purely emotional forms of human empathy. He sought to accomplish this by insisting on the empirical and experiential nature of this activity, implicitly aligning it with the empiricism *(Erfahrung)* of the natural sciences. The mimic method allows one to experience the world *objectively* from the perspective of the individual whose role one has assumed—as a Bedouin, a Frenchman, a Slav, and so on. What distinguishes this mimic identification from simple empathy, however, is the fact that it is combined with a natural distance, and this distance makes the mimic experience "objective." In other words, when applying the mimic procedure, Clauss as racial psychologist assumes a curiously dialectical position: he enters the life of the character he is "mimicking" while simultaneously retaining a kind of distanced self-reflection on this role. What one gains by practicing this method, according to Clauss, is an experience of the *inner* world of the Other; we explore his or her life from the inside, experience it more or less as he or she does, without, however, being totally and uncritically absorbed into it.

The question as to how one attains access to the unsullied inner life of an individual other than the self is, of course, the crucial issue of all psychology. Freud sought to resolve this problem by turning to dreams and other expressions of the unconscious life. Clauss seeks a solution by entering the role of the person he wants to understand and viewing the world from this perspective. The reason this mimic method is especially appropriate to the Nordic attitude—so much so, in fact, that it defines racial psychology as a Nordic science—is that the natural *distance* that, according to Clauss, is typical of the Nordic sensibility assures the scientific and objective nature of this identificatory process. Because of this natural remoteness from others, Clauss as Nordic scientist is incapable of simply "forgetting himself" and disappearing into the role he plays. While he plays his role of empathetic understanding, he is also always *aware* of his role-playing: he stands both within the role and outside it at the same time. Built into Clauss's mimic method, in short, is a dialectical structure of self-conscious alienation similar to the *Verfremdungseffect* (alienation effect) theorized around the same time by Bertolt Brecht (1898–1956) for modern, anti-Aristotelian drama.

The dialectical self-awareness of the racial psychologist makes itself most manifest in the fact that at the same time he ostensibly assumes the role of the people he studies, Clauss surreptitiously photographs their facial expressions and gestures. The external, "objective" stance of the photographer paradigmatically represents the distanced reflection on the analysand that Clauss sees as the necessary counterpart to the analyst's identification with the subject under study. During his four years in the Middle East, for example, Clauss shot over four thousand images, which he developed in a darkroom he constructed himself (*Semiten* 38). One must imagine Clauss, then, as a kind of psychological spy who infiltrates the internal life of an individual of foreign race, plays the role dictated by the style of that life, but at the same time clandestinely takes photographs that will be smuggled out and eventually published so as to reveal the internal, psychic constitution of this racial Other. The Nordic scientist as the practitioner of racial-psychological espionage, the infiltrator of the internal life of other races—that is the scientific ideal Clauss pursues with his mimic methodology. If Günther wanted to observe and visualize the biological and anatomical facts of diverse races, Clauss sought to develop a clandestine, penetrating gaze that would allow him to experience and visualize the *internal* life of the racial subjects he examined.

Clauss's Adaptation of Husserlian Phenomenology

The Nazi Party ideologues had good reason to be skeptical of this racial-psychological theory that seemed to promote an identificatory empathy with other races for the purposes of better understanding them. It is easy to see why the more straightforward theories of Günther slid more easily down their ideologically pampered palates. Clauss's ideas were much more complex and refined than Günther's, and on top of this, Clauss seemed to reject certain ideological principles in which Nazi racial theory was heavily invested. But there was at least one other good reason to reject Clauss's theories, especially his "questionable" procedure of mimic understanding: they were greatly indebted to the thought of a prominent philosopher of Jewish origin, namely, the phenomenological method of Edmund Husserl (1859–1938). Clauss openly acknowledged—at least in his early writings, published prior to the Nazi seizure of power—the influence of Husserl on the thought and methods of his racial psychology. During the First World War and the immediate interwar era, he was one of Husserl's most valued students in Freiburg, a distinction he shared with none other than Martin Heidegger (1889–1976).[11] Already in 1923, in the first edition of *Die nordische Seele,* Clauss identifies Husserl's phenomenological method as the basis of his own research procedure. Pointing in particular to Husserl's *Ideen zu einer reinen Phänomenologie und phänomenologischen Philosophie,* the first book of which appeared in 1913, Clauss praises Husserl's eidetic reduction for its ability to help us penetrate the materiality of the body and train our investigative gaze on the human psyche (9). Husserl's model offered Clauss a manner for distinguishing his own racial methodology from the materialist direction pursued by Günther and his followers. But Clauss is most specific about his debt to Husserl in the preface to the 1926 edition of *Rasse und Seele,* where he remarks: "Where my research is concerned, I am indebted to my previous teacher, Professor *Edmund Husserl* in Freiburg, for most of my best ideas; from him I not only learned the methodology applied in my research, but also received many valuable insights at an early age, for example, regarding the relationship of the soul to the animate body" (vi).

Clauss acknowledges two principal places where Husserl's thought was especially influential: his general methodology—we will see in a moment that the mimic procedure is closely related to phenomenological practices—and his conception of the relationship of the human body to the psyche. But Clauss's debt to Husserl is much broader and more multifaceted than Clauss himself admits, beginning with a general segregation of a human-scientific mode of investigation from the empirical and positivistic research pursued by the natural sciences. Husserl, as is well known, saw himself as the heir to Wilhelm Dilthey's (1833–1911) *Lebensphilosophie* that stressed *Erlebnis,* "lived experience," over the nonparticipatory, detached observation of the empirical scientist. In an addendum to the second book of *Ideen zu einer reinen Phänomenologie und phänomenologischen Philosophie,* Husserl follows Dilthey in distinguishing the human sciences—among which he includes phenomenology—from the natural sciences, on the basis of the nature of the objects they investigate and their procedures. "In the totality of these intellectual subject-relations," Husserl notes, "a field begins to open up for a different type of science, one that is principally distinct from the natural sciences. Subsumed under this new science are human observation and anthropology in all its forms, the study of personalities, of societies, and the formation and transformation of surroundings for these personalities—a complex of sciences that we gather under the collective name of the human sciences *[Geisteswissenschaften]*" (*Ideen II* 347–48). Husserl circumscribes the domain of the human sciences as everything related to the relations and relationships among human subjects, and he specifies anthropology and all the forms of *Menschenbeobachtung,* human observation—among which are included physiognomics and pathognomics—as subdisciplines of this overriding category. He stresses, moreover, the importance of the relationship of humans to their surroundings—what he will later call the *Lebenswelt,* or "life world"—as a coefficient of their nature and their self-understanding. This fundamental embeddedness of human subjects in their natural and cultural environment also underwrites Clauss's theory about the connection of race to a primordial landscape. But on the most general level it is Husserl's valorization of the human sciences over the natural sciences that

Clauss will adopt and deploy as a tactical weapon in his struggle against Günther's racial materialism.

In the early programmatic essay "Rassenkunde im Unterricht an Mittelschulen" (Racial studies in the middle-school classroom), for example, Clauss unequivocally asserts:

> [T]he concept of race as formulated by the natural sciences is no longer sufficient today for grasping the field in its entirety; it proves itself insufficient as soon as we attempt to apply it in the domains of the human sciences. The treatment of the "racial issue" in public life suffers greatly from this evil: People recognize vaguely and instinctually that "race" must also have some meaning in the sphere of intellectual production, but to attain a clearer view they have no other instrument at hand than the concept of race as defined by physical anthropology and biology—that is, as defined by the natural sciences. This concept is just as useless in the realm of the human sciences . . . as is a telescope, a microscope, or any other instrument employed in natural-scientific research. (90)

Clauss's point is clear. Although people are likely to acknowledge that race—as a foundational principle of the human constitution, according to racial theory—must leave its imprint on the psychological and intellectual products of human beings, not just on their anatomies, no distinct methodologies have emerged for gaining access to this psychological expression of race. The only attempts to investigate the impact of race on the spiritual domain have, like Günther's racial physiognomics, applied the inappropriate tools employed by the natural sciences. Clauss's aim is to develop an appropriate instrument for the study of race in the realm of the human sciences—that is, an instrument that will allow him to grasp the racial dimension he believes is inherent in all the expressions of the human spirit. The instrument he has in mind, but which is left unnamed in the cited passage, is the phenomenological method of his teacher Husserl, which was developed precisely as a procedure for the adequate investigation of the human "spirit." Clauss will appropriate Husserl's phenomenological tools for their application to questions of race—an application with which their inventor, Husserl himself, was certainly not in agreement.[12] What is clear, at any rate, is that Clauss believed that the study of race, as practiced in Germany at the time, needed to be reformed and supplemented by a new, nonmaterialist direction. He formulated his racial psychology as a human-scientific alternative to the predominant natural-scientific study of race.

When Clauss expresses his indebtedness to Husserl he explicitly mentions how he profited from his teacher's conception of the interrelation between body and soul. There is good reason for this, since without Husserl's basic notion of the human being as a psychosomatic unity, Clauss's racial psychology would lose its conceptual cornerstone. In the second book of *Ideen* Husserl lays out most succinctly his idea that the human being is structured as a coherent entity in which body and soul are inherently fused. "The psychological dimension [of the human being] is always given to us in its connection with the material domain. Among material objects there are some . . . that are soulless, that are 'merely' material; on the other hand, there are others that have the status of animate bodies *[Leibern]* and as such manifest a connection with a new layer of Being, which we call the psychic dimension" (*Ideen II* 91–92). Things that are purely material, void of all psychic impulses, do exist; they are called *Körper,* "inanimate bodies," and for Husserl these are the proper objects of study for the natural sciences. But animate bodies, which Husserl distinguishes from inanimate bodies by applying to them the German word *Leib,* are distinct from *Körper* in that the materiality of the body is extended by the addition of what Husserl calls "a new layer of Being." This additional layer of Being is, as it were, grafted onto (or into) the body, and it includes all the psychic and intellectual functions. In the third chapter of *Ideen II,* which deals with the constitution of psychic reality as expressed in the body, Husserl describes the human being, using the same metaphor, as "a material body *[Körper]* upon which new layers of Being, the somatic-psychological dimensions, are erected" (143), and his formulation emphasizes that the body serves as the material foundation, and hence as a necessary a priori, for the distinct strata of psychic existence.

Clauss, we should note, adopts in toto Husserl's distinction between the inanimate *Körper* and the animate *Leib,* concentrating his investigations on the latter as the vehicle of psychic expression (see *Die nordische Seele* [1923] 5–6). For Husserl, as for Clauss, body and soul stand in a clearly definable relationship: the body is the necessary medium through which the psychic dimension of the human being gains expression (*Ideen II* 96). In an addendum to the second book of *Ideen,* Husserl attempts to elucidate this conception of the body-soul relationship by turning to the example of a newspaper or similar written text. The paper on which the text is inscribed is the material body; the text itself expresses the psychic layers of the human being; and the newspaper in its entirety is, like the human being, an entity that fuses inanimate material and psychic expression into the animate body, or *Leib* (*Ideen II* 320). Similarly, Clauss asserts the dependency of the material body, as *Leib,* on the expressions of the psyche: for him the animate body is, as he says, *Etwas-für-Seele,* "something-for-psyche" (*Rasse und Seele* [1926] 19), something that exists purely for the sake of the psyche and its self-expression.

Husserl likewise views the psychic expressions of the human being as dependent on the material body as their medium of expression. "In order to be experienced objectively," he asserts, "spirit must be the animation *[Beseelung]* of an objective body. . . . The animate body *[Leib]* is not just a thing, rather it is the expression of spirit" (*Ideen II* 96). Clauss appropriates for his racial psychology this idea of the body as medium for the expressions of the psyche. In the first edition of *Rasse und Seele,* for example, he claims, in genuine Husserlian fashion: "Hence the psyche, which cannot itself be perceived empirically, possesses *an arena [Schauplatz]* in which it can present its expressions. This is the animate body *[Leib]*" (19; cf. *Die Seele des Andern* 97). Aside from transforming Husserl's textual metaphor into a theatrical one *(Schauplatz),* Clauss will also give this basic phenomenological idea a distinctly racial turn. He does this, first of all, by substituting the subcategory of race for Husserl's universal "human being." Husserl claims in *Ideen II* that the analogies which tie together the material body and the psyche in every individual "*are grounded in a commonality of ontological form*" (*Ideen II* 125). General human ontology thus provides the foundation for laws that determine the relationship between the human body and the human psyche. For Clauss, by contrast, there are no human beings pure and simple, but only human beings of this or that race or of such and such a racial intermixture (see "Der germanische Mensch" 8; *Rasse und Seele* [1937] 118–19).

This substitution of race for Husserl's ontological ground leads directly to one of Clauss's most basic ideas: the notion that racial purity can be defined in terms of the interconnection of a specific racial "soul" with the racial body that is most appropriate to its endemic psychic expressions. Clauss explains this relationship in the following way:

> [T]he style of the psyche expresses itself in its arena, the animate body. *But in order for this to be possible, this arena itself must be governed by a style,* which in turn must stand in a structured relationship to the style of the psyche: all the features of the somatic structure are, as it were, pathways for the expression of the psyche. The racially constituted (that is, stylistically determined) psyche thus requires a racially constituted animate body *[Leib]* in order to express the racially constituted style of its experience in a consummate and pure manner. The psyche's expressive style is inhibited if the style of its body does not conform perfectly with it. (*Rasse und Seele* [1926] 20–21)

This concept of psychic and/or bodily style is, of course, foreign to Husserl's thought. As we know, however, for Clauss race is defined as nothing other than this psychological style, which he classifies in terms of broad typological categories that are given the race designations common at the time. But Clauss, in a sophisticated intellectual move, takes this idea even further: in the ideal case, the racial style characteristic of the psychic expressions of any individual would be perfectly congruous with the racial style of the body that serves as medium for these expressions. Clauss is obviously structuring his conception of the internally consistent racial being in terms of traditional aesthetic categories: on the idea that, to be apprised as beautiful, a work of art must be structured according to a single coherent style, and not be a cacophony of diverse or even conflicting styles.

The theme of *kalokagathia,* the belief that ethical and physical beauty inherently converge, which is part and parcel of the physiognomic tradition well before Lavater, returns here with a curious racial twist. This principle will allow Clauss to offer an original—and from the standpoint of Nazi racial ideology, deviant—definition of racial purity. Rather than being based in "pure blood" or in a unitary racial-genetic makeup, as was the case for Günther and the racial materialists, racial purity for Clauss expresses itself in the uniformity of racial style in both body and soul. "We understand under purity of constitution or of race," he explains, "a unitary style. We deem those human beings to be *of pure racial constitution or racially pure* whose soul and body are governed and organized by one single style alone" (*Rasse und Seele* [1926] 24). If his teacher Husserl considered the human being to be composed of a material body onto which are grafted the different layers of psychic existence, then Clauss added to this conception the essentially aesthetic demand that these diverse psychic layers, as well as the body through which they reach expression, must be structured according to the same (racial) style, the same *Gestalt.* Style makes the (racial) man, in Clauss's theory, and coherence of style is the highest attribute of racial purity.

Husserl's specific theory about the relationship of the body, as medium of expression, to the psyche, as the active composer of the expressive "text," is worth examining in more detail here, since his arguments hark back to ideas first brought forward in the context of the post-Lavaterian debate over physiognomics, in particular the position Hegel assumed in his critique of Lavater's and Gall's materialist approaches. One of Husserl's most important distinctions in this regard is that between an understanding of the material body as an inherent and determining part of our existential Being—what he calls *Leib sein,* "being an animate body"—or as a fortuitous possession that individuals employ for the expression of their psychic substance—what Husserl designates as *Leib haben,* "possessing an animate body" (*Ideen II* 94). Husserl identifies *Leib sein* with the erroneous materialist, natural-scientific conception that views the body as the primordial given of the individual, while he associates *Leib haben* with the more malleable conception of the body as expressive medium, which he sees as solely relevant for phenomenological psychology. Clauss takes over not only the terms of this dichotomy, but also Husserl's relative evaluation of both positions. "I *am* not this body," he emphatically maintains in the 1923 edition of *Die nordische Seele,* "rather I *possess* it; it is my field of expression" (34).

If for Husserl the psyche is dependent on the body as its medium of expression, then the animate body, the *Leib,* is likewise thoroughly defined by the manner in which it manifests the psyche: the relationship between body and soul is a wholly reciprocal one. This leads Husserl to a theory of psychic expression reminiscent of Goethe's addendum to the fragment "On Physiognomics" in the first volume of Lavater's *Physiognomische Fragmente* (15). Here, we recall, Goethe claims that it is not merely a person's face or body that reveal character; clothes, household effects, actions—indeed, all cultural expressions—constitute signs of inherent personality. Husserl makes a similarly broad claim in the second book of *Ideen.* "The animate body *[Leib],* as body, is a psychically-imbued body through and through. Every movement of the body is psychically imbued, coming and going, standing and sitting, running and dancing, etc. The same is true for every human accomplishment, every product, etc." (240). There is no *movement* of the body, no physical action, and no human creation or artifact that is not born of, and that does not bear witness to, the psychic substance of the individual who produced it. Clauss will make a similar claim in the first edition of *Rasse und Seele,* explicitly extending the field of psychic expression to cover all cultural products: "The psyche can also express itself in *its products:* these also constitute the arena of its style. This insight opens up immeasurable domains for our research: the domains of *culture*" (23). Characteristically, Clauss identifies *style* or *form,* not content, as the sphere in which the psyche manifests itself in the artifacts of culture.

Over a hundred years prior to the development of Husserl's phenomenological theory of the body, this same idea about the expression of the "soul" in the actions of the body and in the products created by the individual was voiced in the work of another German philosopher—in a text, not coincidentally, that also bore the word "phenomenology" in its title: Hegel's *Phänomenologie des Geistes.* In the section where he takes issue with the materialist positions represented in Lavater's physiognomics and Gall's phrenology, Hegel writes:

> The external totality [of the human being] is constituted not merely by its *primordial Being,* the innate body, but also by the forming of this body that is a function of internal activity. It is the unity of unstructured and structured Being and the reality of the individual, which is permeated by its for-itself. This totality, which contains within it the determined, primordial firm parts of the body as well as the features

> that are only generated by actions, *is,* and this *Being* is *expression* of the internal realm, the individual constituted as consciousness and movement. (234)

The section of the *Phänomenologie* in which this passage is found bears the title "Beobachtung der Beziehung des Selbstbewußtseins auf eine unmittelbare Wirklichkeit" (Observation on the relationship of self-consciousness to an immediate reality), and it contains in rudimentary form many of the ideas about the interconnection between the material body and its underlying psychic substance that Husserl will later formulate in his phenomenological theory. The cited passage circumscribes the human being as a psychosomatic unity in which the somatic material is shaped and creatively (re-)formed by the activity of the psyche. The fundamental existential Being of the individual is identified not with the materiality of the body, but rather with the activities of the psyche that *express themselves through* the body. This psychic expression, as activity and deed, as cultural production, constitutes the essential Being of the individual, his or her "character." This is the same position that Husserl, and following him Clauss, will adopt.

It is important at this point to call to mind Hegel's principal critique of Lavaterian physiognomics and Gallian phrenology as semiotic systems in which bodily forms serve as signs or symbols of transcendental or psychological characteristics. Hegel, we recall, insisted that the acts of consciousness that reveal themselves through the medium of the animate body are more than semiotic indicators pointing to something that lies beyond our grasp; they are immediate symptoms of this higher Being itself, identical with it.

> An action is something simple and determinate, something general, something that can be contained in an abstraction; it is murder, theft or act of charity, courageous act, etc.; and we can *express* what *it is.* It *is* this, and its Being *[Sein]* is not just a sign, but rather the thing itself. The action *is* this, and the individual human being *is* what *this action is.* . . . Thus only action can be conceived as the person's *genuine Being [Sein]*—not his figure, which is supposed to express . . . what one thinks that he merely might do. (*Phänomenologie des Geistes* 243)

The genuine Being of any animate creature cannot be expressed by its static anatomical form, the shape of its skull, the length of its nose, the color of its hair, and so on, but only by its deeds and actions. Expressions that employ the body as medium are, moreover, not simple "signs" that point to an imperceptible transcendental layer of true Being; they are, instead, immediate reflexes of true Being itself. Hegel, in effect, erases the Kantian distinction between the absolute Being of the thing-in-itself and the world of perceptible appearances. Such an argument must serve as the basis of *any* "phenomenology" of spirit; otherwise Hegel's—and Husserl's—project would be a *semiotics* of spirit, not a phenomenology. For what the term "phenomenology of spirit" implies is nothing less than the idea that spirit (or soul, or psyche) is *identical* with its expressions in the phenomenal world. In the instance of the human being, this means that the manifestations of the psychic layers in gesture, action, motion, deeds, and so on are the perceptually ascertainable impulses of the psyche itself: they are the visible, perceptible psyche as such. This argument is clearly of central importance for the theory of physiognomics, since its most basic hypothesis is that appearance manifests essence. Indeed, it is no exaggeration to claim that the emergence of phenomenological theory from Hegel to Husserl provides one of the most solid foundations for physiognomic thought within the German intellectual tradition, thereby helping explain its vitality and persistence within this intellectual-historical formation.[13]

Husserl concerns himself with precisely this dissolution of the Kantian duality between the thing-in-itself and its appearance in §43 of the first book of *Ideen*. "It is a fundamental error to believe," he maintains, "that perception is not able . . . to get hold of the thing itself, to believe that the thing exists in itself and that it is not available to us in its immanent being *[Ansichsein]*" (89). Significantly, he follows through on this assertion by arguing, as Hegel had, against any semiotic relation between the immanence of the thing and the transcendence of its internal Being.

> One can easily be misled by the idea that the transcendence of the thing is that of a *representation* or a *sign*. Often the theory of representation is vehemently attacked and replaced with a theory of signs. However, both these theories are not merely incorrect, but actually nonsensical. The spatial body we see is something that is perceived in all its transcendence, something given to consciousness in all its

> corporeality *[Leibhaftigkeit]*. A representation or a sign does *not* take its place. We should never impute a consciousness of signs or of representations to the act of perception. (*Ideen I* 89–90)

There is a great deal at stake in this argument for Husserl and for the science of phenomenology in general. Phenomenology as method is dependent on the assertion that every perception, as an "intentional act" in the sense defined by Husserl's teacher and mentor Franz Brentano (1838–1917), encompasses the true Being of the perceived object, and is hence not merely a "sign," or second-order representation, of its Being. Phenomenology understands itself as a form of *immediate* perception, immediate *intuition* of the thing's essence, which expresses itself—and can only express itself—in or through the phenomenality of the corporeal entity as such. If sensual appearances are signs at all, Husserl remarks at a later point in *Ideen I*, they are not signs that refer to something other than themselves; instead they are self-referential signs or, in semiotic terminology, wholly motivated and absolutely self-identical signs, in which signifier and signified collapse into one. Perception, for Husserl, recognizes no semiotic "difference."

This excursus on the theoretical principles of Husserlian phenomenology and their relationship to the terms Hegel introduced into the dispute over physiognomics represents more than an intellectual-historical curiosity. The eighteenth- and nineteenth-century debate on physiognomics was a kind of trigger, perhaps even a cover, for arguments about much more deep-seated and consequential philosophical issues. Addressed in this debate were not merely the obvious questions of the connection of body to soul, but fundamental issues about the nature of human perception and consciousness, the relationship of appearance to essence, the phenomenality of the psyche, and the ontological status of the human being as psychosomatic entity. The fact that during the Weimar Republic and Nazi era German racial thought was able to actualize this debate in much of its philosophical profundity—this is one of the things that Clauss, above all, was able to accomplish—contributed greatly to its intellectual standing. By appropriating the terms of this intellectual-historical debate, German racism could credibly pretend that it, too, was concerned with such profound questions as the ontological status of human beings.

If we return now to the indebtedness of Clauss's racial psychology to Husserl's phenomenological method, we can ascertain (aside from the shared fundamental conception of the human being as a unified psychosomatic entity in which the activities of the body express the phenomenality of the spirit, soul, or psyche) three further points of intersection: their theories of intersubjectivity; the concept of mutual understanding and the relationship of the individual to his or her *Lebenswelt* or life world; and the principal of *Anschauung,* perceptually based, immediate intuition.

We have already touched briefly on Clauss's "mimic" method and the practice of *Mitleben,* of identificatory empathy, by which he sought to understand the subjects he studied from their own internal perspective. This procedure represents a methodological variant of one of Husserl's basic principles for the constitution of intersubjectivity: what he calls *Einfühlung.* Usually translated as "empathy," this term actually implies a projection of the self into the position or situation of an Other as a means for comprehending it. Husserl outlines its importance in §21 of the second book of *Ideen.*

> If a psychic entity is to exist, is to have *objective* existence, then the *conditions of possibility for intersubjective givenness* must be fulfilled. However, such intersubjective experientiability is only conceivable through a process of "empathy," which, for its part, presupposes an animate body *[Leib]* that can be intersubjectively experienced. This animate body, moreover, must be recognizable to the individual who is practicing this act of empathy as the animate body of the psychic entity under investigation, and it must, further, appeal in its givenness to an empathetic understanding of its psychic dimension, and demonstrate in subsequent experiences its identity [as a psychosomatic entity]. (95)

Each human being is objectively aware of the existence of psychic and intellectual phenomena in other human beings only through his or her own experience of these phenomena in the self. However, we can never immediately share the psychic experiences of others; we can only project such experiences into them, based on analogies to our own psychic life, working under the assumption that these psychic phenomena will express themselves in physical manifestations that we recognize based on our own psychosomatic integrity. Intersubjectivity, in other words, requires that we interpolate psychic impulses into Others based on the interpretation of symptoms expressed through the medium of the body. Husserl stresses the interpretive nature of this activity when he notes: "*Empathetic understanding of people* is nothing other than the mode of comprehension that *understands meaning,* that, in other words, grasps the meaning of the animate body *[Leib]* in the context of the unity of meaning of which it is the medium. Practicing empathy means nothing other than grasping an *objective spirit,* seeing a human being" (244). To grasp "objective spirit" means to interpret the movements of the animate body as the phenomenal concretization of psychic impulses, as the Being of spirit. We comprehend the "meaning" of the soul by virtue of an interpretive operation that is essentially physiognomic in nature, reading, on the basis of an assumed unity of body and psyche, bodily expression as symptomatic of psychic essence. Clauss similarly stresses the fundamentally *hermeneutic* nature of his racial psychology, emphasizing the researcher's role as an interpreter of bodily expressions, which in turn are viewed as the manifestation of psychic impulses (see *Rasse und Seele* [1926] 19; "Der germanische Mensch" 5).

When Husserl elaborates this notion of *Einfühlung,* he describes it in terms that evoke its proximity to the role-playing of Clauss's mimic method. When I project myself into the psychic Being of an Other, Husserl contends, "I not only feel my way into his thoughts, emotions, and actions, but I must also *follow* him in all these respects; his motives become my quasi-motives, which, however, in the mode of an intuitively realized empathy, prove themselves to be *sensibly motivated.* I share in his temptations, I share in his fallacies, and this "sharing" is indicative of an internal co-experiencing *[Miterleben]* of motivating factors that bear within themselves their own necessity" (*Ideen II* 275). It is not, then, merely a matter of "empathy" in the common sense, but of actual *reenactment* of the situation and motivations of the Other whom I wish to comprehend. I must *share, participate* completely in the logic—or illogic—of his or her actions, thoughts, and emotions. Husserl's word *Miterleben,* "co-experience" or "participatory experience" of the Other, is quite close to Clauss's term *Mitleben.* What these two methodologies have in common, above all, is the idea that profound understanding of a human Other must be grounded in participatory identification with the very structure of that Other's psychic experiences. Clauss takes over this more general conception of *Einfühlung,* which for Husserl serves as the basis for *any* intersubjective understanding, and attempts to hone it into a specific research tool for the (human) science of race.

In Husserl's thinking, human beings have the inherent possibility of mutual intersubjective comprehension because they share the same ontological foundation. By contrast, in his racial psychology Clauss substitutes racial style for Husserl's more general ontological grounding. This has important consequences for Clauss's conception of intersubjective understanding; for him shared *race,* not shared ontological structure, becomes the condition of possibility for mutual understanding. This is one of the most persistent themes in Clauss's writings: true intersubjective comprehension and interhuman community can only be established on the basis of common racial identity. Throughout his works he recounts the same parable, which is intended to elucidate this problem: the story of a brother and sister who have absolutely nothing in common and are constantly at odds with one another. The upshot of this parable for Clauss is that while the siblings are descended from the same parents and hence from the same gene pool, they are governed by absolutely contrary racial identities and hence by conflicting racial styles (see *Die nordische Seele* [1932] 7–9; *Vorschule der Rassenkunde* 7–8). In the tendentious essay "Nordische Glaubensgestaltung" (The form of Nordic belief), Clauss expresses in its most ideologically radical form this notion that mutual understanding can only be predicated on racial selfsameness: "Pure understanding cannot transcend the boundaries of racial constitution. The boundary of internal destiny unites identically constituted racial souls into a potential community of like-minded people, and it simultaneously distinguishes all these like-minded people from those other individuals who do not have the same racial constitution. The bonding boundary of destiny is simultaneously a barrier that separates" (1).

Mutual understanding and the intersubjective community on which it is founded are only possible among racially identical people. Clauss calls this, with obvious ideological pathos, the "bonding boundary of destiny," a force that ties individuals together as a coherent collective. But these traits that fuse commonly constituted individuals into a racial community present an obstacle to the understanding of racially dissimilar people. In cases of racial difference, no community-building understanding can ever exist. This theory, which defines racial segregation as an inevitable natural phenomenon, clearly provided grist for the mills of German nationalism and racism.

Closely related to this idea of intersubjective bonding and the coherent racial collectivity is a conception of the integral bond that joins thc individual with his or her environmental surroundings *(Umwelt),* or in Clauss's terminology, with a particular "landscape." In §50 of *Ideen II,* which bears the subtitle "Die Person als Mittelpunkt einer Umwelt" (The person as focal point of a set of surroundings), Husserl claims that each person, as person, is defined by a particular environmental context integral to his or her personality. "As a person I am what I am (and every person is what he or she is) by virtue of being a *subject in specific surroundings.* The concepts 'I' and 'surroundings' are inseparably connected to one another" (185). Surroundings for Husserl constitute nothing less than the context in which a person becomes what he or she is, and in which he or she functions as a constituent part. This environmental context helps shape the way the person thinks, feels, and acts, and these thoughts, feelings, and actions obtain their specific meaning only within this context. Moreover, as Husserl later explains, a common set of surroundings, or a shared life world, is the prerequisite for mutual comprehension and community; this is what makes individuals into parts of an integrally connected totality (*Ideen II* 191–92). Clauss views the question of community and comprehension through the lens of racial identity. He also transposes this perspective onto Husserl's conception of environmental surroundings, the contextualizing life world, by identifying them with a particular type of natural landscape.

In the chapter entitled "Seele und Landschaft" (Soul and landscape) in the first edition of *Rasse und Seele,* Clauss expands on the Husserlian concept of contextual surroundings in order to define landscape as a natural environment imbued with psychological significance.

> To say that the psyche "lives" is to say that it lives *in a specific set of surroundings*, and these surroundings are part of the psyche just as the psyche is part of these surroundings. The meaning of all sur-roundings *[Um-Welt]* is precisely to be a world that "surrounds" a psyche. Psyche and surroundings form an essential unity: the psyche is shaped and trained by the style of its surroundings, and the psyche, in turn, shapes and places the stamp of its racial style on its surroundings. It thus should be clear that the surroundings of a particular psyche are also structured according to a particular style: *We call a set of stylistically structured psychic surroundings a landscape.* (*Rasse und Seele* [1926] 33)

We recognize immediately the internal consistency of Clauss's argumentation. Just as racial purity is grounded in consistency of racial style and community in the commonality of racial *Gestalt*, so, too, one's proper natural or cultural surroundings share with the racial individual a common stylistic form. Landscape and racial type are structured according to a symbiotic relationship in which the nature of the landscape helps define the features of its indigenous racial type; in turn the racial style of the individuals who live in a particular environment influences the style these surroundings assume. As is clear from its name alone, the Nordic type thrives best, according to Clauss, in the landscapes of northern and central Europe (*Rasse und Seele* [1926] 34–35). Landscape, in fact, takes on such decisive significance in Clauss's theory that displacement from one's racially appropriate surroundings inevitably leads to degeneration and decline (*Rasse und Seele* [1926] 39). It is but a small step from this theory to a legitimation of the Nazis' territorial expansion, their drive for *Lebensraum.* What Clauss implicitly provides is a kind of racial-psychological justification for the recolonization of any "landscape" that once was tied closely to the races that make up the population of the German Reich.

There is yet one more foundational principle of Husserlian phenomenology appropriated by Clauss for his racial psychology: the key concept of *Anschauung* as the medium of human awareness and knowledge of the world. *Anschauung* is one of those nearly untranslatable German philosophical terms whose semantic field is uncommonly extensive. Meaning both "perception" and "intuition," in Husserl's thought the term suggests a manner of "seeing" that penetrates into the inner nature, the very essence or core of the things its observes. Moreover, *Anschauung* for Husserl circumscribes a form of immediate understanding, a mode of givenness that accompanies the act of human perception itself. In the first book of *Ideen* Husserl contends: "*Immediate 'seeing,'* not merely sensual, empirical seeing, but rather *seeing as such, as an immediate dative consciousness of whatever sort,* is the ultimate source of validity for all rational assertions. . . . Thus we substitute for empirical experience the more universal 'intuitive perception' *[Anschauung]*" (*Ideen I* 43). *Anschauung,* or intuitive perception, is distinct from simple empirical observation; it is not restricted to the realm of the sensual, but signals a more fundamental form of vision, a mode of seeing in which the consciousness of the perceiver is actively involved. Indeed, *Anschauung* is identified as the type of perception practiced in the human sciences, as opposed to the sensually oriented, "empirical seeing" of the natural sciences. This leads Husserl to what he calls his "principle of principles," the unquestioned authority and truth of the originary knowledge provided by perceptual intuition. This principle states "*that every immediately dative intuitive perception constitutes a source of validity for knowledge, that everything that presents itself to us immediately in 'intuition'* (in all its physical reality, so to speak) *must simply be accepted as what it makes itself out to be*" (*Ideen I* 51). Perceptual intuition, directed at the objects of animate reality, penetrates the external layers of the sensual being and presents us with domains of *super*sensual knowledge about this being. What is more, rather than having the status of mere transcendental speculation, this supersensual knowledge, according to Husserl, represents a principal level of awareness whose truthfulness and validity should simply be accepted without question. We must embrace this supersensual perception as the bearer of a particular type of knowledge: not knowledge of "facts," for those are the domain of the natural sciences, but rather knowledge of "essences" (*Ideen I* 6).

The supersensual apperception of *Anschauung* requires a special attitude or procedure on the part of the observer: this is

Husserl's famous "eidetic reduction," which he refers to with the Greek word *epoché,* which means "suspending," or as Husserl liked to say, "placing in brackets." Husserl calls this procedure an eidetic reduction because, he argues, what we perceive after we have "bracketed" or "suspended" all the natural attitudes of empirical observation is nothing less than the *eidos,* the internal "essence," of the object under study. Husserl explains how this procedure operates:

> We place out of action the general thetic awareness that constitutes the essence of our natural attitude, we place in brackets everything that this thetic awareness implies in respect to ontology: *hence [we suspend] the natural world in its entirety,* which constantly "exists for us" and is "present," and which will always continue to exist as a "reality" for our consciousness, even if we choose to bracket it. . . . I thereby practice the "phenomenological" ἐποχή [epoché] which *prevents me from passing any judgment whatsoever about spatio-temporal existence.* (*Ideen I* 67–68)

Everything in our "normal" or everyday consciousness—in Husserl's terminology, our general "thetic" attitude—is placed "out of action," which means we bracket off from our awareness the natural—that is, the empirical—world in its entirety. Once I have, in the act of perception, suspended from my consciousness all those aspects of this perceptual act that deal with phenomena of the spatio-temporal world, what we otherwise call physical "reality," I have reduced this perceptual experience to its eidetic core. By performing this phenomenological reduction, the phenomenologist gains access to the transsensual essence of the object of his or her consciousness. To be sure, this "essence" should not be confused with the Kantian thing-in-itself; for Husserl the very consciousness with which one carries out this act of *Anschauung* is part and parcel of the essence one will distill out of it. The object of perceptual intuition is never pure object; it is always an object *of* consciousness, and Husserl's aim, in fact, is to arrive at the pure consciousness at work in any individual perceptual act: "we direct our conceptualizing, theoretically investigative gaze at *pure consciousness in its absolute self-being [Eigensein]*" (*Ideen I* 107).

In one specific sense Husserl's phenomenological reduction can be seen as the ultimate solution to the problems posed by physiognomics in general. I have pointed repeatedly to the paradox that underlies all physiognomic endeavors since Lavater: they seek to employ empirical procedures in order to arrive at trans-empirical knowledge. Physiognomics attempts to study the *physis*, the physical, as a manner for arriving at *meta*-physical insights. Husserl's phenomenological reduction theorizes a mode of perception that, modeled on the gaze of the empirical sciences, "brackets" all the positivist data that is the concern of the natural scientist in order to reveal the true internal essence of the experienced object. The ambiguities of the word *Anschauung*, in fact, encompass and reconcile this apparent paradox. What eidetic reduction is intended to achieve is nothing less than the appropriation of visual perception for the purposes of internal intuition. Phenomenology, in short, theorizes a kind of bi-vision in which every intuitive perception of the animate body is simultaneously an act in which the inherent essence of the psyche animating that body is grasped.

Husserl himself never applies the phenomenological reduction specifically to physiognomic ends; to do so he would have to move from the domain of phenomenological theory, with which his early writings were principally concerned, to the domain of practice. But he does consider the general theoretical issue that revolves around the application of the phenomenological method to the human subject. Indeed, in a certain sense the human being as integral psychosomatic entity is the exemplary instance for applied phenomenology: it is easy to understand on the basis of the human model precisely how the "suspension" of all the empirical, natural, physical data about the phenomenal world is requisite for an understanding of its psychological essence. In the second book of *Ideen* Husserl deals explicitly with this issue: "In a certain sense, the comprehension of the human being passes through the phenomenon of the body *[Körper]*, which in this instance is animate body *[Leib]*. It does not stop, so to speak, at the body *[Körper]*, it does not direct its arrow at it, but rather passes through it—it is also not directed at a spirit connected to that body, but rather simply at the human being itself" (*Ideen II* 240). What Husserl describes here reads almost like a general description of every act of physiognomic interpretation. Such perception does not linger with the human body itself, or if it does, then only so as to transcend it, to penetrate it and arrive at an internal substrate. At the same time, however, Husserl is careful to avoid a dualistic body-spirit conception. When one penetrates and transcends the body in the act of inter-human comprehension, one does not arrive simply at the "spirit" as the other side of the animate body; rather, one grasps the human being as a whole, the particular human being as such. This is, of course, precisely the kind of claim physiognomists have perennially made: what I discern when I subject another human being to my physiognomic gaze is nothing other than the essence of that human being, his or her unitary characterological core.

It is not surprising that Husserl's student Ludwig Ferdinand Clauss would recognize the relevance of phenomenological theory for physiognomic applications. Indeed, Husserl's theories invite their own adaptation to physiognomic practice, since they provide answers to some of the most vexing methodological problems that have plagued modern physiognomics—that is, physiognomics with pretensions to delivering "scientific" knowledge—since Lavater first attempted to define physiognomics as a positivistic science. What *is* surprising, perhaps, is that the *primary* physiognomic application Husserl's theories received at the time lent them a specifically racial cast.[14] As we have seen, Clauss only needed to undertake one fundamental shift in basic principles to accomplish this move: he substituted for Husserl's ontological understanding of human beings as a general species with a common human "essence" the racial conception of human beings as divided into distinct and distinguishable types with discernible and ineradicable differences. In Clauss's view, the essence at which one would arrive when subjecting another human subject to a phenomenological reduction would always be a *racial* essence, never a general human or ontological form. Given the power of typological thinking in Germany during the years of the Weimar Republic, it comes as no surprise that Clauss projects this typological framework onto Husserl's more general ontological model. Indeed, the ultimate basis of this divergence can perhaps be taken back to the controversies surrounding the competing monogenetic and polygenetic theories of human origin. Husserl's ontological ground assumes a monogenetic origin of the human species, whereas Clauss's theory of absolute racial distinctness is implicitly founded on a polygenetic thesis.[15]

Husserlian *Anschauung* as the Ground of Clauss's Racial Panopticism

In a passage from the first edition of *Rasse und Seele* in which Clauss explains his methodological procedure, he describes his mode of observation in terms that invoke Husserl's *Anschauung* as a fusion of visual perception and immediate intuition.

> Our methodology does not principally consist in lying in wait to make fine observations; for we know that such a procedure would only latch onto fragments of the external aspect and never grasp the law and interconnections that govern the deep structure. That is precisely why the drawing of inferences has no place in our method. We do not observe, we experience; we do not draw inferences, we behold. Is this piece of paper on which I am writing white? Yes. Do I infer that it is white? No, I see it. And when I received a nice letter this morning, was it joy that I experienced? Yes. Did I infer that it was joy? No, I experienced joy. And now, reflecting back upon it, I can experience it once more in my memory. And I can intuitively perceive *[anschauen]* it and, based on this perception, arrive at the immediate insight and certainty that we arrive at in our research. Inward gazing is all that matters. ([1926] 28)

What Clauss presents here can be seen as a kind of commonsense explanation of phenomenological *Anschauung,* devoid of its abstract philosophical terminology. The racial psychologist, like the phenomenologist, does not "lie in wait" for the subject it will study, like a hunter for its prey. Such a procedure would reveal only fragments of the external person. What Clauss is after is the "deep structure" and the "law"—Husserl's "essence"—that informs the internal nature of this person. Clauss is careful to distinguish the evidence his method produces from the conclusions generated by deductive reasoning. What he arrives at are not, he insists, the results of logical operations, but rather *immediate* insights, knowledge that is just as certain as is the awareness of our own personal experiences. What is "seen" by this procedure is explicitly not the external being; what is perceived, rather, is its very inwardness. Once again we become aware of how Clauss's psychological procedure invokes the intuitive certainty other Weimar proponents of physiognomics, people like Spengler, Klages, and Kassner, associated with the immediacy of physiognomic perception. Clauss has the added advantage, however, that he can appeal to Husserl's phenomenological theory to provide this notion of inward perception with a solid philosophical grounding. Husserl, after all, developed an explicitly philosophical method for practicing this intuitive gaze.

Husserl applies the term *Wesenserschauung,* the perception of essence, to the phenomenological procedure of eidetic reduction. He describes this perception of essence in a way that openly suggests its relevance for physiognomic observation. "Perception of essence *[Wesenserschauung]* hence is intuitive perception *[Anschauung],* and it is beholding in the profound sense, not a simple or perhaps vague envisioning; it is an *immediately* dative intuitive perception that grasps the essence of the thing in its 'bodily' selfness" (*Ideen I* 15). *Wesenserschauung* describes an immediate form of intuition that grasps the "essence" of what is observed in all its physical "selfness"; it reveals, as it were, the internal identity of the perceived object or person as an animate body. It is no coincidence that Clauss describes his method of mimic identification and *Mitleben* in terms derived from Husserl's eidetic reduction. In *Semiten der Wüste unter sich,* for example, he writes:

> Placing our self in steely brackets—that is part and parcel of every consummate act of mimic understanding, if it is truly a genuine and honest piece of work. Placing something in brackets does not mean abandoning it. If the actor were to abandon his actual role in life when playing a particular stage role, he would only be able to play Othello once in his entire life, for he would actually strangle his leading lady—an act he would scarcely be allowed to repeat. These steely brackets are the brackets we employ when we assume the attitude of playing at something. (24)

Clauss has obviously drawn his metaphor of "bracketing" from his teacher Husserl. Here it is the personal reality of the racial psychologist as mimic role-player that is placed under suspension. But the results are the same as with Husserl's procedure of *Wesenserschauung:* bracketing allows the racial psychologist, like the phenomenologist, to gain immediate, intuitive knowledge of the (human) subject under study, purely on the basis of a disciplined mode of observation. In fact, for Clauss this perceptual intuition becomes the trademark of racial psychology as discipline. He invokes it whenever he is at pains to distinguish his brand of racial anthropology from its statistically, materialistically oriented relative, represented above all by Günther's racial physiognomics. In *Rasse und Seele* he remarks: "[Anthropology] measures and categorizes details and strives for the exactitude of perceptionless *number;* we, by contrast, remain wholly within the domain of intuitive perception *[Anschauung],* we involve ourselves in the totality of the visible phenomenon and ask questions about its *significance*" ([1926] 130; cf.[1937] 116). The key dichotomy around which this passage turns—exactitude, number, and quantification versus intuition, totality, and significance—repeats the terms in which those who championed a humanist form of physiognomics—above all Spengler, Kassner, and Klages—defended their own ostensibly subjectivist methodology and distinguished it from the analytical procedure of the natural sciences. Clauss, too, is intent upon legitimating the nonsystematic, even non-systematizable method by which his new discipline arrives at its data and its evidence. It operates, he asserts, by employing a mode of perception that, like phenomenological *Wesenserschauung,* penetrates the physical surfaces of the subjects it studies and grasps the totality of the internal human being at its core. Since for Clauss this human essence is always *racially* constituted, what this model of intuitive perception ultimately permits him to see is *race.* The application of phenomenological principles allows Clauss to make race visible to the properly trained racial psychologist. When applied to race, however, this valorization of immediate intuition as the medium of absolutely certain knowledge takes on an ominous guise. For what Clauss essentially claims is that the gaze trained to practice *Anschauung* as a rigorous methodology is able infallibly to divulge race on the basis of pre-rational, prelogical observation. In its racial application it is difficult to distinguish this perceptual intuition from subjectivistic prejudice. To put it another way: the belief that one arrives at a basic level of prelogical comprehension by practicing this form of observant *Anschauung* could certainly be marshaled in support of wholly subjectivistic, arbitrary, even capricious opinions. Woe to those who have been penetrated and "discerned" by this racial gaze!

As I have argued throughout this book, physiognomics since Lavater must be conceived as a disciplinary mechanism in a two-fold sense. On the one hand, it attempts to establish itself as science, to structure itself according to a defined set of epistemological principles and practical procedures so as to constitute itself as a knowledge discipline. On the other hand, because it subjects individuals to a certain set of implicit values—under the guise, of course, of revealing hitherto unrecognized "truths" about the inner person—physiognomics also performs a disciplinary function in the sense of control and social coercion. All physiognomic theories imply an ethical norm of one sort or another. Even those physiognomists who appeal to a relativism of ethical values—as do, to take two extreme examples, Lavater and Clauss—implicitly establish an evaluative hierarchy that is then propagated through their physiognomic judgments. The interpretive gaze of the physiognomist manifests a practiced and disciplined observation of others with the ultimate purpose of coercing them—as well as the readers of one's own physiognomic treatises—into accepting and embracing these implicit norms.

In the theories of Hans F. K. Günther and Ludwig Ferdinand Clauss we can discern two distinct yet complementary forms of this physiognomic gaze. In the case of Günther, this disciplinary/disciplining observation is directed at the human being in all his or her physicality, and it attempts to interpret out of these physical features the signs and symptoms of (racial) personality. The gaze that Clauss practices is much more subtle—and perhaps for that reason, more insidious—than that employed by Günther. Clauss's racial-physiognomic gaze is hardly concerned with anatomy at all; indeed, it seeks to penetrate the anatomical veneer of the individual so as to grasp, in a moment of perceptual intuition, the totality of the inner person, the essence of his or her racial "style." What becomes clear when one examines the history of physiognomics, however, especially in the articulations it receives in the German intellectual-historical tradition, is that the intuitive perception that claims to interpret and recognize internal "essence" in fact *creates* and *projects* this essence in its own "hermeneutical" act. Nowhere is this so true as in the case of Clauss's racial psychology. The racial "soul" that the psychologist "uncovers" beneath the facade of the observed subject's body is nothing but an interpolated construct that serves as a self-disciplinary measure for the analyzed "racial" subject itself.

For Michel Foucault, this is the very meaning of the notion of "soul" in the post-Enlightenment era: it names a disciplinary mechanism, born of supervision and surveillance, in which the human being assumes controlled mastery over the self out of fear of outside constraint. "It would be wrong to say that the soul is an illusion, or an ideological effect," Foucault argues in *Discipline and Punish.* He continues:

> On the contrary, it [the soul] exists, it has a reality, it is produced permanently around, on, within the body by the functioning of a power that is exercised on those punished—and, in a more general way, on those one supervises, trains and corrects, over madmen, children at home and at school, the colonized, over those who are stuck at a machine and supervised for the rest of their lives. This is the historical reality of this soul, which, unlike the soul represented by Christian theology, is not born in sin and subject to punishment, but is born rather out of methods of punishment, supervision and constraint. (29)

In his catalogue of the disciplinary mechanisms that produce the "soul," Foucault overlooks one of the most effective—because most universal and most clandestine—forms of coercion by surveillance: the intricate physiognomic theories and practices developed from the end of the eighteenth century to the beginning of the twentieth. If, as Foucault contends, "[t]he panoptic schema, without disappearing as such or losing any of its properties, was destined to spread throughout the social body" (*Discipline and Punish* 207), then physiognomics was one of the primary mechanisms by which this dissemination, the transformation of the panoptic schema into "a generalized function," as Foucault writes (207), took place. In Germany, in particular, we are justified in designating the era from about 1775 to 1945 as the age of physiognomic panopticism. In England and in France, according to Foucault, surveillance tended to travel along the established paths of religious institutions or the police apparatus (213). For the German-speaking world, which throughout the modern age was never held together by a common religion, and only rarely by a unifying state apparatus, other avenues for the coherent self-disciplining and social definition of the general population had to be found. Physiognomics was one of the primary forms this mechanism of social constraint took in the German-speaking world. Jeremy Bentham's (1748–1832) panopticon—which, invented in 1787, is approximately contemporaneous with the development of Lavater's physiognomic theories—is simply the most concrete manifestation, as Foucault demonstrates in the chapter of *Discipline and Punish* entitled "Panopticism" (195–228), of this more generalized will to surveillance and social supervision. In physiognomic practice this drive becomes more universal, more abstract, and, above all, more surreptitious, subjecting the general populace to a set of norms established in the name of Christian "love," moral "goodness," humanistic faith, individuality, beauty, self-knowledge, and ultimately racial purity. Each of these ideological mechanisms attempts to establish a hierarchy of values that define the good, the bad, and the ugly, and that assign each individual a place in a highly detailed taxonomical grid.

Clauss's penetrating racial gaze, schooled on the eidetic reduction and intuitive perception of Husserlian phenomenology, represents the culmination of an ambition expressed already in Houston Stewart Chamberlain's *Grundlagen des 19. Jahrhunderts:* the cultivation of a perspicacious "*gaze [Blick]*" defined as "an intuition, born of a great deal of incessant *observation.* We should train ourselves to practice such a form of observation" (590). Clauss embraces this challenge to develop methods for training and practicing this all-encompassing, all-penetrating intuitive gaze. Moreover, since Chamberlain viewed this art of systematic observation as a special characteristic of the Teutonic race and of Germanic science in particular (*Grundlagen* 936), Clauss had additional justification for defending his racial psychology as a research endeavor especially appropriate to the Nordic race. If Günther's materialist physiognomics of race established a panoptic schema for cataloging the racial body, Clauss's racial psychology extended this panoptic schema inward to encompass the racial "soul."

But because it was more complex and harder to practice than Günther's relatively simplistic anatomical taxonomy, Clauss's methodology was also more difficult to disseminate.

With his training in phenomenology, Clauss viewed the (racially) observant gaze as a systematically defined instrument crucial to the basic procedure by which the racial psychologist operates. In the popularizing pamphlet *Rassenseelenforschung im täglichen Leben* (Racial psychology in everyday life), Clauss calls the "gaze" of the racial psychologist, which grasps the essential "significance" of whatever it is trained upon, "a tool that is more consummate than any man-made instrument" (12). If the gaze of the racial researcher is a precision tool, however, then people must be taught how to use it properly. This is precisely the project Clauss sets for himself after the Nazi seizure of power; he moves away from the theoretical direction of his work, which had more or less attained conceptual fruition by the late 1920s and which was reiterated in revised and reorganized form in the later editions of his basic theoretical writings *Rasse und Seele* and *Die nordische Seele,* and gives his work a decidedly more pedagogical and didactic bent. This new direction is marked by the emergence of a novel theme: learning (or teaching) to see.

Clauss's didactic turn is made possible, of course, by the new opportunities for developing instructional materials about race for implementation in the public schools after the National Socialist takeover of the state apparatus. Clauss was one of the first to take advantage of this new opportunity; in 1934 he published, with the cooperation of a certain Arthur Hoffmann (b. 1889), a primer on racial anthropology intended for classroom use. The title of this work, *Vorschule der Rassenkunde auf der Grundlage praktischer Menschenbeobachtung* (Primer for racial anthropology on the basis of practical observation of human beings), points both to the centrality of coercive observation as well as to its general application in everyday life. Clauss was obviously intent upon spreading his form of racial panopticism throughout the population of the Third Reich. The structure of this particular work clearly indicates its didactic purpose. Composed of a teacher's manual, a workbook for students, and a set of illustrative photographs—all of which, not insignificantly, were shot and selected by Clauss himself—this work was ideally suited for classroom use. In the opening paragraph of the preface to the teacher's manual, Clauss and Hoffmann lay out their aim: a systematized training of the students' racial gaze.

> Not much can be accomplished with the traditional, textbook-like report about the racial peculiarities of well-known types (Nordic, Phalian, Eastern, etc.). Here, if anywhere, *observation and its systematic training* must constitute the first step. . . . The practice questions [included in the student textbook], which refer the students to people with whom they have daily contact . . . , provide a means for training the students' *powers of racial observation and comprehension.* Because of this didactic-methodological emphasis, which gives absolute priority to observation and places reading entirely in its service, this work is able to break new ground as compared with the already existing "Introductions to Specific Racial Ethnology." (3)

The remark about the "traditional" materials with their model photographs of individuals who exemplify the anatomical traits of the various racial types, is, of course, one more swipe at Günther and the many classroom materials created on the basis of his *Rassenkunde des deutschen Volkes.* For Clauss and Hoffmann, it is not a matter of having students memorize lists of physical features that are confirmed by illustrative photographs, but rather of offering a more practical training of the students' gaze so they will learn to apply a racially discriminating—in both senses of that word—mode of observation in their daily lives. In other words, if Günther and his followers operated deductively, moving from typological definitions to specific examples, Clauss and Hoffmann want to structure their racial-physiognomic training program inductively, having the students first work with individual examples, from which they can derive systematic categories based on perceived similarities. It is consistent with this inductive procedure that the students are given practical activities to pursue outside of class. They are told, for example, to practice by observing the people in their immediate environment and attempting to classify them according to the categories they have established. They are even encouraged to try to take photographs of these individuals and collect their data on index cards, thereby facilitating review and revision of their original findings (38). The purpose of these exercises is to hone the students' skills in their use of the new "instrument" Clauss has invented: the penetrating racial gaze.

Clauss took to the lecture circuit in order to disseminate his ideas and promote the kind of practical training in racial observation he was advocating. One of his foundational lectures,

Rassenseele und Einzelmensch (Racial soul and the individual), provided brief introductions—accompanied, of course, by illustrative photographs—of the main ideas and principles of racial psychology in its Claussian form. This lecture was also distributed in published form as early as 1938. In this lecture one finds the programmatic statement: "We will learn to see what we have in common" (9). Learning to see: that was the Rilkean theme with which this chapter opened. This is also the theme of Clauss's works for the rest of his life, even in the book *Die Seele des Andern,* which was published well after the Second World War and reiterates the fundamental positions of Clauss's racial psychology. In *Rasse und Charakter,* for example, published in 1936, Clauss defines the aim of the book as "nothing other than *teaching people to see*" and "teaching people the composure that is part and parcel of productive seeing" (8). And in *Die Seele des Andern* we similarly read: "Ultimately it is only a matter here of *learning to see:* with one's eyes and with one's reason" (224). Clauss's expertise as a photographer, of course, contributed to his ability to teach others to see; indeed, he believed that his photographs, and the photographic techniques they implemented, were integral parts of his research method (see *Rasse und Seele* [1937] 122). Ultimately, Clauss's works added an entirely new dimension to the racial panopticism and social disciplining that dominated the Nazi social order. His intention was to train the German people to use their powers of observation as a precision instrument for the revelation of racial style. Appropriating the theories and practices of phenomenology, Clauss developed a sophisticated racial psychology that propagated the intuitive perception of race based on sensitive and disciplined observation. The gaze of the racial psychologist is a penetrating gaze that purports to detect the racial essence of the individuals upon whom it is trained by bracketing all anatomical features and grasping their internal racial "essence." Clauss's disciplined "gaze," the tool of his trade, was, in effect, a kind of X-ray vision, a psychological version of the Zeiss company's precision optics, for the revelation of race. "Learning to see," the motto of Clauss's pedagogical program, means training people to see *race,* transforming the German population into a cadre of practiced racial spies whose penetrating gazes no individual can possibly escape.

Racial Physiognomics and the German Physiognomic Tradition

One of the main contentions of this work, a thesis that the cases of Hans F. K. Günther and Ludwig Ferdinand Clauss exemplify, is that contrary to the common scholarly view, racial physiognomics is not a simple aberration of the otherwise intellectually sound and innocent intellectual tradition of German physiognomic thought.[16] Nor can the ideology of race simply be hypostatized as a separate intellectual-historical line that has nothing but passing and coincidental connections to the mainstream of physiognomic theory.[17] On the contrary, the racial theories of Günther and Clauss—and they stand merely as the two most prominent representatives of a much larger group of racial physiognomists—are the direct heirs to central theoretical tenets and methodological practices generated by German physiognomists since Lavater. While it is certainly true that racial ideology appropriated or even *mis*appropriated ideas developed in the almost two-hundred-year debate on physiognomics in Germany, it is just as correct to assert that these ideas *lent themselves to* and even *invited* interpretation along racially discriminatory lines. The chauvinistic underside that emerges already in the physiognomic theories of Lavater and Carus gives ample evidence of this. However, the ability of racial physiognomics to adapt and effectively instrumentalize both sides of the fundamental physiognomic divide, the split between the materialism of the immutable body (physiognomics proper) and the communication of psychic impulses through the body as expressive medium (pathognomics), clearly demonstrates what might be called, only somewhat facetiously, the Darwinian adaptability of racial ideology. In the opening decades of the twentieth century the idea of race was, without doubt, a flourishing parasite that exhibited an astonishing ability to feed off myriad intellectual hosts. Although based primarily on the materialist principles and the doctrine of inequality promulgated by Gobineau and his ilk, modern racism did not require these tenets in order to survive and thrive. As the case of Clauss emphatically demonstrates, racist ideology was able to appropriate and put to its own use even deeply humanistic traditions, such as the intellectual heritage of German *Lebensphilosophie* and

Husserlian phenomenology. Clauss's example also reveals that racism is not always the expression of narrowness, a limited horizon, or even of ignorance. The science of racial physiognomics in Germany often worked with subtle intelligence, even with sophisticated strategy, toward the adaptation of mainstream ideas and methodologies that could be adapted to its purposes and placed in the service of its ideology. My concluding chapter will examine this facility for adaptation and appropriation on the specific example of technological innovations in the creation and reproduction of images that heightened physiognomists' abilities to visually scrutinize and analyze their chosen subjects, and communicate their findings through the persuasive power of concrete illustrations.

Conclusion

Envisioning the Invisible

Technologies of Seeing in the History of Physiognomics

Objective Representation: From Silhouette to Photograph

The history of modern physiognomics is inseparable from the history of technological innovations that permit the replication of the human face and its multiple reproduction in exact copies. As early as 1586, Giambattista della Porta employed illustrations in his influential physiognomic treatise, *De Humana Physiognomonia* (On the human physiognomy) (Fig. 52), in order to lay before his readers eyes concrete examples of the physiognomic theories of the ancient Greeks, which his work sought to summarize. What made these illustrations possible was the relatively recent emergence of a new representational technology, the woodcut, which provided a first rudimentary form for the serial reproduction of images. In the case of della Porta's work, there can be no doubt that its tremendous popularity—it became one of the best-sellers of the sixteenth century—can be attributed to thc artistry and thc novclty of thc skillfully cxccutcd woodcuts (Borrmann 62). (Fig. 53) A little more than a hundred years later, in 1687, the famous physiognomic work of the French painter Charles Le Brun (1619–1690), *Conférence sur l'expression générale et particulière des passions* (Study of the general and particular expression of the human passions) appeared. Like della Porta, Le Brun also employed the print technology of the woodcut in order to present to his readers concrete representations of the facial expressions associated with specific emotional states. Le Brun was the official painter for the French court of King Ludwig XIV (1638–1715) and a student of the artist Nicolas Poussin

DELLA·FISONOMIA
DI·TVTTO·IL·CORPO·HVMANO
DEL·S·GIO·BATTA·DELLA·PORTA
ACC·LINCEO
Libri Qvattro
Ne' quali si tratta di quanto intorno a questa materia
n'hanno i Greci, Latini e gli Arabi scritto.
Hora breuemente in tauole sinottiche
ridotta et ordinata
DA FRANCESCO STELLVTI
ACC LINCEO
DA FABRIANO
FRANC·BARBERINO

Fig. 52. Title page, Giambattista della Porta, *Della Fisonomia di Tutto il Corpo Humano*, 1637. (Courtesy of Special Collections, University of Washington Libraries)

(1594–1665), the prominent representative of French Classicism; the illustrations in his physiognomic study eclipse those in della Porta's work, being distinguished above all by their greater artistry and refinement of detail. (Fig. 54)

Although della Porta's and Le Brun's works are among the first to employ technical means to elucidate and elaborate on the written word by means of illustrative images, they cannot yet be reckoned as part of the tradition of *modern* physiognomics, whose specific German-language tradition I have attempted to outline throughout this study. To be sure, to the extent that they employed new representational media, they must be considered significant historical precursors to the richly illustrated physiognomic volumes produced by Lavater, his contemporaries, and those who followed. But della Porta's and Le Brun's works lack a

Fig. 53. Physiognomic comparison of human and animal, from Giambattista della Porta, *La Physionomie Humaine,* 1655. (Courtesy of Special Collections, University of Washington Libraries)

decisive trait peculiar to Enlightenment and post-Enlightenment physiognomics: the conscious will to portray by means of mimetic representation an exact and faithful copy of the *individual* human physiognomy. By contrast, della Porta is chiefly concerned with producing pictures that exemplify the interrelationships between human and animal physiognomy; in this regard, he is strongly indebted to the ancient physiognomic tradition since (pseudo-) Aristotle, which demonstrated a particular fascination for this type of comparative study. For his part, Le Brun as painter was primarily interested in studying and reproducing the facial expressions of the human passions in general, not their manifestation in specific individuals. Le Brun's studies, which should be seen as painterly etudes, served the more pragmatic purpose of providing guidelines for portraying the passions, paradigms that could be followed and applied by other artists. In this sense, his depictions present overdrawn, magnified, even exaggerated representations of

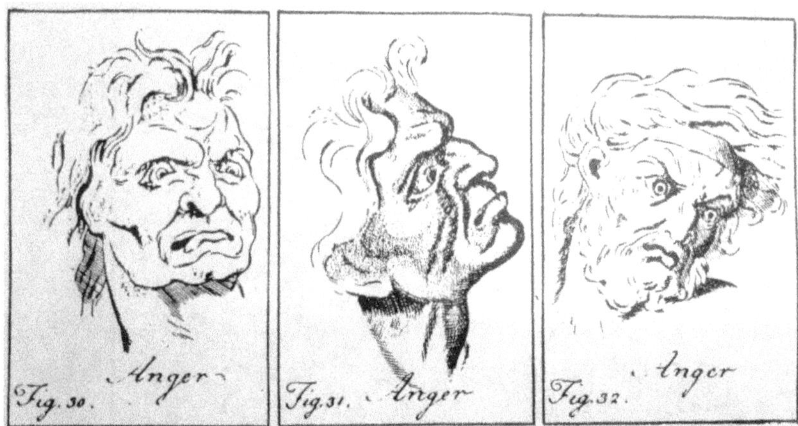

Fig. 54. Etchings from Charles Le Brun, *A Method to Learn to Design the Passions,* 1734. (Courtesy of Special Collections, University of Washington Libraries)

the human passions and their expression. The same can be said—to be sure, for different reasons—of the illustrations found in della Porta's *De Humana Physiognomonia.* In both instances we are dealing with conscious constructions, which, although not yet moving to the extreme form of caricature, make no pretense to offering objective representations of empirical individuals for the purpose of analysis and examination. This will change about a hundred years after the publication of Le Brun's *Conférence* with the appearance in 1775 of Johann Caspar Lavater's *Physiognomische Fragmente.*

Already the title of Lavater's work—"Physiognomic fragments for the promotion of human understanding and human love"—points to the narrower, more focused aim of physiognomic perception that Lavater will pursue: the kind of human understanding and knowledge *(Menschenkenntnis)* Lavater seeks to promote is specifically that of individual character, with all its fortés and foibles. In this project aimed at character identification, the truth and faithfulness of mimetic representations to the individuals they portray will for the first time play a significant role. It is completely in line with this emphasis on the individual that beginning with Lavater famous personalities—people like Goethe, Hamann, and Herder, to name just a few—are pictorially portrayed and their well-known characters established on the basis of physiognomic features. The illustration gracing the title page of the first volume of the *Physiognomische Fragmente* thematizes not only the fundamentally hermeneutic nature of the physiognomic endeavor, but also the central role that illustrations will play in this hermeneutics of disclosure. (Fig. 55) It portrays two human beings and an angel sitting in an isolated landscape, constructed according to the tropes of the romanticized idyll, perusing a panel held out in front of them on which a series of human faces are portrayed. Presumably the angel has been sent to fulfill the pedagogical task of teaching human beings the art of interpreting the physiognomies of their fellow beings, which, according to Lavater, articulate the characters of a divine language. This illustration reveals in a single image—employing the persuasive immediacy of visual depiction to enhance its communication—the ideological program of Lavater's physiognomic project. It would probably not be incorrect to assume that Lavater saw himself in the role either of the instructing angel or the privileged human being who receives this divine lesson. What is certain, at least, is that with Lavater physiognomics is staged as a dramaturgy of revelation and unmasking in which the physiognomist not only plays the leading interpretive part but, as physiognomic theorist, also directs and choreographs the dramatic events. Physiognomic exposé—that is what is presented for the first time in Lavater's *Physiognomische Fragmente*—and visual illustrations that appeal directly to the senses and sensibilities of the readers fulfill a fundamental role in this strategy of disclosure.

The vignette found on the title page of the first volume of Lavater's *Physiognomische Fragmente* also alludes to the crucial place that representational images of human subjects will assume in his physiognomic hermeneutics. In "Von der Physiognomik" (On physiognomics), the initial physiognomic treatise in which he sketched the general outlines of the larger project he would ultimately pursue, Lavater points for the first time to the special role illustrations will play in this endeavor, helping to lend physiognomics the credibility and validity of the

Physiognomische Fragmente,
zur Beförderung
der Menschenkenntniß und Menschenliebe,
von
Johann Caspar Lavater.
Gott schuf den Menschen sich zum Bilde!
Erster Versuch.
Mit vielen Kupfern.
Leipzig und Winterthur, 1775.
Bey Weidmanns Erben und Reich, und Heinrich Steiner und Compagnie.

Fig. 55. Title page, volume 1 of Johann Caspar Lavater, *Physiognomische Fragmente*, 1775.

empirical sciences. Laying out the properties that are required if physiognomic observation is to attain objectivity and exactitude, Lavater remarks:

> But my observations must be exact; they must be repeated and tested often. How can that be possible if I have to make these observations on the sly? Isn't it presumptuous to analyze faces? And if a humble person notices that she is being observed, won't she turn away and hide her face? Indeed, it is here that I encountered one of the greatest obstacles to my studies; anyone who notices that he or she is being observed either puts up resistance or dissimulates. How can I get around this problem? Perhaps in part in the following way.
>
> I retire into solitude; I place before me a medallion or a piece of antique sculpture, the sketches of a Raphael, the apostles as depicted by Van Dyck, the portraits of Houbraken. These I can observe at will, I can turn them and view them from all sides. (176)

The ideal conditions for physiognomic analysis, as described here by Lavater, are precisely those depicted in the title-page vignette in volume one of the *Physiognomische Fragmente:* the subjects under analysis have been transformed into objects insofar as they are "present" solely in the form of visual re-presentations that can be manipulated, turned this way and that, studied at will and with uninterrupted perseverance by the physiognomic analyst. Moreover, as depicted in the vignette, this examination occurs in nearly absolute isolation, the only other participants being the angel who divulges the secret language of the human physiognomy and a human figure who, passively gazing at the table of represented faces, assumes the role of the recipient of knowledge and hence represents the readers of Lavater's treatise. In other words, this vignette portrays in emblematic form the pragmatic and pedagogical methodology Lavater will pursue in the *Physiognomische Fragmente:* a Hermes in the realm of physiognomic cognizance, Lavater will mediate between his readers and the angelic revelations of the physiognomic language naturally ordained in divine creation. His principal tool in transmitting this knowledge will be the tables and illustrations that are so liberally strewn throughout these volumes.

As in the cases of della Porta and Le Brun, it is in large part the wealth and the quality of the illustrations found in the *Physiognomische Fragmente* that account for the tremendous popularity of Lavater's physiognomic writings in the final decades of the eighteenth century. Moreover, these illustrations were executed by some of the most noted artists of the day, people such as Johann Heinrich Lips (1758–1817) and Daniel Chodowiecki (1726–1801).[1] But what made such profuse employment of precise and detailed images possible was once again a major advance in print technology: the development of the cop per etching, which permitted the relatively inexpensive reproduction of serial images—images that stood out because of the artistic skill they evinced and the refinement and high quality of the prints they produced. However, it is a second innovation in the means of mechanical reproduction, one that Lavater strategically exploited, that is of most interest to us here: the development of the art of silhouette, which emerged in the middle of the eighteenth century and bears the name of the French minister of finance, Étienne de Silhouette (1709–1767). (Fig. 56)

In order to understand the importance of the silhouette as technological advance in Lavater's physiognomics, we have to

Fig. 56. Machine for creating silhouettes, from volume 4 of Johann Caspar Lavater, *Physiognomische Fragmente,* 1778.

recall the major theoretical argument he introduced into physiognomic thought: the idea that it is not facial expression, gesture, or the movements of the body—as was the case, for example, for Le Brun—that reveal the essential, otherwise invisible character of the human being, but rather the firm and unchanging features such as bone structure, shape of the skull, placement of eyes, mouth, nose, ears, and so on. As we have seen, Lavater valorizes physiognomics as the only certain and objective interpretive approach to human character precisely because the firm parts of the body are not under the control of the will and hence cannot be falsified or dissimulated: only the *indelible* traits of the face and body can be seen as *definitive* signs of human character (see *Physiognomische Fragmente* 2: 56; 4: 30–32; 4: 39). There is, as I have argued, a direct intellectual-historical line that runs from this theory, through the phrenology of Franz Josef Gall and the human "symbolics" of Carl Gustav Carus, to the materialistically oriented racial anthropologies of proto-fascist and fascist thinkers such as Hans F. K. Günther and Bruno K. Schultz. (Fig. 57)

Given Lavater's preference for what he calls "standing character" over the dynamism of the face (*Physiognomische*

Fig. 57. Silhouettes with analytical lines, from volume 2 of Johann Caspar Lavater, *Physiognomische Fragmente,* 1776.

Fragmente 4: 39), we can easily understand the significance the silhouette assumed as the representational device most appropriate to his project. For the silhouette, as mode of representation, systematically excludes all details of facial expression and all manifestations of the passions so as to stress the stable and unchanging outlines of the face and head. Lavater was well aware that his claim that the silhouette of a human face represents the true and objective manifestation of the personality and "color" of the individual relied on a counterintuitive, even paradoxical conception. In the segment in the second volume of the *Fragmente* entitled "On Silhouettes," Lavater openly addresses the paradox that this form of portrayal, which literally reduces the human subject to a shadow of itself, simultaneously offers its most objective representation: "The silhouette of a human being, or of a human face, is the feeblest, the emptiest image, but simultaneously the most truthful and most faithful image that one can attain of a human being; the *feeblest* because it does not represent anything positive; . . . the *most faithful* because it is an immediate copy of nature itself" (2: 90). Not only does the silhouette highlight precisely those features Lavater sees as characterologically significant, it represents them truthfully and with exactitude. As an early form of mechanical reproduction, the silhouette guarantees for Lavater the "objectivity" of his empirical evidence.

For Lavater it is nothing other than the im-mediacy—the absence of mediation by any subjective variables such as the relative skill of the artistic representation, for example—that guarantees the objective quality of the silhouette and defines it as an exact representation or, in his words, "an immediate copy of nature itself." The silhouette is the physiognomic equivalent of the "lucida," the semitransparent canvas with a rectilinear grid that was introduced into painting to allow the perfect perspectival graphing of a distant object onto the canvas. When mechanically translated into a silhouette, the human face is schematized, mapped out in such a way that its physiognomically significant qualities are emphasized. By screening out certain traits, in other words, the silhouette makes other characteristics more visible, and hence more interpretable. The silhouette delivers, as it were, the necessary laboratory conditions in which the individual human physiognomy can be repeatedly subjected to experimental analysis and manipulation.

In his investigation into the paradigmatic forms of analysis produced by what he terms "Classical" thought, Michel Foucault describes the reflex for observation characteristic of empirical scientism in words that perfectly articulate the form of systematic seeing that Lavater's physiognomics sought to achieve.

> To observe, then, is to be content with seeing—with seeing a few things systematically. With seeing what, in the rather confused wealth of representation, can be analysed, recognized by all, and thus given a name that everyone will be able to understand. . . . Displayed in themselves, emptied of all resemblances, cleansed even of their colours, visual representations will now at last be able to provide natural history with what constitutes its proper object, with precisely what it will convey in the well-made language it intends to construct. (*The Order of Things* 134)

The silhouettes and other illustrations presented in Lavater's *Physiognomische Fragmente* are functionally deployed so as to institutionalize just such a form of systematic seeing that highlights certain features while intentionally eclipsing others. In this context Lavater's partiality for the silhouette takes on a special significance. As a mode of systematic representation, the silhouette exhibits certain traits that are particularly advantageous for a scientifically conceived physiognomics. Above all, the art of the silhouette represents a first and major step in the direction of that type of objective and mechanical representation that will culminate less than a hundred years later in the technology of the daguerreotype and the photograph. This belief in the infallibly mimetic quality of the silhouette allows Lavater to claim, with overly exaggerated certainty, that physiognomics has "no proof of its objective truthfulness that is more reliable and more incontrovertible than silhouettes" (*Physiognomische Fragmente* 2: 91). Already for Lavater, seeing was believing; and the believability of his physiognomic theories relied heavily on his ability to employ silhouettes and other forms of illustration to make his readers "grasp" with their own eyes the physiognomic "truths" he sought to promulgate.

The appeal to representations as the proper analytical object of physiognomics is just one example of the way in which Lavater's demand for scientific exactitude motivates his exploitation of technologies intended to make the individual more visible and penetrable to the examining gaze of the physiognomist. Another significant example is found in Lavater's invention of his *Stirnmaaß*, an instrument capable of generating precise measurements of various dimensions of the human cranium. (Figs. 58 and 59) Lavater himself drew up detailed blueprints of this machine, which he hoped would help him fulfill his dream of transforming physiognomics into a science that operated with the precision and objectivity of mathematics. It is certainly no coincidence that Lavater introduced this machine in the fourth volume of the *Physiognomische Fragmente* when trying to fend off the objections to his theory that were voiced by the physicist Georg Christoph Lichtenberg. The description of this anthropometric device allows Lavater to play a game of rhetorical one-upmanship in which he, the Protestant theologian, demonstrates his reliance on technologically derived

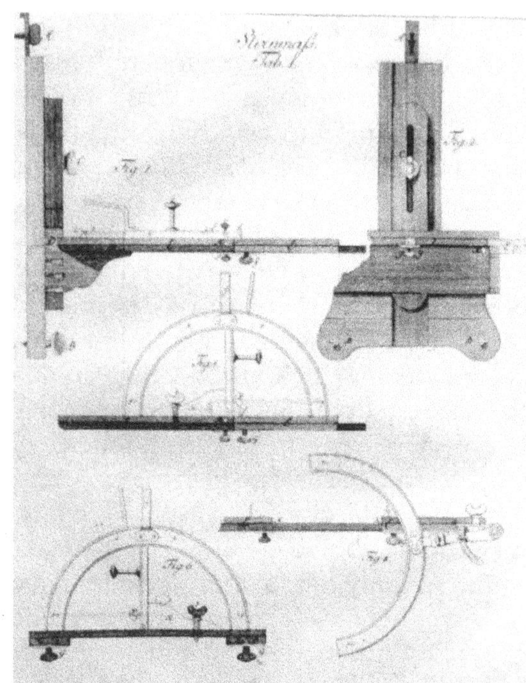

Fig. 58. Schematic drawing of instrument for cranial measurement, from volume 4 of Johann Caspar Lavater, *Physiognomische Fragmente,* 1778.

empirical data, thereby making himself look more "scientific" than the scientist Lichtenberg himself. Indeed, the passage in which Lavater describes this machine and its virtues carries a subtle barb against the scientist whose objections Lavater is attempting to parry. Alluding to Lichtenberg's training in mathematics, he writes:

> If I were a mathematician . . . , then it would be a simple matter for me to draw up a proportional table graphing the abilities inherent in all human skulls. . . . As I write this, I am busy with the plans for a machine that will replicate, even without a silhouette, the form of every forehead and will simultaneously determine exactly the measure of its capacity. In particular, it will allow us to discover the significant relationship that obtains between the basic line of the forehead and the profile. The use of this [machine] will allow us to generate, over time, a universally comprehensible and practical proportional table for all the capacities of the human soul. (4: 23–24)

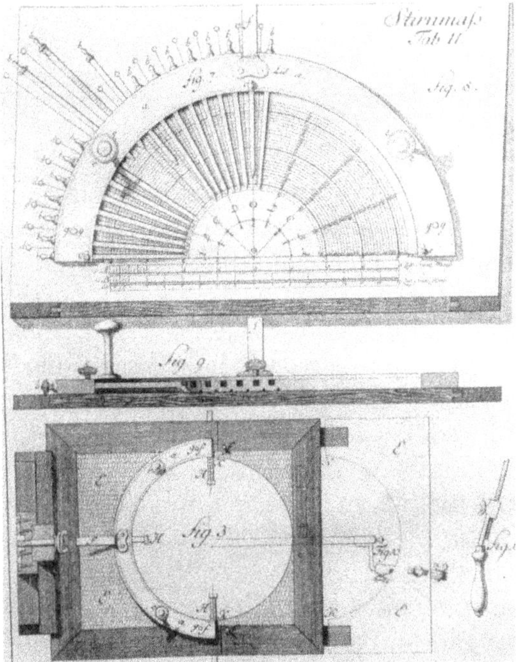

Fig. 59. Schematic drawing of instrument for cranial measurement, from volume 4 of Johann Caspar Lavater, *Physiognomische Fragmente,* 1778.

Lavater implicitly criticizes Lichtenberg for not applying his scientific abilities to solutions for the practical problems faced by empirical physiognomics. But more important in the present context, Lavater's statement makes clear that he sees this anthropometric instrument in a technological continuum with the technique of silhouetting: the *Stirnmaaß* becomes an improvement upon, and hence a replacement for, the mechanical reproduction made possible by the silhouette. The advance Lavater has in mind is a significant one. The greater abstraction of mathematics and the proportional table would ultimately allow one to produce a general taxonomy of the human skull and the intellectual and psychological capacities associated with its shape. As we noted in chapter 3, these ambitions tie Lavater closely to anthropological developments that emerged from Enlightenment thought, in particular to Petrus Camper's theory of the *linea facialis* and its relationship to evolutionary biology.

Lavater also anticipates developments in anthropometry that will culminate a century later in Adolphe Quetelet's (1796–1874) systematization of human body measurements in his *Anthropométrie* (1870). (Fig. 60)

One hundred and fifty years later, during the Weimar Republic, Lavater had no dearth of imitators where his insistence on anthropometric data and the development of appropriate measuring devices were concerned. The racial ethnologist Bruno K. Schultz (1892–1942), for example, oriented his investigations almost completely around numerical data derived from measurements of the human body. In this regard, he took the materialist emphasis of Hans F. K. Günther to its logical, if extreme, conclusion. Indeed, Schultz sought to promote anthropometry as practice by assembling a handbook describing the instruments and techniques employed for measuring the human form, his *Taschenbuch der rassenkundlichen Meßtechnik: Anthropologische Meßgeräte und Messungen am Lebenden* (Handbook for the technique of racial-ethnological measurements: Anthropological measuring instruments and the techniques for measuring living things), which was published in 1937. (Fig. 61) Among other things, this work provides a summary of all the quantifiable dimensions of the human body and describes the instruments used to measure these somatic features. More closely related to Lavater's model is the work of the portrait painter Robert Burger-Villingen (b. 1865), who invented a machine he called the "plastometer," which was able to measure with great precision all the dimensions of the human head. (Fig. 62) But Burger-Villingen went a great deal farther than did Lavater. Not content with developing blueprints for this machine and imagining the advances it would allow, he produced the instrument itself and employed it in the flourishing physiognomic practice he established in his studio in Berlin. Following the tendency of the time, Burger-Villingen gave his physiognomic interpretations a decidedly racial bent, promising his "patients" the determination of their exact racial makeup. An advertising leaflet he produced to promote his racial-physiognomic business depicts Burger-Villingen himself, demonstrating his brainchild. (Fig. 63) The text of the leaflet reads in part: "The racial scientist Robert Burger-Villingen discovered the laws of the human form and

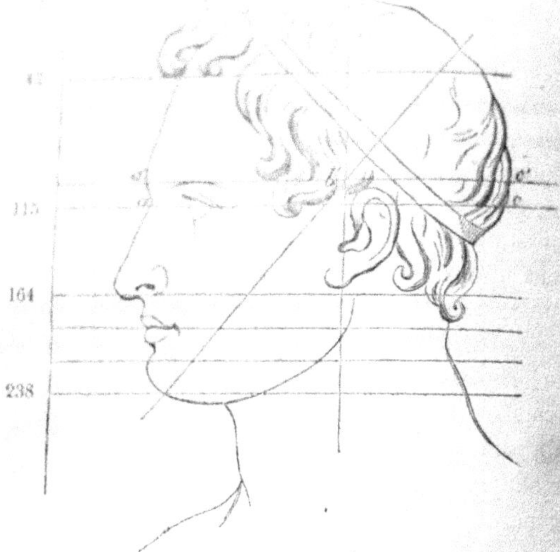

Fig. 60. Mapping of the head for measurement, from Adolphe Quetelet, *Anthropométrie,* 1870. (Courtesy of the Hessische Landesbibliothek, Darmstadt)

founded a popular, nationalist *[volkstümliche]* brand of human understanding whose principles can be taught and applied to all races; [he] invented the patented plastometer that gives these formal laws a scientific basis."[2] Burger-Villingen transformed Lavater's theory of a "proportional table" into a concrete—and profitable—practice that could be applied in daily life. Moreover, he did not shrink from deploying his "scientifically founded" physiognomic theories and the technologies they spawned in the racial struggle that consumed the hearts and minds of so many Germans at this time. He disseminated his ideas through the publication of several books replete with his own illustrations, many of which approach the form of blatant caricatures of allegedly "lower" races such as blacks and Jews. In the 1921 edition of his *Das Geheimnis der Menschenform* (The secret of the human form), for example, Burger-Villingen prints a stereotyped sketch of an African tribesman under the title "Negro-beast *[Negerbestie],*" in which both the heading and the caricature-like sketch clearly betray his racist intentions and prejudices. (Fig. 64) But as we saw in chapter 3, even in this regard Burger-Villingen could appeal to Lavater's model, in particular to the section on

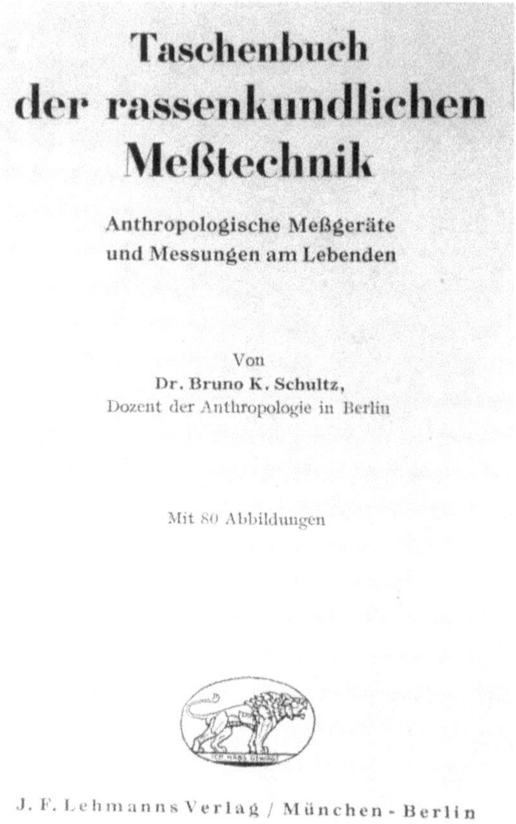

Taschenbuch
der rassenkundlichen
Meßtechnik

Anthropologische Meßgeräte
und Messungen am Lebenden

Von
Dr. Bruno K. Schultz,
Dozent der Anthropologie in Berlin

Mit 80 Abbildungen

J. F. Lehmanns Verlag / München - Berlin

Fig. 61. Title page, Bruno K. Schultz, *Taschenbuch der rassenkundlichen Meßtechnik,* 1937.

"National Physiognomies" in the last volume of the *Physiognomische Fragmente* (4: 265–340), in which national and racial stereotypes are played off against one another.

This union of scientific-anthropometric methodologies with the application of new technological means employed both for the greater mechanical reproduction of individual human beings as well as their reduction to measurable but ultimately abstract quantities manifests itself in paradigmatic fashion in the forensic physiognomics that emerged in the latter part of the nineteenth century. This field was dominated by the theories,

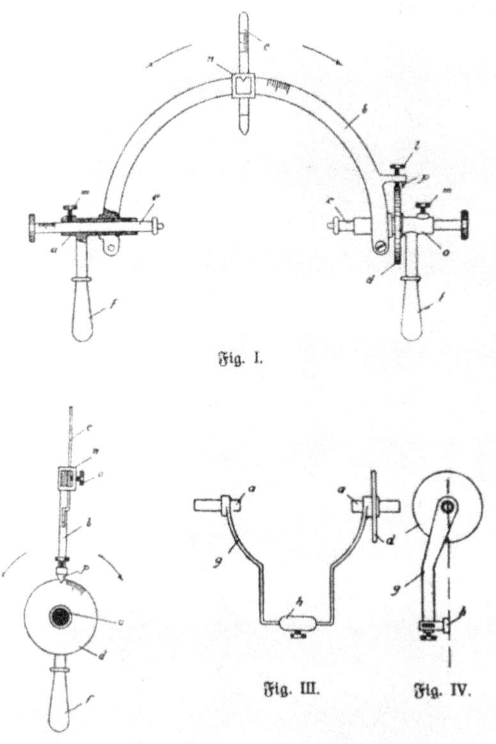

Fig. 62. Schematic drawing of "plastometer," from Robert Burger-Villingen, *Geheimnis der Menschenform,* 1912.

Fig. 63. Robert Burger-Villingen with his plastometer, advertising prospectus. (Courtesy of the Bundesarchiv, Coblenz.)

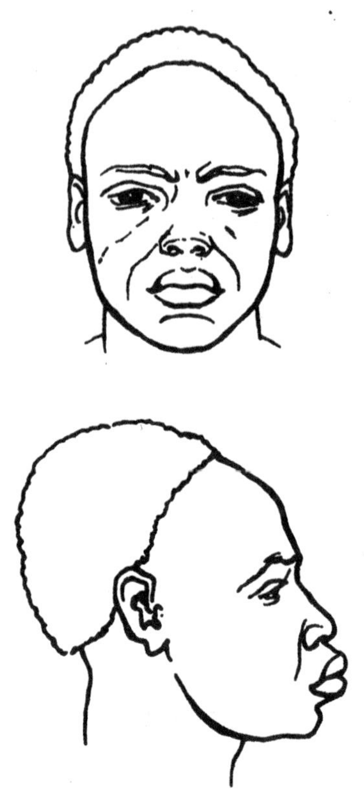

Fig. 64. "Negro-Beast," from Robert Burger-Villingen, *Geheimnis der Menschenform,* 1912.

Fig. 172. Negerbestie

the creative implementation of technology, and the drive toward systematization evinced in the work of the French criminologist Alphonse Bertillon (1853–1914). Bertillon, whose father and grandfather were both anthropologists, came into contact with the instruments and strategies of anthropological measurement at an early age. Although he rebelled against systematic learning and did not distinguish himself at school, he nonetheless absorbed from his background a fascination for the dimensions and proportions of the human skeleton. During his stint in the French military, this personal obsession led him to complete a metrical study—it is unclear how he derived his data—of the 222 components of the human skeletal structure (Rhodes 62–63). In 1879, when Bertillon became a minor police clerk in a Paris precinct, he immediately began to deliberate on how the unique bone features of every individual human being could be applied to the identification of criminals. Just a few months after assuming his police duties, Bertillon worked out an anthropometric system that he believed would allow him to incontrovertibly identify and reidentify any given individual. This system was based on eleven distinct body measurements for which the probability of all eleven occurring in the exact same proportions in more than one individual was extremely minute. By 1883 Bertillon was able to prove the practical effectiveness of his system, which later came to be called "Bertillonage" in his honor, when he succeeded in identifying a recidivist by consulting the measurements he had begun to systematize (see Rhodes 93–95). Just five years later he was appointed chief of judicial identity for all of Paris.

Bertillon managed to develop an extremely exact and detailed taxonomy that facilitated the identification of repeat criminals. Aside from the organized collection of anthropometric data, he also relied on his own brand of forensic photography and devised an ingenious system that allowed him to use his vast collection of data in an efficient and effective manner. He invented an intricate index-card system that classified criminals according to their physiognomic features and specific anthropometric data. When an alleged criminal was arrested, Bertillon used the data from pictures and measurements to locate in his anthropometric catalogue the individual features of the person under arrest, thereby recognizing whether the person in question was a recidivist and for which crimes he or she had previously been arrested. With each bodily feature organized into three broad groups based on average or typical dimensions, Bertillon was able to sort through the increasingly voluminous data easily and employ a process of elimination to identify the criminal in his records. More than anything else, it was this tremendous rationalization of the process of criminal identification that explains Bertillon's success. His index cards were organized in such a way as to form, as it were, a kind of encyclopedia of anthropometric measures, in which the record of any particular individual could be "looked up" simply by following the clues manifest in the physical form and proportions of his or her body.

In the present context, Bertillon's establishment of a well-defined and precise methodology for the photographing of criminals is even more significant than his encyclopedic system of anthropometric measures, since the motivations and practices that underlie his photographic techniques point both backward to Lavater's preference for the silhouette and forward to the practices employed by the Nazis for identifying racial characteristics. Bertillon established exact and detailed guidelines for the use of the camera so as to transform it into an effective tool for the identification of criminals. As a result, he not only prescribed the desired posture the photographed subject should assume and the requisite position in which the head must be held, he also calculated the precise distance the subject should sit from the camera, the angle at which light should fall on the subject, the type of photographic lens to be employed, the proper amount of light, and even the preferred color for the photographic backdrop. The basic parameters Bertillon established are still in use today, with the result that criminal photography employs an almost unitary format throughout the world.

The emphasis forensic photography still places on the profile shot derives from Bertillon's system. The reason for this preference goes back to arguments strikingly reminiscent of those brought by Lavater in defense of the usefulness of silhouettes in capturing the characteristic physiognomic features of an individual. For Bertillon, the profile shot constitutes an indispensable tool for the purposes of criminal identification precisely because it captures the durable, unalterable features of the face. In other words, the profile image presents a strategic antidote and countermeasure to the pervasive drive of the lifelong criminal to disguise his or her physical features in order to evade detection. Forensic photography accomplishes this by recording precisely those firm somatic traits, such as the shape and position of the ear—to which Bertillon ascribed particular importance—the length of the chin, the form of the skull, and so on. The virtues of the profile shot for Bertillon thus are completely coherent with the arguments Lavater made a hundred years earlier in order to valorize the expressive power of firm and permanent "physiognomic" features of the body over the ephemeral "pathognomic" signs reflecting passion or emotion. Like Lavater's silhouettes, Bertillon's forensic photographs, which concentrate on the profile, reveal the nonchanging, inescapable "Being" of the photographed subjects. Like Lavater before him, Bertillon clearly subscribed to this essentialist doctrine of the human being, applying it in the domain of criminology. For Bertillon, criminals are born, not made.

Toward the beginning of the twentieth century another technological advance, the development of the half-tone plate, promoted the inclusion of photographs in diverse print media by making possible for the first time their unlimited and inexpensive reproduction (Lalvani 86). This led to a boom in the production of illustrated books and magazines in the 1920s and 1930s, and these new potentials were cleverly exploited by authors and publishers in Germany who dedicated themselves to an examination of the racial issues that had captured the imagination of intellectuals and the general populace alike. The number of illustrated books from this period that, directly or indirectly, presented schematic racial typologies based on photographs of human "specimens" can scarcely be estimated. Wilhelm Böhle's *Die Körperform als Spiegel der Seele* (Body form as mirror of the soul) represents one of the more harmless, and hence less known, variants. Hans F. K. Günther's many books on race, in particular his best-selling *Rassenkunde des deutschen Volkes,* were far and away the best known and most influential works of this type in Germany during this period. There can be little question that the profuse illustrations with which he exemplified his racial theories contributed in significant ways to their broad acceptance and popularity. Günther both drew on and contributed to the development of a particular photographic genre, the so-called "racial face" or "characterological face," which enjoyed growing popularity during the years of the Weimar Republic and the Nazi regime. This genre emerged in large part out of a neo-Romantic fascination with the populace and customs of Germany's rural areas and in reaction against the eradication of territorial distinctions brought on by industrialization and the rise of the modern metropolis. Erna Lendvai-Dircksen's (1883–1965) photographic volume *Das Gesicht des deutschen Ostens* (The face of the

German Eastern territories) can be taken as prototypical of this nostalgic attempt to capture and preserve the "face" of Germany's rural populations. (Fig. 65) Indeed, her veritably encyclopedic photographic project, which emerged under the collective title *Das deutsche Volksgesicht* (The face of the German rural populace), sought to document in photographs the "typical" facial features of the populations that inhabited each and every region of Germany.[3] In the introduction to this volume she describes the ideology motivating this project in the following way: "The rural person [*Volksmensch,* who in Lendvai-Dircksen's vocabulary stands in direct contrast to the *Stadtmensch,* the city-dweller], who in everything he is and owns stands close to nature, still retains a true face, a face that is genuine down to the core of his being. He himself, as well as his attitude toward life, has a specific physiognomy that speaks about existence in a different and deeply persuasive manner" (*Das deutsche Volksgesicht* 5–6). Clearly, the values Lendvai-Dircksen stresses—nature, essential being, genuine existence, authenticity—are identical in many ways to those promulgated by Lavater one hundred and fifty years earlier.

The overwhelming significance and popularity this genre of physiognomic-photographic documentary achieved in this period is perhaps best demonstrated by the fact that it thrived not only in German-nationalist and *völkisch* circles, but actually crossed over more generally into ideological programs that sought to rescue rural communities. As early as 1920, for example, the Jewish writer Arnold Zweig (1887–1968) published a volume entitled *Das ostjüdische Antlitz* (The face of Eastern European Jewry), illustrated with drawings instead of photographs, that celebrated the "typical" faces of rural Jews drawn from the diaspora in Eastern Europe. (Fig. 66) But for the most part, such volumes tended to pursue a more incendiary tactic, fueling either hatred of those identified as physiognomic "Others"—as is the case with Otto Stiehl's (1860–1940) *Unsere Feinde: 96 Charakterköpfe aus deutschen Kriegsgefangenenlagern* (Our enemies: Ninety-six characterological faces from German prisoner of war camps; 1916)—or feeding nationalist sentiments by glorifying figures of the past—the approach taken in Karl Richard Ganzer's (b. 1903) *Das deutsche Führergesicht:*

Fig. 65. Young farmer, from Erna Lendvai-Dircksen, *Das deutsche Volksgesicht,* 1930.

200 Bildnisse deutscher Kämpfer und Wegsucher aus zwei Jahrtausenden (The face of German leadership: 200 images of German battlers and pathfinders from two millennia; 1935).[4] Exemplary for the attempt to exploit the faddish popularity of these books with characterological faces for explicitly racial-ideological ends is a volume published in 1930 and coedited by the biologist Eugen Fischer (1874–1967) and the racial anthropologist Hans F. K. Günther, which bears the title *Deutsche Köpfe nordischer Rasse* (German faces representing the Nordic race). Especially curious is the manner in which this book came about. The publishing house owned by Julius Friedrich Lehmann (1864–1935)—responsible, not coincidentally, for printing the lion's share of the racial literature of the Weimar and Nazi period, including the books of Günther and Clauss—sponsored a public competition in 1927 for the submission of the best "characterological face" of an individual representing the Nordic race. Fischer and Günther were charged with reviewing the submitted photographs and selecting the winning pictures in several categories. The published volume contains their selection of the most representative portraits. (Fig. 67)

Ludwig Ferdinand Clauss, Günther's primary competitor for dominance in the field of racial anthropology, laid great emphasis on the fact that the photographs printed in his books were taken by the author and racial investigator himself. This, according to Clauss, guaranteed that the pictures he provided

Fig. 66. Eastern European Jew, lithograph by Hermann Struck, from Arnold Zweig, *Das ostjüdische Antlitz,* 1920. (Courtesy of the Hessische Landesbibliothek, Darmstadt)

were more accurate and had a greater illustrative power than those found in Günther's books, which were gathered almost serendipitously from archives and miscellaneous contributors (Clauss, *Rasse und Seele* [1937] 122; Clauss and Hoffmann, *Vorschule der Rassenkunde* 3). If, as we have seen, Clauss represented a heretical, if yet ideologically vociferous, strain of German racial-ethnological thought in this period, his works also stand apart from the bulk of illustrated race books with regard to the photographic techniques they employ. In large measure, the purveyors of racial physiognomics simply adapted the photographic techniques developed by Bertillon and forensic photography in general. This is perhaps best evident in the frequency of profile shots throughout these works, since, once again, the profile was generally believed to be more revelatory of permanent—that is, in this instance, racially determined—physiognomic traits. Although exceptional in other respects, in this even Clauss follows mainstream tendencies, and profile images assume a prominent place in his works. (Fig. 68) But in other regards Clauss resisted what he viewed as the generally unprofessional and unscientific application, in the racial literature of

Fig. 67. Example of Nordic type, from *Deutsche Köpfe nordischer Rasse,* 1930. (Courtesy of the Hessische Landesbibliothek, Darmstadt)

the day, of techniques drawn from traditional portrait photography. Clauss, in fact, is one of the only racial theoreticians who actually reflected upon the precise purpose and objectives photographic illustrations ought to have for the racial ethnologist.

In a telling passage from his book *Rasse und Charakter* (Race and character), Clauss expresses his principal objections to the way images have been employed in the predominant racial ethnologies of the time, carefully distinguishing this practice from the role of illustrative photography in his own racial psychology. Here he writes:

> In the field of racial psychology, photographs are nothing but a means of representation, a mnemonic tool, an explanatory device. Sometimes people assume that the methodology practiced in our area of investigation takes photographs as its point of departure, as though our research were nothing other than the interpretation of these images. That is not the case. Knowledge about what transpires in the photographs must be present before the photograph is shot, or at least occur simultaneously with it, and the photo must be based on a living knowledge of the photographed individual. We do not base our knowledge of the human being on these photographs, rather we base these photographs on our knowledge of the human being. (34)

Fig. 68. Profile photos, from Ludwig Ferdinand Clauss, *Die Seele des Andern,* 1958.

Photography for Clauss is not in and of itself a means for identifying human beings or races; such identification must precede the photographic study itself. Only after one has arrived at an understanding based on empirico-psychological investigation is it even possible to use photography to create a "speaking likeness"—to apply the term used to describe Bertillon's forensic photographs—of the person under examination. The racial psychologist must already know what characteristics the photograph is supposed to illuminate *before* the photo is shot. According to Clauss, traditional racial ethnology, especially in its Güntherian variant, substitutes the interpretation of images for the interpretation of living beings. By contrast, he insists on the photograph as a supplementary tool, one that helps the racial researcher communicate the knowledge he has discovered through empirical means. For Clauss, illustrations serve a primarily didactic purpose, providing the investigator with a manner of allowing his readers to see and experience secondhand what the researcher saw and experienced firsthand. In addition, these photographs take on the role of training devices that perform the ultimate function of teaching others to see with the expert eyes of the racial psychologist, and we saw in chapter 7 how important this pedagogical mission increasingly became for Clauss.

In a subsequent passage in *Rasse und Charakter,* Clauss articulates the pedagogical aim associated with his photographs, and he goes on to detail the revelatory logic that underwrites his own photographic technique.

> Our photographs do not teach us something uncommon and unusual, something that merely occurs here and there and that hence must be sought out. It is something everyday and is relevant to almost all of us. But we usually do not pay any attention to it, since we only see transitions. The photograph, however, accentuates the moment in a fraction of a second and captures it; it grasps what the eye cannot grasp and presents it to the eye. The photograph reveals the rupture that divides so many of us into two, three, or more parts: that secret rupture that we call the *rupture of race [Artriß].* (56)

The rupture of race: this idea constitutes Clauss's peculiar contribution to German racial theory. This is basically a simple notion. Since most modern human beings are racial "bastards," composed of the combination of more than one racial element, it is possible, according to Clauss, to discern—with the help of the camera—the breaches between one racial style and another. The assumption here, of course, is that racial styles by definition do not merge and intermingle, but somehow remain distinct and recognizable. According to Clauss's theory, the naked eye is incapable of discerning these "ruptures" in the dominant expressive style of an individual; only the photograph, which reduces the indistinct flow of expressive motions into distinct momentary still lives, is capable of documenting this racial rupture and making it visible. (Fig. 69) This explains why the photographic practice Clauss develops is based not on individual photographs, but rather on a pictorial series shot in immediate succession. Such

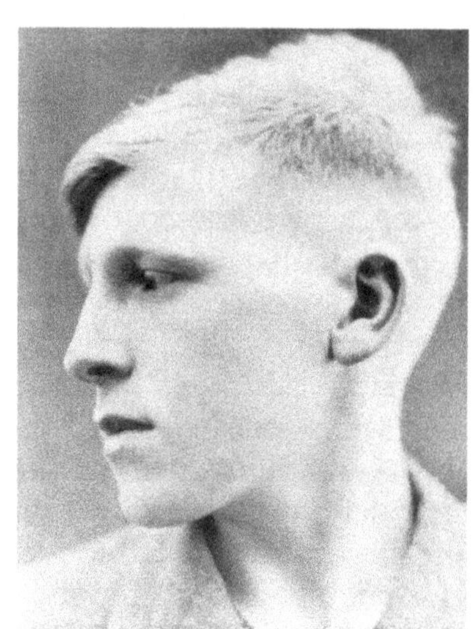

Fig. 69. Example of stylistic rupture, from Ludwig Ferdinand Clauss, *Rasse und Charakter,* 1936.

photos are able to capture what Clauss calls the "transitions" between one racial style and another.

Significantly, it is decidedly not the *cinematic* camera that Clauss has in mind. On the contrary, the cinematic camera, like the naked eye, passes over the transitions and ruptures Clauss wants to document in his photography. This points to a curious peculiarity in the development of modern German physiognomics with regard to its appropriation of emergent visual technologies: its tendency to play up the role of the still photograph and ignore, for the most part, the potentials of the cinematic camera for the purposes of physiognomic study. Indeed, Béla Balázs's (1884–1949) *Der sichtbare Mensch oder Die Kultur des Films* (The visible human being, or The culture of film; 1924) is the only treatise of note that deals with the relationship of cinematic portrayal to questions of human physiognomy. This is all the more surprising given the central role that facial and bodily expression played as the predominant communicative medium in silent film. But as Anton Kaes has shown (164–65), the physiognomic orientation of early silent film concentrated predominantly on the close-up, which reduces the cinematic medium in many respects to the stasis of the photograph. Among the prominent expressive psychologists working in Germany at the time, only one, Philip Lersch (1898–1972), employed film rather than still photographs to produce visual documentation for his studies. Lersch's *Gesicht und Seele* (Face and psyche), first published in 1932, is, to my knowledge, the only work that relies on motion pictures; yet even in this instance, Lersch exploits the cinematic medium not for the generation of a continuous stream of images, but to reduce the motion-picture flow to individual, momentary snippets. (Fig. 70) For Lersch, cinematic photography serves the same purpose as did the photographic succession for Clauss: it highlights single moments that can be extracted from the continuum of motion and analyzed for their psychological content.

One of the central theses of this book is that throughout the history of physiognomics, the borderline between scientific research and chauvinistic, even propagandistic racial ideology is relatively fluid. This is most obviously the case for people like Hans F. K. Günther and Ludwig Ferdinand Clauss, who openly defended their theories in the context of Nazi racial policies. Indeed, the "sciences" of racial ethnology and racial psychology functioned as laboratories or proving grounds for many of the tenets championed by Nazi racial ideologues. There is perhaps no better place to witness the fluidity of this transition between science and propaganda than in the exploitation of visual technologies. It is generally recognized, of course, that the Nazis were expert at appropriating technological advances and placing them in the service of their ideological platform. This is no less true for the technologies of seeing that emerged out of the obsession to study and interpret human physiognomy. During the Third Reich the two primary agencies responsible for policies and practices regarding race and ethnic minorities were the *Rassenpolitisches Amt der NSDAP* (National Socialist Office for Racial Politics) and the *Rasse- und Siedlungshauptamt SS* (SS Office for Racial and Settlement Issues). The Office for Racial Politics was primarily responsible for the development and dissemination of the Nazi Party line on all matters of race; in this sense, it was the ideological dynamo that powered all the racial conceptions of the Nazi state. One of its main tasks was the production of propaganda materials that promoted National Socialist views on race and racial politics. It was responsible for the creation and distribution,

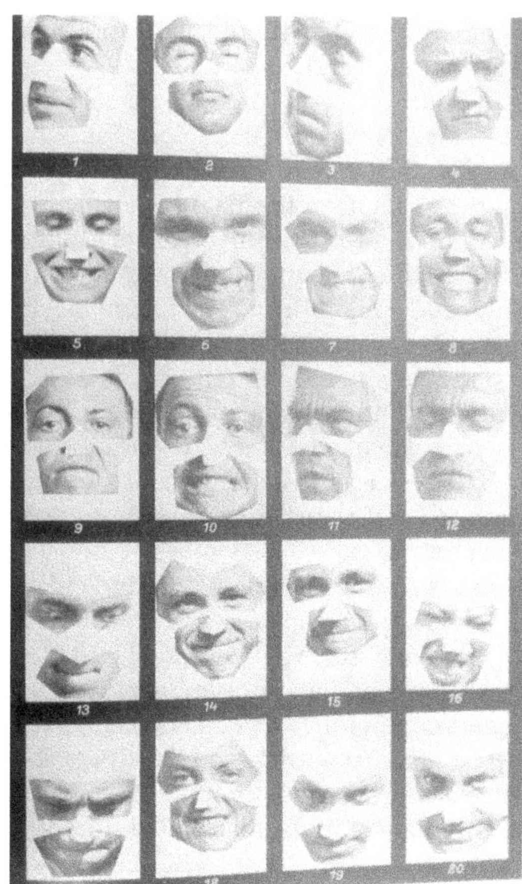

Fig. 70. Photographic table of facial expressions, from Philipp Lersch, *Gesicht und Seele,* 1932.

for example, of the documentary films produced for the so-called "racial-political enlightenment" of the German populace that bore such telling titles as *Die Sünden der Väter* (The sins of the fathers), *Abseits vom Wege* (Off the beaten track), *Erbkrank* (Genetic illness), or *Opfer der Vergangenheit* (Victims of the past). In addition, this bureau was in charge of the publication of illustrated journals such as *Neues Volk* (New nation), as well as the production of agitprop pieces such as the infamous *Deutschland treibt Rassenpolitik* (Germany pursues racial politics) and other equally propagandistic documents, including racially incendiary posters and leaflets. This agency mercilessly exploited visual media such as film and photograph in order to convey strictly black-and-white—or Aryan-and-Jew—racial stereotypes. Indeed, it systematically pursued the production and collection of stereotypical racial portraits for use in its various publications. (Fig. 71) It also generated "educational" materials on issues of race and eugenics for distribution and use among the various grassroots organizations that formed the ideological safety net of Nazi society, especially the two primary youth organizations, the *Hitlerjugend* for boys and the *Bund deutscher Mädel* for girls.

The tremendous importance the Nazis placed on visual media for the purposes of indoctrination is evident throughout the culture of the Third Reich. One only need think of the significant ideological function of the films of Leni Riefenstahl (b. 1907), especially *Der Triumph des Willens,* or consider that Adolf Hitler had his own personal photographer, Heinrich Hoffmann (b. 1885), whose sole duty consisted in compiling a sympathetic photographic documentation of the Führer's life and activities, such as that presented in the volume *Hitler wie ihn keiner kennt* (Hitler as no one knows him). (Fig. 72) Indeed, immediately following the Nazi seizure of power, Hoffmann compiled a photo-documentary of the emergence and rise of Hitler and the National Socialist Party, which appeared in 1933 under the title *Deutschland erwacht: Werden, Kampf und Sieg der NSDAP* (Germany awakens: Emergence, struggle, and victory of the National Socialist Party). (Fig. 73) But the optico-centrism of the Nazi propaganda machinery can perhaps best be illuminated by one striking example: the development and production of a special projector, the "Hitler Youth picture projector" (*HJ-Bildgerät*), created for exclusive distribution to local chapters of the *Hitlerjugend.* (Fig. 74) The advertising brochure, which urges—indeed, declares mandatory—the purchase of this projector by all chapters of the Hitler Youth, quotes the following passage from Hitler's *Mein Kampf* as its epigraph: "The image provides people with enlightenment in a much shorter period of time—I am tempted to say, as a bolt out of the blue—something they could only achieve from written material by means of protracted and wearisome reading."[5] The body of the advertisement goes on to provide what can be seen as a succinct statement of

Der Jude kriminell

Fig. 71. "The Jew: Criminally Inclined," anti-Semitic propaganda piece from *Neues Volk*, 1935. (Courtesy of the Bundesarchiv, Coblenz)

Nazi views on the significance of visual materials for the purposes of propaganda and indoctrination. It argues:

> Over 80% of our boys and girls are visually inclined. The immediate experience and the observation of events are essential prerequisites for the formation of correct [!] ideas as the basis of important recognitions and firm knowledge. Thus, ideological education will be successful above all when the written and spoken word is effectively enhanced by visual means, by images and films, maps, graphic representations, and models. The image is one of the most significant educational tools, hence its application in the political work of the Hitler Youth has been planned and prepared . . . for quite some time. With the "Hitler Youth Picture Projector" . . . we have created ideal preconditions for the employment of projected images in the work of the Hitler Youth.

The Nazis were perfectly aware that the immediacy of visual images lent the ideas they were intended to concretize a more persuasive and palpable form, effectively shutting down any critical reflexes that might otherwise arise in their students.

If the Office for Racial Politics had the more theoretical, educational, and propagandistic aim of disseminating Nazi racial

Fig. 72. "The Chancellor," from Heinrich Hoffmann, *Deutschland erwacht,* 1933. (Courtesy of Special Collections, University of Washington Libraries)

Deutschland erwacht

Werden, Kampf und Sieg

der

NSDAP

501.—600. Tausend

Die Auswahl und künstlerische Durcharbeitung der Lichtbilder übernahm Heinrich Hoffmann, München
Der Verfasser des Textes ist Wilfrid Bade, Berlin. Sonderbeiträge sind eingereiht

Fig. 73. Title page, Heinrich Hoffmann, *Deutschland erwacht,* 1933. (Courtesy of Special Collections, University of Washington Libraries)

Fig. 74. Hitler-Youth picture-projector, advertising prospectus. (Courtesy of the Bundesarchiv, Coblenz)

thought, the SS Office for Racial and Settlement Issues assumed the more applied task of translating this ideology into specific policies in the foreign territories under German occupation. This bureaucracy was charged, above all, with a kind of racial cartography of the populace in Germany and the occupied territories. In keeping with this commission, one of its primary tasks was the examination of the general population and the categorization of individuals according to their racial constitution. To this end, it was responsible for the training of so-called *Eignungsprüfer,* testers who studied the physiognomic features of individuals and established their racial constitution according to a preordained taxonomy. It is certainly no coincidence that this agency adopted almost in toto the methods of forensic identification developed by Bertillon. The infamous *R-Karte,* or racial index card, which contained a cross section of bodily measurements, was a copy of

Bertillon's anthropometric index cards, adapted for the purposes of racial categorization rather than criminal identification. It documented various information about the individual, including such traits as hair and eye color, shape of the nose, contour of the forehead, and so on. Moreover, the procedures for these racial-physiognomic examinations were laid out in detail in manuals developed for training the racial examiners, and the mandatory photographs that supplemented the anthropometric data were taken in a carefully prescribed manner, one that closely resembled the technical specifications Bertillon established for forensic photography. These "Richtlinien für die Bildarbeit an den RuS-Dienststellen" (Guidelines for photographic work at the centers of the Office for Racial and Settlement Policy), encompassing more than thirty typed pages, begin with the remark: "Without photographs of the individuals and clans under examination, effective work at the centers of the Office for Racial and Settlement Policy would no longer be conceivable. . . . Photography is particularly well suited for this task because it makes feasible the greatest possible exactitude in the reproduction of the face and the physical form of the human being."[6] This document goes on to claim that these technologically standardized photographs are "entirely truthful" and for this reason they must be considered "absolute proof" of the racial constitution of the photographed subject. The circle closes. Just like the silhouette Lavater held up as the exemplary analytical tool for his physiognomics, these racial photographs are not merely believed to be wholly "objective": they ostensibly reveal a fundamental substrate of the human being—in this instance, his or her inherent racial essence—that evades observation by the naked eye. In both cases it is a matter of rendering visible what is otherwise invisible.

In his "Kleine Geschichte der Photographie" (Brief history of photography), Walter Benjamin (1892–1940) reflects on a new dimension of nature that the photograph produces. He writes: "The form of nature that speaks to the camera is different from that which speaks to the eye; above all it is different insofar as a space permeated by consciousness is replaced by one permeated by the unconscious" (371). With this remark Benjamin suggests that the dimension of the human unconscious purportedly discovered by this new optical technology is actually *produced* by this technology itself. In other words, photography does not bring a hitherto invisible dimension to light; rather, it constructs an entirely new world of the visible, just as Freudian psychoanalysis did not so much discover as create a specifically psychological life of the instincts. But one thing we can learn from the history of physiognomics, in particular from the way it employed visual technologies, is that this optical unconscious is not introduced, as Benjamin believed, with the advent of photography. It is present already in Lavater's use of the silhouette, and it is part and parcel of the physiognomic tradition from the end of the eighteenth century onward. In their reliance on optical media for the construction of racial insiders and outsiders, the Nazi ideologues could appeal to this long and sometimes venerable tradition.

The propaganda of the *Rassenpolitisches Amt* and the popularizing racial textbooks of people like Günther and Clauss demonstrate just how important the photograph became in Nazi culture as an instrument for training a disciplinary gaze, for developing a form of technologized seeing whose purpose was to strip away the visible veneer of human beings and expose or interpolate an otherwise "invisible" racial foundation that purportedly undergirded it. This gaze, trained by the exploitation of specific representational and photographic techniques, ultimately played a decisive role in the pragmatic strategy of Nazi racial policy. It contributed to the transformation of Nazi society into a racial panopticon in which the eyes of the common citizens were schooled in methods conceived explicitly to lay bare every individual's racial essence, exposing it to the eyes of the ever watchful political apparatus. This obsession with panoptic observation is best concretized in the bevy of "professional physiognomists" the Nazis trained and deployed: their task was to drive through cities in the occupied territories in order to descry racially suspicious individuals (Blumenberg, "Menschenkenntnis" 3). Similarly, the aim of the Nazi Office of Racial Politics was to transform every German citizen into just such a physiognomic surveillance machine, in order to ensure the total racial-political supervision of the populace under Nazi control. Every individual was supposed to view his fellow citizens with the eyes of the state apparatus, so as to deliver anyone with the features of racial—that is, of course, ideological—Otherness over to the political authorities. In principle, this is not very far removed from the moral program, dictating the symptoms of virtue and vice, that Lavater's physiognomics sought to institute at the end of the eighteenth century. In both instances, the exploitation of visual media played a decisive role in making possible and fueling the popular pursuit and broad dissemination of these fundamentally ideological programs that sought to institutionalize a particularly penetrating and oftentimes demeaning mode of human scrutiny.

Counter-Racist Physiognomics: The Photography of August Sander

The broad manner in which the marriage of physiognomics and photographic technique was brought into complicity with the Nazis' racial-ideological program can perhaps best be thrown into relief by examining the example of a practitioner who sought to exploit a physiognomically oriented portrait photography to undercut the racist and nationalist direction that had come to dominate the field: I am thinking of the work of August Sander (1876–1964), especially his book *Antlitz der Zeit* (Face of the time; 1929), part of his monumental and unfinished photographic documentary *Menschen des 20. Jahrhunderts* (People of the twentieth century). In my discussion in chapter 5 of Rudolf Kassner's questionable collaboration with the Atlantis publishing house on the illustrated volume *Das deutsche Antlitz in fünf Jahrhunderten deutscher Malerei* (The German face in five centuries of German painting), I pointed out how one German representative of humanistic physiognomics succumbed—perhaps unwittingly—to the temptation to piggyback on the popularity of dominant trends in racial physiognomics to find a larger audience for his own physiognomic theories. Although in retrospect it seems as though it was nearly impossible in Germany during the 1920s and 1930s for those with interests in human physiognomy to resist being drawn into the vortex of racial ideology, it seems fitting to end this conclusion with the example of an artist whose photographic practice was consciously gauged as a counter to the ruling racial physiognomics of the day.[7] It was left to August Sander to carve out a critical space in this ideologically overburdened domain of physiognomic-photographic study by developing an exemplary practice that ran counter to mainstream developments in the Germany of the Weimar Republic.

Sander was keenly aware of both the pragmatic use and abuse to which the art of photography lent itself. In the fifth lecture in his 1931 series of radio broadcasts on the topic "Wesen und Werden der Photographie" (The nature and emergence of photography), Sander remarks: "besides its enormous importance in demonstrating truth, photography makes very dangerous kinds of deceptions possible" ("Photography as a Universal Language" 49). Given Sander's penchant for physiognomically exact photographic portraiture, there can be little doubt that among the dangerous deceptions to which he is alluding are the misuses of photographic technique in the racially oriented physiognomic literature of the time, in particular the works of Günther and Clauss. To be sure, Sander was an unabashed advocate of the revelatory power of physiognomic observation, and in this sense he was a true child of his age (Brückle 162). Indeed, if in his radio addresses he defends photography as a "universal language" with "so great a power of expression that [verbal] language can never approach it" ("Photography as a Universal Language" 47), what constitutes this power of photographic language is its ability to capture on film the essence of the human physiognomy. Sander conceived his magnum opus, the documentary collection *Menschen des 20. Jahrhunderts,* as a physiognomic cross section of the contemporary German population. In retrospect he describes this project as "a declaration of faith in photography as universal language," claiming that in this work he sought to "arrive at a physiognomic definition of the German people of the period" (49). A physiognomic definition of the German people—no doubt, Hans F. K. Günther or Erna Lendvai-Dircksen could have employed this very phrase to describe the purpose of their racial ethnologies with their ostentatiously *völkisch* orientation. But Sander's physiognomic anthropology of the German populace explicitly provides a critical alternative to the racist physiognomics of Günther and his ilk. Sander's opposition to the practices of mainstream German physiognomics of the period expresses itself on various levels of his work: in photographic technique; in the composition and choreography of his images; and in the nature of the human subjects he chooses.

Begun in 1910, *Menschen des 20. Jahrhunderts* was intended to encompass five to six hundred photographs of individuals, divided into forty-five separate portfolios, each composed of twelve photographs.[8] Although Sander never completed this project, in 1929 he published under the title *Antlitz der Zeit* a kind of prospectus that sketched in rudimentary form the outlines of this larger photo-documentary. This title already indicates the purported exemplariness of the photographic images presented in this collection: the faces of a small sampling of individuals are taken as representative of the physiognomy—and hence of the entire mentality—of the time. Sander, in short, subscribed to the typological thinking that dominated physiognomic thought during this period. But this is where the similarities end. Whereas, for example, Kretschmer's psychological types or Günther's racial types were grounded in the biological-genetic constitution of the individual, and hence were taken to be facts of nature, Sander constructs his typology along purely sociological, not racial lines. This is already evident in the seven broad categories into which he divides the material of *Menschen des 20. Jahrhunderts,* which bear titles such as "The Farmer," "The Worker," "The Artists," "The Woman," and "The Professions." These headings, in turn, are subdivided into smaller groups; the category "The Professions," for example, contains sections on "The Official," "The Doctor and the Pharmacist," "The Priest," "The Businessman," and "The Politician," among others, and it even presents a separate category for "The National Socialist," whom Sander treats as a sociohistorical type unto itself. The inclusion of a distinct subdivision entitled "Persecuted" under the larger grouping dedicated to "The City" gives a first indication of Sander's oppositional stance vis-à-vis the Nazi movement and its racial ideology. This resistance expressed itself above all in Sander's opposition to the biological determinism advocated by mainstream German racial anthropologists. He made this clear in his 1931 radio addresses, in which he openly maintained: "Human beings, unlike animals, live in societies that are constantly changing. Thus people develop, adjusting to their changing conditions, and subjected to more change in their environment than other living beings" ("Photography as a Universal

Language" 46). Sander thereby implies that the ontological difference distinguishing human beings from other animal species is distinctly *sociological* rather than biological: what sets humans apart is the self-constructed sociological environment in which they live, act, and realize themselves. The German writer and neurologist Alfred Döblin (1878–1957), who composed an introduction to the 1929 edition of *Antlitz der Zeit,* acknowledges this sociological component when he remarks in the following words on the implications of Sander's physiognomic portraits: "Diet has a formative influence on the human being, as do the air and the light in which he moves, the work he accomplishes or does not accomplish, and finally the special ideology of his social class" (14). Sander thus takes sides in one of the most vociferously contested ideological debates of the period: whether the human being is predetermined by natural-genetic dispositions, as the racial ideologues maintained, or by immediate environmental factors conditioned by milieu, social standing, and historical variables.[9] Sander clearly comes down on the side of the defenders of the so-called "milieu theory" and against the genetic determinism defended by the proponents of racial purity. He subscribes, in short, to a dynamic, developmental view of the human being as an entity that is transformed in its dialectical interaction with the sociocultural environment it helps to produce. This conception is in keeping with the strain of humanist physiognomics, descended from Goethe, that interprets physiognomics in a broad manner to include the surroundings and cultural attributes of the individual.

This more dynamic understanding of the human being and his or her characteristic physiognomy informed Sander's photographic procedure. In one radio address he asserts: "Not only a person's face, but his movements, define his character. It is always the photographer's responsibility to stabilize and record characteristic movement, which will then express physiognomy in a single comprehensible image" ("Photography as a Universal Language" 50). This argument places Sander's method in a certain proximity with that advocated by Ludwig Ferdinand Clauss, who, as we have seen, similarly employed photography to capture characteristic likenesses extracted from the fluid movement of the human subject. But once again this congruity on the broader conceptual level stands in contrast to profound differences in photographic and compositional method. Most significantly, of course, Clauss was a practitioner of the snapshot, often clandestinely taken, which was intended to reveal, almost like a kind of photographically recorded Freudian slip, the unconscious essence or "truth" of the photographed individual. Sander's practice could scarcely be more different. He was a vehement opponent of the unrehearsed, purportedly revelatory snapshot, favoring instead a method that emphasized the conscious staging of the photograph both by the photographer himself and by his photographed subjects. We can study this technique on the example of plate 13, "Jungbauern. Westerwald" (Young Farmers of Westerwald) from *Menschen des 20. Jahrhunderts.* (Fig. 75) The three young farmers stand on a path through an open field decked out in almost identical clothing: from white shirt, to broad-brimmed black hat, to black suit and shoes, to curve-handled walking stick, the "costumes" in which they appear underscore the extent to which they are, so to speak, cut from the same cloth. Moreover, in direct contrast to the photographs of Lendvai-Dircksen, who captures her farmers in local peasant dress, Sander's farmers indeed appear in costume: the ill-fitting, formal dark suits dictated by the economic logic of fashion, not by the physiognomic-racial logic of rural existence (see Berger 34–35). Their fundamental identity with one another highlights, of course, Sander's broader typological theme. In fact, we might read this single photograph as a microcosm for the method of concatenation Sander exploits throughout this documentary volume. Just as in this image the replication of costume and props brings out what is "typical" in these three farmers, so, too, Sander's arrangements of individual photographs in typologically ordered groups has exactly the same effect, stressing the paratactic connection among the figures representative of a particular social caste (see Keller 65). Sander himself emphasizes the importance of this typological arrangement for his overall project when he claims that "it is possible to record an era's physiognomic image, articulating it in the photo through physiognomy. This image of an age becomes even more comprehensible if we string together photos of types from the most diverse human social

Fig. 75. "Young Farmers," 1914, from August Sander, *Menschen des 20. Jahrhunderts.* © 2003 Die Photographische Sammlung/SK Stiftung Kultur—August Sander Archiv, Cologne; ARS, New York.

groups" (quoted in Susanne Lange 112). The typological similarities made evident in the cluster of photographs from a single group would enter into a contrastive relationship with the characteristics manifest in other groups. In his introductory essay for *Antlitz der Zeit,* Alfred Döblin accurately calls Sander's methodology "comparative photography" (14), stressing its relationship to the scientific practices of disciplines such as comparative anatomy. This procedure allowed Sander to generate what Ulrich Keller has called a systematic social inventory of German society at the beginning of the twentieth century (11).[10]

The similarities in the three figures in the photograph of the three young farmers goes much deeper than their clothes and accoutrements. All three men stand in rather rigid, almost identical poses, their feet planted firmly and in the very same configuration on the ground, their right hands resting on the handles of their canes, their faces turned slightly across their right shoulders to meet the photographic lens with their eyes, and their faces with a blank, unsmiling, but somewhat inquisitive stare. Everything about this photograph points to the fact that it has been carefully choreographed. Even the minor differences that distinguish the figures—the uplifted, partially clenched left hand of the man in the middle, the cigarette in the mouth of the man on the left, the unequal distances at which the three men are spaced—serve above all to highlight through contrastive effect their overriding similarities. More important is the fact that Sander enlisted the participation of his subjects in this choreography. The poses and expressions his characters strike are not dictated to them by the photographer, rather they are encouraged to engage in an act of self-dramaturgy in which they play out, for the camera, their own self-understanding. As Ulrich Keller points out, such a practice could only be predicated on an extensive exploratory dialogue between the photographer and his subjects, and the interactive sessions that preceded the actual photographs sometimes stretched out for hours (39). In direct contrast to the desire of the snapshot photographer to catch his or her subjects in unreflective moments that betray their otherwise hidden unconscious self, Sander sought to encourage and capture precisely the reflected, self-conscious dimensions of his subjects' personal self-understanding. Ulrich Keller has suggested that in this regard Sander's photographic technique has certain conscious or unconscious affinities with the alienation effect his contemporary Bertolt Brecht (1898–1956) demanded of the actors in his epic theater (43). Sander's photographic subjects, in other words, choreograph themselves, but they do so in a manner that consciously thematizes this self-stylized pose. This allows Sander's photography to reveal not so much what his individuals *truly are*—the aim of the clandestine snapshot and of physiognomics—but instead to bring to light the habitus associated with their sociohistorically conditioned self-understanding. We witness this, for example, in the attitude of the pastry cook (Fig.76), who looks out at the world with provocative self-assurance, surrounded by the tools and artifacts of his trade, or in the photograph of the jobless man (Fig. 77), in which, as a sign of his

Fig. 76. "Pastry Cook," 1928, from August Sander, *Menschen des 20. Jahrhunderts.* © 2003 Die Photographische Sammlung/SK Stiftung Kultur—August Sander Archiv, Cologne; ARS, New York.

socioeconomic alienation, the surrounding world appears out of focus and the photograph concentrates its crystal clarity on the image of the man's shorn head, drawn face, and submissive pose.

There is one more feature of Sander's photographic technique that both locates him in the general attitudes of his time and place, yet distinguishes his practice as a critical countermodel to the photographic approach pursued by the majority of his contemporaries: his belief in the faithfulness, indeed, in the quasi-scientific objectivity of the images his methodology produced. In an advertising flyer for his photographic practice produced as early as 1904, Sander claims "that—as distinct from the common approach—it is my aim to let stand all that is characteristic, everything that disposition, life, and time have im-

Fig. 77. "Jobless," 1928, from August Sander, *Menschen des 20. Jahrhunderts.* © 2003 Die Photographische Sammlung/SK Stiftung Kultur—August Sander Archiv, Cologne; ARS, New York.

pressed upon the face; and that is why I produce verisimilar, expressive, and characteristic portraits that completely correspond to the nature of the photographed subject" (quoted in Keller 23). What Sander emphasizes here is that his photographs are explicitly "unretouched." They do not strive for an idealized representation of the individual, reduced to a set of standard norms, but reproduce instead what is "typical"—that is, what is endemic to the human type to which the individual belongs—by capturing everything that is peculiar and characteristic of that person. What makes the photographic subject "typical" is not its reduction to a set of standardized conventions, but rather the traits that "life" and "time," as commonly shared sociohistorical parameters, have stamped upon it. This desire to replicate the reality of the human physiognomy with all its coarseness, blemishes, and scars, is reflected on the level of Sander's photographic instrumentarium as well. In a letter to Erich Stenger dated 21 July 1925, he remarks on the specific photographic tools adapted for the pursuit of what he calls "pure photography": "In order to achieve a clear, pure photography, I use Zeiss lenses, an orthochromatic plate with corresponding light filter, and clear, fine-grained glossy paper. I make my photos on 12 × 16½ or 13 × 18 plates, enlarging them to 18 × 24 (quoted in Susanne Lange 108). Sander preferred the then-antiquated technology of the orthochromatic plate precisely because it highlighted details, stressed impurities, and lent his photographs a less idealized, more critical cast (Keller 37). His insistence on the clarity of Zeiss lenses, the proper light filter, and high-gloss paper likewise supports the orientation to detail and verisimilitude that he valued in his photographic technique. More than anything else, this technique marked Sander and his work as representative of the artistic movement dubbed *Neue Sachlichkeit,* the "new objectivism" so prominent in Germany at the time, especially among left-leaning artists and intellectuals. Sander's photographic practice can stand as a model for the exploitation of specific technologies and artistic practices in support of a physiognomic project specifically conceived as an ideological counterforce to the reactionary physiognomics practiced so widely throughout Germany in his day.

This oppositional stance was not ignored by the Nazis after they came to power. In 1936 the Gestapo entered Sander's studio, confiscated all copies of the 1929 edition of *Antlitz der Zeit,* which had been banned by the Nazi Party, and destroyed the printing plates on which this edition was based so as to prevent any further reproduction of the work to which the new political masters took such ideological umbrage. The Nazi ideologues were only too aware that Sander's photographs presented realistic counter-models to the idealized images of racially pure individuals that were the stock in trade of the Nazis' own publications that exploited the photographic medium (see Kozloff 159; Keller 30). It is to Sander's credit that despite the political persecution he suffered at the hands of the Nazis, he continued throughout the Third Reich to assemble portfolios with photographs of the victims of Nazi crimes (Keller 30). At a time when physiognomic theories and practices were being mercilessly exploited for questionable ideological and political ends, Sander was one of the few Germans who, without abandoning his belief in the verity of physiognomic portrayal, sought to develop a physiognomic practice with an outspoken ideology-critical intent. Walter Benjamin was perhaps the first person to recognize this. In the 1931 essay "Kleine Geschichte der Photographie," Benjamin points to the significance of Sander's accomplishment by alluding to the political and socioeconomic context in which it emerged:

> It would be a pity if economic considerations were to prevent the further publication of this extraordinary corpus. Aside from this principal encouragement, we can offer the publisher a more precise form of encouragement. Overnight works like the one Sander has produced could acquire unsuspected relevance. Shifts in power like those that are overdue in our society tend to make the cultivation and sharpening of physiognomic modes of comprehension into a vital necessity. Regardless of whether we are on the left or the right—we will have to get used to being observed with an eye intent on detecting our stance. And we, in turn, will have to observe others in the same way. Sander's work is more than a picture book: it is a training manual. (381)

Benjamin's remarks lead us back to the theme of the previous chapter: learning to see. The proliferation of physiognomic theories and practical physiognomic primers in Germany during the early decades of the twentieth century represents a fundamental response to the sociological, political, and cultural disorientation experienced by Germans at this time. As Benjamin indicates, the Germans felt an irrepressible need to turn to physiognomic training manuals that might offer them clues about how to interpret the desires, designs, intentions, emotions, and even the political sentiments of the individuals with whom they came into contact. Sander might have been pleased to see his photographic documentation acknowledged by someone with the intellectual stature of Walter Benjamin as a critical counterweight to those other physiognomic training manuals, such as the ones produced by Günther and Clauss, that were proliferating so wildly throughout Germany. In a review of *Antlitz der Zeit,* a certain F. Worm summarized succinctly the physiognomic ambitions voiced by many prominent Germans not only at the beginning of the twentieth century, but from the publication of Lavater's

Physiognomische Fragmente in the 1770s onward: "We find portrayed here German people of today. An emerging science of physiognomics and of typological research will one day know how to outline in conceptual terms everything that today merely makes itself apparent to the observer by means of our gaze and our feelings" (quoted in Keller 67). This desire to elevate physiognomic investigation to the certainty and objectivity of scientific knowledge is one of the most persistent leitmotifs of the history of German physiognomics. It culminated during the Third Reich in the pseudo-sciences of racial discrimination, the generation of practical racial-physiognomic handbooks, and ultimately in the widespread massacre of those whose physiognomies betrayed their biological, cultural, or political Otherness. August Sander's work exemplifies this obsession with the development of a scientifically founded physiognomic taxonomy and erects a monument against the perverse ideological direction this pursuit often took.

Notes

Introduction

1. Throughout this examination I follow historians such as Isabel Hull in employing the more inclusive and ideologically neutral term "civil society" to designate the sociopolitical formation that emerged in late-eighteenth century Germany with the dissolution of the absolutist state and its social order of well defined estates. As Hull has argued (201–4), the tendency of social critics, following the lead of Jürgen Habermas, to narrowly identify German *bürgerliche Gesellschaft* with the middle class and with capitalist economic practices is both anachronistic and reductionist when applied to the situation of German-speaking Europe at the end of the eighteenth century and beyond. The phrase "civil society" indicates that the practitioners of these new forms of social and political interaction were more diverse than has often been assumed, encompassing hordes of state and city officials, the German *Bildungsbürgertum* composed of scholars, educators, doctors, lawyers, and other professionals, and finally, as just one subgroup, the economically productive bourgeoisie involved in commerce, manufacturing, and finance.

2. Musäus's *Physiognomische Reisen,* which were published anonymously, enjoyed enough popularity to warrant reissues in 1781, 1788, and 1803.

3. See especially pp. 1–40 in the second volume of Lavater's *Von der Physiognomik.*

4. Excerpts from this so-called "physiognomic cabinet," which is currently held in large part at the Portrait Collection of the Austrian National Library in Vienna, have recently been made available by Gerda Mraz and Uwe Schlögl in *Das Kunstkabinett des Johann Caspar Lavater,* the catalogue to the first exhibition of Lavater's private physiognomic collection. On the substance and nature of this collection, see Mraz and Schlögl's introduction (7–9).

5. On the emergence of the fashion system and the mentality of consumerism in German-speaking Europe in the final decades of the eighteenth century, see Purdy (esp. 1–73).

6. Musäus parodies this tendency toward the formation of societies centered around the study of Lavater's treatises when he has one of the characters of his *Physiognomische Reisen* form a physiognomic academy in his native village (1: 59).

7. Lichtenberg's treatise was first published in the *Göttingischer Taschen-Kalender für 1778* and later appeared as an independent pamphlet.

8. This parody first appeared in the *Neues Magazin für Ärzte* 5 (1783): 3–11.

9. Lavater himself gives an extended reply to Lichtenberg's critique in the fourth volume of the *Physiognomische Fragmente* (3–38). These remarks are reprinted with an introduction by Zimmermann in the *Deutsches Museum* (1778, 2: 289–317). Among Lavater's most ardent supporters, the poet Johann Michael Reinhold Lenz counterattacked Lichtenberg in his "Nachruf zu der im Göttingschen Almanach Jahrs 1778 an das Publikum gehaltenen Rede über Physiognomik" (Answer to the public address on physiognomics presented in the Göttingen Almanac of 1778), which was first published in Christoph Martin Wieland's *Teutscher Merkur* (1777, 4: 106–19). Zimmermann assaulted Lichtenberg with a barrage of ad hominem attacks in various submissions to the journal *Deutsches Museum* of 1778.

10. The persistence of this oversimplified understanding of the controversy between Lavater and Lichtenberg is repeated even in the most recent scholarship on this debate. See especially Gurisatti and Huizing, who, pursuing a Foucauldian archaeological analysis, invert the traditional hierarchy and valorize Lavater as the representative of a prerational sensibility that is mercilessly eradicated by the intolerance of enlightened reason. This transvaluation implicitly accepts the conventionalized terms in which this debate has been understood and overlooks the fact that Lavater himself appropriated the discourse of enlightened rationality in order to legitimate his physiognomic project.

11. See Eduard von der Hellen, *Goethes Anteil an Lavaters Physiognomischen Fragmenten*; Reinhold Steig gives a survey of Herder's relations to Lavater's physiognomics; Fr[iedrich] Waldmann summarizes Lenz's contributions.

12. Nicolai affirms his fundamental belief in the scientific basis of physiognomics in a letter to Lichtenberg dated 15 April 1778, published in Lichtenberg's *Briefwechsel* 1: 815–17. See also Nicolai's reviews of Lavater's physiognomic writings in his *Allgemeine Deutsche Bibliothek* 23 (1775): 313–46; 29 (1776): 349–414; and the supplement to volumes 25–36, pp. 1251–73.

13. On the connection of physiognomics to periods of sociopolitical disorientation see, for example, Arburg (42), Mattenklott (*Der übersinnliche Leib* 17–18), Schmölders (*Der exzentrische Blick* 12–13).

14. For an examination of the reflexes in style and fashion that contribute to the production of the civil subject, see Halpern (32).

15. Regarding the focus of physiognomics on the male and its general disinterest in issues of gender and women, see Regener ("Frauen," esp. 90–91).

16. I principally disagree with Andreas Käuser's view ("Die Physiognomik des 18. Jahrhunderts als Ursprung der modernen Geisteswis-

senschaft" 136) that the development from physiognomics to psychoanalysis is marked by a rupture or discontinuity characterized by a turn away from bodily to linguistic expression. Although the medium that reveals the "unconscious" does change from physical gesture to dream and linguistic slippage, the *metaphor* of language for conceiving the systematic, revelatory aspect of the unconscious remains constant.

17. For a definition of the epistemic structure of the enlightened world, see Foucault (*Order of Things* 50–63).

18. This motif is present throughout the *Fragmente;* see, for example, 3: 9–10; 3: 229.

19. On Carus as a precursor of Freud's theory, see Buser (68–79).

20. On this obsession with natural, "primordial" languages in this period, especially in the domain of art, see Herrmann (71–78).

21. The proximity of the "naive" to a trans-intentional unconscious is brought out best in Moses Mendelssohn's "Ueber das Erhabene und Naive in den schönen Wissenschaften" (esp. 240–42).

22. On the role of "Protestant" self-discipline in the constitution of modern socioeconomic practices, see Max Weber, "Die protestantische Ethik und der Geist des Kapitalismus" (esp. 47–48; 135–36; 187).

23. Stallybrass and White (149–70) have made especially persuasive arguments about this displacement of socioeconomic considerations by familial relationships in Freudian theory.

Chapter 1

1. Anon., Review of *Physiognomische Fragmente* in *Neue Bibliothek der schönen Wissenschaften und der freyen Künste* (144).

2. The *Aussichten in die Ewigkeit* (Outlooks on eternity) were a set of theological essays in epistolary form that Lavater published between 1768 and 1778.

3. In his *Physiognomisches Cabinet,* a work modeled on Lavater's *Physiognomische Fragmente,* Christian Friedrich Müller affirms the semiotic character of physiognomics, explicitly calling it a "semiotic science" (1: 222).

4. For a more detailed sketch of this semiotic teleology of Enlightenment culture see Wellbery (26–29).

5. Jacques Derrida exposes the semiotic presuppositions of Husserlian phenomenology—which, we should note, are not at all unlike those of Lavaterian physiognomics—in *Speech and Phenomena.*

6. The phrase "affective theory" for the hypothesis represented by Leibniz is taken from Aarsleff (65).

7. On this future-oriented aspect of Lavater's physiognomics see Kuzniar.

8. Although this connection between skull size and intelligence is often attributed to the facial angle theory of the Dutch scientist Petrus Camper (1722–1789), Meijer (173–76) has shown that this is a false attribution and that Soemmerring was one of the primary initiators of this

thesis. She overlooks, however, the importance this notion already has in Lavater's physiognomic theories.

9. One finds a further example of this iconic relationship in the third volume of the *Fragmente,* where Lavater presumes that the talent of a painter, because painting is a static art, will express itself in static features, whereas the face of a musician, whose art is composed of flowing tones, will manifest itself in fluid features (see *Physiognomische Fragmente* 3: 195).

10. Schopenhauer reiterates Lavater's arguments, claiming that the objectivity of physiognomic judgment is compromised by any social contact with the subject under analysis, and hence that physiognomic observation must occur under conditions of strict solitude (749).

11. On the difficulties artists experienced in trying to conform to Lavater's impossible expectations, see Herrmann (20–28), and Goritschnig, "Lavaters auserwählter Künstlerkreis" (97).

12. Moses Mendelssohn presents the typical arguments for this idealizing, transfiguring task of art and the artist in his *Ueber die Hauptgrundsätze der schönen Künste und Wissenschaften* (431–36).

13. Lavater would probably justify this procedure by pointing out that he believes painters are, and must be, the best physiognomists. According to him, painters master more fully than other human beings the primal language of physiognomics, and they make this language speak in their art (see *Physiognomische Fragmente* 2: 78–85). That belief would allow him to claim that even the fantasy images of historical personalities created by great painters would have some degree of physiognomic accuracy, since these painters would render the somatic traits that correspond to the historically inscribed character of these individuals. This is, however, an extremely tenuous argument, one based on the initial and unproven hypothesis that painters by definition possess this mysterious physiognomic intuition. But more weighty in critical terms, perhaps, is the obvious circularity of this argument, which presupposes the physiognomic identity between character trait and physical feature that Lavater is supposed to be trying to prove.

14. See Käuser, "Die Physiognomik des 18. Jahrhunderts als Ursprung der modernen Geisteswissenschaften" for an examination of the connections that link physiognomics with the hermeneutically oriented human sciences. Stadler (92) also places Lavater's physiognomics in the tradition of German hermeneutics, but he erroneously names Lavater's presumed aesthetic opposition to the natural sciences as part of this hermeneutic context. As we have seen, Lavater is more intent on appropriating the authority of the natural sciences than he is on opposing them.

15. Karl Pestalozzi ("Physiognomische Methodik" 143) discusses the aspects of Lavater's physiognomics that align it with textual studies.

16. To be sure, both these traits are also tied to the empirical sciences in some traditions, for example in the experimental method of Francis Bacon, who was skeptical of the truth of systems. But they are

not typical of the thought of the German Enlightenment philosophers on whom Lavater largely relied.

Chapter 2

1. For good general introductions see Davies, Lesky, and Young.

2. Although scholars have at times noted Gall's reliance on Lavater's ideas (see, for example, Geitner, "Klartext" 376; Stafford 103), Brooks and Johnson (17–19) are to my knowledge the only ones who offer a rudimentary analysis of selected points of immediate contact.

3. Oehler-Klein ("Franz Joseph Gall" 99) views this segmentation into distinct organs as a genuinely revolutionary idea on Gall's part, since prior to this the brain was always viewed as a unitary whole.

4. Comparing Lavater's use of silhouettes to Petrus Camper's dissection of actual skulls, Rauchensteiner (177) reverses this valuation, noting that Lavater was able to accomplish in effigy what Camper (and by extension Gall) could only achieve on the basis of actual human specimens. The primary difference, however, lies in the contrast between Lavater's aesthetic orientation and Camper's and Gall's physiological emphasis.

5. Volrad Deneke provides a great deal of background information on Scheve and the popularization of phrenology in nineteenth-century Germany.

6. On the broad popularity of physiognomics called forth by Lavater's theories see Siegrist's remarks ("Nachwort" 387–90) on their immediate reception.

7. For a historical overview of this development of modern physiognomics into the psychology of expression, see Buser.

8. On the semantic opposition of the words "culture" and "civilization" in the self-distinction of the civil subject, see Elias (1: 7–64, esp. 9–10).

9. On the problem of the counterfeit in the discourse of this period see Baudrillard (83–86; 93–94; 153).

10. Gotthold Ephraim Lessing's *Emilia Galotti* or Friedrich Schiller's inaugural drama *Die Räuber* (The robbers) are prototypical for the many texts of this period that revolve around problems of dissimulation and the counterfeit. See my *Stations of the Divided Subject* (45–101 and 102–45) for detailed interpretations of these texts.

11. In *Distinction,* Pierre Bourdieu has brilliantly illuminated the processes that define sociocultural distinction.

12. Karl Pestalozzi ("Physiognomische Methodik" 147) has elaborated this point more fully.

13. See Wolff, *Thun und Lassen* (132).

14. On the physiognomist as mortician see Fischer and Stumpp (124–25).

15. Horkheimer develops this theory of the authority-orientation of the modern civil subject in "Autorität und Familie."

16. Schmölder's argument (*Das Vorurteil im Leib* 19) that Schopenhauer's comments on physiognomics take it *ad absurdum* and hence should be seen as a critique of the same sort as Lichtenberg's fails to take the larger context—above all Schopenhauer's opposition to Hegel—into consideration and hence must be regarded as untenable.

17. This is the position defended by Gurisatti and Huizing.

18. Neumann advocates this view in "'Rede, damit ich dich sehe.'"

19. A similar conception of the body as the site at which individuality is constituted in a process of dialectical contestation has recently been advanced by post-Lacanian psychoanalysis. For an elaboration of this thesis see Küchenhoff.

20. Already the Enlightenment philosopher Christian Wolff took note of this problem, which he viewed as particularly intractable; see *Thun und Lassen* (136–39).

21. This is the position advocated by Neumann, who makes his arguments on the basis of Lichtenberg's interpretations of Hogarth ("'Rede, damit ich dich sehe'" 78; 88).

22. Hegel consistently associates the word "Zeichen" with arbitrary signs, those whose signifying function is ascribed to them independent of their material being. Natural signs, in which signification is related to the organic makeup of the signifying object, he designates with the word "Symbol," under which he understands what contemporary semiotic theory would call an "icon." See Hegel, *Theorie-Werkausgabe* (10: 270–77; 13: 394–96).

23. See especially Frank, *Was ist Neostrukturalismus?*, and also his *Die Unhintergehbarkeit von Individualität*, as well as the essays collected in the volume edited by Frank and Haverkamp.

24. See, for example, Coward and Ellis, Kristeva, and Paul Smith.

Chapter 3

1. Blankenburg ("Rassistische Physiognomik" 136) stresses that physiognomic theory is not by definition racist, but that it often takes on racist implications when it is put into practice.

2. On the development of forensic physiognomics see especially the essays by Becker, as well as Schneider, and Regener, "Verbrecherbilder."

3. Schmölders must be credited with presenting the first outlines of such an investigation; see especially her chapter in *Das Vorurteil im Leibe* entitled "Physiognomik als Dilemma" (155–64), and also her "Einleitung" to *Der exzentrische Blick* (7–18).

4. An important link between physiognomics and Lamarckian theory is forged by Charles Darwin (1808–1882) in his *The Expressions of the Emotions in Man and Animals* (1882), in which he argues that expression is a second nature that, gradually acquired, becomes habit and thereby leaves permanent traces on the human physiognomy. Hartley (161–63) notes that Darwin's corollary axiom that habits can become instincts has a close proximity to Lamarck's belief that

acquired traits can assume a genetic basis and become inheritable from one generation to another.

5. This propaganda piece is contained in the pamphlet "Rassenpolitik" (Racial politics), a copy of which is preserved in the German Federal Archive in Coblenz, file number NSD 41/117, pp. 32–33.

6. Lavater's physiognomic "cabinet," his collection of physiognomic portraits and sketches, contained an extensive subdivision devoted to "nationalities." See Swoboda (76), and also Lachs, "Nationalphysiognomien."

7. Lachs emphasizes that Lavater's judgments about nationalities merely confirm the stereotypes that prevailed at that time in Europe ("Nationalphysiognomien" 183).

8. For a further example of Lavater's standardized prejudices toward the "Moor," see *Physiognomische Fragmente* 4: 309, "Appendix D: A Standing Moor." On the depiction of blacks in eighteenth-century physiognomics, see Gilman, "Lavater, Lichtenberg, and the Physiognomy of the Black."

9. Sander Gilman has brought ample evidence that confirms the persistence of these prejudices about the typical "Jewish" physiognomy. See especially *The Jew's Body.*

10. See Camper's *Über den natürlichen Unterschied der Gesichtszüge in Menschen verschiedener Gegenden und verschiedenen Alters . . . ,* which was translated into German by the prominent anatomist Samuel Thomas Soemmerring. The most thorough introduction to Camper's theories and their reception is presented by Meijer.

11. Meijer justifiably insists on this correction to the common reception of Camper's theories (1), documenting Camper's belief in the fundamental equality of the races (3–6). Meijer points out that it was the interpretation by Camper's contemporaries of his theory of racial gradation through the lens provided by the notion of a chain of being that lent his position a hierarchizing implication (43–46)

12. Carus's first cranioscopic treatise, *Grundzüge einer neuen und wissenschaftlich begründeten Cranioscopie* (Fundamentals of a new and scientifically grounded cranioscopy), appeared in 1841; it was followed by the *Proportionslehre,* and subsequently by the *Neuer Atlas der Cranioskopie* (New atlas of cranioscopy).

13. On this reifying tendency in Carus's procedure, see Fischer, Schrader, and Stumpp (11–58).

14. This direction is pursued with truly exaggerated consequence in the works of the racial anthropologist Bruno K. Schultz, especially his *Taschenbuch der rassenkundlichen Meßtechnik* (Handbook of racial anthropometrics).

15. Carus is referring to his book *Goethe: Zu dessen näherem Verständnis* (Goethe: Toward understanding him better), which was published six years earlier, in 1843.

16. Gobineau's treatise on human inequality appeared from 1853–1855.

17. On this tendency of racial thought to biologize social conditions, see Claussen (2).

18. See line 95 of the poem "Resignation" in Schiller's *Sämtliche Werke* (1: 133).

19. On the relationship between physiognomics and colonialism, see Blankenburg, "Rassistische Physiognomik" (136).

20. See, for example, Schultz, *Erbkunde, Rassenkunde, Rassenpflege* (70), or Hans F. K. Günther, *Adel und Rasse* (50–60), where all the traits of aristocracy and nobility are identified with the "Nordic" human being. This line of argumentation was initiated, of course, by Gobineau, and pursued in exaggerated form by Chamberlain in his *Grundlagen des neunzehnten Jahrhunderts* (Foundations of the nineteenth century).

21. Note, in this regard, that the Jena anatomist Emil Huschke, writing in 1854, found it necessary to define his own cranioscopic theories in the context of those developed by Carus; see Huschke (45).

22. Meijer (173) elaborates on this association between skull size and intellectual ability. She identifies Samuel Thomas Soemmerring as the originator of this idea, not Camper, to whom it is often attributed.

23. Carus's most important German predecessor in the establishment of a racial typology based on cranioscopic data was Johann Friedrich Blumenbach (1752–1840). Blumenbach's dissertation *De generis humani varietate nativa* (On the native varieties of the human species) appeared in 1775, and his *Beyträge zur Naturgeschichte* (Contributions to natural history) was published in 1790.

24. See Klages, "Einführendes Wort des Herausgebers."

25. Kern's book first appeared in 1926 under the title *Die Philosophie des Carl Gustav Carus: Ein Beitrag zur Metaphysik des Lebens.* A second edition, with the revised title *Carl Gustav Carus: Persönlichkeit und Werk* was published in 1942. The chapter on racial psychology can be found on pages 169–70 of the second edition.

26. The chapter devoted to Carus's theory of race can be found on pages 153–60 of Voegelin's historical survey.

27. For documentation on the dissertations treating Carus see Michael (85–86).

28. Theodor Lessing published a new edition of the *Symbolik der menschlichen Gestalt* (Celle: Kampmann, 1925), which was reprinted in 1932 and 1938. Hans Kern edited a collection of excerpts from Carus's works under the title *Natur und Seele* (Nature and soul; Jena: Diederichs, 1936), and Paul Stöcklein published excerpts with commentaries in the volume *Carl Gustav Carus: Menschen und Völker* (Carl Gustav Carus: Human beings and nations; Hamburg: Hoffman & Campe, 1943).

29. Carl Gustav Carus, *Gesammelte Schriften,* ed. R.[udolf] Zaunick and W.[olfgang] Keiper (Berlin: Keiper, 1938–1944). This edition was never completed.

30. Carl Gustav Carus, *Goethe-Denkschrift,* vol. 6 of his *Gesammelte Schriften* or of his *Werke, Abhandlungen,* the general title under which this edition appeared in the 1943 printing.

31. Blankenburg, "Rassistische Physiognomik," is the one notable exception to this.

32. Representative of this tendency are the arguments of Rüdiger Campe and Manfred Schneider in the "Preface" to their anthology *Geschichten der Phyiognomik* (11).

33. See the section "Physiognomik und Systematik" (Physiognomics and systematics) in Spengler's *Untergang des Abendlandes* (125–52), or Kassner's *Das physiognomische Weltbild.*

34. See especially Klages's *Die Grundlagen der Charakterkunde,* which first appeared in 1910 as *Prinzipien der Charakterologie.*

Chapter 4

1. The diverse areas in which this physiognomic Renaissance occurred have recently been documented in the essays collected by Claudia Schmölders and Sander Gilman in the volume *Gesichter der Weimarer Republik.*

2. Klages, who pays tribute to Lavater's role as a model for characterology, constitutes the only partial exception; see his essay "Prinzipielles bei Lavater" (Principal recognitions in Lavater; *Sämtliche Werke* 6: 3–12). Despite this acknowledgment of Lavater's insights, Klages consistently distanced his own kinetically oriented physiognomics from Lavater's and Gall's "organic physiognomics," as he was inclined to call this materialistic strain of physiognomic thought.

3. For an extended discussion of this issue see chapter 1 above.

4. Gert Mattenklott ("Goethe als Physiognomiker" 135) points out the epistemological significance of this essay for Goethe's concept of *Anschauung,* or intuition.

5. Concerning the problematic of mortification in Carus, see Fischer and Stumpp (124–25).

6. See *Symbolik* (185–88), where Carus first develops these thoughts; but compare also his *Proportionslehre,* to which he appends typological sketches of racial crania. For more on Carus's significance for the subsequent "racial psychology" of the Weimar period, see Hans Kern (169–70), and chapter 3 above.

7. Klages conveniently ignores the Hegel of the *Phänomenologie des Geistes* in this intellectual-historical reconstruction, although Hegel is clearly more deserving than Goethe of being called the first phenomenologist.

8. As early as 1933 Richard Loewenberg warned against the political-ideological thrust indicative of physiognomic practices in Germany prior to, and during, the rise of fascism ("Der Streit um die Physiognomik" 29–32).

9. On this culturally pessimistic line of thought in German physiognomics, see chapter 2 above.

Chapter 5

1. Critics have only recently taken note of this resurgence of physiognomic theories in Weimar and Nazi Germany; see, for example, Campe and Schneider (9), Lethen (7–9), but particularly Schmölders, *Das Vorurteil im Leib* (15–16), who makes a first, rudimentary attempt to explain the fascination physiognomics held for German intellectuals at this time. See, in addition, the introduction to Schmölders and Gilman, *Das Gesicht der Weimarer Republik* (8).

2. Klages's characterological psychology was carried on by psychologists such as Philipp Lersch and Hans Prinzhorn.

3. For an examination of the influence of Balázs's theory and of silent film in general on the resurgence of physiognomics in the Weimar period, see Kaes (esp. 162–65).

4. Günther republished some of his books after the war, although he was banned from further teaching. He did, however, receive a pension from the West German government. Clauss also published a book on physiognomics as late as 1958, *Die Seele des Andern.* Although cleansed of explicit references to racial ideology, this book replicates in all major respects the theories propounded in his prewar works, even recycling many of the same illustrations. Another example of the continuation of ethnological physiognomics with a nationalist tendency beyond the end of the war is Willy Hellpach's *Deutsche Physiognomik,* which was published in a second edition in 1949.

5. The essays collected in the volume by Schmölders and Gilman, *Das Gesicht der Weimarer Republik,* present an excellent cross section of the areas in which physiognomics came to the fore during this period.

6. On Dilthey's role as a mediator of the morphological worldview with its insistence on a mode of perception consistent with organic structures, see Rodi (38–42).

7. See also *Maximen und Reflexionen* no. 279, where Goethe defines the poetic approach to the world as the envisioning of the universal in the particular (*Gedenkausgabe* 9: 528–29).

8. See Schröter, who criticizes Spengler for not fully developing the opposition between systematic and physiognomic methodologies (85).

9. Schulze (137) maintains that *Untergang* had a shaping influence on the thought of Weimar Germany.

10. On the reception of *Untergang* see Schröter (25), and also Felken (114–16).

11. Kassner translated several of Plato's major dialogues into German, and he was strongly influenced by his dialogic dialectic; see Paeschke (10).

12. This theory of the physiognomically "split" face has certain affinities with Ludwig Ferdinand Clauss's theory of *Artriß,* the rupture of race. On Clauss and this principle, see chapter 7 below.

13. Michael Schmidt (63–65) sees this merging of seer and seen through the shared power of imagination as the basis for the autobiographical structure of Kassner's physiognomics.

14. On the fluidity of Kassner's key concepts see Rychner (198).

15. Cited in Ernst Zinn's "Nachwort" to his edition of *Zahl und Gesicht* (248). See also *Das physiognomische Weltbild,* where Kassner writes of the "unity of *Gesicht* (visage) and *Gesicht* (vision)" (*Sämtliche Werke* 4: 339).

16. Böschenstein (368) is to my knowledge the only critic who has recognized that for Kassner the type represents a higher form of human being.

17. In this and other citations from these posthumous texts I have consciously deleted the interpolations added by the editors of Spengler's notebooks.

18. On the significance of the nose as a signal of race, see *Physiognomik* (*Sämtliche Werke* 5: 90) and *Das physiognomische Weltbild* (4: 460). Cf. also Kassner's remarks on the Jewish face in *Grundlagen der Physiognomik* (4: 24). On the traits identified by racial propaganda as characteristic of the Jewish physiognomy see Gilman, *The Jew's Body* and *The Visibility of the Jew in the Diaspora.*

19. For the background history of this volume and Kassner's input, see the editors' notes in Kassner, *Sämtliche Werke* (10: 951–58).

20. See, for example, the propagandistic volume *Deutschland treibt Rassenpolitik* or journals such as *Volk und Rasse.* Ganzer's *Das deutsche Führergesicht* has affinities with the project Kassner participated in, as does the illustrated volume by Heinsius and Ebert, *Sonne und Schatten im Erbe des Volkes.* Fischer and Günther's *Deutsche Köpfe nordischer Rasse* has a more strictly racial bent, but the art history studies of Schultze-Naumburg are filled with propagandistic fervor tied to the masters of German art and architecture.

21. See Rudolf Kassner and W. R. Deutsch, *Das deutsche Antlitz in fünf Jahrhunderten deutscher Malerei;* Kassner's introduction "Die Physiognomik des Porträts" appears on pages 5–26. This essay is reprinted in Kassner's *Sämtliche Werke* (10: 385–404).

22. Schmölders (*Das Vorurteil im Leib* 40) makes a similar point when she refers to the monologic aspect of physiognomic voyeurism, its avoidance of mutuality and reciprocity between the seer and the seen.

Chapter 6

1. The best summary of Günther's life and thought can be found in Lutzhöft (28–47). Lutzhöft's book also gives a detailed analysis of the ideological positions of the Nordic Movement and its diverse representatives.

2. Meijer (173) attributes the subsequent transformation of Camper's theory into a distinct racial hierarchy to the thought of Cuvier.

3. Soemmerring's treatise was republished in revised and expanded form one year later, in 1785, under the title *Über die körperliche Verschiedenheit des Negers vom Europäer* (On the anatomical differences distinguishing the Negro from the European). In this version Soemmerring, reacting to the controversy his book had engendered, mollifies the racial qualities of his argument.

4. This notion of an intuitive, innate physiognomic sensibility is still used as an explanation for physiognomics in the scientific literature of today. In the article on physiognomics for the volume devoted to *Ausdruckspsychologie* (Psychology of expression) in Robert Kirchhoff's encyclopedic *Handbuch der Psychologie* (Handbook of psychology), for example, Franz Kiener postulates an *Urverstehenstheorie,* a "theory of primordial comprehension," as the basis of people's inexplicable ability to grasp human character on the basis of physiognomic interpretation (480).

5. This identification of nobility and beauty with the Nordic race was carried out most thoroughly by Günther's friend, the art historian Paul Schultze-Naumburg (1869–1949), in his books *Kunst und Rasse* (Art and race; 1928) and *Nordische Schönheit: Ihr Wunschbild im Leben und in der Kunst* (Nordic beauty: Its ideal in life and in art; 1937). On the development of Schultze-Naumburg's life and his turn from an aesthetic to a racial orientation, see Sauerländer.

6. This general tendency toward the valorization of types can also be found, for example, in the thought of Ernst Jünger, especially in his essay *Der Arbeiter* (The laborer; 125–207). But the seductive appeal this notion had for intellectuals during the Weimar period can perhaps best be gauged by the fact that even the Jewish intellectual Arnold Zweig, in the book *Das ostjüdische Antlitz* (The face of Eastern European Jewry; 1920), positively stresses the significance of the typical as an eradication of all individual features (78).

7. Compare Husserl's formulation, for example, to Lavater's assertion that the body is the "cloak and the image of the soul" (*Physiognomische Fragmente* 1: 4). This is a standard idea among eighteenth-century intellectuals. In his *Allgemeine Theorie der schönen Künste* (Universal theory of the fine arts) Johann Georg Sulzer (1720–1779) asserts: "the body [is] nothing other than the soul made visible" (quoted in Pollnow 163). Similarly, in his "Sokratische Denkwürdigkeiten" (Socratic memoirs) Johann Georg Hamann (1730–1788) calls the human body *"a figure or an image of the soul"* (66).

8. Günther himself articulates this spiral in which each master race inevitably experiences decline—a phenomenon we might call the fatalism of mastery—in his description of the collapse of Greek and Roman civilizations, described in *Rassengeschichte des hellenischen und des römischen Volkes* (92).

9. A further telling example of Günther's appropriation of Nietzschean ideas and discourse can be found in his *Herkunft und Rassen-*

geschichte der Germanen, where he asserts that the decline of the powerful Teutonic tribes was engineered by the weak but cunning representatives of Christianity (175).

10. Even Adolf Hedler, one of Günther's most adamant critics, concedes the significant role the illustrations play in Günther's book (52).

11. For a summary of Dühring's position and an excerpt of his treatise, see Claussen (44–66).

12. Hans Blumenberg has rightly argued that physiognomic discourses operate according to deceptions based on their tendency to "deck themselves out with theories"; see his *Die Lesbarkeit der Welt* (202).

13. At the points in his argument when he acknowledges the possibility that a fundamental element of an individual's racial constitution might be hidden on the non-manifest level of genotype, Günther simply calls for a thorough examination of that person's family tree, a so-called *Ahnentafel.* Anatomy, he claims in this context, merely gives a strong "indication" of one's racial constitution, and certainty can be achieved only by compiling a complete hereditary-genetic chart (*Rassenkunde* 249; *Kleine Rassenkunde* 80). This is another example of one of Günther's theories that was directly implemented under Nazi rule in the infamous *Ahnenpaß*, the racial-hereditary identification book laying out genetic heritage, which each German citizen was required to possess if he or she wanted to advance in the hierarchies of the Third Reich.

14. Weingart, Kroll, and Bayertz see Günther as one of the two most politically effective representatives of the Nordic Movement (452), the other being Richard Walther Darré (1895–1953), who defended the German peasant stock as the bearers of healthy "Nordic" genes and assumed the significant title of *Reichsbauernführer* (imperial leader of the peasantry), a ministerial post in Hitler's regime.

15. These guidelines were used for training those officials who had the task of cataloging the racial features of individuals, detailing specific anatomical features on the notorious racial index cards created expressly for such examinations. These guidelines are contained in file NS 2/161 at the German Federal Archive in Coblenz.

16. "Pressebericht des Rassenpolitischen Amtes der NSDAP," 28 November 1935; German Federal Archive Coblenz, document NS 2/155, p. 37.

Chapter 7

1. The philosopher Joachim Küchenhoff uses the terms "inscribed body" and "speaking body" to designate these two conceptions (169). Although I have borrowed his terminology here, my categories, which rely on the eighteenth-century distinction between "physiognomics" and "pathognomics," are more inclusive than his.

2. *Rasse und Seele* has a curious publication history. The first edition appeared under this title in 1926 with the subtitle "Eine Einführung in die Gegenwart" (An introduction to the contemporary world). A second, heavily revised edition appeared in 1929 under an entirely different title, *Von Seele und Antlitz der Rassen und Völker* (On the soul and face of races and nations). A third revised edition, which returned to the original title *Rasse und Seele,* was published in 1934, this time, however, with the subtitle "Eine Einführung in den Sinn der leiblichen Gestalt" (An introduction to the meaning of somatic form), and this latter edition remained the basis for all subsequent printings, including the 1937 edition I cite. The content of the three books is similar, although the various editions tend to organize this material in very different ways. In order to avoid confusion I will include the year of publication in brackets when citing from the different editions of this and other works by Clauss. In general, Clauss's oeuvre is characterized by the constant reworking, reformulation, and reorganization of a relatively stable core of ideas. These basic principles remain constant throughout the pre-Nazi publications, the works published during the Third Reich, and even in Clauss's book that appeared after the Nazi defeat, *Die Seele des Andern: Wege zum Verstehen im Abend- und Morgenland* (The soul of the other: Paths to understanding in Occident and Orient), published in 1958. What changes is the ideological context in which these ideas are placed, and this tends to underscore the impression that Clauss was above all an opportunist who tried to take advantage of the changing intellectual climate in order to garner support for his research (Weingart 21).

3. A typical example of the sanctimonious reference to the idea that each race has its own value and its own standard of worth can be found in the article "Wert der Rasse," written by Walter Gross, the head of the Nazi Office for Racial Politics, and published in the popular illustrated magazine *Neues Volk* in June 1934.

4. Little is known about the connections between Clauss and Rosenberg prior to the Nazi seizure of power; it is documented, however, that Rosenberg took sides against Clauss in 1941 when Clauss was denounced for protecting his Jewish coworker Margarete Landé. See Weingart (69).

5. Clauss's expulsion is reported in a flyer from the *Informationsdienst des Rassenpolitischen Amtes der NSDAP* 7 (1943): 415.

6. My account of the Nazi Party proceedings against Clauss, which eventually led to his expulsion, is largely indebted to Peter Weingart's masterful biography of Clauss, especially pp. 45–148, which supplies the fundamental information about and the relevant Party documents surrounding these proceedings.

7. The idea that race makes itself manifest in artistic styles was pursued most vigorously by a close friend of Hans F. K. Günther, Paul Schultze-Naumburg (1869–1949), in his books *Nordische Schönheit* (Nordic beauty) and *Kunst und Rasse* (Art and race).

8. Erich Voegelin (b. 1901), one of the most insightful German analysts of race during the period of the Weimar Republic, refers to Clauss's notion of racial style as a *Gestalt-Idee* (form-idea), and he locates Clauss in an intellectual tradition that debated differing conceptions of what Voegelin calls the *Leib-Idee*, the "idea of the animate body" (*Rasse und Staat* 92–104; 122–42). Clauss was clearly aware that the stress he placed on style or form as the determining dimension of racial personality had close theoretical affinities with the characterology and graphology of Ludwig Klages. See especially *Rasse und Charakter* (14, 82, and 106), and *Die Seele des Andern* (97), where Clauss refers positively to Klages's theories.

9. Throughout his writings Clauss is exceedingly careful not to fall into the standard rhetoric of anti-Semitic discourse. For the most part, his critique of the Jews is based on his belief that they exemplify the negative traits of racial mixture and that they threaten the German populace because of their alien style (see *Rasse und Seele* [1926] 74–76; *Die nordische Seele* [1923] 234). Only in *Rasse und Charakter*, which was published in 1936, does Clauss employ some of the standard derogatory rhetoric typical of the Nazi propaganda against the Jews, words such as *Schmarotzertum* (parasitism), which was one of the code terms for the Jews favored, for example, by Alfred Rosenberg. See Clauss, *Rasse und Charakter* (101–4).

10. George Mosse has examined in general terms Nietzsche's influence on the major proponents of the Nordic Idea; see his *Crisis of German Ideology* (205–12).

11. On Clauss's relationship to his teacher Husserl, especially Clauss's decision to break away from this respected mentor and set off in his own direction, despite Husserl's offer of continued support, see Weingart (11–18).

12. Despite this major difference of opinion, Husserl apparently valued Clauss's engagement and intelligence enough to consider him a potential successor to the professorial chair of philosophy Husserl himself held in Freiburg (Weingart 15).

13. Husserl was clearly aware of this connection between his phenomenological theory and the ambitions of physiognomists to establish systematic rules for the interpretation of character. See, for example, *Ideen II* (166), where Husserl comments positively on the possibility of developing a "grammar of expression," similar to the grammar of language, that would allow the systematic study of the psychic lives of humans.

14. The expressive psychology of Phillip Lersch is one of the only other examples of the impact of phenomenology on a major and influential figure of this period. See Lersch's *Der Aufbau des Charakters*, first published in 1938, which frequently refers to the thought of Dilthey and to phenomenology.

15. For a brief history of the competition between monogenetic and polygenetic theories, especially among Enlightenment anthropologists, see Poliakov (179–208).

16. A particularly illuminating manifestation of this position can be found in an essay by Richard D. Loewenberg, himself an exile from Hitler's Germany, published in 1941. In "The Significance of the Obvious," Loewenberg notes the misuse of physiognomics for the ends of political barbarism, but asserts that this does not "wipe out the soundness of the original conception" (677). Loewenberg speaks for the majority of scholars on this subject, who for the most part avoid evoking the specter of race as an inherent ingredient of the tradition since Lavater—indeed, since (pseudo)-Aristotle.

17. This view, which tends to hold physiognomics harmless in the rise of fascist racial ideologies and practices, is represented above all by Rüdiger Campe and Manfred Schneider, who intentionally leave racial physiognomics out of their collection of scholarly essays that purports to relate the many "histories" of physiognomic thought, *Geschichten der Physiognomik* (11).

Conclusion

1. On the artists Lavater employed and the relationships he maintained with them see Goritschnig, "Künstlerkreis" and Herrmann (21–25).

2. A copy of this advertising leaflet is contained in file NS26, number 503, at the German Federal Archive in Coblenz.

3. Lendvai-Dircksen initially published a single volume under the title *Das deutsche Volksgesicht.* Subsequently, however, she brought out under this same collective title a series of individual volumes keyed to specific regions of Germany.

4. For other interesting examples of this popular genre, see Bruno K. Schultz, *Deutsche Rassenköpfe* (German racial faces); Heinsius and Ebert, *Sonne und Schatten im Erbe des Volkes* (Sun and shadow in the heritage of the Volk); or even Ernst Jünger's photo-documentation of the First World War, *Antlitz des Weltkrieges* (The face of the World War).

5. This advertising prospectus is contained in file R18, document 3610, in the German Federal Archive in Coblenz.

6. "Richtlinien für die Bildarbeit an den RuS-Dienststellen," file NS2, document 161, p. 63, German Federal Archive in Coblenz.

7. Brückle (132–33) makes a case for the politically progressive character of Sander's physiognomic project.

8. For detailed background on the plan for this project, see Ulrich Keller's introduction to *Menschen des 20. Jahrhunderts* esp. 33–46).

9. On the centrality of this issue as the flash-point around which the primary ideological conflicts of the day emerged, see Lutzhöft (13–15).

10. Kozloff similarly emphasizes that Sander's collection presents "a roll call of stock figures that moves horizontally through the professions or trades, and vertically, up or down, through the progress of generations and the division of classes" (158).

Select Bibliography

Aarsleff, Hans. *From Locke to Saussure: Essays on the Study of Language and Intellectual History.* Minneapolis: University of Minnesota Press, 1982.

Adorno, Theodor W. *Ästhetische Theorie.* Frankfurt am Main: Suhrkamp, 1970.

———. "Wird Spengler recht behalten?" *Vermischte Schriften I.* Vol. 20.1 of his *Gesammelte Schriften.* Ed. Rolf Tiedemann. Frankfurt am Main: Suhrkamp, 1986. 140–48.

———. "Zum Verhältnis von Soziologie und Psychologie." *Soziologische Schriften I.* Ed. Rolf Tiedemann. Frankfurt am Main: Suhrkamp, 1979. 42–85.

Aerni, Fritz. *Huter und Lavater: Von der Gefühlsphysiognomik zur Psychologie und Psycho-Physiognomik.* Zurich: Kalos-Verlag, 1984.

Allentuck, Marcia. "Fuseli and Lavater: Physiognomical Theory and the Enlightenment." *Studies on Voltaire and the Eighteenth Century* 55 (1967): 89–112.

Althaus, Karin. "Lavaters Begegnungen und die Formen seiner Kommunikation." In Mraz and Schögl. 30–39.

Anon. *Darstellung der neuen, auf Untersuchungen der Verrichtungen des Gehirns gegründeten Theorie der Physiognomik des Herrn Dr. Gall in Wien.* 2nd, expanded ed. Weimar: Verlag des Industrie-Comptoirs, 1801.

Anon. Review of Lavater's *Physiognomische Fragmente. Neue Bibliothek der schönen Wissenschaften und der freyen Künste* 22.1–2 (1778): 118–65 and 191–260.

Anon. Review of Lavater's *Physiognomische Fragmente,* volumes 1 and 2. *Ephemeriden der Menschheit* 1(1776): 58–71; 1(1777): 46–54.

Anon. Review of Lavater's *Physiognomische Fragmente. Neue litterarische Unterhaltungen* (1775): 545–61; 609–31; 762–64.

Anon. Reviews of Lavater's *Physiognomische Fragmente. Gothaische gelehrte Anzeigen* (1775): Stück 50, 409–13; (1776): Stück 65, 527–29; (1777): Stück 49, 401 5; (1778): Stück 54–55, 441–45 and 449–51.

Anon. Review of Lichtenberg's "Über Physiognomik; wider die Physiognomen." *Der teutsche Merkur* (April 1778): no. 2, 80–81.

Arburg, Hans-Georg von. "Johann Caspar Lavaters Physiognomik: Geschichte—Methodik—Wirkung." In Mraz and Schögl. 40–59.

Aristotle [Pseudo-Aristotle]. *Physiognomica.* Trans. T. Loveday and E. S. Forster. *Aristotle: Complete Works.* Ed. Jonathan Barnes. Princeton: Princeton University Press, 1984. 1: 1237–50.

Armstrong, A. M. "The Methods of the Greek Physiognomists." *Greece and Rome* 5 (1958): 52–56.

Ash, Mitchell G., and Ulrich Geuter, eds. *Geschichte der deutschen Psychologie im 20. Jahrhundert: Ein Überblick.* Opladen: Westdeutscher Verlag, 1985.

Die Aufklärung und ihr Körper: Beiträge zur Leibesgeschichte im 18. Jahrhundert. Special issue of *Das Achtzehnte Jahrhundert* 14.2 (1990).

Balázs, Béla. *Der sichtbare Mensch oder Die Kultur des Films.* Vol. 1 of *Schriften zum Film.* Vienna: Deutsch-österreichischer Verlag, 1924.

Barkan, Leonard. *Nature's Work of Art: The Human Body as Image of the World.* New Haven: Yale University Press, 1975.

Baudrillard, Jean. *Simulations.* Trans. Paul Foss et al. New York: Semiotext(e), 1983.

Baumgarten, Alexander Gottlieb. *Metaphysica. Texte zur Grundlegung der Ästhetik.* Ed. Hans Rudolf Schweizer. Hamburg: Meiner, 1983. 1–65.

Baur, Erwin, Eugen Fischer, and Fritz Lenz. *Menschliche Erblehre und Rassenhygiene.* 2 vols. 4th ed. Munich: J. F. Lehmann, 1936.

Becker, Peter. "Randgruppen im Blickfeld der Polizei: Ein Versuch über die Perspektivität des 'praktischen Blickes.'" *Archiv für Sozialgeschichte* 32 (1992): 283–304.

———. "Vom 'Haltlosen' zur 'Bestie': Das polizeiliche Bild des 'Verbrechers' im 19. Jahrhundert." *"Sicherheit" und "Wohlfahrt": Polizei, Gesellschaft und Herrschaft im 19. und 20. Jahrhundert.* Ed. Alf Lüdke. Frankfurt am Main: Suhrkamp, 1992. 97–131.

Behrens, Rudolf, and Roland Galle, eds. *Leib-Zeichen: Körperbilder, Rhetorik und Anthropologie im 18. Jahrhundert.* Würzburg: Königshausen & Neumann, 1993.

———. "Vorwort." *Leib-Zeichen: Körperbilder, Rhetorik und Anthropologie im 18. Jahrhundert.* 7–9.

Bell, Charles. *The Anatomy of the Brain, Explained in a Series of Engravings.* London: Whittingham, 1802.

———. *Essays on the Anatomy and Philosophy of Expression.* London: Longmans, 1806.

Benjamin, Walter. "Kleine Geschichte der Photographie." *Gesammelte Schriften: Werkausgabe.* Ed. Rolf Tiedemann and Hermann Schweppenhäuser. 12 vols. Frankfurt am Main: Suhrkamp, 1980. 4: 368–85.

———. "Das Paris des Second Empire bei Baudelaire." *Gesammelte Schriften: Werkausgabe.* Ed. Rolf Tiedemann and Hermann Schweppenhäuser. 12 vols. Frankfurt am Main: Suhrkamp, 1980. 2: 511–604.

Benthall, Jonathan, and Ted Polhemus, eds. *The Body as Medium of Expression.* New York: E. P. Dutton, 1975.

Benz, Ernst. "Swedenborg und Lavater: Über die religiösen Grundlagen der Physiognomik." *Zeitschrift für Kirchengeschichte* 57 (1938): 153–216.

Berger, John. *About Looking*. New York: Pantheon, 1980.

Bernoulli, Christoph. *Die Psychologie von Carl Gustav Carus und deren geistesgeschichtliche Bedeutung*. Jena: Diederichs, 1925.

Bertillon, Alphonse. *Die gerichtliche Photographie*. Halle: Knapp, 1895.

Blankenburg, Martin. "Rassistische Physiognomik: Beiträge zu ihrer Geschichte und Struktur." In Schmölders, *Der exzentrische Blick*. 133–61.

———. "Seelengespenster: Zur deutschen Rezeption von Physiognomik und Phrenologie im 19. Jahrhundert." In Mann and Dumont, *Gerhirn—Nerven—Seele*. 211–37.

[Bloede, Karl August]. *F. J. Galls Lehre über die Verrichtungen des Gehirns*. Dresden: Arnoldsche Buchhandlung, 1805.

Blumenberg, Hans. *Die Lesbarkeit der Welt*. Frankfurt am Main: Suhrkamp, 1981.

———. "Menschenkenntnis." *Frankfurter Allgemeine Zeitung* 124 (30 May 1990): Beilage Natur und Wissenschaft, 3.

Bock, Werner. "Rudolf Kassner und die moderne Physiognomik." *Universitas* 10 (1955): 715–19.

Böhle, Wilhelm. *Die Körperform als Spiegel der Seele*. Leipzig: Teubner, 1929.

Böhme, Hartmut. "Der sprechende Leib: Die Semiotiken des Körpers am Ende des 18. Jahrhunderts und ihre hermetische Tradition." In Kamper and Wulf, *Transfigurationen des Körpers*. 144–81.

Borrmann, Norbert. *Kunst und Physiognomik: Menschendeutung und Menschendarstellung im Abendland*. Cologne: DuMont, 1994.

Böschenstein, Bernhard. "Anmerkungen zu Rudolf Kassners Personenbeschreibungen, ausgehend von seiner *Physiognomik*." In Groddeck and Stadler. 360–72.

Bourdieu, Pierre. *Distinction: A Social Critique of the Judgment of Taste*. Trans. Richard Nice. Cambridge, Mass.: Harvard University Press, 1984.

Braungart, Georg. *Leibhafter Sinn: Der andere Diskurs der Moderne*. Studien zur deutschen Literatur, Bd. 130. Tübingen: Niemeyer, 1995.

Brednow, Walter. "Symbol und Symbolik in der Biologie Goethes." *Goethe: Neue Folge des Jahrbuchs der Goethe-Gesellschaft* 28 (1966): 236–62.

———. *Von Lavater zu Darwin*. Sitzungsberichte der sächsischen Akademie der Wissenschaften zu Leipzig, Bd. 108, Heft 6. Berlin: Akademie-Verlag, 1969.

———. "Wesen und Bedeutung der *Physiognomischen Fragmente* J. C. Lavaters." *Physiognomische Fragmente*, Faksimile-Druck. Zurich and Leipzig: Orell Füssli, 1969. 4: 1–47.

———. "Wilhelm von Humboldt und die Physiognomik." *Clio medica* 4 (1969): 33–42.

Breitenfellner, Kirstin. *Lavaters Schatten: Physiognomie und Charakter bei Ganghofer, Fontane und Döblin.* Dresden: Dresden University Press, 1999.

Breitenfellner, Kirstin, and Charlotte Kohn-Ley, eds. *Wie ein Monster entsteht: Zur Konstruktion des anderen in Rassismus und Antisemitismus.* Bodenheim: Philo, 1998.

Breitling, Rupert. *Die nationalsozialistische Rassenlehre: Entstehung, Ausbreitung, Nutzen und Schaden einer politischen Ideologie.* Meisenheim am Glan: Hain, 1971.

Brooks, G. P., and R. W. Johnson. "Johann Caspar Lavater's *Essays on Physiognomy.*" *Psychological Reports* 46 (1980): 3–20.

Bruce, Vicki, and Andy Young. *In the Eye of the Beholder: The Science of Face Perception.* Oxford: Oxford University Press, 1998.

Brückle, Wolfgang. "Kein Portrait mehr? Physiognomik in der deutschen Bildnisphotographie um 1930." In Schmölders and Gilman. 131–55.

Brunswik, Egon, and Lotte Reiter. "Eindruckscharaktere schematischer Gesichter." *Zeitschrift für Psychologie* 142 (1938): 67–134.

Bühler, Karl. *Ausdruckstheorie: Das System an der Geschichte aufgezeigt.* Jena: Gustav Fischer, 1933.

Burger-Villingen, Robert. *Das Geheimnis der Menschenform.* 2 vols. Leipzig: Scholz, 1912.

———. *Die menschlichen Formgesetze als Schlüssel zur Rassenkunde: Der körperliche Formenbau als sichtbarer Ausdruck der Rasse.* Leipzig: Hermann Eichblatt Verlag, 1935.

Burleigh, Michael, and Wolfgang Wippermann. *The Racial State: Germany 1933–1945.* Cambridge: Cambridge University Press, 1991.

Buser, Remo. *Ausdruckspsychologie: Problemgeschichte, Methodik und Systematik der Ausdruckswissenschaft.* Munich and Basel: Ernst Reinhardt, 1973.

Buttkus, Rudolf. *Physiognomik: Ein neuer Weg zur Menschenkenntnis.* Munich: Reinhard, 1956.

Campe, Rüdiger. "Rhetorik und Physiognomik oder Die Zeichen der Literatur." *Rhetorik* 9 (1990): 68–83.

———. "Zufälle im physiognomischen Urteil: Ein Aspekt der 'Aristoteles'—Lektüre zwischen Della Porta und der Barockphysiognomik." In Campe and Schneider. 125–51.

Campe, Rüdiger, and Manfred Schneider, eds. *Geschichten der Physiognomik: Text, Bild, Wissen.* Freiburg im Breisgau: Rombach, 1996.

Camper, Petrus. *Discours prononcés par feû en l'acadêmie de dessein d' Amsterdam.* Ed. Adrien Gilles Camper. Utrecht: Wild & Altheer, 1792.

———. *Dissertation physique, sur les différences réelles que présentent les traits du visage chez les hommes de différents pays et de dif-*

férents âges. Ed. Adrien Gilles Camper. Utrecht: Wild & Altheer, 1791.

———. *Über den natürlichen Unterschied der Gesichtszüge in Menschen verschiedener Gegenden und verschiedenen Alters.* Ed. Adrian Gilles Camper. Trans. Samuel Thomas Soemmerring. Berlin: Vossische Buchhandlung, 1792.

Carus, Carl Gustav. "Goethe und seine Bedeutung für diese und die künftige Zeit." *Goethe Denkschrift.* Berlin: Keiper, 1943. 1–32.

———. *Goethe: Zu dessen näherem Verständnis.* Ed. Rudolf Marx. Leipzig: Kröner, n.d.

———. *Grundzüge einer neuen und wissenschaftlich begründeten Cranioscopie.* Stuttgart: Balz'sche Buchhandlung, 1841.

———. *Neuer Atlas der Cranioskopie enthaltend dreissig Abbildungen merkwürdiger Todtesmasken und Schädel.* 2nd ed. Leipzig: Brockhaus, 1864.

———. *Physis: Zur Geschichte des leiblichen Lebens.* Stuttgart: Scheitlin, 1851.

———. *Die Proportionslehre der menschlichen Gestalt.* Leipzig: Brockhaus, 1854.

———. *Psyche: Zur Entwicklungsgeschichte der Seele.* 2nd ed. Stuttgart: Scheitlin's Verlagsbuchhandlung, 1851.

———. *Symbolik der menschlichen Gestalt.* 2nd ed. 1858; rpt. Hildesheim: Olms, 1977.

———. "Symbolische Rhapsodien: Fragmente zur Symbolik menschlicher Gestalt." *Betrachtungen und Gedanken vor auserwählten Bildern der Dresdner Galerie.* Berlin: Keiper, 1943. 102–26.

———. *Über die typisch gewordenen Abbildungen menschlicher Kopfformen namentlich auf Münzen in verschiedenen Zeiten und Völkern.* Jena: Frommann, 1863.

———. *Über Grund und Bedeutung der verschiedenen Formen der Hand in verschiedenen Personen.* Ed. Julius Schuster. Berlin: Breslauer, 1927.

———. *Über ungleiche Befähigung der verschiedenen Menschheitsstämme für höhere geistige Entwickelung.* Leipzig: Brockhaus, 1849.

Chamberlain, Houston Stewart. *Die Grundlagen des 19. Jahrhunderts.* 16th ed. 2 vols. Munich: Bruckmann, 1932.

Christians, Heiko. "Gesicht, Gestalt, Ornament: Überlegungen zum epistemologischen Ort der Physiognomik zwischen Hermeneutik und Mediengeschichte." *Deutsche Vierteljahrsschrift für Literaturwissenschaft und Geistesgeschichte* 74 (2000): 84–110.

Ciocco, Antonio. "The Background of the Modern Study of Constitution." *Bulletin of the Institute of the History of Medicine* 4 (1936): 23–38.

Clauss, Ludwig Ferdinand. *Als Beduine unter Beduinen.* Freiburg im Breisgau: Herder, 1933.

———. "Der germanische Mensch." *Rasse: Monatsschrift der Nordischen Bewegung* 1.1 (1934): 2–20.

———. "Nordische Glaubensgestaltung." *Deutschlands Erneuerung* 8.7–8 (July–Aug. 1924): 1–16.

———. *Die nordische Seele: Artung, Prägung, Ausdruck.* Halle: Niemeyer, 1923.

———. *Die nordische Seele: Eine Einführung in die Rassenseelenkunde.* Munich: J. F. Lehmann, 1932.

———. *Rasse und Charakter.* Frankfurt am Main: Diesterweg, 1936.

———. *Rasse und Seele: Eine Einführung in den Sinn der leiblichen Gestalt.* 8th ed. Munich: J. F. Lehmann, 1937.

———. *Rasse und Seele: Eine Einführung in die Gegenwart.* Munich: J. F. Lehmann, 1926.

———. "Rassenkunde im Unterricht an Mittelschulen." *Deutschlands Erneuerung* 9.2 (Feb. 1925): 90–99.

———. *Rassenseelenforschung im täglichen Leben.* Erfurt: Kurt Stenger, 1934.

———. *Rassenseele und Einzelmensch: Lichtbildvortrag.* Munich: J. F. Lehmann, 1938.

———. *Die Seele des Andern: Wege zum Verstehen im Abend- und Morgenland.* Baden-Baden: Grimm, 1958.

———. *Semiten der Wüste unter sich.* Munich: J. F. Lehmann, 1937.

———. *Von Seele und Antlitz der Rassen und Völker.* Munich: J. F. Lehmann, 1929.

Clauss, Ludwig Ferdinand, and Arthur Hoffmann. *Vorschule der Rassenkunde auf der Grundlage praktischer Menschenbeobachtung: Lehrerheft.* Erfurt: Kurt Stenger, 1934.

Claussen, Detlev. *Was heißt Rassismus?* Darmstadt: Wissenschaftliche Buchgesellschaft, 1994.

Cooper, Helen, and Peter Cooper. *Heads, or The Art of Phrenology.* London: London Phrenology Company, 1983.

Courtine, Jean-Jacques. "Körper, Blick, Diskurs: Typologie und Klassifizierung in der Physiognomik des Klassischen Zeitalters." In Campe and Schneider. 211–43.

Courtine, Jean-Jacques, and Claudine Haroche. *Histoire du visage.* Paris: Editions Rivages, 1988.

Coward, Rosalind, and John Ellis. *Materialism and Language: Developments in Semiology and the Theory of the Subject.* London: Routledge & Kegan Paul, 1977.

Cruikshank, George. *Phrenological Illustrations, or An Artist's View of the Craniological System of Doctors Gall and Spurzheim.* London: Frederick Arnold, 1873.

Cunningham, Andrew, and Roger French, eds. *The Medical Enlightenment of the Eighteenth Century.* Cambridge: Cambridge University Press, 1990.

Danow, D. K. "Physiognomy: The Codeless 'Science.'" *Semiotica* 50 (1984): 157–71.

Darré, Richard Walther. *Neuadel aus Blut und Boden.* Munich: J. F. Lehmann, 1930.

Darwin, Charles. *The Expression of the Emotions in Man and Animals.* London: J. Murray, 1872.

Davies, John D. *Phrenology—Fad and Science: A Nineteenth-Century American Crusade.* New Haven: Yale University Press, 1955.

Deleuze, Gilles, and Felix Guattari. "Das Jahr Null—Gesichtlichkeit." *Bildlichkeit: Internationale Beiträge zur Poetik.* Ed. Volker Bohn. Frankfurt am Main: Suhrkamp, 1990. 431–67.

Della Porta, Giambattista. *Della Fisionomia di Tutto il Corpo Humano.* Ed. Francesco Stelluti. Rome: Vitale Mascardi, 1637.

———. *La Physionomie Humaine.* Rouen: Jean & David Berthelin, 1655.

Derrida, Jacques. *Speech and Phenomena and Other Essays on Husserl's Theory of Signs.* Trans. David B. Allison. Evanston: Northwestern University Press, 1973.

Descartes, René. *The Passions of the Soul. The Philosophical Works of Descartes.* Trans. E. S. Haldene and G. R. T. Ross. 2 vols. 1911; rpt. Cambridge: Cambridge University Press, 1968. 1: 329–427.

Deutschland treibt Rassenpolitik. Ed. Rassenpolitisches Amt der NSDAP. Munich: Verlag NSDAP, n.d.

Diehl, Otto. *Mimik im Film: Leitfaden für den praktischen Unterricht in der Filmschauspielkunst.* Munich: Müller, 1922.

Diez, Karl August. *Versuch einer theoretischen Begründung der Physiognomik.* Freiburg: Verlag Friedrich Wagner, 1830.

Dilthey, Wilhelm. *Die geistige Welt: Einleitung in die Philosophie des Lebens.* Vol. 5 of *Gesammelte Schriften.* Stuttgart: Teubner, 1957.

Disraeli, Isaac. "Physiognomy." *Curiosities of Literature.* 2 vols. London: Frederick Warne, 1863–1866. 1: 148–50.

Döblin, Alfred. "Von Gesichtern, Bildern und ihrer Wahrheit." In August Sander, *Antlitz der Zeit.* 1929; rpt. Munich: Schirmer/Mosel, 1976. 6–15.

Dougherty, Frank W. P. "Christoph Meiners und Johann Friedrich Blumenbach im Streit um den Begriff der Menschenrasse." In Mann and Dumont, *Natur des Menschen.* 89–111.

Duchenne, G.-B. *Mécanisme de la physiognomie humaine.* Paris: Jules Renouard, 1862.

Dürkop, Marlis. "Zur Funktion der Kriminologie im Nationalsozialismus." *Strafjustiz und Polizei im Dritten Reich.* Eds. Udo Reifner and Bernd-Rüdiger Sonnen. Frankfurt am Main: Campus, 1984. 97–120.

Dürre, Konrad. *Erbbiologischer und rassenhygienischer Wegweiser für Jedermann.* 6th ed. Berlin: Alfred Metzner, 1935.

———. *Wege zur Menschenkenntnis.* Berlin: Verlag für Standesamtswesen, 1938.

Eco, Umberto. "Die Sprache des Gesichts." *Über Spiegel und andere Phänomene.* Trans. Burkhart Kroeber. Munich: Hanser, 1988. 71–82.

Ekman, Paul. "Facial Signs: Facts, Fantasies, and Possibilities." *Sight, Sound, and Sense.* Ed. Thomas Sebeok. Bloomington: Indiana University Press, 1978. 124–56.

Elias, Norbert. *Über den Prozeß der Zivilisation: Soziogenetische und psychogenetische Untersuchungen.* 2nd ed. 2 vols. 1969; rpt. Frankfurt am Main: Suhrkamp, 1976.

Engel, Johann Jakob. *Ideen zu einer Mimik.* 2 vols. 1785–1786; rpt. Darmstadt: Wissenschaftliche Buchgesellschaft, 1968.

Erb, Rainer. "Die Wahrnehmung der Physiognomie der Juden: Die Nase." *Das Bild des Juden in der Volks- und Jugendliteratur vom 18. Jahrhundert bis 1945.* Ed. Heinrich Pleticha. Würzburg: Königshausen & Neumann, 1985. 107–26.

Europa, Europa. Dir. Agnieszka Holland. CCC Filmkunst, 1990.

Evans, Elizabeth C. "The Study of Physiognomy in the Second Century A.D." *Transactions and Proceedings of the American Philological Association* 72 (1941): 96–108.

[Feder, Georg Heinrich]. Review of Lavater's *Von der Physiognomik. Göttingische gelehrte Anzeigen,* 107 Stück (5 Sept. 1772): 919–20.

Felken, Detlef. *Oswald Spengler: Konservativer Denker zwischen Kaiserreich und Diktatur.* Munich: Beck, 1988.

Fielding, Henry. "An Essay on the Knowledge of the Characters of Men." *Miscellanies.* Ed. Henry Knight Miller. 2 vols. Middletown, Conn.: Wesleyan University Press, 1972. 1: 153–78.

Fischer, Eugen, and Hans F. K. Günther. *Deutsche Köpfe nordischer Rasse.* Munich: J. F. Lehmann, 1930.

Fischer, Rotraut, and Gabriele Stumpp. "Das konstruierte Individuum: Zur Physiognomik Johann Kaspar Lavaters und Carl Gustav Carus'." In Kamper and Wulf, *Transfigurationen des Körpers.* 123–43.

Fischer, Rotraut, Gerd Schrader, and Gabriele Stumpp. *Natur nach Maß: Physiognomik zwischen Wissenschaft und Ästhetik.* Marburg: Soznat, 1989.

Fishberg, Maurice. *Die Rassenmerkmale der Juden.* Munich: Ernst Reinhardt, 1913.

Foucault, Michel. *Discipline and Punish: The Birth of the Prison.* Trans. Alan Sheridan. New York: Vintage, 1979.

———. *The Order of Things: An Archaeology of the Human Sciences.* New York: Vintage, 1973.

Frank, Manfred. *Die Unhintergehbarkeit von Individualität.* Frankfurt am Main: Suhrkamp, 1986.

———. *Was ist Neostrukturalismus?* Frankfurt am Main: Suhrkamp, 1984.

Frank, Manfred, and Anselm Haverkamp. *Individualität.* Vol. 13 of *Poetik und Hermeneutik.* Munich: Fink, 1988.

[Franz, Johann Georg Friedrich]. *Versuch einer Geschichte der Physiognomik und der damit verbundenen Wissenschaften.* Vienna & Leipzig: Friedrich August Hartmann, 1784.

Freud, Sigmund. "Notiz über den 'Wunderblock.'" *Freud Studienausgabe.* Ed. Alexander Mitscherlich et al. Frankfurt am Main: Fischer, 1967–1979. 3: 363–69.

Fülleborn, Georg Gustav. "Abriß einer Geschichte und Litteratur von der Physiognomik." *Beyträge zur Geschichte der Philosophie* 8 (1797): 1–188; 9 (1798): 164–69; 10 (1799): 116–19.

Gall, Franz Joseph. "Des Herrn Dr. F. J. Gall Schreiben über seinen bereits geendigten Prodromus über die Verrichtungen des Gehirns der Menschen und Thiere, an Herrn Joseph Friedrich von Retzer." *Neuer teutscher Merkur* (1798), Stück 12: 311–32.

———. *Meine Reise durch Deutschland, nebst pathognomischen Bemerkungen über meine gemachten Bekanntschaften und einzig wahre Darstellung meiner Lehre.* n.p.: n.p., 1806.

Gall, Franz Joseph, and Johann Gaspar Spurzheim. *Recherches sur le système nerveux en général, et sur celui du cerveau en paticulier.* Paris: Schoell & Nicolle, 1809.

Gallagher, Catherine, and Thomas Laqueur, eds. *The Making of the Modern Body.* Berkeley: University of California Press, 1987.

Galton, Sir Francis. *Inquiries into Human Faculty and its Development.* London: Macmillan, 1883.

Ganzer, Karl Richard. *Das deutsche Führergesicht: 200 Bildnisse deutscher Kämpfer und Wegsucher aus zwei Jahrtausenden.* Munich: J. F. Lehmann, 1935.

Gauch, Hermann. *Neue Grundlagen der Rassenforschung.* Leipzig: Alfred-Klein-Verlag, 1933.

Gebauer, Gunter. "Ausdruck und Einbildung: Zur symbolischen Funktion des Körpers." In Kamper and Wulf, *Wiederkehr des Körpers.* 313–29.

Geitner, Ursula. "Die 'Beredsamkeit des Leibes': Zur Unterscheidung von Bewußtsein und Kommunikation im 18. Jahrhundert." *Das achtzehnte Jahrhundert* 14 (1990): 181–95.

———. "Klartext: Zur Physiognomik Johann Caspar Lavaters." In Campe and Schnieder. 357–85.

———. *Die Sprache der Verstellung: Studien zum rhetorischen und anthropologischen Wissen im 17. und 18. Jahrhundert.* Tübingen: Niemeyer, 1992.

Gerhart, Dieter. *Kurzer Abriß der Rassenkunde.* Munich: J. F. Lehmann, 1933.

Gilman, Sander L. *The Face of Madness: Hugh W. Diamond and the Origin of Psychiatric Photography.* New York: Brunner and Mazel, 1976.

———. *The Jew's Body.* New York: Routledge, 1991.

———. "Lavater, Lichtenberg, and the Physiognomy of the Black." *On Blackness without Blacks: Essays on the Image of the Black in Germany.* Boston: G. K. Hall, 1982. 49–56.

———. *The Visibility of the Jew in the Diaspora: Body Imagery and Its Cultural Context.* Syracuse, N.Y: Syracuse University Press, 1992.

Glas, Norbert. *Die Formensprache des Gesichts: Neue Wege zu einer Physiognomik des Menschen.* Vienna: Weidmann, 1935.

Goethe, Johann Wolfgang von. *Aus meinem Leben: Dichtung und Wahrheit. Goethes Werke: Hamburger Ausgabe.* Ed. Erich Trunz. 6th ed. Munich: Beck, 1976. 9: 7–598 and 10: 7–187.

———. *Gedenkausgabe der Werke, Briefe und Gespräche* (Artemis Ausgabe). Ed. Ernst Beutler. 26 vols. Zürich: Artemis, 1950ff.

[Goethe, Johann Wolfgang von]. Review of Lavater, *Aussichten in die Ewigkeit,* vol. 3. *Frankfurter gelehrte Anzeigen* (1772), No. 88. In *Deutsche Literaturdenkmale des 18. und 19. Jahrhunderts.* Eds. Wilhelm Scherer and Bernard Seuffert. 150 vols. Heilbronn: Henninger, 1882–1883. 7–8: 579–82.

Goethes Briefe. Ed. Karl Robert Mandelkow. 2nd ed. 4 vols. Hamburg: Wegner, 1968.

Goethe und Lavater: Briefe und Tagebücher. Ed. Heinrich Funck. Schriften der Goethe-Gesellschaft, Bd. 16. Weimar: Verlag der Goethe-Gesellschaft, 1901.

Goldberg, David Theo. *Racist Culture: Philosophy and the Politics of Meaning.* Oxford: Blackwell, 1993.

Goldberg, David Theo, ed. *Anatomy of Racism.* Minneapolis: University of Minnesota Press, 1992.

Gombrich, Ernst H. "On Physiognomic Perception." *Meditations on a Hobby Horse and Other Essays on the Theory of Art.* London: Phaidon, 1963. 45–55.

Goritschnig, Ingrid. "Faszination des Porträts." In Mraz and Schögl. 138–51.

———. "Lavaters auserwählter Künstlerkreis." In Mraz and Schögl. 96–109.

Gould, Stephen Jay. *The Mismeasure of Man.* New York: Norton, 1981.

Graf, Jakob. *Biologie für Oberschule und Gymnasium.* 2 vols. Munich: J. F. Lehmann, 1940.

———. *Familienkunde und Rassenbiologie für Schüler.* Munich: J. F. Lehmann, 1934.

———. *Vererbungslehre, Rassenkunde und Erbgesundheitspflege: Einführung nach methodischen Grundsätzen.* 2nd ed. Munich: J. F. Lehmann, 1934.

Graf, Ruedi. "Utopie und Theater: Physiognomik, Pathognomik, Mimik und die Reform von Schauspielkunst und Drama im 18. Jahrhundert." In Groddeck and Stadler. 16–33.

Graham, John. *Lavater's Essays on Physiognomy: A Study in the History of Ideas.* Berne: Peter Lang, 1979.

Gräntz, Fritz. "Spengler und Goethe." *Westermanns Monatshefte* 66 (Dec. 1921): 325–31.

Gray, Richard T. *Stations of the Divided Subject: Contestation and Ideological Legitimation in German Bourgeois Literature, 1770–1914.* Stanford: Stanford University Press, 1995.

Groddeck, Wolfram, and Ulrich Stadler. *Physiognomie und Pathognomie: Zur literarischen Darstellung von Individualität.* Berlin: de Gruyter, 1994.

Grohmann, Johann Christian August. *Ideen zu einer physiognomischen Anthropologie.* Leipzig: Dykische Buchhandlung, 1791.

Gross, Walter. "Wert der Rasse." *Neues Volk* 2.6 (June 1934): 20–23.

Gruber, Max, and Ernst Rüdin. *Fortpflanzung, Vererbung, Rassenhygiene: Katalog der Gruppe Rassenhygiene der Internationalen Hygiene-Ausstellung 1911 in Dresden.* Munich: J. F. Lehmann, [1911].

Gruhler, Hans W. "Historische Bemerkungen zum Problem Körperbau und Charakter." *Zeitschrift für die gesamte Neurologie und Psychologie* 84 (1923): 444–49.

Günther, Hans F. K. *Adel und Rasse.* Munich: J. F. Lehmann, 1926.

———. *Führeradel durch Sippenpflege: Vier Vorträge.* Munich: J. F. Lehmann, 1936.

———. *Herkunft und Rassengeschichte der Germanen.* Munich: J. F. Lehmann, 1935.

———. *Kleine Rassenkunde des deutschen Volkes.* Munich: J. F. Lehmann, 1929.

———. *Der nordische Gedanke unter den Deutschen.* Munich: J. F. Lehmann, 1925.

———. *Rassengeschichte des hellenischen und des römischen Volkes.* Munich: J. F. Lehmann, 1929.

———. *Rassenkunde des deutschen Volkes.* 16th ed. Munich: J. F. Lehmann, 1939.

———. *Rassenkunde des jüdischen Volkes.* Munich: J. F. Lehmann, 1930.

———. *Rassenkunde Europas.* Munich: J. F. Lehmann, 1929.

———. *Rasse und Stil: Gedanken über ihre Beziehungen im Leben und in der Geistesgeschichte.* 2nd ed. Munich: J. F. Lehmann, 1926.

———. *Ritter, Tod und Teufel: Der heldische Gedanke.* 2nd ed. Munich: J. F. Lehmann, 1924.

Gurisatti, Giovanni, and Klaus Huizing. "Die Schrift des Gesichts: Zur Archäologie physiognomischer Wahrnehmungskultur." *Neue Zeitschrift für systematische Theologie und Religionswissenschaft* 31 (1989): 271–87.

Habermas, Jürgen. *Erkenntnis und Interesse.* Frankfurt am Main: Suhrkamp, 1968.

———. *Strukturwandel der Öffentlichkeit: Untersuchungen zu einer Kategorie der bürgerlichen Gesellschaft.* 13th ed. Darmstadt: Luchterhand, 1982.

Hagner, Michael. "Zur Physiognomik bei Alexander von Humboldt." In Campe and Schneider. 431–52.

Hake, Sabine. "Zur Wiederkehr des Physiognomischen in der modernen Photographie." In Campe and Schneider. 475–513.

Hall, Stephen S. "Fear Itself." *New York Times Magazine.* 28 February 1999. 40–47, 69–72, 88–91.

[Haller, Albrecht von]. Review of 2nd and 3rd vols. of Lavater's *Physiognomische Fragmente. Göttingische gelehrte Anzeigen* (1777): Zugabe, 50–54; (1777): 993–98.

Halley, Anne. "August Sander." *Massachussetts Review* (1978): 35–45.

Halpern, Richard. *The Poetics of Primitive Accumulation: English Renaissance Culture and the Genealogy of Capital.* Ithaca: Cornell University Press, 1991.

Hamann, Johann Georg. "Sokratische Denkwürdigkeiten." *Sämtliche Werke.* Ed. Josef Nadler. 6 vols. 1949–1957; rpt. Wuppertal: Brockhaus, 1999. 2: 57–82.

Hanneford, Ivan. *Race: The History of an Idea in the West.* Baltimore: Johns Hopkins University Press, 1996.

Hartley, Lucy. *Physiognomy and the Meaning of Expression in Nineteenth-Century Culture.* Cambridge: Cambridge University Press, 2001.

Hau, Michael, and Mitchell G. Ash. "Der normale Körper, seelisch erblickt." In Schmölders and Gilman. 12–31.

Hecht, Günther. *Kannst du rassisch denken?* Schriftenreihe des Rassenpolitischen Amtes der NSDAP und des Reichsbundes der Kinderreichen, Heft 14. Berlin: Rassenpolitisches Amt der NSDAP, n.d.

Hedler, Adolf. *Rassenkunde und Rassenwahn: Wissenschaft gegen demagogischen Dilettantismus.* Berlin: Dietz, 1932.

Hegel, Georg Wilhelm Friedrich. *Phänomenologie des Geistes.* Vol. 3 of *Theorie-Werkausgabe.* Eds. Eva Moldenhauer and Karl Markus Michel. Frankfurt am Main: Suhrkamp, 1970.

———. *Theorie-Werkausgabe.* 20 vols. Eds. Eva Moldenhauer and Karl Markus Michel. Frankfurt am Main: Suhrkamp, 1970.

Heidegger, Martin. *Sein und Zeit.* 15th ed. Tübingen: Niemeyer, 1979.

Heinsius, Fritz, and Georg Ebert. *Sonne und Schatten im Erbe des Volkes.* Berlin: Verlag der deutschen Ärzteschaft, 1935.

Hellpach, Willy. *Deutsche Physiognomik: Grundlagen einer Naturgeschichte der Nationalgesichter.* 2nd ed. Berlin: de Gruyter, 1949.

———. *Studien zur Ethnophysiognomik und Ethnopathognomik.* Abhandlungen der Heidelberger Akademie der Wissenschaften, Jahrgang 1951, Abhandlung 1. Heidelberg: Winter, 1951.

———. "Der völkische Aufbau des Antlitzes." *Die medizinische Welt* 7.2 (1933): 1546–49.

Helm. Carl. *Arier, Wilde und Juden: Ihre Rassen, Kulturen und Ideen.* Leipzig: C. W. Stern, 1923.

Herder, Johann Gottfried. "Ist die Schönheit des Körpers ein Bote von der Schönheit der Seele?" *Sämtliche Werke.* Ed. Bernhard Suphan. Berlin: Weidmannsche Buchhandlung, 1877ff. 1: 43–56.

———. Review of vol. 1 of Lavater's *Physiognomische Fragmente. Sämtliche Werke.* 9: 411–24.

———. "Vom Erkennen und Empfinden in der menschlichen Seele." *Sämtliche Werke.* 1: 165–333.

Herland, Leo. *Gesicht und Charakter: Handbuch der praktischen Charakterdeutung.* Zurich: Rascher, 1938.

Herrmann, Sabine. *Die natürliche Sprache in der Kunst um 1800: Praxis und Theorie der Physiognomik bei Füssli und Lavater.* Frankfurt am Main: Fischer, 1994.

Hitler, Adolf. *Mein Kampf.* Munich: Zentralverlag der NSDAP, 1943.

Hofer, Walter. *Der Nationalsozialismus: Dokumente 1933–1945.* Frankfurt am Main: Fischer, 1957.

Hoffmann, Heinrich. *Hitler wie ihn keiner kennt.* Berlin: Zeitgeschichte, 1935.

Hoffmann, Heinrich, and Wilfrid Bade. *Deutschland erwacht: Werden, Kampf und Sieg der NSDAP.* Altona-Bahrenfeld: Cigaretten-Bilderdienst, 1933.

Horkheimer, Max. "Autorität und Familie." *Gesammelte Schriften.* Ed. Alfred Schmidt et al. Frankfurt am Main: Fischer, 1985ff. 3: 336–417.

Horkheimer, Max, and Theodor W. Adorno. *Dialektik der Aufklärung: Philosophische Fragmente.* Frankfurt am Main: Fischer, 1969.

Hull, Isabel. *Sexuality, State, and Civil Society in Germany.* Ithaca: Cornell University Press, 1996.

Humboldt, Wilhelm von. "Das achtzehnte Jahrhundert." *Werke in fünf Bänden.* Eds. Andreas Flitner and Klaus Giel. 3rd ed. 5 vols. Darmstadt: Wissenschaftliche Buchgesellschaft, 1980. 1: 376–505.

Huschke, Emil. *Schädel, Hirn und Seele.* Jena: Mauke, 1854.

Husserl, Edmund. *Ideen zu einer reinen Phänomenologie und phänomenologischen Philosophie.* First Book. Vol. 3 of *Gesammelte Werke.* Ed. Karl Schumann. The Hague: Nijhoff, 1976.

———. *Ideen zu einer reinen Phänomenologie und phänomenologischen Philosophie.* Second Book. Vol. 4 of *Gesammelte Werke.* Ed. Marly Biemel. The Hague: Nijhoff, 1952.

Huter, Carl. *Menschenkenntnis durch Körper-, Lebens-, Seelen- und Gesichts-Ausdruckskunde auf neuen wissenschaftlichen Grundlagen.* 2nd ed. Althofnass bei Bresgau: Carl Huter Verlag, 1929.

Jaensch, Erich Rudolf. "Die biologisch fundierte psychologische Anthropologie, ihre Stellung zur Rassenkunde und Kulturphilosophie, ihr Gegensatz zur unbiologischen Anthropologie." *Zeitschrift für Psychologie* 137 (1936): 1–50.

———. *Der Gegentypus: Psychologisch-anthropologische Grundlagen deutscher Kulturphilosophie, ausgehend von dem, was wir überwinden wollen.* Leipzig: Barth, 1938.

Jaensch, Walther. *Körperform, Wesensart und Rasse: Skizzen zu einer medizinisch-biologischen Konstitutionslehre.* Leipzig: Thieme, 1934.

Janentzky, Christian. *J. C. Lavaters Sturm und Drang im Zusammenhang seines religiösen Bewußtseins.* Halle: Niemeyer, 1916.

Jaspers, Karl. *Die geistige Situation der Zeit.* Berlin: de Gruyter, 1931.

Jauffret, Louis-François. "Einführung in die 'Memoires' der 'Société des Observateurs de l'homme.'" *Beobachtende Vernunft: Philosophie und Anthropologie in der Aufklärung.* Ed. Sergio Moravia. Trans. Elisabeth Piras. Munich: Hanser, 1973. 209–19.

Jordan, Leo. "Physiognomische Abhandlungen." *Romanische Forschungen* 29 (1911): 680–721.

Judt, J. M. *Die Juden als Rasse: Eine Analyse aus dem Gebiet der Anthropologie.* Berlin: Jüdischer Verlag, 1903.

Jünger, Ernst. *Das Antlitz des Weltkrieges: Fronterlebnisse deutscher Soldaten.* 2 vols. Berlin: Neufeld und Hensius, 1930.

———. *Der Arbeiter: Herrschaft und Gestalt. Sämtliche Werke.* 18 vols. Stuttgart: Klett-Cotta, 1981. 8: 9–317.

Junker, C.[arl] L.[udwig] "Anlage zu einem Familiengespräch über die Physiognomik." *Deutsches Museum* (1776) 2: 791–809.

Kaes, Anton. "Das bewegte Gesicht: Zur Großaufnahme im Film." In Schmölders and Gilman. 156–74.

Kafka, Franz. "Betrachtungen über Sünde, Leid, Hoffnung und den wahren Weg." *Hochzeitsvorbereitungen auf dem Lande und andere Prosa aus dem Nachlaß.* Ed. Max Brod. Frankfurt am Main: Fischer, 1953. 39–54.

Kamper, Dietmar, and Christoph Wulf, eds. *Das Schwinden der Sinne.* Frankfurt am Main: Suhrkamp, 1984.

———. *Transfigurationen des Körpers: Spuren der Gewalt in der Geschichte.* Berlin: Dietrich Reimer Verlag, 1989.

———. *Die Wiederkehr des Körpers.* Frankfurt am Main: Suhrkamp, 1982.

Kant, Immanuel. *Anthropologie in pragmatischer Hinsicht. Theorie-Werkausgabe.* Ed. Wilhelm Weischedel. Frankfurt am Main: Suhrkamp, 1968. 12: 397–690.

———. "Aus Sömmering: Über das Organ der Seele." *Theorie-Werkausgabe.* 11: 255–59.

———. "Bestimmung des Begriffs einer Menschenrasse." *Theorie-Werkausgabe.* 11: 65–82.

———. *Die Metaphysik der Sitten.* Vol. 8 of *Theorie-Werkausgabe.*

———. "Von den verschiedenen Rassen der Menschen." *Theorie-Werkausgabe.* 11: 11–30.

Kassner, Rudolf. *Buch der Erinnerung.* Leipzig: Insel, 1938.

———. "Das Gesicht Beethovens." *Sämtliche Werke.* 9: 689–97.

———. "Gespräche mit Alfons Clemens Kensik." *Rudolf Kassner zum 80. Geburtstag: Gedenkbuch.* Eds. A.[lfons] Cl.[emens] Kensik and D.[aniel] Bodmer. Winterthur: Rentsch, [1953]. 181–234.

———. *Die Grundlagen der Physiognomik (Von der Signatur der Dinge). Sämtliche Werke.* 4: 5–73.

———. "Das Menschengesicht." *Sämtliche Werke.* 6: 265–70.

———. *Physiognomik.* Munich: Delphi-Verlag, 1932.

———. *Physiognomik. Sämtliche Werke.* 5: 5–153.

———. *Das physiognomische Weltbild. Sämtliche Werke.* 4: 301–538.

———. *Sämtliche Werke.* Eds. Ernst Zinn and Klaus E. Bohnenkamp. 10 vols. Pfullingen: Neske, 1969–1991.

———. "Schicksalsahnung im Gesicht. Ein neuer Cäsarkopf: Physiognomische Deutung." *Sämtliche Werke.* 6: 358–62.

———. "Über Physiognomik." *Sämtliche Werke.* 6: 416–28.

———. *Die Verwandlung: Physiognomische Studien. Sämtliche Werke.* 4: 75–143.

———. *Zahl und Gesicht. Sämtliche Werke.* 3: 185–378.

———. "Zur Physiognomik des Porträts." In Kassner and Deutsch. 5–26.

Kassner, Rudolf, and W. R. Deutsch. *Das deutsche Antlitz in fünf Jahrhunderten deutscher Malerei.* Zurich: Atlantis Verlag, 1954.

Käuser, Andreas. "Anthropologie und Ästhetik im 18. Jahrhundert: Besprechung einiger Neuerscheinungen." *Das 18. Jahrhundert* 14 (1990): 196–206.

———. "Die anthropologische Theorie des Körperausdrucks im 18. Jahrhundert: Zum wissenschaftshistorischen Status der Physiognomik." In Behrens and Galle, *Leib-Zeichen.* 41–60.

———. "Die Physiognomik des 18. Jahrhunderts als Ursprung der modernen Geisteswissenschaften." *Germanish-Romanische Monatsschrift* 41 (1991): 129–44.

———. *Physiognomik und Roman im 18. Jahrhundert.* Frankfurt am Main: Peter Lang, 1989.

Kaye, Howard L. *The Social Meaning of Modern Biology: From Social Darwinism to Socio-Biology.* New Haven: Yale University Press, 1986.

Keller, Ulrich. "Einführung." In August Sander, *Menschen des 20. Jahrhunderts.* Munich: Schirmer/Mosel, 1980. 11–76.

Kern, Hans. *Carl Gustav Carus: Persönlichkeit und Werk.* Berlin: Widukind, 1942.

Kern, Stephen. *Anatomy and Destiny: A Cultural History of the Human Body.* Indianapolis: Bobbs-Merrill, 1975.

Kessler, Frank. "Photogénie und Physiognomie." In Campe and Schneider. 515–34.

Kiefer, Annegret. *Das Problem einer "jüdischen Rasse."* Frankfurt am Main: Peter Lang, 1991.

Kiener, Franz. "Physiognomik." *Ausdruckspsychologie: Handbuch der Psychologie.* Vol. 5. Ed. Robert Kirchhoff. Göttingen: Hogrefe, 1965. 465–529.

Klages, Ludwig. "Einführendes Wort des Herausgebers." In Carl Gustav Carus, *Psyche.* Jena: Eugen Diederichs, 1926. i–xx.

———. *Der Geist als Widersacher der Seele.* Vols. 1 and 2 of his *Sämtliche Werke.*

———. "Goethe als Seelenforscher." *Sämtliche Werke.* 4: 564–67.

———. *Goethe als Seelenforscher. Sämtliche Werke.* 5: 218–59.
———. *Die Grundlagen der Charakterkunde. Sämtliche Werke.* 4: 191–428.
———. *Grundlegung der Wissenschaft vom Ausdruck. Sämtliche Werke* 6: 315–673.
———. *Handschrift und Charakter: Gemeinverständlicher Abriss der graphologischen Technik.* 24th ed. Bonn: Bouvier, 1956.
———. "Prinzipielles bei Lavater." *Sämtliche Werke.* 6: 3–12.
———. *Sämtliche Werke.* Ed. Ernst Frauchiger et al. 8 vols. Bonn: Bouvier, 1964ff.
———. "Die Seelenkunde des Carl Gustav Carus." *Zur Ausdruckslehre und Charakterkunde.* Heidelberg: Niels Kampmann, [1927]. 287–311.
———. "Stammväter der Seelenkunde." *Sämtliche Werke.* 4: 568–78.
Kleist, Heinrich von. "Über das Marionettentheater." *Werke in einem Band.* Ed. Helmut Sembdner. Munich: Hanser, 1966. 802–807.
Kloos, Gerhard. *Die Konstitutionslehre von Carl Gustav Carus mit besonderer Berücksichtigung seiner Physiognomik.* Basel: S. Karger, 1951.
Koktanek, Anton Mirko. *Oswald Spengler in seiner Zeit.* Munich: Beck, 1968.
König, Helmut. *Zivilisation und Leidenschaft: Die Masse im bürgerlichen Zeitalter.* Reinbek: Rowohlt, 1992.
Koselleck, Reinhart. *Kritik und Krise: Eine Studie zur Pathogenese der bürgerlichen Welt.* 1959; rpt. Frankfurt am Main: Suhrkamp, 1973.
Kozloff, Max. "The Uncanny Portrait: Sander, Arbus, Samaras." *Photography and Fascination.* Danbury, N.H.: Addison, 1979. 150–63.
Kraitschek, Gustav. *Rassenkunde: Mit besonderer Berücksichtigung des deutschen Volkes.* Vienna: Burgverlag, 1924.
Kretschmer, Ernst. "Konstitution und Rasse." *Zeitschrift für die gesamte Neurologie und Psychologie* 82 (1923): 139–47.
———. *Körperbau und Charakter.* 19th ed. Berlin: Springer, 1948.
Kristeva, Julia. *Revolution in Poetic Language.* Trans. Margaret Waller. New York: Columbia University Press, 1984.
Kroh, Otto. "Das physiognomische Verstehen in seiner allgemein-psychologischen Bedeutung." *Neue psychologische Studien* 12.2 (1934): 23–40.
Krukenberg, Hermann. *Der Gesichtsausdruck des Menschen.* Stuttgart: Ferdinand Enke, 1913.
Küchenhoff, Joachim. "Der Leib als Statthalter des Individuums?" In Frank and Haverkamp. 167–202.
Kuhn, Dorothea. "Grundzüge der Goetheschen Morphologie." *Goethe-Jahrbuch* 95 (1978): 199–211.
Kunz, Reinhard. *Johann Caspar Lavaters Physiognomielehre im Urteil von Haller, Zimmermann und anderen zeitgenössischen Ärzten.* Zurich: Juris, 1970.

Kupfer, Amandus. *Grundlagen der praktischen Menschenkenntnis nach Carl Huters Psycho-Physiognomik.* 2 vols. 5th ed. Malmsbach-Schwaig: Selbstverlag, 1920–21.

Kuzniar, Alice. "Signs of the Future: Reading (in) Lavater's *Aussichten.*" *Seminar* 22 (1986): 1–19.

LaCapra, Dominick, ed. *The Bounds of Race: Perspectives on Hegemony and Resistance.* Ithaca, N.Y.: Cornell University Press, 1991.

Lachs, Daniela. "Lavaters Frauenbild—Lavaters Frauenbilder." In Mraz and Schögl. 152–61.

———. "Nationalphysiognomien." In Mraz and Schögl. 182–89.

Lalvani, Suren. *Photography, Vision, and the Production of Modern Bodies.* Albany: State University of New York Press, 1996.

Lambert, Johann Heinrich. *Neues Organon oder Gedanken über die Erforschung und Beziehung des Wahren und dessen Unterscheidung vom Irrthum und Schein.* 2 vols. 1764; rpt. Hildesheim: Olms, 1965.

Lange, Fritz. *Die Sprache des menschlichen Antlitzes: Eine wissenschaftliche Physiognomik und ihre praktische Verwertung im Leben und in der Kunst.* 3rd ed. Munich: J. F. Lehmann, 1940.

Lange, Susanne. "A Testimony to Photography: Reflections on the Life and Work of August Sander." *August Sander 1876–1964.* Ed. Manfred Heiting. Cologne: Taschen, 1999. 105–15.

Lavater, Johann Caspar. "Anmerkungen zu einer Abhandlung über Physiognomik im Göttingschen Taschenkalender aufs Jahr 1778." *Deutsches Museum* (1778) 1: 289–317.

———. Announcement of *Physiognomische Fragmente. Neue Bibliothek der schönen Wissenschaften* 17 (1775): 337–41. The same Announcement appeared in *Der teutsche Merkur* 8 (1774): 265–72.

———. *Aussichten in die Ewigkeit, in Briefen an Herrn Johann Georg Zimmermann.* 4 vols. Zurich: Orell, Geßner, 1768–1778.

———. *Physiognomische Fragmente zur Beförderung der Menschenkenntniß und Menschenliebe.* 4 vols. Leipzig and Winterthur: Weidmanns Erben & Reich, 1775–1778.

———. "Verantwortung gegen eine ehrsame Meisterschaft der Schuster in Zürich . . . " *Deutsches Museum* 2 (1777): 24–32.

———. "Von der Physiognomik." *Hannoverisches Magazin* (1772): columns 145–92.

———. *Von der Physiognomik.* 2 vols. Leipzig: Weidmanns Erben & Reich, 1772.

Le Brun, Charles. *Abhandlung über den Ausdruck der bildenden Künste.* Prague: Johann Ferdinand Edlen von Schönfeld, 1781.

———. *A Method to Learn to Design the Passions.* Trans. John Williams. London: J. Huggonson, 1734.

———. *Méthode pour apprendre à dessiner les passions, proposée dans une conférence sur l'expression générale, et particulière.* 1702; rpt. Hildesheim: Olms, 1982.

Leibniz, Gottfried Wilhelm. *Les principes de la philosophie ou la Monadologie.* Vol. 1 of *Philosophische Schriften.* Ed. Hanz Heinz Holz. Darmstadt: Wissenschaftliche Buchgesellschaft, 1965.

———. *Unvorgreifliche Gedanken, betreffend die Ausübung und Verbesserung der teutschen Sprache. Hauptschriften zur Grundlegung der Philosophie.* Ed. Ernst Cassirer. 2 vols. Hamburg: Meiner, 1966. 2: 519–55.

Lendvai-Dircksen, Erna. *Das deutsche Volksgesicht.* Berlin: Zeitgeschichte, [1930].

———. *Das deutsche Volksgesicht: Schleswig-Holstein.* Bayreuth: Gauverlag, 1939.

———. *Das Gesicht des deutschen Ostens.* Berlin: Zeitgeschichte, [1934].

Lenz, Johann Michael Reinhold. "Nachruf zu der im Göttingschen Almanach Jahrs 1778 an das Publikum gehaltenen Rede über Physiognomie." *Werke und Briefe.* Ed. Sigrid Damm. 3 vols. Munich: Hanser, 1987. 2: 761–68.

Lerner, Richard M. *Final Solutions: Biology, Prejudice, and Genocide.* University Park: Pennsylvania State University Press, 1992.

Lersch, Philipp. *Der Aufbau des Charakters.* Leipzig: Barth, 1938.

———. *Gesicht und Seele: Grundlinien einer mimischen Diagnostik.* Munich: Reinhardt, 1932.

Lesky, Erna. "Einleitung." *Franz Joseph Gall: Naturforscher und Anthropologe.* Berne: Hans Huber, 1979. 9–35.

Lessing, Gotthold Ephraim. *Gesammelte Werke.* Ed. Paul Rilla. 10 vols. Berlin: Aufbau, 1954–1957.

———. *Laokoön.* Vol. 14 of *Sämtliche Werke.* Ed. Karl Lachmann and Franz Muncker. 3rd edition. Stuttgart: G. J. Göschen'schen Verlagshandlung, 1894.

Lethen, Helmut. "Neusachliche Physiognomik: Gegen den Schrecken der ungewissen Zeichen." *Der Deutschunterricht* 49.2 (1997): 6–19.

Lichtenberg, Georg Christoph. "Bericht von den über die Abhandlung wider die Physiognomen entstandenen Streitigkeiten." *Schriften und Briefe.* 3: 563–68.

———. *Briefwechsel.* Ed. Ulrich Joost und Albrecht Schöne. Munich: Beck, 1983.

———. "Dritte Epistel an Tobias Göbhard." *Schriften und Briefe.* 3: 539–50.

———. "Fragment von Schwänzen: Ein Beitrag zu den *Physiognomischen Fragmenten.*" *Schriften und Briefe.* 3: 533–38.

———. *Schriften und Briefe.* Ed. Wolfgang Promies. Munich: Hanser, 1968–1972.

———. *Sudelbücher.* Vols. 1 and 2 of *Schriften und Briefe.* Ed. Wolfgang Promies. Munich: Hanser, 1968–1971.

———. "Über Physiognomik; wider die Physiognomen: Zu Beförderung der Menschenliebe und Menschenkenntnis." *Schriften und Briefe.* 3: 256–95.

———. "Wider Physiognostik: Eine Apologie von G. C. L." *Schriften und Briefe*. 3: 533–62.

Die literarische Welt. Special Issue on "Psychologie und Charakterologie," 3.19 (13 May 1927).

Locke, John. *An Essay Concerning Human Understanding*. Ed. Maurice Cranston. London: Collier-Macmillan, 1965.

Loewenberg, Richard Detlev. "The Significance of the Obvious: An Eighteenth Century Controversy on Psychosomatic Principles." *Bulletin on the History of Medicine* 10 (1941): 666–79.

———. "Der Streit um die Physiognomik zwischen Lavater und Lichtenberg." *Zeitschrift für Menschenkunde* 9 (1933): 15–33.

Lohmann-Siems, Ilsa. "J. C. A. Grohmanns 'Ideen zu einer physiognomischen Anthropologie' aus dem Jahre 1791." *Jahrbücher der Hamburgischen Kunstsammlungen* 8 (1963): 67–84.

———. "Der universale Formbegriff in der Physiognomik des 18. Jahrhunderts." *Jahrbücher der Hamburgischen Kunstsammlungen* 9 (1964): 49–74.

Lombroso, Cesare. *Der Verbrecher (Homo Delinquens) in anthropologischer, ärztlicher und juristischer Beziehung*. Trans. M. O. Fraenkel and H. Kurella. 3 vols. Hamburg: Verlagsanstalt und Druckerei, 1890–1896.

Lutzhöft, Hans-Jürgen. *Der nordische Gedanke in Deutschland 1920–1940*. Stuttgart: Klett, 1971.

MacRae, Donald G. "The Body and Social Metaphor." In Benthall and Polhemus. 59–73.

Madlener, Elisabeth. "Ein kabbalistischer Schauplatz: Die physiognomische Seelenerkundung." *Wunderblock: Eine Geschichte der modernen Seele*. Vienna: Löcker, 1989. 159–79.

Malter, Rudolf. "Der Rassebegriff in Kants Anthropologie." In Mann and Dumont, *Die Natur des Menschen*. 113–22.

Mann, Gunter. "Franz Joseph Galls Natur- und Geisteslehre des Menschen und der Völkerschaften (Lehre von den 'Nationalschädeln')." In Mann and Dumont, *Die Natur des Menschen*. 301–23.

———. "Franz Joseph Gall (1758–1828) und Samuel Thomas Soemmerring: Kranioskopie und Gehirnforschung zur Goethezeit." In Mann and Dumont, *Samuel Thomas Soemmerring und die Gelehrten der Goethezeit*. 149–89.

———. "Organ der Seele—Seelenorgan: Kranioskopie, Gehirnanatomie und dic Geisteskrankheiten in der Goethezeit." In Mann and Dumont, *Gerhirn—Nerven—Seele*. 133–57.

Mann, Gunter, and Franz Dumont, eds. *Gehirn—Nerven—Seele: Anatomie und Physiologie im Umfeld S. T. Soemmerrings*. Soemmerring-Forschungen, Bd. 3. Stuttgart: Gustav Fischer, 1987.

———. *Die Natur des Menschen: Probleme der physischen Anthropologie und Rassenkunde (1750–1850)*. Soemmerring-Forschungen, Bd. 6. Stuttgart: Gustav Fischer, 1990.

———. *Samuel Thomas Soemmerring und die Gelehrten der Goethezeit.* Soemmerring-Forschungen, Bd. 1. Stuttgart: Gustav Fischer, 1985.

Mann, Thomas. "Über die Lehre Spenglers." *Gesammelte Werke in zwölf Bänden.* Frankfurt am Main: Fischer, 1960. 10: 172–80.

Marcuse, Herbert. "Über den affirmativen Charakter der Kultur." *Kultur und Gesellschaft I.* Frankfurt am Main: Suhrkamp, 1965. 56–101.

Märker, Friedrich. *Charakterbilder der Rasse: Rassenkunde auf physiognomischer und phrenologischer Grundlage.* Berlin: Frundsberg-Verlag, 1934.

———. *Die Kunst aus dem Gesicht zu lesen.* Erlenbach-Zurich: Rentsch, 1971.

———. *Symbolik der Gesichtsformen: Physiognomik und Mimik.* Zurich: Rentsch, 1933.

———. *Typen: Grundlagen der Charakterkunde.* Erlenbach-Zurich: Rentsch, 1932.

Mason, Eudo C. "Rudolf Kassner zum Gedächtnis." *Exzentrische Bahnen: Studien zum Dichterbewußtsein der Neuzeit.* Göttingen: Vandenhoeck & Ruprecht, 1963. 168–80.

Matt, Peter von. *fertig ist das Angesicht: Zur Literaturgeschichte des menschlichen Gesichts.* Munich: Hanser, 1983.

Mattenklott, Gert. "Goethe als Physiognomiker." *Goethe: Vorträge aus Anlass seines 150. Todestages.* Eds. Thomas Clasen and Erwin Leibfried. Frankfurt am Main: Peter Lang, 1984. 125–41.

———. *Der übersinnliche Leib: Beiträge zur Metaphysik des Körpers.* Reinbek: Rowohlt, 1982.

Mau, Friedrich. *Warum Rassen- und Bevölkerungspolitik?: Bilder sprechen!* Schriftenreihe des rassenpolitischen Amtes der NSDAP und des Reichsbundes der Kinderreichen, Heft 15. Berlin: Rassenpolitisches Amt der NSDAP, n.d.

Meijer, Miriam Claude. *Race and Aesthetics in the Anthropology of Petrus Camper.* Amsterdam: Rodopi, 1999.

Meiners, Christoph. *Grundriß der Geschichte der Menschheit.* 2nd, expanded ed. Lemgo: Meyer, 1793.

Mendelssohn, Moses. "Ueber das Erhabene und Naive in den schönen Wissenschaften." *Ästhetische Schriften in Auswahl.* Ed. Otto F. Best. Darmstadt: Wissenschaftliche Buchgesellschaft, 1974. 207–46.

———. *Ueber die Hauptgrundsätze der schönen Künste und Wissenschaften. Gesammelte Schriften: Jubiläumsausgabe.* Ed. Alexander Altmann et al. 29 vols. Berlin and Stuttgart: Frommann, 1971–1998. 1: 425–52.

Merkenschlager, Friedrich. *Götter, Helden und Günther: Eine Abwehr der Güntherschen Rassenkunde.* Nuremberg: L. Spindler, [1927].

———. "Rasse und Volkstum im Lichte der Biologie." *Der Morgen* 6 (1930): 527–41.

———. "Streifzüge durch die wissenschaftliche und scheinwissenschaftliche Rasseliteratur." *Der Morgen* 8 (1932): 163–80.

Michael, Erika. *Carus-Fibel.* 2nd ed. Wiesbaden: Privatdruck, 1975.

Michel, Karl Markus. *Gesichter: Physiognomische Streifzüge.* Frankfurt am Main: Hain, 1990.

Moravia, Sergio. *Beobachtende Vernunft: Philosophie und Anthropologie in der Aufklärung.* Trans. Elisabeth Piras. Munich: Hanser, 1973.

Moritz, Karl Philipp. "Die Signatur des Schönen." *Schriften zur Ästhetik und Poetik.* Ed. Hans Joachim Schrimpf. Tübingen: Niemeyer, 1962. 93–103.

Mosse, George L. *The Crisis of German Ideology: Intellectual Origins of the Third Reich.* New York: Grosset & Dunlap, 1964.

———. *Towards the Final Solution: A History of European Racism.* London: Dent, 1978.

Mraz, Gerda, and Uwe Schögl, eds. *Das Kunstkabinett des Johann Caspar Lavater.* Vienna: Böhlau, 1999.

Muckermann, Hermann. *Grundriß der Rassenkunde.* Paderborn: Schöningh, 1935.

Mühlen, Patrik von zur. *Rassenideologien: Geschichte und Hintergründe.* Berlin: Dietz, 1977.

[Müller, Friedrich Christoph]. *Physiognomisches Cabinet für Freunde und Schüler der Menschenkenntniß.* 2 vols. Frankfurt & Leipzig: Philipp Heinrich Perrenon, 1777–1778.

Müller-Friedenfels, Richard. "Zur Problematik des Rassebegriffes." *Der Morgen* 6 (1930): 279–89.

Murr, Erich. *Einführung in die deutsche Rassenkunde.* Berlin: Brehm, n.d. [ca. 1935].

Musäus, Johann Karl August. *Physiognomische Reisen.* 4 vols. Altenberg: Richtersche Buchhandlung, 1778–1779.

Nakdimen, Kenneth A. "The Physiognomic Basis of Sexual Stereotyping." *American Journal of Psychiatry* 141 (1984): 499–503.

Neumann, Gerhard. "'der Mensch ohne Hülle ist eigentlich der Mensch': Goethe und Heinrich von Kleist in der Geschichte des physiognomischen Blicks." *Kleist-Jahrbuch* (1988–1989): 259–79.

———. "'Rede, damit ich dich sehe': Das neuzeitliche Ich und der physiognomische Blick." *Das neuzeitliche Ich in der Literatur des 18. und 20. Jahrhunderts: Dialektik der Moderne.* Eds. Ulrich Fülleborn and Manfred Engel. Munich: Fink, 1988. 71–108.

Nicolai, Friedrich. Letter to Georg Christoph Lichtenberg dated 15 April 1778. In Lichtenberg, *Briefwechsel.* 1: 815–16.

[Nicolai, Friedrich]. Review of Lavater's *Physiognomische Fragmente. Allgemeine deutsche Bibliothek* 29 (1776): 379–414; and supplement to vols. 25–36: 1251–73.

[Nicolai, Friedrich]. Review of Lavater's *Von der Physiognomik. Allgemeine deutsche Bibliothek* 23 (1775): 313–46.

Niehaus, Michael. "Physiognomie und Literatur im 19. Jahrhundert (von Poe bis Balzac)." In Campe and Schneider. 411–30.

Niekerk, Carl. "'Individuum est ineffabile': Bildung, der Physiognomikstreit und die Frage nach dem Subjekt in Goethes *Wilhelm-Meister*-Projekt." *Colloquia Germanica* 28 (1995): 1–33.

Niestroy, Brigite H. E. "Der Körper im 18. Jahrhundert: Essays zur historischen Anthropologie." *Das 18. Jahrhundert* 14 (1990): 153–58.

Noghe, Karl. *In jedes Menschen Gesichte steht seine Geschichte: Eine Einführung in die Physiognomik.* Oranienburg: Orania, [1920].

Nordau, Max. *Entartung.* 2nd ed. Berlin: Dunker, 1893.

Norton, Robert. "Racism, History, and Physiognomy: Herder and the Tradition of Moral Beauty in the Eighteenth Century." *Ethik und Ästhetik: Werke und Werte in der Literatur vom 18. bis zum 20. Jahrhundert.* Ed. Richard Fischer. Frankfurt am Main: Peter Lang, 1995. 43–54.

Oehler-Klein, Sigrid. "Franz Joseph Gall, der Scharlatan—Samuel Thomas Soemmerring, der Wissenschaftler?" In Mann and Dumont, *Gehirn—Nerven—Seele.* 93–131.

———. "Samuel Thomas Soemmerrings Neuroanatomie als Bindeglied zwischen Physiognomik und Anthropologie." In Mann and Dumont, *Die Natur des Menschen.* 57–87.

Ohage, August. "Von Lessings 'Wust' zu einer Wissenschaftsgeschichte der Physiognomik im 18. Jahrhundert." *Lessing Yearbook* 21 (1989): 55–87.

Ortner, Eduard. *Biologische Typen des Menschen und ihr Verhältnis zu Rasse und Wert.* Leipzig: Thieme, 1937.

Pack, R. A. "Artemidorus and the Physiognomists." *Transactions and Proceedings of the American Philological Association.* 72 (1941): 321–34.

———. "Physiognomical Entrance Examinations." *Classical Journal* 31 (1935): 42–43.

Paeschke, Hans. *Rudolf Kassner.* Pfullingen: Neske, 1963.

Pallot, Peter. *Menschen ohne Maske: Wie man Wesen und Charakter der Menschen erkennt.* Büdingen-Gettenbach: Lebensweiser-Verlag, 1953.

Parrinello, Giuli Liebmann. "La fisiognomica di J. C. Lavater." *Annali Sezione Germanica, Studi Tedeschi* 22 (1979): 7–26.

Pascal, Blaise. *Pensées.* Vol. 2 of *Oeuvres.* Ed. Léon Brunschvicg. Paris: Hachette, 1904.

Pestalozzi, Karl. "Lavaters Utopie." *Literaturwissenschaft und Geschichtsphilosophie: Festschrift für Wilhelm Emrich.* Eds. Helmut Arntzen et al. Berlin: de Gruyter, 1975. 283–301.

———. "Physiognomische Methodik." *Germanistik aus interkultureller Perspektive.* Eds. Adrien Finck and Gertrud Gréciano. Strasbourg: Université des Sciences Humaines, 1988. 137–53.

Petermann, Bruno. *Das Problem der Rassenseele: Vorlesungen zur Grundlegung einer allgemeinen Rassenpsychologie.* Leipzig: Barth, 1935.

Peters, Emil. *Menschengesicht und Charakter: Lehrbuch der praktischen Menschenkenntnis. Erster Teil: Kopf und Gesicht.* Konstanz: Volkskraft-Verlag, 1922.

Peukert, Kurt Werner. "Physiognomik in Goethes Morphologie." *Deutsche Vierteljahrsschrift für Literaturwissenschaft und Geistesgeschichte* 47 (1973): 400–19.

Picard, Max. *Die Grenzen der Physiognomik.* Erlenbach-Zurich: Eugen Rentsch, 1937.

———. *Das letzte Antlitz: Totenmasken von Shakespeare bis Nietzsche.* Munich: Knorr & Hirth, 1959.

———. *Das Menschengesicht.* Munich: Delphin-Verlag, 1929.

Pick, Daniel. *Faces of Degeneration: A European Disorder, c. 1848–c. 1918.* Cambridge: Cambridge University Press, 1989.

Piderit, Theodor. *Grundsätze der Mimik und Physiognomik.* Braunschweig: Friedrich Vieweg und Sohn, 1858.

———. *Wissenschaftliches System der Mimik und Physiognomik.* Detmold: Klingenbergsche Buchhandlung, 1867.

Polhemus, Ted. *Social Aspects of the Human Body.* Harmondsworth: Penguin, 1978.

———. "Social Bodies." In Benthall and Polhemus. 13–35.

Poliakov, Léon. *Der arische Mythos: Zu den Quellen von Rassismus und Nationalismus.* Trans. Margarete Venjakob. Hamburg: Junius, 1993.

Pollnow, Hans. "Historisch-kritische Beiträge zur Physiognomik." *Jahrbuch für Charakterologie* 5 (1928): 157–206.

Poole, Roger. "Objective Sign and Subjective Meaning." In Benthall and Polhemus. 74–106.

Popkin, Richard H. "The Philosophical Bases of Modern Racism." *The High Road to Pyrrhonism.* Eds. R. A. Watson and James E. Force. San Diego: Austin Hall Press, 1980. 79–102.

Prinz, W. "Ganzheits- und Gestaltpsychologie und Nationalsozialismus." *Psychologie im Nationalsozialismus.* Ed. Carl Freidrich Graumann. Berlin: Springer, 1985. 89–111.

Prinzhorn, Hans. *Charakterkunde der Gegenwart.* Berlin: Junker & Dünnhaupt, 1931.

Purdy, Daniel L. *The Tyranny of Elegance: Consumer Cosmopolitanism in the Era of Goethe.* Baltimore: Johns Hopkins University Press, 1998.

Purmann, Johann Georg. *Etwas über die moralische Physiognomik.* Frankfurt am Main: Bayrhoffer, 1776.

Quetelet, Adolphe. *Anthropométrie ou mesure des différentes facultés de l'homme.* Brussels: Muquardt, 1870.

Rauchensteiner, Meinhard. "Dein Körper, diese Karte, mein Herz: Johann Caspar Lavaters analytische Anthropologie." In Mraz and Schögl. 172–81.

Rauchensteiner, Meinhard, and Gudrun Swoboda. "Physiognomische Rhetorik I." In Mraz and Schögl. 110–17.

Reche, Otto. "Das Rassebild des deutschen Volkes." *Rassenhygiene für Jedermann.* Ed. Ernst Wegner. Dresden: Steinkopff, 1934. 30–43.

Regener, Susanne. "Frauen, Phantome und Hellseher: Zur Geschichte der Physiognomik des Weiblichen." In Schmölders, *Der exzentrische Blick.* 187–212.

———. "Verbrecherbilder: Fotoportraits der Polizei und Physiognomisierung des Kriminellen." *Ethnologia Europaea* 22 (1992): 67–85.

Retzer, Joseph Friedrich von. "Antwort an Herrn Doktor Gall." *Neuer teutscher Merkur* (1798), Stück 12: 332–35.

Rhodes, Henry T. F. *Alphonse Bertillon: Father of Scientific Detection.* London: Harrap, 1956.

Rieger, Stefan. "Literatur—Kryptology—Physiognomik: Die Lektüren des Körpers und die Dekodierung der Seele bei Johann Kaspar Lavater." In Campe and Schneider. 387–409.

Rilke, Rainer Maria. *Die Aufzeichnungen des Malte Laurids Brigge.* Frankfurt am Main: Insel, 1963.

Rittershaus, Ernst. *Konstitution oder Rasse?* Munich: J. F. Lehmann, 1935.

———. *Die Rassenseele des deutschen Volkes, ihr Wesen, ihr Wirken und ihre Geschichte im europäischen Raum.* Halle: Marhold, 1937.

Rivers, Christopher. *Face Value: Physiognomical Thought and the Legible Body in Marivaux, Lavater, Balzac, Gautier, and Zola.* Madison: University of Wisconsin Press, 1995.

Rodi, Frithjof. *Morphologie und Hermeneutik: Zur Methode von Diltheys Ästhetik.* Stuttgart: Kohlhammer, 1969.

Roesler, Christoph. "Beitrag zur Frage 'Zusammenhang zwischen Rasse und Konstitutionstypen.'" *Zeitschrift für die gesamte Neurologie und Psychologie* 95 (1925): 108–19.

Rohden, Friedrich von, and W. Gründler. "Über Körperbau und Psychose." *Zeitschrift für die gesamte Neurologie und Psychologie* 95 (1925): 37–78.

Rohracher, Hubert. *Kleine Einführung in die Charakterkunde.* Leipzig: Teubner, 1934.

Rosenberg, Alfred. *Der Mythus des 20. Jahrhunderts.* Munich: Hoheneichen-Verlag, 1934.

Ross, Stephanie. "Painting the Passions: Charles Le Brun's *Conférence sur l'expression.*" *Journal of the History of Ideas* 45.1 (Jan.–Mar. 1984): 25–47.

Rutkowski, Erik von. "Die Wurzeln der modernen Populärphysiognomik." *Allgemeine Zeitschrift für Psychiatrie* 89.20 (1928): 20–61.

Rutz, Ottmar. *Grundlagen einer psychologischen Rassenkunde.* Tübingen: Heine, 1934.

———. *Vom Ausdruck des Menschen: Lehrbuch der Physiognomik.* Celle: Niels Kampmann, 1925.

Rychner, Max. "Rudolf Kassner." *Arachne: Aufsätze zur Literatur.* Zurich: Manesse, 1957. 195–205.

Saller, Karl. *Die Rassenlehre des Nationalsozialismus in Wissenschaft und Propaganda.* Darmstadt: Progress-Verlag, 1961.

Saltzwedel, Johannes. *Das Gesicht der Welt: Physiognomisches Denken in der Goethezeit.* Munich: Fink, 1993.

Sander, August. *Antlitz der Zeit: 60 Aufnahmen deutscher Menschen des 20. Jahrhunderts.* 1929; rpt. Munich: Schirmer/Mosel, 1976.

———. *Menschen des 20. Jahrhunderts.* Munich: Schirmer/Mosel, 1980.

———. "Photography as a Universal Langauge." Trans. Anne Halley. *Massachussetts Review* (1978): 46–51.

Sauerländer, Willibald. "Vom Heimatschutz zur Rassenhygiene: Über Paul Schultze-Naumburg." In Schmölders and Gilman. 32–50.

Schemann, Ludwig. *Die Rassenfrage im Schrifttum der Neuzeit.* Vol. 3 of *Die Rasse in den Geisteswissenschaften: Studien zur Geschichte des Rassengedankens.* Munich: J. F. Lehmann, 1931.

Scheve, Gustav. *Phrenologische Bilder: Zur Naturlehre des menschlichen Geistes und deren Anwendung auf Wissenschaft und Leben.* 2nd, expanded ed. Leipzig: J. J. Weber, 1855.

Schiller, Friedrich von. *Die Räuber. Sämtliche Werke.* 1: 481–618.

———. *Sämtliche Werke.* Eds. Gerhard Fricke and Herbert G. Göpfert. 2nd ed. 5 vols. Munich: Hanser, 1960.

———. "Versuch über den Zusammenhang der tierischen Natur des Menschen mit seiner geistigen." *Sämtliche Werke.* 5: 287–324.

Schlesinger, Louis B. "Physiognomic Perception: Empirical and Theoretical Perspectives." *Genetic Psychology Monographs* 101 (1980): 71–97.

———. "Physiognomic Sensitivity: Its Development and Modification." *Journal of Genetic Psychology* 134 (1979): 107–23.

[Schlosser, Johann Georg]. Review of Lavater's *Von der Physiognomik. Frankfurter gelehrte Anzeigen* (1772), No. 66. In *Deutsche Literaturdenkmale des 18. und 19. Jahrhunderts.* Eds. Wilhelm Scherer and Bernard Seuffert. 150 vols. Heilbronn: Henninger, 1882–1883. 7–8: 434–37.

Schmid, Niklaus. "Der Einfluß von J. C. Lavaters Physiognomik auf die Anfänge der Kriminologie im 19. Jahrhundert." *Zeitschrift für schweizerisches Recht* 125 (1984): 465–88.

Schmidt, Michael. "Autobiographie und Physiognomik: Probleme der Darstellung im Werk Rudolf Kassners." Diss. University of Munich, 1970.

Schmölders, Claudia. *Hitlers Gesicht: Eine physiognomische Biographie.* Munich: Beck, 2000.

———. *Das Vorurteil im Leib: Eine Einführung in die Physiognomik.* Berlin: Akademie Verlag, 1995.

Schmölders, Claudia, ed. *Der exzentrische Blick: Gespräch über Physiognomik.* Berlin: Akademie Verlag, 1996.

Schmölders, Claudia, and Sander L. Gilman, eds. *Gesichter der Weimarer Republik: Eine physiognomische Kulturgeschichte.* Cologne: DuMont, 2000.

Schneider, Manfred. "Die Beobachtung des Zeugen nach Artikel 71 der 'Carolina': Der Aufbau eines Codes der Glaubwürdigkeit 1532–1850." In Campe and Schneider. 153–82.

Schögl, Uwe. "Vom Frosch zum Dichter-Apoll: Morphologische Entwicklungsreihen bei Lavater." In Mraz and Schögl. 164–71.

Schopenhauer, Arthur. "Zur Physiognomik." *Parerga und Paralipomena. Sämtliche Werke.* Ed. Wolfgang von Löhneysen. Stuttgart: Cotta-Insel, 1965. 5: 744–52.

Schröter, Manfred. *Metaphysik des Untergangs: Eine kulturkritische Studie über Oswald Spengler.* Munich: Leibniz, 1949.

Schubart, Christian Friedrich Daniel. "Etwas Physiognomisches." *Teutsche Chronik* 2 (1775): 445–46.

———. "Lavater und sein Recensent." *Teutsche Chronik* 4 (1777): 726–27.

———. "Politische Physiognomik." *Teutsche Chronik* 3 (1776): 145–47.

Schultz, Bruno K. *Deutsche Rassenköpfe: 43 preisgekrönte Bilder der fünf in Deutschland vertretenen Hauptrassen.* Munich: J. F. Lehmann, 1935.

———. *Erbkunde, Rassenkunde und Rassenpflege: Ein Leitfaden zum Selbststudium und für den Unterricht.* Munich: J. F. Lehmann, 1933.

———. *Rassenkunde deutscher Gaue: Bauern im südlichen Allgäu, Lechtal und Bregenzer Wald.* Munich: J. F. Lehmann, 1935.

———. *Taschenbuch der rassenkundlichen Meßtechnik: Anthropologische Meßgeräte und Messungen am Lebenden.* Munich: J. F. Lehmann, 1937.

Schultze-Naumburg, Paul. *Kunst und Rasse.* Munich: J. F. Lehmann, 1935.

———. *Nordische Schönheit: Ihr Wunschbild im Leben und in der Kunst.* Munich: J. F. Lehmann, 1937.

Schulze, Hagen. *Weimar: Deutschland 1917–1933.* Berlin: Severin und Siedler, 1982.

Sennett, Richard. *The Fall of Public Man.* Cambridge: Cambridge University Press, 1976.

Shaftesbury, Anthony Ashley Cooper, 3rd Earl of. *Characteristics of Men, Manners, Opinions, Times.* 2 vols. Ed. John M. Robertson. London: Grant Richards, 1900.

Shookman, Ellis, ed. *The Faces of Physiognomy: Interdisciplinary Approaches to Johann Caspar Lavater.* Columbia, S.C.: Camden House, 1993.

Shortland, Michael. "The Body in Question: Some Perceptions, Problems, and Perspectives of the Body in Relation to Character, c. 1750–1850." Diss. Leeds University, 1985.

———. "The Power of a Thousand Eyes: Johann Caspar Lavater's Science of Physiognomical Perception." *Criticism* 28 (1986): 379–408.

———. "Skin Deep: Barthes, Lavater, and the Legible Body." *Economy and Society* 14 (1985): 273–312.

Siebels, Eva. "Sprache und Dichtung im physiognomischen Weltbilde Rudolf Kassners." *Deutsche Vierteljahrsschrift für Literaturwissenschaft und Geistesgeschichte* 19 (1941): 218–39.

Siegrist, Christoph. "Nachwort" to Lavater's *Physiognomische Fragmente.* Stuttgart: Reclam, 1984. 377–94.

———. "Satirische Physiognomikkritik bei Musäus, Pezzl und Klinger." In Groddeck and Stadler. 95–112.

Sihler, Wilhelm. *Symbolik des Antlitzes.* Berlin: F. Lauer, 1829.

Simmel, Georg. "Die ästhetische Bedeutung des Gesichts." *Aufsätze und Abhandlungen 1901–1908.* Vol. 7 of *Gesamtausgabe.* Ed. Otthein Rammstedt. Frankfurt am Main: Suhrkamp, 1995. 36–42.

Simms, Joseph. *Physiognomy Illustrated; or, Nature's Revelations of Character.* 9th ed. New York: Murray Hill, 1889.

Sloterdijk, Peter. *Kritik der zynischen Vernunft.* 2 vols. Frankfurt am Main: Suhrkamp, 1983.

Smith, Paul. *Discerning the Subject.* Minneapolis: University of Minnesota Press,1988.

Soemmerring, Samuel Thomas. *Über das Organ der Seele.* Königsberg: Nicolovius, 1796.

———. *Über die körperliche Verschiedenheit des Mohren vom Europäer.* Mainz: n.p., 1784.

———. *Über die körperliche Verschiedenheit des Negers vom Europäer.* Mainz: n.p., 1785.

Spengler, Oswald. *Briefe 1913–1936.* Ed. Anton M. Koktanek. Munich: Beck, 1963.

———. *Frühzeit der Weltgeschichte: Fragmente aus dem Nachlaß.* Ed. Anton Mirko Koktanck. Munich: Beck, 1966.

———. "Heraklit: Eine Studie über den energetischen Grundgedanken seiner Philosophie." *Reden und Aufsätze.* Munich: Beck, 1937. 1–47.

———. *Jahre der Entscheidung. Erster Teil: Deutschland und die weltgeschichtliche Entwicklung.* Munich: Beck, 1933.

———. *Der Mensch und die Technik: Beitrag zu einer Philosophie des Lebens.* Munich: Beck, 1931.

———. "Pessimismus?" *Reden und Aufsätze.* Munich: Beck, 1937. 63–79.

———. *Der Untergang des Abendlandes: Umrisse einer Morphologie der Weltgeschichte.* Vollständige Ausgabe in einem Band. Munich: Beck, 1963.

———. *Urfragen: Fragmente aus dem Nachlaß.* Ed. Anton Mirko Koktanek. Munich: Beck, 1965.

Spieß, Christian Heinrich. "Der gläserne Ökonom." *Biographien der Wahnsinnigen.* Ed. Wolfgang Promies. Neuwied: Luchterhand, 1966. 44–61.

Spoerri, Theophil. "Rudolf Kassner." *Jahresring* (1959–1960): 300–306.

Spranger, Eduard. *Lebensformen: Geisteswissenschaftliche Psychologie und Ethik der Persönlichkeit.* 9th ed. Tübingen: Niemeyer, 1966.

Spurzheim, Johann Gaspar. *The Anatomy of the Brain with a General View of the Nervous System.* Trans. R. Willis. London: Highley, 1826.

———. *Phrenology, in Connexion with the Study of Physiognomy.* 2 vols. Boston: Marsh, Capen & Lyon, 1833.

———. *Phrenology, or the Doctrine of the Mental Phenomena.* 2 vols. New York: Harper, 1846.

Stadler, Ulrich. "Der gedoppelte Blick und die Ambivalenz des Bildes in Lavaters *Physiognomischen Fragmenten zur Beförderung der Menschenkenntniß und Menschenliebe.*" In Schmölders, *Der exzentrische Blick.* 77–92.

Staemmler, Martin. *Rassenpflege im völkischen Staat.* 2nd ed. Munich: J. F. Lehmann, 1935.

———. *Rassenpflege und Schule.* 2nd ed. Manns Pädagogisches Magazin, Heft 1379. Langensalza: Beyer & Söhne, 1934.

Stafford, Barbara Maria. *Body Criticism: Imaging the Unseen in Enlightenment Art and Medicine.* Cambridge, Mass: M.I.T. Press, 1991.

Stallybrass, Peter, and Allon White. *The Politics and Poetics of Transgression.* Ithaca: Cornell University Press, 1986.

Steig, Reinhold. "Herders Verhältnis zu Lavaters *Physiognomischen Fragmenten.*" *Euphorion* 1 (1894): 540–57.

Steinbrucker, Charlotte. *Lavaters Physiognomische Fragmente im Verhältnis zur bildenden Kunst.* Berlin: Borngräber, 1915.

Stern, Fritz. *The Politics of Cultural Despair: A Study in the Rise of the Germanic Ideology.* Berkeley: University of California Press, 1961.

Stern-Piper, Ludwig. "Konstitution und Rasse." *Zeitschrift für die gesamte Neurologie und Psychologie* 86 (1923): 265–73.

———. "Zur Frage der Bedeutung der psycho-physischen Typen Kretschmers." *Zeitschrift für die gesamte Neurologie und Psychologie* 84 (1923): 408–14.

Stiehl, O[tto]. *Unsere Feinde: 96 Charakterköpfe aus deutschen Kriegsgefangenenlagern.* Stuttgart: Julius Hoffmann, 1916.

Stingelin, Martin. "Der Verbrecher ohnegleichen: Die Konstruktion 'anschaulicher Evidenz' in der Criminal-Psychologie, der forensischen Physiognomik, der Kriminalanthropometrie und der Kriminalanthropologie." In Groddeck and Stadler. 113–33.

Stöcklein, Paul. *Carl Gustav Carus: Menschen und Völker.* Hamburg: Hoffmann & Campe, 1943.

Sturz, [Helferich Peter]. "Des Herrn Staatsrath Sturz Erklärung über die Physiognomik, mit Anmerkungen von Johann Caspar Lavater." *Deutsches Museum* (1777) 1: 399–408.

———. "Rezensionen der Lavaterschen Physiognomik." *Die Reise nach dem Dreister: Prosa und Briefe.* Ed. Karl Wolfgang Becker. Berlin: Roetten & Loening, 1976. 203–13.

Sulzer, Johann Georg. "Gedanken über einige Erscheinungen der Seele, in sofern sie mit den Eigenschaften der Materie eine Aehnlichkeit haben, zur Prüfung des Systems des Materialismus." *Vermischte philosophische Schriften.* Leipzig: Weidmanns Erben und Reich, 1773. 348–76.

Swoboda, Gudrun. "Die Sammlung Johann Caspar Lavater in Wien." In Mraz and Schögl. 74–95.

Synnott, Anthony, and David Howes. "From Measurement to Meaning: Anthropologies of the Body." *Anthropos* 87 (1992): 147–66.

Timm, Hermann. "Von Angesicht zu Angesicht: Das theologische Interesse an der Physiognomik." *Wege zum Menschen* 38 (1986): 195–207.

Trebeck, Richard. "Die Anthropologie des Johann Caspar Lavater." *Zeitschrift für Psychologie* 147 (1939–1940): 274–327.

Tucker, William H. *The Science and Politics of Racial Research.* Urbana: University of Illinois Press, 1994.

Tytler, Graeme. *Physiognomy in the European Novel: Faces and Fortunes.* Princeton: Princeton University Press, 1982.

Venzmer, Gerhard. *Dein Kopf—dein Charakter: Was Schädelform und Antlitzbildung über die Wesensart des Menschen verraten.* Stuttgart: Franckh, 1934.

———. *Körpergestalt und Seelenanlage: Ein Überblick über die biologische Verwandschaft zwischen Körperform und Wesenskern des Menschen.* Stuttgart: Kosmos, 1930.

———. *Sieh dir die Menschen an!* Stuttgart: Franckh, 1937.

Virchow, Rudolf. *Untersuchungen über die Entwicklung des Schädelgrundes.* Berlin: Reimer, 1857.

Visser, Robert. "Die Rezeption der Anthropologie Peter Campers (1770–1850)." In Mann and Dumont, *Die Natur des Menschen.* 325–35.

Voegelin, Erich. *Die Rassenidee in der Geistesgeschichte von Ray bis Carus.* Berlin: Juncker & Dünnhaupt, 1933.

———. *Rasse und Staat.* Tübingen: Mohr, 1933.

Volrad Deneke, J. F. "Die Phrenologie als publizistisches Ereignis: Galls Schädellehre in der Tagespublizistik des 19. Jahrhunderts." *Medizinhistorisches Journal* 20 (1985): 83–108.

von der Hellen, Eduard. *Goethes Anteil an Lavaters Physiognomischen Fragmenten.* Frankfurt am Main: Rütten & Loening, 1888.

———. "Lavaters Physiognomik." *Westermanns Illustrierte Deutsche Monatsschrift* 92 (1902): 691–701.

Walch, Johann. *Philosophisches Lexikon.* 2 vols. 1775; rpt. Hildesheim: Olms, 1968.

Waldmann, Friedrich. "Lenz' Stellung zu Lavaters Physiognomik." *Baltische Monatsschrift* 40 (1893): 419–36; 482–97; 516–33.

Walsh, Anthony A. "Is Phrenology Foolish? A Rejoinder." *Journal of the History of the Behavioral Sciences* 6 (1970): 358–61.

Weber, Max. "Die protestantische Ethik und der Geist des Kapitalismus." *Die protestantische Ethik I.* Ed. Johannes Winkelmann. Gütersloh: Verlagshaus Mohn, 1984. 27–317.

Wechsler, Judith. *A Human Comedy: Physiognomy and Caricature in Nineteenth Century Paris.* Chicago: University of Chicago Press, 1982.

Wegner, Ernst, ed. *Rassenhygiene für Jedermann.* Dresden: Steinkopff, 1934.

Weidenreich, Franz. "Das Problem der jüdischen Rasse." *Der Morgen* 7 (1931): 78–96.

———. *Rasse und Körperbau.* Berlin: Springer, 1927.

Weindling, Paul. *Health, Race and German Politics between National Unification and Nazism, 1870–1945.* Cambridge: Cambridge University Press, 1989.

Weingart, Peter. *Doppel-Leben. Ludwig Ferdinand Clauss: Zwischen Rassenforschung und Widerstand.* Frankfurt am Main: Campus, 1995.

Weingart, Peter, Jürgen Kroll, and Kurt Bayertz. *Rasse, Blut und Gene: Geschichte der Eugenik und Rassenhygiene in Deutschland.* Frankfurt am Main: Suhrkamp, 1992.

Weinländer, Karl. *Rassenkunde, Rassenpädagogik und Rassenpolitik: Der naturgesetzliche Weg zu Deutschlands Aufstieg.* Weißenburg: Orion, 1933.

Wellbery, David. *Lessing's Laokoön: Semiotics and Aesthetics in the Age of Reason.* Cambridge: Cambridge University Press, 1984.

Wellek, Albert. "Willy Hellpachs 'Deutsche Physiognomik' und die Probleme einer Physiognomik überhaupt." *Zeitschrift für angewandte Psychologie und Charakterkunde* 66 (1943): 1–41.

Wenzel, Manfred. "Johann Wolfgang von Goethe und Samuel Thomas Soemmerring: Morphologie und Farbenlehre." In Mann and Dumont, *Samuel Thomas Soemmerring und die Gelehrten der Goethezeit.* 11–33.

Werner, Heinz. *Einführung in die Entwicklungspsychologie.* 3rd ed. Munich: Barth, 1953.

Wieland, Christoph Martin. Review of vol. 1 of Lavater's *Physiognomische Fragmente. Gesammelte Schriften.* Ed. Deutsche Kommission der Preußischen Akademie der Wissenschaften. 25 vols. Berlin: Weidmann, 1909–1940. Part 1; 21: 184–86.

Wittgenstein, Ludwig. *Tractatus logico-philosophicus.* Frankfurt am Main: Suhrkamp, 1979.

Wittich, Wilhelm Heinrich von. *Physiognomik und Phrenologie.* Berlin: Lüderitz, 1870.

Wittlich, Bernhard. *Wörterbuch der Charakterkunde.* 4th ed. Munich: Barth, 1965.

Wolff, Christian. *Vernünfftige Gedancken von der Menschen Thun und Lassen.* 4th ed. Part 1, vol. 4 of *Gesammelte Werke.* Ed. J. École et al. 1752; rpt. Hildesheim: Olms, 1976.

———. *Vernünfftige Gedancken von Gott, der Welt und der Seele des Menschen, auch allen Dingen überhaupt.* 11th ed. Part 1, vol. 2 of *Gesammelte Werke.* Ed. J. École et al. 1751; rpt. Hildesheim: Olms, 1983.

Young, Robert M. *Mind, Brain and Adaptation in the Nineteenth Century.* Oxford: Clarendon, 1970.

Zelle, Carsten. "Physiognomie des Schreckens im 18. Jahrhundert: Zu Johann Caspar Lavater und Charles Lebrun." *Lessing Yearbook* 21 (1989): 89–102.

[Zimmermann, Johann Georg]. "Über einige Einwürfe gegen die Physiognomik, und vorzüglich gegen die von Herrn Lavater behauptete Harmonie zwischen Schönheit und Tugend." *Deutsches Museum* (1778) 1: 193–98.

Zinn, Ernst. "Nachwort." Rudolf Kassner, *Zahl und Gesicht.* Bibliothek Suhrkamp 564. Frankfurt am Main: Suhrkamp, 1979. 247–52.

Züst, Ruth. *Die Grundzüge der Physiognomik Johann Caspar Lavaters.* Bülach: Steinemann-Scheuchzer, 1948.

Zweig, Arnold. *Das ostjüdische Antlitz.* Berlin: Welt-Verlag, 1920.

Index

www.ingramcontent.com/pod-product-compliance
Lightning Source LLC
LaVergne TN
LVHW010355080826
844660LV00016B/982/J